Page: 256

" 4

" 63

UNDER FIVE FLAGS

Pre-war Secretariat, Sandakan, 1940.

Under Five Flags

Ronald. J. Brooks

The Pentland Press
Edinburgh – Cambridge – Durham – USA

First published in 1995 by
The Pentland Press Ltd
1 Hutton Close
South Church
Bishop Auckland
Durham

ISBN 1-85821-322-3

Typeset by Carnegie Publishing, 18 Maynard St, Preston
Printed and bound by Antony Rowe Ltd, Chippenham

Contents

List of Ilustrations	vii
Prologue	ix
Under the Sabah Jack	1
Under the Poached Egg	87
Under the Australian Flag	147
Under the Union Jack	163
Under the Malaysian Flag	237
Epilogue	251
Obituary	256

Illustrations

Pre-war Secretariat, Sandakan, 1940	Frontispiece
River crossing, Pensiangan District	29
Murut warrior of old	31
Tapai drinking	34
Kedazan lass at Kota Belud Tama	71
Sandakan before the War	150–1
Sandakan after the Allied bombing	150–1
The pre-war Jesselton Post Office	159
Kompong Benoni: Ceremony of *Tutop Kuala*	181
Party celebrating opening of Radio Sabah in old Rest House building incl. Donald Stephens	193
The Royal Yacht *Britannia* alongside Sandakan Wharf	204
Last photograph taken of the Countess Mountbatten	216
Broadcasting House, Jesselton, 1962	226
Sabah Museum	248

Prologue

I WAS looking over the taffrail of the M.V. *Darvel* gazing at the lights of Singapore as they twinkled against the dying embers of a blazing tropical sunset, when an elderly, dapper gentleman of medium build came over to me and asked: 'What's your destination, young fellow?' I was a bit taken aback that anyone so distinguished looking should take an interest in me.

'North Borneo, Sir!' I replied, and went on to explain that I had been newly recruited to the Administrative Service of the Chartered Company which was the Government of that country in pre-war days.

'Oh, pity,' he replied, 'you are going to the wrong place! You should be coming to me!'

He then briskly turned on his heels and went over to a group who were already seated at a table, being served with a round of drinks.

Shortly afterwards, when at dinner, I observed that he and his party were seated at the Captain's table. My companion was able to tell me that he was Rajah Brooke, who was destined to become the last white Rajah of Sarawak. Had I known that earlier, when in conversation with him, I could have explained to him that it had been his family which had inspired me to seek a post in North Borneo, being the nearest place to Sarawak that had offered me employment. I could have told him, too, that from my bedroom window in the house in which I lived as a boy, I could look across the Tamar and up the Tavy towards Sheepstor and clearly see the tower of the nearby church.

One day, when my father had had a holiday, he had taken me to Burrator and, after crossing the wall of the reservoir, we reached the church cemetery where he had shown me the tomb of the first Rajah of Sarawak, Sir James Brooke, a visit which was to inspire my boyhood imagination.

Since that day, school texts notwithstanding, I had read every book about Sarawak and Borneo that I could find. There had been no doubt in my mind where I wished to seek a career. Luck was with me in my secret endeavours! In my last term at Oxford, the North Borneo Chartered Company advertised that they required a Cadet for their Administrative Service. I immediately applied. I clearly remember the reply I gave to the President of the Court of Directors of the Chartered Company, Sir Neil Malcolm, when he asked: 'Why, Mr Brooks, would you like a post like this?'

The reply I gave him came quite naturally and truthfully: 'Because, Sir, I believe it to be a job worth doing!'

'Quite right, my boy,' the President had replied, 'It is!'

I immediately knew the job was mine!

Now I was on my way, nearing my destination, and doubly thrilled since I was travelling on the same boat as the Rajah! We sailed up Kuching River on the tide and anchored in mid-stream, with the colourful town on our port side and, on our starboard bow, carefully tended lawns rising from the river bank to a beautiful house atop the slope: the Astana, the Rajah's home! Many, many years later, I was to dine at the same table at which the Rajah had once presided!

Much, however, was to intervene, and this is the story I have to tell, some fifty-five years later.

Under the Sabah Jack

THE *Darvel* did not tarry long in Kuching. By mid-afternoon and taking advantage of an ebb tide, she glided quickly downstream and long before sunset was over the sand-bar and out into the South China Sea, setting course for Miri. The following evening, a dull red glow appeared in the skies directly ahead of us. It was the oil-field burning off excess gases. A few years before the Shell Oil Company had started developing Borneo's oil resources here, and we were soon to learn that the main items in the cargo which the *Darvel* carried were 3–4 inch pipes destined for the oil field!

The coastline shelved very, very gradually here, and we were anchored at least some three miles off the coast. The South China Sea is by no means a calm sea, and when its deep waters hit the shallow bank of an exposed part of the Borneo Coast it can cause a very heavy ground swell. The crack Japanese landing forces were to learn this much to their cost a few years later. A fierce north-easterly monsoon was blowing when they headed for their principal objective on the Borneo coast: the oilfields of Miri. Their wooden landing barges, hastily constructed in Saigon for the Japanese thrust to the south, quickly disintegrated in the swell and it is said that more than half their invasion force perished here before they reached the shore.

All next day and most of the next night we lay off Miri, any conversation almost drowned by the incessant clattering of the seemingly endless cargo of pipes. At last one was able to fall into a fitful sleep, and it was pleasant to wake up in the morning conscious of the pulsating throb of the engine and thankful that the cacophony of Miri was behind us! The sea was calmer now, and on deck we could discern the green outline of Labuan where we were heading.

Translated from the Malay, its name means 'an anchorage' and quite a number of ships can shelter in its expansive harbour. It has been a focal point of the north-west coast of Borneo, but its history has been like that of a football. It had been ceded to Britain by the Sultan of Brunei on Christmas Eve 1846, and became the first British connection with the island of Borneo.

At this midway point of the nineteenth century the Sultanate of Brunei, which had once had political and military power over all of Sarawak and its northern province Sabah, was going through one of its most troubled periods in its history. To rule his comparatively vast territory the Sultan had appointed Pengirans—overlords—and as long as they paid tribute to him the Sultan was happy! As evidence of his once thriving influence, the Sultan had imported elephants from Siam to add pomp and circumstance to the occasions when he appeared amongst his people. By now, however, in spite of a very long period of affluence, he had begun to feel the effect of the incursions from his biggest rival in the north, the Sultan of Sulu.

Sulu had begun to claim territory in Sabah, which Brunei had always regarded as its own. The matter did not end there, as raiding parties were destroying villages, plundering crops and capturing the womenfolk as slaves. Costly punitive expeditions were necessary, demanding resources of manpower and wealth which Brunei could ill-afford. The impoverished countryside was in a state of turbulence. Not only that, but the Sultan also had domestic problems with his own chosen area representatives, the Pengirans. Communications had perforce to be by sea and were stretched, so that the Sultan was finding that tribute due to be paid him was not reaching his coffers. The governance of his Sultanate had reached its decline. Other powers, greater than he had known before, were to offer more acceptable alternatives.

It was the expansionist Victorian age of the British Empire. 'Trade' was the name of the game; the word 'colonialism' had not yet been invented. First on the scene was James Brooke. Investing an inheritance in a ship going by the name of *Royalist*, he arrived in Kuching, Sarawak, in 1839, with a handful of men, at an opportune moment for the Sultan of Brunei. The Rajah Muda Hashim, the uncle of the then reigning Sultan, was in charge of this south-western province of the Sultanate, and a formidable band of Land Dyaks, acting with good reason, were causing considerable harassment. The reason was that they were being exploited relentlessly by the Sultan's uncle, and it was believed that they were endeavouring to seek help from the Dutch. It was into this scenario that James Brooke entered when he reached Kuching.

The *Royalist* slowly wound its way up the river and on arrival at the township, fired a royal salute of twenty-one guns. Brooke then went ashore, bearing presents for the Rajah, and sought an audience. This was duly granted and pleasantries were exchanged. The next morning the Rajah Muda paid a return visit to the *Royalist*. A friendly relationship was established and arrangements were made for Brooke to visit some of the surrounding villages. From what he saw Brooke reached the conclusion that this was a suitable base from which to establish commercial operations.

However, Brooke discovered that the political scene in Sarawak was not a happy one. The Rajah Muda was a weak ruler and there were many rival notables warring against him and each other. The Rajah Muda was shrewd enough, however, to recognize in his visitor qualities of leadership that might bring some unity and prosperity to the area. As for Brooke, he had endeavoured to assess the position from the point of view of trade and had concluded that possibilities existed. He was, nevertheless, on a voyage of exploration and, having come so far, he felt he should continue with the second part of his project and carry on with his voyage to the Celebes. The Rajah Muda gave him an affectionate farewell but entreated him to return.

Brooke travelled by way of Singapore where he called on the Governor and met several of the leading merchants, all of whom would be of benefit to him in later years. He then set sail for the Celebes, but although it brought him into contact with friendly people and beautiful scenery, his voyage was otherwise uneventful.

With his funds beginning to run low, he decided it would be better for him to keep his promise to the Rajah Muda and return once more to Kuching. If he could not establish a trading base there, he would abandon any further endeavours and return to England.

His return was well received in Kuching, but he found the country in the same state of turmoil. It would take a lot of time, patience and resources to establish a successful trading base. He became very hesitant about staying, an attitude that the Rajah Muda was quick to perceive, and when a rather disillusioned Brooke made overtures regarding his departure, he encountered a very unexpected suggestion.

If Brooke would only agree to stay and bring peace to the area, then the Rajah Muda would agree to cede the territory, its governance and its trade and bestow on Brooke the title of Rajah. This was a proposal very far from James' thought and his intentions. He had only wanted a trading post! However, the thought must have flattered him, as he did not leave as he had intended but instead sought to formalize the offer. A document was duly prepared conveying the administration of the province of Sarawak to Brooke in return for a small annual tribute to the Sultan of Brunei. The deal took time to arrange, but all came out of it in a happy frame of mind. The Rajah Muda would be able to enjoy a more peaceful life and a happier retirement, the Sultan of Brunei was more certain of his income and Brooke had received something which he never could have anticipated! On 24 November 1841, Brooke was ceremoniously proclaimed Rajah of Sarawak. His dynasty was to last just over one hundred years.

Five years were to elapse before Britain took any notice of the island of Borneo, but in 1846 HMS *Iris*, commanded by Captain Mundy, sailed into Labuan harbour and hoisted the British flag. This led to a Treaty of Friendship and Commerce being concluded between the British Government and the Sultan of Brunei, who at the same time ceded the island in perpetuity to Britain.

This could have been an imaginative move on the part of the British Government as the position of Labuan made it a natural gateway to most of the trade along the North Borneo coast. In fact, it turned out to be an isolated incident. Another twenty years were to pass before any outside interest was shown, not by the British but by American and Chinese merchants who formed in Hong Kong a company calling itself the 'American Trading Company of Borneo'. They again acquired concessions from the Sultan of Brunei, and opened a trading post on the Kimanis River. For various reasons the venture proved unprofitable and was soon abandoned. A monument marking the grave of one of the representatives of the Company may still be seen on Kimanis Estate.

The next European incursion into Borneo came from the north and involved the Sultan of Sulu. Another gentleman adventurer by the name of Cowie conducted an arms deal with the Sultan of Sulu, in the course of which he learnt about North Borneo and its apparent potential. On his return to Hong Kong he contacted other businessmen with interests in London and the Far East. These included the Dent brothers and an unlikely starter, a certain Baron Overbeck, who was at that time Austrian Consul General in Hong Kong. It was the latter who entered into negotiations with both the Sultan of Sulu and the Sultan of Brunei and by applying the same time-honoured formula he obtain the cession of all the disputed territory of North Borneo by means of promising annual tribute to them both. After this success the Baron surprisingly withdrew from further participation, sold his interests to the Dent brothers and retired to Europe.

Cowie and the Dent brothers, however, pursued their intentions, formed a Provisional Association and addressed a petition to the Secretary of State for the Colonies in London for the grant of a Royal Charter. The application found favour, and provided that the Company should always remain British, that slavery should be abolished, that justice should be administered with due regard to customs and native laws, that there should be no interference with the religion of the inhabitants, and that the Secretary of State should retain certain powers of supervision including the appointment of a Governor, the Charter was granted on 1 November 1881. A few years later, in May 1888, the new State, together with Brunei and Sarawak, became a British Protectorate.

Having read the history of the territories, it was not without some interest that I looked forward to our arrival in Labuan. This brought us so much closer to the hub of all the activity, the Sultanate of Brunei! After the nightmare that had been Miri, it was calm and peaceful on deck the next morning. Dead ahead, I could make out the wharf, the few red roofs of the little township and the inevitable fringe of coconut trees by the water's edge. The sun was just rising and on the starboard bow lay Brunei Bay, the shore-line looking a foreboding dark green, unlit as yet by the sun's rays, the mountains behind appearing dark blue enshrouded with the morning mist as it mingled with the sky.

Labuan harbour was rapidly becoming clearer; the figures of men were ambling slowly towards the wharf. The engine-room telegraph rang down for half speed and the ship's vibrations eased. After a minute or so, the Captain shouted for the anchor to be let go. The engines stopped, and the tide, combined with the *Darvel's* own momentum, gradually brought the ship broadside to the wharf. A bow line was thrown to a coolie who languidly caught it and strode off in the direction of a bollard with the rope over his shoulder. Slowly he hauled the rope until the loop of the ship's hawser to which it was attached reached him. He heaved until the loop was over the bollard and then his job was done. The donkey engine in the ship's bow gradually hauled in the hawser and slowly and gently we came alongside the wharf.

The gangway was lowered and a smart white-suited Chinese comprador came on board; with a brief smile at the few passengers around, he went quickly up the companionway to the bridge. Shortly afterwards a notice-board was attached to the top of the gangway reading: 'Ship sails at 5 p.m.'

I had written a few letters to friends and relatives in England so I thought I would post them here even though they would wait in the Post Office until the *Darvel's* return trip to Singapore. Anyhow, it was time to practise some of the Malay I had been endeavouring to learn on the ship coming out to the East!

A small group of freshly painted black and white buildings set out by the sea towards the right of the wharf, with a Union Jack flying at a flag-pole in their midst, indicated the Government Offices. The Post Office was one of these buildings, and I thought the larger building of the group, with a large brass gong hung at the top of the steps and an armed policeman outside, was probably that of the District Officer. As I had no business with him I did not wish to waste his time by calling on him.

I was most impressed by the neatness and the tidiness of the place: the grass was all freshly cut and little two-foot posts, newly painted white and linked by black painted chains, were by the roadside encircling the Government buildings. The grass around it was like a lawn as it stretched to the sea-shore. It was almost like a well-kept village green in England.

The commercial part of the town was on the opposite side of the wharf; all the activity which the *Darvel* had brought was taking place here. The doors to the godowns were wide open, and coolies were trotting to and from the ship, sacks of rice on their backs, dumping them in the godown. The bustle of it all made one glad to get back to the ship and call for a nice cool beer!

At dinner that evening, the Captain had said we would be due in Jesselton at dawn the next morning. I was determined to be on deck for the first glimpse of my new home. It proved to be one of those moments that one never forgets. The buoy marking the channel as we rounded Pulau Tiga was still flashing, its light weakening as the morning glow slowly began to reveal the islands and the little town to which we were heading. Behind the string of flickering street lights the ridge of hills showed up against the brightening sky whilst the gentle off-shore morning breeze carried the perfume of frangipane blossom.

Suddenly, the giant mass of Kinabalu, thrusting its way up to the skies, its outline looming darkly on the western skyline, became aglow with reddening fire as the early rays of the rising sun reflected off it. This first glimpse of the highest mountain east of Everest is most impressive when first seen at dawn from the sea. It would have been the first sight of Sabah that the earliest Chinese settlers would have seen as they reached a land which promised them hope: 'New China'! For this, through 'Kina-Baharu', is the derivation of its name: 'k' is the old orthographical way of writing 'ch', whilst *baharu* is the Malay word for 'new', the substitution of 'r' for 'l' being a common philological phenomenon; the adjective always follows the noun in Malay. In splendour, Kinabalu should rank as one of the natural wonders of the world; it rises almost perpendicularly from the foothills of the Crocker Range to a height of 13,450 feet, shyly showing its summit only at dawn before it is hidden by the clouds as, with the intensifying warmth of the sun, the moisture-laden mist quickly rises around it, and again at sunset, when the clouds may lift for five or possibly ten minutes, and the dying embers of the sun's rays light up the cascades of sparkling water as they rush down its glowing red slopes. The sight of the early morning dawn behind Kinabalu was spell-binding.

The sudden clanking of the anchor chain brought me out of my reverie: the engines had stopped and we were slowly drifting towards the wharf. Then, in response to the engine-room telegraph, the propeller threshed hard astern and very slowly the *Darvel* drifted broadside to the quay.

The scene which met me was very different from what I had seen at Labuan. There was a line of railway tracks on the approach to the jetty and a turntable which enabled them to come alongside the cargo hatches, allowing the ships' derricks to unload directly on to the trucks. A telephone was immediately brought on board, not the hand cranking variety one would expect, but an automatic dialling phone such as I had not seen before in the East.

There were two or three Europeans who had come on board. One was the Straits Steamship Company's agent who went straight on up to the bridge to see the Captain, and another came over to me and enquired if I were Mr Brooks. I confessed I was.

'Welcome to Sabah!' he said. 'My name is Peter Edge, and I've been asked by the Resident to come and meet you and bring you along to see him.'

I thought this was a very kind gesture. I glanced at my watch—it was just seven o'clock and I knew they would be serving breakfast in the ship's dining saloon, so I asked him if he would care to join me. He agreed, and that was the beginning of a very long friendship.

I was naturally eager to learn where I would be posted and what my duties would be. I had been appointed as an Administrative Cadet and I knew I could serve anywhere and be called upon to do anything.

'My guess,' said Peter, 'is that you will be stationed on this Coast. Sam Chisholm is due to go on leave, and they'll want a replacement; but I'm sure H.E. and the Government Secretary will first want to meet you in Sandakan. Anyhow, my instructions are to bring you along to meet the Resident, Dick Evans, and he may be able to tell you more!'

After breakfast, Peter rang for a taxi, and we walked to the end of the jetty where it was waiting for us. It was Jesselton's only taxi and its owner-driver, Mr Chin, was known to everyone. On the way, Peter had said to me: 'You won't be sailing until late tonight, so come and have an early dinner with me. I'll ask Mr Chin to meet you at the wharf at six o'clock, and he'll bring you along to the house. Oh, and don't pay him! I will sign for it.'

It was a relatively short drive along the waterfront to a block of one-storey offices with a wide verandah stretching seaward. I remember that the first office which had an overhanging sign reading 'District Office' had quite a few people waiting nearby. We passed that and right at the end of the verandah was a sign: 'Resident'. Peter led the way into the outer office, where three or four Chinese clerks were busy at their desks. He went over to one who nodded with complete understanding and offered me a seat. He went through swinging half doors, and almost immediately came out and said: 'The Resident will see you now.' He held the door open whilst I walked through with Peter following.

The man who stood up to greet me with outstretched hand, I instantly recognized as one of the finest types of Englishman one could ever hope to meet: tall, well-built, and with eyes as steady as a rock.

'I shall be wanting you over here; we're very short staffed, but first the Governor will want to meet you, and I daresay they'll give you a short spell in the Secretariat!'

He was decisive and very economical with words, albeit friendly. Later, in adversity and happier times, I came to recognize him as the finest man it has ever been my privilege to know. He had always been a West Coast man, just as I was always to be a West Coast man, but those who didn't know him, or had not benefited at some time or other from his unfailing help or good advice, were very few indeed; he was a living legend.

It had been a brief interview and very much to the point; obviously the Resident was a very busy man. On leaving, I felt the gentle cool breeze coming off the sea, and looked out across the colourful bay to Gaya Island. 'If this is a sample of Borneo,' I thought, 'then it won't be too bad!'

Peter, so he told me, was Assistant Commissioner of Customs, so it was a busy day for him. He was wanting to get back to his office so he indicated other places whither I could wander.

'If you go down the road as far as you can, you'll come to Ban Guan. He has the European provision shop which supplies all the up-line people. You'll be needing him when you come round here. Then the road to the left will take you to the railway station and the *padang*, and on the corner there, you'll find Sakai. He has the only Japanese store in town, but you'll find that he stocks many useful things like thermos flasks—oh, and he has a good line in cans of tuna fish, caught by the Japanese at Si-Amil Island—excellent in *nasi goreng*!'

At that point, I bade him farewell until the evening and set off to explore the rest of the town. I spotted Ban Guan's emporium but there was no point in introducing myself at this juncture. I rounded the corner at Sakai's shop, and went to the junction with South Road from which I was face to face with the Town *padang*, a large building on a hill on the right which I was to learn later was the Sports Club, while on the left, by the side of a road bearing the sign Atkinson Road, was the Jesselton Recreation Club. That advertised itself with a large sign over the foot of the staircase.

I was delighted to linger awhile and absorb for the first time the lovely little town which was to become my home for so many years, but at the time I couldn't have guessed it. It had all the sights, sounds, and smells of the East. In the middle of the streets was a line of flame trees, planted only some forty years before when Jesselton was founded, which now gave brilliant colour to the scene with their cascades of scarlet flowers.

I walked along the *kaki lima*, the five-foot covered way, approached by four or five steps, forming a verandah for the shops, all open to their full width with their wares displayed to catch the eye of any passer-by: opened sacks of rice; boxes of salt fish; great stone-ware jars from China, brown with garish yellow decoration, containing 100-year-old pickled eggs; boxes of rough soap in bars two feet long. Inevitably, there were flies everywhere! Next to this general merchant, a tin-smith displayed all his wares: tin baths of all sizes, buckets and dippers, and the smith himself hammering away at a length of galvanized metal. Next to him a shoemaker displayed all the sandals he had made, hides hanging from the walls. In all the shops there seemed to be dozens of young children with the eldest girl carrying the youngest baby in a piece of cloth slung round her neck, and all of them staring at the European who was a stranger in their midst!

Immediately in front of me, but slightly to the left, was the station. There were no trains around and slight activity, but a low platform and rail-lines signified its function. By this time it was getting rather warm, and I thought a return to the ship would be more advantageous than exploring the little town any further. However, I couldn't help noticing the Jesselton Hotel on my return journey, set back against a rising hill, and further along, about half-way to the wharf I passed a stone-built building which housed both the Treasury and the Post Office. It was a longer walk than I had anticipated getting back to the ship, and I was glad to be on board again!

Well before six o'clock I was ready waiting for Mr Chin. He came promptly, and in ten minutes or so I was sitting on the lawn outside Peter's house, ice tinkling against the glass of whisky-water I held in my hand as I gazed spellbound at the dazzling, radiant, horizon-spanning embers of the dying sun, just dipping below Pulau Tiga.

We were due to sail at ten o'clock that evening, so we did not linger long over dinner. It was a very nice introduction to Sabah life, and if all my colleagues were to be like those I had met today, then indeed, I couldn't have chosen a nicer group of people to work with, nor a nicer country to work in! Mr Chin duly arrived about nine-thirty to take me back to the wharf; I bade farewell to Peter and I was soon back amongst the hubbub of a ship preparing to sail. I had already spotted Captain 'Winky' Johnston on the bridge. The telephone had been taken off the ship; dockers were standing by the bollards, and seamen were on deck ready to lift and secure the gangway. On the dot of 10 p.m., I heard the Captain's voice boom out: 'Let go aft!' followed by the clanging of the engine-room telegraph. The water churned at the stern and gradually the *Darvel* edged away from the quay whilst still being held at the bow. When we were some 20° to the wharf, the donkey engine paid out the forward hawser, enabling the dockers to lift it free from the bollard: we were away! The propeller stopped its vibration aft, and for a minute or so we drifted in the same direction; the engine-room telegraph clanged again, and with the rudder hard over we slowly nosed out to sea. I've never ceased to wonder at the dexterity with which the Captains of these Straits Steamship Company's vessels manoeuvred their charges in such confined waters.

At sea again, with a pleasantly cool land breeze coming off the shore, it felt quite invigorating after the stifling heat of the afternoon. It happened to be full moon and the shoreline was clearly visible as we pushed our way northward, but dominating everything was the uncloaked mass of Kinabalu, stark and barren in the half light, almost sinister in its silence. Perhaps that is why the pagans of Borneo believe it to be the abode of the dead.

I had quickly developed the habit of rising early, and I cannot remember a day of my life in Borneo in which I had not witnessed the first rays of dawn. It was the coolest, the freshest and the loveliest of moments. I was just going on deck the next morning to see the sun rise when I felt the ship heeling over to starboard. When I looked over the side of the vessel, we seemed almost to be turning into our wake. We were rounding the most northerly tip of Borneo and entering Marudu Bay with Kinabalu almost due south. The land towards the east was just a low-lying green fringe, and it appeared the same in the distant southern edge of the Bay. It was still quite an hour's sailing time before we were due to reach the township of Kudat, so I went into the saloon to have breakfast. John Massey was already there. He had come out on the same boat with me from Tilbury, but as the new Manager of the State Bank he had travelled First Class while I, as a lowly Cadet, had had to travel Second. On the *Darvel*, once the passengers had begun to thin out after Kuching and Jesselton, we had struck up a friendship and, if I remember rightly, we were now the only remaining passengers! After breakfast, we went on deck together and saw the little town of Kudat coming up on our starboard bow. It displayed the same by now familiar pattern of shop-houses, here some four rows neatly painted white with red-painted galvanized iron roofs. On a hillock of its own, on a promontory jutting into the bay, stood a large house, overlooking the harbour and dominating the town. I recalled that when the Chartered Company was first founded, Kudat had been the State's capital for the earlier years of its life, so probably the present District Officer had the advantage of living in a house built originally for the new State's principal officer!

Manoeuvrability seemed even tighter here, but with the same dexterity we were soon tied up alongside the wharf, with our bow pointing seaward. There was the usual clamour and jostling on the quayside, but I was quick to notice a tall well-built, hatless, fair-haired European picking his way toward the ship. He came on board and came over to where we were standing. With a glance at John Massey, he turned to me and said: 'You must be Brooks. I'm John Dingle.' I, in turn, introduced John Massey. He paused and looked around him.

'It soon gets sticky here, so shall we have a beer? It's cheaper on the ship than it is on shore!'

The steward, I noticed, spotting John's arrival, was already hovering in the background, so I thought John might well be accustomed to this habit.

From what Peter had told me about him in Jesselton, I gathered that John had been born here, and that his father had been Principal Medical Officer in the Chartered Company Service. He had had a public school education in England, gone to Cambridge, and won a blue playing rugger; he played forward and was unfortunate enough to have lost an eye in the scrum. Although not terribly noticeable at first, his glass eye seemed to become more obvious as the drinks succeeded each other! Soon we were knocking back pink gins, so it was inevitable John stayed on board for lunch. We were still sitting in the saloon when the steward came over to John and said that the ship was about to sail.

'Well,' said John, rather the worse for wear, 'I had better go and answer the mail!'

As soon as John had reached the quayside, the Captain ordered: 'Let go forward!

Let go aft!' and we were away, heading into the incoming tide and out to sea. After that session, there was no alternative but to lie off in my cabin! The sun was already beginning to set when I came on deck again, and I just spotted Banggi Island to the north where a small cluster of dwellings indicated a Japanese fishing settlement. A short while afterwards, the bridge telegraph rang and the engine stopped. Moments later, I heard the rattling of chains forward: we had anchored.

The Captain joined us at dinner that evening and explained why we were at anchor.

'The Malawali channel,' he said. 'It's all shifting sand around here. There are markers we can follow by daylight, but there are no lighted buoys. Lying up is the best thing. Pirates don't usually operate this far from the islands.' He pointed in the direction of the Philippines, and to Zamboanga just on the skyline. 'We're too near shore, but the Jardine boats have trouble. They pick up cargo in the small ports of the Philippines, and they have to have grills to keep pirates out of the crew's quarters, and iron spars over the side and at all entrances to the deck house.' The Captain was in a more talkative mood this evening. 'Steam pipes are at the ready all the time,' he went on. 'The one thing they don't like! Scalding steam! That puts paid to their lark! They came from Tawi Tawi and Jolo: those are their hide-outs. The Sulu Sea,' he concluded, 'that's a nasty one to be in. We could keep further out, but we'd use more fuel, and we'd be too near those islands. We're better off where we are.'

After hearing that, I thought to myself that those were the same chaps who were a scourge to the Sultan of Brunei; they must be still around today making a nuisance of themselves!

I heard the engines start up just as I was waking the next morning, and by the time I was on deck we were under way. I looked over the side, and sometimes the water seemed so shallow it seemed as if we might run aground, but I noticed that the Captain had a man forward using a plunger and taking the depth all the time. We were obviously sailing at half speed, but there was rougher water ahead and that seemed to indicate that we would soon be out of the channel. My thoughts proved correct: very shortly afterwards the Captain rang down for full steam. It wasn't long before the high bluff of Berhala Island was easily discernable on the starboard bow. I went down to my cabin and quickly finished off my packing; I wanted to make sure I was on deck when Sandakan came into view!

As we rounded the sheer red laterite cliff of Berhala Island, an immense bay, almost completely surrounded by a dark low-lying greenish-blue fringe of distant mangrove swamp, came into view. We were able to see Sandakan sprawling on its eastern bank. It was said at the time that all the ships of the then British Navy could have sheltered here as a fleet. When we arrived it was certainly the busiest port we had encountered since leaving Singapore. There were at least two other freighters in mid-stream, each with a pool of logs buoyed to it; one of these freighters was in the process of hoisting one of the logs aboard: it was swinging slowly in mid-air and was gigantic! We were heading for the wharf which, judging by the activity in progress, was clearly awaiting our arrival.

Quite a stream of people came aboard as soon as the gangway was lowered, among them a couple of Europeans: one to meet John Massey and the other to meet me. Stanley Hill was Under-Secretary in the Secretariat and had come down from the office as soon as he was told the *Darvel* was berthing.

'The Chief Justice has kindly offered to put you up,' he said, 'but it will only be for a few days. The hotel where you will be quartered has all its rooms taken by Japanese business men. You'll find Mr Mackaskie a very nice man, and easy to get on with. The Japanese will be returning on this boat and as soon as they have left, you can transfer to the hotel. In the meantime, I'll arrange for all your heavy baggage to be kept in the Customs, because I believe you'll be posted to the Interior later on.'

Stanley helped me ashore with my hand baggage, and we wended our way through the Customs to a waiting taxi. He spoke in Malay to the driver, and we were soon passing the Post and Telegraph Office on our right, and then the Treasury and State Bank. On the left a road led to the Secretariat and in front of it the Town *padang*. We carried on up, the *padang* on our left and directly ahead the Sandakan Hotel. On reaching it, we turned left and slowly started climbing. Large buildings were on our right: the Sandakan Club and the Chinese consulate flying the Chinese flag. At the top of our climb, we came to a crossroads where a policeman was standing under a sheltered platform directing traffic. As we passed, he came smartly to attention and saluted, Stanley responding.

'You'll get used to that,' Stanley commented, 'they are all trained to salute European officers!'

As we drove along, I noticed little boxes like letter boxes at the entrance to each driveway. I didn't ask anything then, but there was a query in my mind regarding their purpose: I was to learn later!

'There's no need to come down to the office today,' Stanley said. 'Get sorted out a bit first. The C.J. has a car and chauffeur which, I am sure, the C.J. will put at your disposal whenever he is not using it himself. Most often he works at home. Very few of us have cars; three of us who live close by share a taxi. We call it the "tiffin-car". There is an excellent taxi service. There will be telephones wherever you are likely to be—all free—so when you need a taxi, just ring for one. And another thing: don't pay for it, just sign! This is a cashless society as we are all known. If you go to the cinema, just sign! The bills come along at the end of the month, then you just take half an hour writing out the cheques and give them to the office orderly the next morning. I've already nominated you to all the clubs, so whenever you feel like going along to any, just meet the Secretary and introduce yourself. There's the Sandakan Club, which we passed just now. That's the main one; then there's the Recreation Club to which we all belong, Asian staff as well as European, and if you play golf, there's a nice little nine-hole golf course at Mile 3.'

I was glad to hear about that, as I had been a keen golfer in my university days.

By this time we had reached a point where we turned left off the main road and up a ridge to a big two-storey house and drove into a large shady porch. Mr

Macaskie was on the steps to greet us. A white-uniformed boy came out of the house to collect the bags. Mr Macaskie greeted us quite affably:

'The boy will take your bags up to your room. Go up with him, freshen yourself up, and then come down and have a beer!'

I went upstairs into a delightfully spacious room, had a wash, as it was already getting a bit sticky, and then came down to where Mr Macaskie was already seated in the lounge. Stanley had departed, but I was immediately put at ease. There was plenty to talk about and lunch was soon served.

'We all have a lie-off until about 4.30-ish, then it's usual to take exercise of some sort till sundown.'

The pattern in my mind was set: one got up early and worked hard, took it easy during the hottest part of the day, and then played. The only difference in my case was that I was destined eventually not to have time for play!

That evening, Mr Mackaskie suggested we should go down to the Club 'to meet a few of the chaps!' We were driven down and Mr Macaskie introduced me to those who were there, mostly commercial men. Holding centre stage was a well built, broad of beam, gentleman who, apparently, was the skipper off one of the timber boats in harbour. He was narrating the story of one of his colleagues who seemed to be known to most of his audience.

'He always said to me: "When I die, I want to die between the legs of a big black whore!" And do you know,' he continued, 'that is exactly how he did die!'

This story was greeted with guffaws all round, and someone called for another round of drinks. This, I thought to myself, is certainly a man's world! I was right. I was to find out in the next year or so that Borneo was a tough country to live in.

Before retiring, Mr Macaskie asked if I would like to go for a ride the next morning. I eagerly accepted, thinking that he meant a drive around the highways and by-ways of the environs of Sandakan. I came down very shortly after dawn, to find Mr Macaskie was already seated, eating papaya and drinking tea. I noticed that my host was dressed in jodhpurs and I began to suspect it was a pony ride he had meant. I was a bit taken aback, for I hadn't been on horseback for years, and I wasn't prepared for it in the same way as he was! However, it went off very well. My pony was quiet-natured, and it was very pleasant ambling along some of the little used bridle-paths around Sandakan. The morning air was cool and refreshing, and I enjoyed the 'ride' very much.

That was how my first morning's work began! On returning, I had a shower, tucked into a good breakfast, and then was driven down to the Secretariat. I mounted a broad staircase with double swing doors of glass at the top, which were opened by an orderly who was posted inside the office. I thought this was a good start: arriving late! I spotted Stanley, went over to him and apologised.

'No need to explain,' said Stanley. 'We know Mr Macaskie's habits, and we expected you to arrive late! The first thing I want you to do is to meet the Government Secretary, Mr Gray.'

It was one big office where Stanley worked, with about half a dozen clerks busy at different tables facing him. I figured that my desk was to be the one in front of

Stanley, which was vacant, facing the rest of the office staff. Stanley took me to an office, separated by the usual swing half-doors, at the front of the building. We went in and I was introduced to an obviously very busy gentleman. After the usual pleasantries, Mr Gray told me I would probably be here two or three months 'to learn the ropes' and then be posted back to the West Coast where the Resident urgently needed relief staff. He added that it was a very busy time of the week for the Secretariat, as quite a bundle of correspondence had arrived from the Secretary to the Court of the Chartered Company, which had to be answered by the out-going mail. I took my cue and withdrew. On my desk I found a printed form asking for my religion and the type of burial I preferred! I couldn't help suppressing a smile, but I obediently completed it and handed it back to Stanley. The first act in my working life had begun.

I was then handed a whole bundle of very thick files to devil. They formed what must have been one of the oldest subjects in the Chartered Company's archives: the Birds' Nests Caves of Gomantang. In the very earliest days of the Chartered Company, the collection and export of the nests of the swift living in the caves of Gomantang and Medai to provide for the expensive tastes of Chinese cuisine was one of the main sources of revenue for the country, and they were still the most valuable of all the minor forest products to be exported. A petition had been made to the Government and, as in all democracies, precedent had to be followed. This was to involve much 'devilling' of the file, and I immediately became involved with dealing with letters in Malay, in Arabic or Jawi script! Certain families had the rights to the gathering of these nests, rights which had always to be protected by the Government. I was immediately made aware of the necessity of the Government's Malay examinations which included a working knowledge of Arabic script! Much of my subsequent work whilst in the Secretariat was to be that of general dogsbody.

The out-going *Darvel* took with it all the Japanese guests who had been occupying the eight rooms of the hotel, so I took leave of my very kind host the Chief Justice and made myself as comfortable as I could in my new quarters. I was in the bar on my first Saturday having a quiet pre-lunch drink when a young smart-looking European Police officer came in and introduced himself as Mike Edge, Peter's younger brother. We had a drink or two together and thus began a truly remarkable friendship which in happy days or adversity, in Borneo or in England, has lasted over fifty-five years!

'Why not come over to the house tomorrow?' he suggested. 'One or two of the lads are dropping in for curry tiffin, come along and join us!'

I willingly accepted, and so began my introduction to Borneo society.

Stanley, however, introduced me to the correct and more formal approach expected of a young Government officer. I had to have visiting cards printed, and then call on all the Europeans by leaving a card in their 'box', the funny little things I had spotted at the entrance to every driveway.

'The Printing Office will do them for you,' he said, 'Just given them your particulars.'

At this point, I thought of John Massey and wondered how he had been faring. He had been met on the boat by the Treasurer, and had stayed with him for the first few days. He had been allocated a house and had moved straight into it, having acquired a cook-boy into the bargain! The State Bank was on the way to the Printing Office so I called in to see him. He didn't seem all that happy, as his house hadn't been lived in for a while and had acquired a rat or two, one of which had found a way under his mosquito net on his first night there. I chatted to him about the oddities of the social graces and the need to have cards printed; he had been given similar advice so we decided that when they were ready we would do the rounds together. That, in fact, is what we did. We also joined the Golf Club; I retrieved my golf clubs from the Customs, and every evening when we left the office, I would get a taxi, go to his house, pick him up and go straight on out to the Golf Club. The telegraph station was at Mile 3 too. I recall that they were both sited there as each required cleared and open grassland. We spent many hours that way and soon began to make a number of friends.

It was customary for the Government Secretary to spend a few weeks at a time on the West Coast, about once every eight or nine months, to clear up all outstanding matters with the Resident. He would stay at a house called Government Cottage and there he would entertain the planters and heads of local commercial firms so that they could keep in touch with the capital and Government proposals in general. When that visit occurred, it was the practice of the Governor, Sir Charles Smith, to occupy the Government Secretary's chair in the Secretariat. This ensured that all correspondence was dealt with expeditiously.

Sir Charles was a Chartered Company man; he had been recruited as a Cadet and had served on most stations in the country, ending up as Resident. Normally, the Secretary of State for the Colonies, under the terms of the Charters, would appoint the Governor, and in this case he had appointed Sir Charles. He was one of a line of good Governors the country had been fortunate enough to acquire.

It was a point of honour that replies to the Court which came in on the weekly mail boat went out on her return voyage to Singapore. Whilst the steamer was in port, life was hectic! On one of the slacker mid-week days, a note in red ink was placed on my desk. It read simply: 'Mr. Brooks. Please speak. C.S.' I showed it to Stanley who simply said, nodding his head towards the Governor's office: 'You'd better go on in!'

So I went over to the swing doors and gently knocked.

'Come on in, Brooks!' I heard the Governor say.

On entering, the Governor looked up from his desk, glanced at me longer than I thought necessary, then said: 'Come back and see me when you are properly dressed!'

I was a bit astonished and withdrew, feeling as if I had forgotten to do up my flies! I returned to Stanley, naturally telling him.

'Oh!' he said, 'he means you to put on a tie and jacket and then go and see him!'

It was customary for European officers to wear a tie, white suit jacket and long trousers to the office, and as soon as they got there, off would come the tie and the jacket would go on the back of the chair. Because I was quartered so near, I was in the habit of not bothering to put on jacket or tie, but had to return for them on that occasion feeling very small!

When I returned and was granted entry on the second occasion, the Governor was extremely pleasant. We had a chat about things in general, and then the Governor said: 'The Resident, West Coast, is urgently pressing me to transfer you to his Residency. A pity, as you are getting very useful here! But I know he is badly below strength, so I shall have to let you go. Please arrange to travel on the next boat.'

Stanley may have been aware of my impending departure, but he was genuinely sorry to lose my assistance. Coded cables about the deteriorating situation in Europe were arriving in an endless stream, and decoding took time. Those coming in groups of letters were relatively straightforward and one began to recognize groups which were repeated frequently, but the mathematical codes were devils! One mistake, and you had to do the whole lot again! A couple of evenings later, on returning from golf, the hotel boy summoned me to answer a phone call. It was the Governor asking me to come up to Government House immediately. I suspected the reason as Stanley had warned me earlier of the possibility. It was pages and pages of the mathematical code system to be deciphered. When decoded it raised the likelihood of the Japanese joining the Axis powers and the immediate action to be taken if this possibility proved correct.

The question which immediately arose concerned Japanese objectives. Japan had been at war with China since 1937 and by the following year the Japanese armies had captured most of the large Chinese cities and ports. It could be poised for greater things.

In the late nineteenth century, after the first Sino-Japanese War, China had ceded Taiwan to Japan, and even though Korea had been awarded independence, it too was occupied by Japan.

It seemed as if, by joining the Axis powers, Japan's ultimate goal was sparsely populated Australia. As in the case of all island nations and as a sea-going country, it would look overseas for territorial expansion. The riches of Australia seemed its obvious target. The capture of Australia would give Japan the resources it need and *Lebensraum* (to use Hitler's then current excuse for any aggression).

The key to this situation, as far as we were concerned, appeared to be America, and with American territory in the shape of the Philippine Islands on our northern and eastern flank, and their main port defended by Corregidor, the island fortress in Manila Bay, we felt our position was reasonably secure. No nation could make a sea-borne attack on such a fortress as Corregidor, defended as it was by the American Pacific Fleet. Such was our line of thought.

The United States had not yet entered the European theatre of war, although their sympathies were manifest in the Lease-Lend Act and the subsequent sale to Britain of fifty destroyers surplus to the needs of its Navy. It seemed unlikely however that America would still remain on the touch-line if Japan were to enter the war. She had closer ties with Japan than we did, and had a large number of Japanese amongst her own citizens. If war did break out, then it appeared probable that the war would be mostly fought at sea. Land attacks might possibly occur on Malayan territory which was mainly defended by Australian forces and the Singapore Naval Base. North of us there was Hong Kong.

It was, therefore, with some equanimity that we viewed this latest threat, and, at the worst, assessed our position as the centre of a whirlpool. It was, of course, only with Stanley that I was able to have any discussion, and I recall that he viewed the prospect with more apprehension than I. From the look on his face, it definitely bothered him, and with hindsight I sometimes wonder if he had fore-knowledge of things to come.

The information was 'top-secret', and in no way could it be discussed with anyone for fear of causing alarm and despondency. Certain officers, however, for reasons of security, had to be advised; certain plans had to be made. The impact the eruption of a war would make on the State had to be assessed. To that extent, there was an awareness that something was 'in the air'.

Of immediate concern to me personally was that my posting to the West Coast Residency was imminent. The *Marudu* was in port and Mr Vun Hon Kyong, the Chief Clerk in the Secretariat, who was to become my very good friend, had booked my passage. So I bade a hasty farewell to all my friends in Sandakan and found my way on board in time for dinner. I was looking forward to this trip for I had heard very good reports of Captain Findlay. In those days, the owners, the Straits Steamship Company, made a personal allowance to their Captains for passengers' victuals. It was up to him and his head chef how he disposed of it. There was no 'penny-pinching' with Captain Findlay. He was a tall, jovial and corpulent man, and he enjoyed his food! The dinner was excellent.

The same meticulous time-table was followed by the Straits boats each week. On the dot of midnight the *Marudu* cast off and by the judicious use of engine speed reached the Malawali Channel by dawn. We were in Kudat in time for John Dingle to come down to the ship and have his beer, but this time he had to forego lunch as we were away by noon. The skipper wanted to make good progress so as to ensure that we passed Banggi Island and rounded the Batu Mandi rocks, which were only visible when they were awash at low tide, well before sunset. Our out-going cargo was rubber with a certain amount of copra which we had picked up at Kudat, so we were only half laden and were fairly shallow in the water; consequently we rolled quite a bit. I didn't notice the movement greatly as I had had an early night in readiness for the dawn arrival in Jesselton.

Peter again met me and arranged for all my baggage to be brought ashore and taken to the railway station godown to be loaded on to the train the next morning. He guessed I would know the ropes by now so went straight back to the office, just passing the message that the Resident would like to see me during the morning. I rang for Mr Chin, walked with my hand baggage to meet him and asked him to take me straight to the hotel, where I had a wash, sorted myself out a bit and walked down to the Resident's office.

'To start with, I am posting you to the Interior,' the Resident told me. 'One of our best District Officers is there, George Robertson, and if you make out all right, I shall give you a District of your own in about a year's time.'

That was great news and I was delighted. When I rose to leave he said:

'You'll be leaving on tomorrow morning's train. When you get to Beaufort, go to the Club and have lunch and sign on my book. Also Benita and I would be very pleased if you would have lunch with us today. Just come along here at 12.30 p.m.'

Dick Evans drove his own car, and he went up Ridge Road to the Residency. A young uniformed boy with a *songkok* on his head came out of the house as we entered under the porchway and sprang forward to open the car doors; we walked straight into the lounge where Benita was sitting on a reclining lounge chair before a wide open window overlooking Gaya Island. A glorious scene lay before us: beyond the crimson flowers of the tulip trees on the lower slopes of the lawn surrounding the house we gazed on to the fringe coastal village of Api-Api, built on stilts over the water, and the varying azure colours of the sea where it drifted over the coral reefs stretching across the bay to Gaya Island. Benita was a tall fair haired lady of Grecian beauty. She was wearing a white open-neck blouse and slacks, and held a gin-tonic in her hand. Her repose at that moment belied her character: that morning, so she told Dick, she had done various jobs in the garden, kneaded the bread and made arrangements for their weekend visit to Kota Belud. She was a great conversationalist and immediately put me at my ease. Whilst we were seated at the lunch table, a young deer walked through the open doorway and into the dining room.

'Oh,' said Benita, 'we can't have you in here! He thinks it's time he had his milk.'

So she called to the boy waiting near the kitchen entrance to lead the deer by its collar out into the garden and around to the kitchen.

In the early evening, I paid my first visit to Ban Guan's shop and placed an order for canned food, spirits and a case of beer. I gave him the destination: the District Office, Keningau, and took out my cheque book with which to pay him.

'No, no, Sir!' exclaimed the clerk. 'We shall send you an account at the end of the month! You may need something else before then, and if you need anything from any other shop, like the tailor or the shoe-maker, just ask them to send the bill to us: we will pay it for you and put it on your account.' Nothing could have been more simple, nor a salesman more obliging!

The one 'up' train per day left at seven o'clock in the morning. I was having an early breakfast when I heard an engine whistle blow; I stood up and saw that the train had arrived from the depot at Tanjong Aru, so I hurriedly finished, signed the voucher for my hotel bill and ambled with all my gear in the direction of the railway station. I edged my way into the stationmaster's office where all pandemonium seemed to have been let loose: clerks shouting instructions to porters, native and Chinese peasants noisily jostling for their tickets, bamboo cages stuffed full of live poultry, all clucking away nervously! I went over to a Sikh, in white uniform with S.M. on his epaulette, whom I took to be the stationmaster; he was busily engrossed in filling forms, but as I approached, he stood up.

'Oh, yes, Sir, you are going to Melalap! Very busy now, Sir, preparing to get the train away! I'll make out your ticket!'

With that, he sat down again, reached for another bill-book and wrote my ticket.

'Will you sign here, Sir?' he asked as he tore out the counterfoil to give me. 'The train will leave in ten minutes time, Sir. All your baggages are in the truck!'

Anyhow, I was glad to know that! I thanked him, found the first class section and got aboard.

Most of the train was built for third class passengers and were not styled for comfort. Seats were slatted, with vertical backs, and the passengers sat back to back in groups of four with a central open corridor or passageway for access where most of their belongings seemed to be piled. Certainly it was colourful, with the Malay ladies wearing *sarong kebayas* bedecked with gold sovereigns which laced their bodices as they mingled with Chinese wearing their best *san foo*, or everyday dress resembling bright pyjamas.

I peeped into the second class compartment, and there the passengers did have cane seats to sit on: two benches each backing on to the side of the carriage with a central gangway. It shared half the carriage with the first class compartment where passengers had the privilege of enjoying the luxury of half a dozen green-leather padded bucket seats fixed on swivels which didn't look too uncomfortable! I made myself as easy as possible and was joined by a Chinese gentleman who introduced himself as the Inspector of Chinese Schools. He spoke very good English and it was good to be able to talk to someone about the countryside through which we were to pass.

Suddenly a whistle blew! I looked out of the window and the stationmaster had come out of his office, holding a green flag; that set the scene for all the intending passengers who had been milling about on the platform to hurry back to the seat they had each picked for themselves. The platform which had been so busy just a few minutes before gradually emptied as people boarded the train, leaving just the hawkers of Chinese sweetmeats doing late business through the carriage windows. Another long blast on his whistle, and the stationmaster had done his big job for the day! The engine, which had been hissing away in response to the raising of steam by the engine-driver for the long journey ahead, blew a shrill whistle and snorted in a cloud of steam, followed immediately by a jerk as it began its journey. I was bumped back into my seat with a bang as the train began to move forward, interrupted only by the sudden spinning of the wheels on the rails, damp with the morning dew, as the engine took the strain of the groaning, loaded carriages behind it. The journey had begun!

It seemed to be the one moment in the morning that all Jesselton had been waiting for! Children waved their handkerchiefs from the doors in which they were standing, men on bicycles waved their hand in greeting, groups talking in South Road also turned and raised their hands. Puffing and steaming, whistling at every bend, we gradually gathered speed.

The railway ran mostly in a southerly direction, never very far from the sea until we reached Kinarut, just a row of shops with a few natives strolling around; rubber-gardens intermingled with *padi*-fields until we reached Kawang, and shortly after there was a gentle rising approach to Pengalut tunnel. Here the engine puffed and grunted and slowed to a snail's pace as it climbed the slope; then there was a long loud blast as the engine disappeared into the hillside, puffing its way through and then, triumphantly emerging, it raced down the slope to a well earned stop, where there was a water tank for it to take on water and stacks of firewood, near which the felling contractors were gathered to load the tender.

Knowing this to be a longish stop, quite a number of the passengers descended from the carriages and disappeared into the nearby scrub, presumably to obey the calls of nature. After the needs of the engine were replenished, a whistle bade them all return, and soon we were progressing through *padi*-fields and rubber gardens of a very prosperous and productive region. After a few miles the train slowed and whistled as we came up to the biggest engineering feat in the building of the railway some thirty-five years before: the Papar Bridge!

This was the widest river we had to cross; the bridge had a length of two large spans with approaches on both banks. It had, running on either side of the track, pedestrian walk-ways which were in constant use as they were the only links between several large villages and Papar town.

Papar itself was a flat, well cultivated plain—the word as an adjective in Malay means 'flat'—and it was one of the oldest settled areas on the West Coast. It was located at a point where the Moslem coastal races met the Kedazan natives who had for many long years tilled the fertile *padi*-fields running up to the foothills of the Crocker Range. It also had a large immigrant Chinese population: some of the earliest Chinese immigrants had settled here in the early days of the Chartered Company. Well-established fruit trees were everywhere, so much so that it had gained the reputation of being the country's finest fruit district.

This was very evident as soon as the train pulled into the station, its journey of twenty-four miles having been completed in an hour and a half! Dozens of Hakka women, each wearing wide flat-brimmed hats edged with little black bobbles, flocked around the passenger compartments as soon as the train stopped. On their heads they carried shallow palm-leaf plaited trays loaded with all types of exotic fruit. They were offering mangoes, mangosteen, three or four different types of bananas, pineapples and a very pleasant jungle fruit known as rambutan with a red skin from which smooth hairs extruded, a fruit which you could easily handle by squeezing open the skin and find inside fleshy white segments pleasantly sweet. It was all a noisy and colourful scene.

Here at Papar, my Sinophile Inspector of Schools having failed, I fear, to instruct me in some of the rudiments of Chinese characters because of my interest in the passing scenery, descended from the train to undertake two visits to Chinese schools and I was left alone to ponder on the fortitude of the builders and engineers of this little railway, as it snaked its way through at times seemingly impenetrable mangrove swamps. Sometimes its path passed over easier terrain: the hard white sandier soil of the coast, and at other times we passed through cuttings of hard red laterite.

It was built to open up land for commercial exploitation, linking up the territorial concessions for which the rubber companies had applied and which lay mostly along the river valleys. It was now the railway which provided their only means of communication with commercial Jesselton. The estates themselves were usually in the *ulu*, that is 'upstream' from the railway itself where the more fertile land was to be found. At the rail-head of these estates little townships had grown. Papar was not one of these; this was a town in itself, a long-settled area with most of the amenities one would expect of a market town. For example, as the train pulled off the bridge, I noticed amongst the shop-houses and market places the Gaiety cinema, prominently displaying its sign. There were large godowns too, probably rice stores, as Papar was the pre-eminent district for rice growing, and also possessed rice-mills usually owned and operated by Chinese entrepreneurs. They were more often than not shopkeepers too, and very often 'bankers' to the local rice-growers, who, as soon as their rice crops were planted, would go along to them and obtain a loan, usually based on a *pikul* of rice at a price probably lower than the market value would have been, to provide his immediate cash requirements whilst his rice was growing! Such was the market economy of the more sophisticated native rice farmer.

It was another thirty-two miles before we reached Beaufort. We had passed several townships on the way, but none as colourful as Papar. An event of some interest to travellers on this unique little railway occurred at Kimanis. When we had made our call, we shunted into a loop line, and awaited the arrival of the 'down' train from Beaufort. Why it was always called the 'down' train when it was going northwards, I've never quite understood, but that was the custom! We were well aware of its imminent arrival by its whistle as it turned a distant bend and hove into view. It had left Beaufort at the same time as we had left Jesselton, so we were now passing approximately the half-way point.

At the moment, we were running on hard sandy soil, close to the sea; there was little vegetation beyond a fringe of coastal firs on the seaward side, and on the landward side, stunted palms, mostly *mandanus* from which local native ladies would make highly coloured sleeping mats.

The halts or stations we slowly jerked through were usually by the side of small rivers, which in turn lent their names to those of the rubber estates sited on their banks perhaps eight or ten miles upstream. Communication to the estate headquarters would be by road, but some had their own light railway.

In the early days of the Chartered Company, in order to attract capital for the development of the territory, estate land had been granted in the offices of the Chartered Company in London by drawing lines on a map, calculating the acreage and charging £1 per acre. A tracing was then sent out to the Lands and Survey Department for registration in their records with subsequent land survey and the fixing of boundary stones. For the newly formed Companies paying the money, it was fairly safe to assume that the river valleys were fertile areas, and they were seldom wrong. To businessmen in London it might have seemed good commercial practice, but to subsequent administators on the ground there was one vital flaw: there was no cultivation clause! There was, in fact, nothing to prevent the Company buying the land and just sitting on it; they had the freehold right to do so. There was a notable case on the East Coast where quite a large area had been purchased for tobacco planting; a little tobacco had been planted but didn't prosper, whereupon the estate was abandoned.

The typical practice of rubber companies operating on the West Coast was to apply for 10,000 acres and plant up about 2,500. I believe the worst example was Sapong Estate with an area of 25,000 acres of which only 5,000 was planted, yet it was the largest estate operating on the coast, and once had a staff of the Manager with ten or twelve European assistants. The slump of the thirties changed all that! However, the practice did in the main achieve its objectives which were to the immediate financial advantage of the Chartered Company and, indirectly, of the territory too.

On leaving Bangawan and Membakut, the nature of the terrain changed. We left the coast and the hard white sand on which the railway line had been laid and ran inland amongst mangrove swamp. We were cutting across the Klias peninsula; very slowly the mangrove gave way to drier land and we began to pass through rubber gardens with the odd smoke-house or two where the owners processed their crop. The train began to gather speed as we emerged from the jungle of 'no man's land' and we entered a well settled and developed township; paths appeared, and Chinese Hakka ladies with their usual characteristic headgear were walking along them balancing a *pikul* stick on their shoulders which bore sheets of smoked rubber on either end. The engine-driver was triumphantly whistling the train's arrival into Beaufort.

When we stopped, I carried my bags into the stationmaster's office, quickly identified him, asking if I might leave my bags with him and checking on the departure time of the train to Melalap. He was very friendly and helpful and, busy as he was, he took time to show me the path which led to the Club 'where you will have time for food and a drink, Sir!' And he concluded, 'I'll ask the engine driver to blow the whistle ten minutes before the train is due to leave.' What, I thought, could be more civilized!

Two planters were in the Club when I reached it and they introduced themselves to me. One was 'Pedlar' Palmer, and the other Mark Linggard who, with a shock of red, bushy hair, looked like and was a mad Irishman! They had, so it transpired, both been into the District Office to collect money as it was their estate's pay day on the following day. They both kept the money in haversacks at the bottom of their bar-stools, whilst they were knocking back pink gins! I had a couple of drinks with them but, wary of the passing of time, I ordered some sandwiches. I had just finished them when another European came into the Club and introduced himself to me. He was John Macartney, the District Officer. 'I heard you were on the train,' he said, 'so come on up to the house and have a drink! There will be plenty of time before the train leaves: they won't go without you,' he added, when I glanced at my watch apprehensively. I took his word for it and went with him up to his house. 'I've never been posted to the Interior myself,' he said, 'I reckon you are lucky!'

He had a beautiful house overlooking the town and with a lovely view of the Padas valley and the river which had just completed its whirlwind journey through the gorge, and was slowing down and broadening in its flood plain. We quickly had a pink gin together, but he noticed that I was looking at my watch and probably getting anxious, so he said: 'I'll walk down with you to the station and go to the office from there. You'll have Marcus Clark with you. He's been visiting the hospital today.' He went on to tell me that Marcus was an Australian, 'a good type', and was stationed in Keningau, but was actually Medical Officer for Beaufort and District and the whole of the Interior.

Marcus was already at the station with his Medical Assistant talking 'shop' together. I thought it odd that he should have a shot-gun tucked underneath his arm, and he may have noticed my odd glance at him! 'I carry this to take a pot shot at any croc I might see. It passes the time going through the gorge!'

The stationmaster looked at us, saying: 'We are ready to leave now, gentlemen!' so without further ado, I sought out my bags and thanked Mac for meeting me. We boarded the train. It was quite different from that in which I had travelled from Jesselton: the carriages were much shorter, almost the size of trucks, and the first class seats just benches. I had become used to the creaking and swaying of the first train, but this little thing was something different! Every rail-joint seemed to jar me; I felt that after an hour or so of this I would be left bruised and battered. The driver, though, knew what was ahead better than I did. He sped along while he could through the short stretch of flat plain, and then, as I began to hear the sound of rushing water, we began to climb, with a roaring torrent on our right-hand side. These were the last rapids as the River Padas emerged from its gorge. The puffing of the engine became louder and less frequent, and our rate of progress was considerably reduced. We were running quite close to the river now, with the water splashing against the rocks which were the rail-tracks' defence. The roar of the water was deafening. As we rounded a bend, I had a glimpse of the steepening sides of the valley, covered in dark green forest. We were following the course of the river which turned a complete semi-circle in its progress through the gorge. As we edged along the base of the northern cliff there was a spit of rocks between which there were pools of water. 'When it's in spate all this disappears under the water!' Marcus shouted to me above the din. 'It's not so much the level of the river which gives the trouble, it's the edge of the ravine slipping on to the line which is the danger! Sometimes the line is closed for up to a month at a time before it is cleared for use again. Always buy in not less than a month's supply of all your gin, whiskey and beer. You never know when it'll open again!'

There was a halt at Rayoh, at a place where there was high ground for a moment 'twixt us and the river, but it was only for the benefit of the railway workers whose families were also here, together with quarters for the men and their families who maintained the track. We were soon away again!

This next section became more and more spectacular; it bore every feature one would expect of a gorge. Around some bends little sunlight would penetrate and we felt the cold damp air as it hit us. Then we would pass over a short bridge, underneath it a drop of some sixty or seventy feet to a torrent, as it collected the early afternoon's rainfall. It was very shortly after this point when, on rounding a curve, the engine came to a abrupt halt, with our luggage falling all over the place. Marcus was instantly on his feet and down the carriage steps.

'A tree across the line!' he shouted up, 'That'll take 'em the best part of an hour to shift!'

I learnt that the line was always inspected twice daily, half an hour before the down train was due, and half an hour before the up train arrived, so this fall was very recent. The driver, the fireman and the spare man carried on the foot-plate for emergencies like this had their cross-cuts out and were hard at it. A number of passengers got out of other carriages, not to lend a hand, but to watch the progress being made. Eventually, all was cleared, and with a whistle, we were away again.

I noticed that Marcus reached for his gun, slipped in a couple of cartridges and held it at the ready through the carriage window. 'This is the spot you can often see a croc!' Marcus said. We continued crawling our way up the gorge, when suddenly Marcus raised his gun to his shoulder and fired a shot.

'Got him!' he cried excitedly.

I must confess I saw nothing, but there was a little disturbance in the water, where a crocodile could have slid off a sand-spit. Anyway, it satisfied Marcus, he was well pleased!

The noise of the shot brought cries of 'Wow!' from some young bloods further down the carriages. I don't think they had had a clue what the intention had been. Just another mad white man or *orang puteh*! For my part I just sat glued in wonder at the really spectacular scenery as we wound our way up the gorge; there was a different view-point at every bend. I became busy with my camera, as never before had I seen anything so beautiful in natural grandeur. Soon we made another stop at a place called Panggi where there were one or two other railway quarters, but I think there must have been a village fairly close at hand, because it was here I saw my first Murut—one of a tribe of headhunters of not so long ago! His sleek black hair was combed straight back with a plait hanging down behind his neck which was garlanded with large beads. His well developed bare chest was brown, tattooed and sleek; he wore just a scarlet *chawat*, or loin-cloth, around his middle; he was, of course, bare-footed, and he held a blow-pipe in his right hand. There were a group of two or three with their women-folk in the background, one or two of whom carried an infant slung in a piece of cloth hanging around their shoulder. They boarded the train somewhere at the rear.

After a few miles the chasm through which we were crawling, just hanging on to the side of its sheer wall of rock, gradually began to widen; on the opposite bank the hills were receding, and more riverine land was appearing, with vegetation and shrubs which, a little further on, blended into forest. On the other side of the rail track, the slopes had become far less precipitous too; we had passed through the gorge. There was one more halt, at a point where the Padas, emerging from its flood plain and just beginning to gather speed before entering the race to the gorge, again came near to the railway line. This was the ferry point to Sapong Estate. There was a small red galvanized iron godown here, where the Estate housed its smoked rubber sheets before sending them down the line, a truckful at a time. Quite a number of people descended here. 'Probably looking for work on Sapong!' Marcus suggested. He obviously knew the form.

Shortly afterwards we reached Tenom. This was quite a bustling little town of some maturity. I got out to stretch my legs. 'We've probably got time for some tea and a biscuit at the rest-house,' Marcus suggested; he obviously knew what to do. 'I'll just let the stationmaster know where we are going, and then he'll give us a whistle when the train's ready to go!'

There were about three blocks of shop-houses around two sides of the *padang*, two of them running across the bottom end of the *padang* and one at right-angles to the station. We walked along a well-kept path between the rail and the *padang*, turning at the bottom end, and approached the rest-house which ran across the other short side of the *padang*. We entered straight into the lounge. From this, wide steps rose to the dining-room which was flanked by a couple of rooms on either side, with access by a wide verandah the entire length. It was a pleasing and well proportioned building. Marcus rang the bell and the rest-house cook appeared. I think he may have anticipated that he would have guests coming off the train, because with the tea he also brought a plate of freshly baked buns, and cucumber and tomato sandwiches. I was quite hungry as lunch seemed to have been a long time ago so the food was particularly welcome. Just as we were walking back to the station, the engine blew its whistle, so we were dead on time!

The last part of our journey was interesting, not so much from the scenic point of view, as from the virility and variety of the cash crops being grown, particularly maize. Although in the environs of the town rubber still predominated, the further one progressed, the more recent cultivation had concentrated on peanuts, soya-bean and plantations of coffee. All the people we saw were the industrious Hakka, and around their homesteads they kept their livestock, pigs, mostly in sties, hens and the occasional cow. We stopped here and there at halts and crossed one or two earth roads, but we were soon to arrive at the train's final destination, the rail-head at Melalap, a journey of ninety-six miles from Jesselton, completed, including the stops, in eleven hours! Not exactly the Flying Scot, however much it had appeared on occasion to equal it, but at the same time the terrain through which it had passed was a little different!

George Robertson was at the rail-head to meet me; there was no doubting as to who was who. 'Don't bother about all your gear. I've got a boy looking out for all that, and it will come along in the bus.' Then turning to Dr Clarke, he said: 'There's room in my car, get in too. I think the Lacks are expecting us to drop in.' So we all piled into George's little red sports car, and drove half a mile or so down the earth road through rubber trees to a dark-green painted house on the right hand side standing on very high stilts and all mosquito-proofed.

Horry and his wife rose from their chairs as we mounted the staircase and came forward to greet us. They were very affable and pleasant people and were, I was to learn, our nearest European 'neighbours'! We just stayed long enough for a couple of drinks, but it was already past sunset and although he didn't say anything, I don't think George relished the thought of a twenty-mile drive through the jungle in darkness. The bus had already gone on ahead whilst we were chatting, but I could appreciate that the Lacks felt the need to exchange news with others of their kind whenever they had the opportunity. The land around their house was all flat and planted with rubber, almost up to the door, and it must have been monotonous to have lived in circumstances of that nature.

The drive to Keningau proved to be quite straightforward; we went over a couple of low-level bridges and I think it was these that had been bothering George because if the afternoon rains had been very heavy, and they often were, the rivers would have been in spate, and would have presented quite a worrying obstacle in a light car. At length we descended on to a gently rising plain, and I noticed a few lights ahead. 'Those are the lights of the *kedai*!' George shouted out, and very soon we were passing through the little township. We overtook the bus which had stopped to disgorge its passengers, and climbed the hill to the District Office, the focal point of the Government's Headquarters for the Interior District. The long passage from England had, at last, come to an end.

All whom I had spoken to in the Chartered Company service prized the Interior. It was in entire contrast to any other District, with the possible exception of Kota Belud. It had its jungle areas in the south, as I was soon to learn, but the station of Keningau was in the middle of vast open country. To the north, with hills and patchy jungle intervening, was the fertile Tambunam plain, narrow and not so broad as the Keningau plain, and further away lay Ranau, nestling by the foothills of Kinabalu and the mountain itself. It was much cooler at night than the coastal areas, and you needed more than a sheet to cover you. Insects, though, were rife, especially at night, when the lamp-lit room seemed to attract everything that lived in the jungle. It was remote and it felt remote! There was plenty to do, and much in which to take an active interest, yet the feeling of isolation seemed to get on top of you. I in no way blame George who was a loner too, but when one reflects, it was an odd life! Marcus was living in the Cadet's house on the other side of the station, and in any case was travelling more than three weeks out of four, so I had to live in the annexe to the D.O.'s house, separated from it by a length of gravelled footpath, a small bridge over a tiny stream, and then a slope up to the house. He was kind enough to put me up for the first couple of nights I was there, and I was grateful for that. He also had obtained for me the services of an excellent cook-boy, Linituk, Ituk for short, to whom for his tolerance, good humour, fortitude and help I shall always be most grateful. In a day he had cleaned the two-roomed annexe and made it habitable for me to move into. It stood on stilts about three feet high, and at the back there was a two-roomed bamboo erection, one room of which was Ituk's sleeping and living quarters for himself and his family while the other was the kitchen: just a mud hearth for a wood fire to cook on. There was a small lean-to against my bedroom which served as a bathroom, and outside there was a pit latrine: just the basics!

The message that I read loud and clear was that I should get off my backside and travel. In Jesselton, I had bought a saddle, and on my first day Ituk brought along a spirited pony for me to ride. He threw me once or twice, so when I called him 'Firefly', I felt he had been very aptly named! He turned out to be a very faithful friend, and I had him for all my time in the Interior. When we parted company, I calculated that he had carried me for over a thousand miles! On my first ride with him, he proved that he had a will of his own; once he got going, I had one almighty job to stop him!

On my first day's work, George asked me to come with him to Bingkor, an experiment in Native Administration some six miles north of Keningau. We trotted out, and I felt only stiff and sore when we reached there and was able to walk around and take an interest in all I saw, but George, naturally leading the way along the bridle-path, cantered back, followed by my pony. Whatever I did to ease him up was ignored—if the other pony was doing it, he was going to do it too! By the time I got back, my backside was raw! George saw me limping along. I'm sure he guessed what was wrong, but he said: 'Dab a little methylated spirits on it; that'll harden it up!' Like a fool I did, and nearly hit the roof!

My next task had a definite purpose. A section of bridle-path had slipped in a heavy rainstorm fifteen miles north of Keningau, as it left the Keningau plain and started climbing over a range of hills leading to Tambunam. I was allocated the task of first cutting a new trace, surveying it if necessary, and building a new section of path. I was given permission to take a *mandor*, or foreman with me; he would recruit labour from the nearby village of Apin Apin, and I was to issue them with chits for the number of days' work they had done. These they would bring to the office where the Chief Clerk would then arrange to pay them. I was allowed to take three pack-ponies with me to carry my gear. I was told the job shouldn't take more than three or four days but in any case I had to be back at the end of the month to close the account ledger, and despatch copies to the Treasury.

So my caravan set off! I led the way (never having been there before) on Firefly, followed by Ituk on his pony, the *mandor* and the syce in charge of the pack ponies. We passed through Bingkor and then I entered country unfamiliar to me. It was fairly open country, certainly not jungle, but there was a goodish bit of scrub land where secondary growth predominated. Occasionally, we would pass enormous bushes of giant bamboo; the natives call it bamboo *poring*, and to them it is a most useful growth. It can be split open along one side, and by a series of short cuts on the inside, it can be flattened and used like planks in the building of a house. It makes excellent walls, facilitating the air to percolate gently through, keeping the air inside cool, and it also makes an excellent floor, with a little give in it to give comfort when they lay out their sleeping mats for the night. Soon we reached the fifteenth mile post, and sure enough, as we rounded a bend, a bamboo halting bungalow came into view: this was our destination!

As it was now past three o'clock in the afternoon, and rain clouds were building up, I didn't propose to do anything more than make ourselves comfortable for that night. Ituk proved what a good lad he was and, in less than no time, had set up my camp bed and mosquito net, had a fire going and had brought along a refreshing cup of tea! It was an extremely pretty place in which to camp. There was a clear, rocky river giving a pleasant refreshing atmosphere, and after the rainstorm was over, it was cool and invigorating. I had brought a few bottles of beer with me, and these I tied to string and dropped into the cool river water, which acted like a refrigerator. This was my first night out alone in the jungle, and I was determined to enjoy it. I was able to have a refreshing bath in the river, and I vividly remember there was a most colourful sunset.

Word soon seemed to get around that there was an *orang prentah* camped in the village, i.e. a Government officer, for I heard quite a murmur of conversation emerging from the back quarters. I decided I would go behind and have a chat; I had to learn Malay anyhow, and the best way to do it (apart from a methodical practice of learning twenty words a day) was trying to comprehend it as it was spoken, and speak it myself however haltingly!

It was very dim and smoky when I entered the small area which served as a hearth and living space for all my followers. As soon as they noticed my arrival, there seemed to be a bit of a hush. Ituk broke the silence by finding a place where I could sit, and having entered the forum the talking gradually recommenced. Unfortunately, they weren't speaking Malay but chatting in their own language, Murut. Ituk himself was a Murut of the Keningau plain, but having served as cook-boy to European officers on previous occasions, and having gone with them to the coast, he had picked up enough Malay to be used, as on this occasion, as an interpreter. There were some three or four old men from the village who seemed to be quite old and infirm, who had come to seek dispensation from poll tax, *wang kepala*. This was a nominal levy of M$1.50 which, right from the inception of its rule, the Chartered Company had levied on all the able-bodied working natives in the territory. In origin it replaced the tribute demanded of old by the Sultan of Brunei; in a way, it represented the authority of Government, which was more vigorously imposed in former days, but now was gradually being relaxed, so that any working person who paid more revenue to the Government, e.g. in land rent, known locally as 'quit' rent, than $1.50 was automatically exempted. Anyhow, one look at these poor old chaps convinced me that clemency was the order of the day, and I wrote out little notes which they would then give to their village headman who would take them into the District Office on the next occasion of a visit, and on the strength of my chit, their names would be erased from the Poll Tax Register. I left them all happy, and we had no difficulty in getting labourers for the work that had to be undertaken on the bridle-path!

I had just settled down to sleep when there was a grunting sound outside the hut and a munching of grass. I flashed my torch and discovered that a herd of buffaloes from the village were grazing outside. I think they had come down to drink water from the river, and wallow in it; they were, after all, water buffaloes! It was just as well I found out what they were, because one or two of them decided to rub their hindquarters against the bamboo walls of the halting bungalow and I'll swear that the whole structure wobbled.

I was up at dawn with the others, had a cup of tea and some fruit, and straight away with the *mandor* went to inspect the reported damage to the path. I had to walk further than I had bargained for; the slip which had occurred was nearly at the top of the hill, almost three miles from the camp-site. Fortunately, a new trace didn't appear to be necessary, but the overhang had to be dealt with. It meant cutting away the upper slope to a width of ten or twelve feet, and bringing it down to a path width of some six feet, with good drainage on the side of the slope. This involved the construction of small bridges over the drains that I indicated should be built. I think I made everything clear to the *mandor*, and we both went back to the halting bungalow. On arriving there, I found that last night's softening up process had worked, and there were some twenty labourers, with their tools, ready and waiting to commence the job. The *mandor* went over to them and sorted them out, whilst I did justice to a magnificent cooked breakfast that I was ready and waiting for!

There was no purpose in returning to the scene of activity. The *mandor* had received his instructions, and I was content to let him carry them out. For my part, I had law exams pending in a month or so; it was essential to pass these to permit me to sit in court and undertake magisterial work, an essential part of one's duties as a District Officer. So I spent the rest of the morning and early afternoon familiarizing myself with the Indian Penal Code and the Criminal and Civil Procedure Codes. Later, after the usual rainstorm had passed, I walked up the path to inspect progress. I met the *mandor* and his gang as they were returning to their village. Their working schedule was to start shortly after daybreak, do a long morning's work, shelter when the rain came and then knock off for the day. That was the custom and who was I to vary it? They had, in fact, made reasonably good progress, but the real drudge was still to come. They had quite rightly started at the top, and had pulled the earth down the slope. Now it had to be shifted into earth baskets and thrown down the other side of the path. I reminded the *mandor* that they would need earth baskets on the following day, and he assured me this was being taken care of! I felt confident that he was quite capable of doing the job without my assistance. On my visit on the third morning, I assessed that the job would be successfully completed by the afternoon, signed all the necessary chits which would give the labourers their pay, entrusting them to the *mandor*, and made my return to Keningau.

It must have been the end of the month, since I recall my task on returning was to close the accounts. Whilst I was engaged on this, George asked me to go into Dalit country for a couple of weeks. 'Nobody's been there for many a long year,' George had said. 'Good: that's exactly what I am waiting for,' I had replied and basically I spoke the truth, but I must confess that I did nurse a little apprehension. A policeman was to travel with me, and I could take five pack-ponies to Pedawan, on the Pensiangan path.

It was to take a long two days' travelling to reach Pendewan and meant an

River crossing, Pensiangan District.

overnight stop at Sook. Here there was shelter, similar to that provided at Apin Apin. A journey of some twenty miles or so along the bridle-path was quite a stretch for poor old Firefly! I was familiar with the first four or five miles or so, as by this time, I had done quite a bit of riding around the station with George when he did his morning rounds overseeing gangs in their various duties of public works around the station. Telephones were vital links, and the telephone-line *mandor* and his gang had to be kept on the job. Bridle-path maintenance was equally important in keeping open lines of communication, and endeavouring to prevent incidents like the Apin Apin land-slip. Initially all proceeded without incident, but it was a wet start the next day. Before we could continue, we had to cross the Sook river! I was expected to lead the way, so, gritting my teeth, I nudged a rather reluctant Firefly down the slope and into the water. He decided on a path of his own choosing, and gradually, with a little coaxing, step by cautious step, he made his way across the rocky bottom, the water flopping against his under-belly. Like a human, I think he would have welcomed it more if the crossing had occurred at the end of the journey, rather than at the beginning. Fortunately, the rippling level of the river didn't reach the saddle, and only my feet were splashed. Soon all the ponies were across, and we pushed our way south.

Pedawan was located in real deep jungle and there was no bamboo around with which to construct an over-night shelter. Instead tree-bark had been used; it was quite amazing to judge the effectiveness of this material. The smooth bark of very large trees had been used and gradually flattened out, rather in the same way as bamboo *poreng* had been turned into a gently resistant flooring. News of my intended arrival was obviously known to the people of the local village, since they had been asked to supply porters, and it was not long before people began to appear out of the forest. By nightfall, which in the dense forest had fallen quickly without any sign of a sunset, a crowd appeared similar to that at Apin Apin, but here they were, without any doubt, Muruts, the head-hunters whose notoriety had travelled the world! Soon the kitchen fires were going, and tongues were wagging fast. The policeman who had accompanied me appeared to be the master of ceremonies; unfortunately, I was only just beginning to learn Malay. I was no expert, but I recognized that they were speaking a language I had never heard before! Apparently, so Ituk told me later, they were planning the route I should take in the Dalit country, and estimating the number of days the journey would take. This was quite a sensible matter, as there was no feed for all the ponies here, and they had to be taken back to Keningau. So that there should be no confusion over the number of days we would be in the forest, someone had obtained a length of very pliable creeper, and was tying it in knots along its length: each knot, so Ituk explained to me, represented a day. They were to return in twenty days! I think now, looking back, I must have felt horrified! Twenty days in the jungle like this, and with people like these! Well, this was my lot, and I had chosen it, so I had to get on with the job, and show the flag, with a brave face.

The next day the ponies started on their return trip to Keningau, and I started jungle-bashing! And what jungle it was! Down, over and up the edge of razor-backed

Murut warrior of old.

hills, then wading through rivers, first on one bank, and then, balancing on the edge of an overturned tree trunk which had fallen across the river and served as a bridge, recrossing it again! Then the mud on the flats, squelching over the top of my boots! But the worst horror were the leeches; they seemed to be everywhere, on every leaf that touched you. I can see them now—wriggling brown devils about two to three inches long, with a broadened snout at one end attached to a leaf, and the other end gyrating around in a semi-circle waiting to pounce on any passing human! You wouldn't feel them at all; it was only at the end of a journey that you saw the ugly things, gorged and bloated with your own blood. If you pulled them off, they exuded a poison which would cause the wound created by their bite to become septic. The most common way of ridding yourself of them was to apply a burning cigarette end to the beast. It didn't like that! But as a non-smoker, I devised another method which was possibly a little slower, but had the same desired effect. I carried an iodine pencil with me and applied it just above the wound, allowing the iodine to trickle down the affected limb on to the leech's snout. It would very quickly loosen itself from you, and the iodine, whilst it gave you hell momentarily, also had the beneficial effect of sterilizing the bite.

I found it extremely hard to judge the distance you had travelled. From your watch, you knew the number of hours you had taken on the journey, but it wasn't a march, or even a ramble! It was a slow foot-slogging ordeal! The maps may have resembled accuracy at the time they were drawn, but rivers in this part of the world, unlike in Europe, have a habit of changing their course, and the villages, by virtue of the shifting cultivation they employed, frequently changed location too. I had a good pocket compass and could tell the general direction in which we were heading, and I could only judge our progress to be about one mile per hour at the most. I felt a diary of my journey would be of great value to anyone who travelled in my footsteps, and every evening I carefully wrote it up, with other matters of interest which I will mention later.

Eventually, we reached the village in which it had been decided to stay the first night. The inhabitants may have had some foreknowledge of an impending visit, as they very probably had been asked to supply the bearers for my caravan, but they certainly didn't greet me with the village band. There was scarcely a soul in sight. I almost felt an intruder as my porters carried my gear up the sloping pole which served as a staircase to the great long-house built high on stilts. It was *padi*-planting time and all the able bodied men and women alike were out on the *ladang*, or cultivated area which had been cleared of forest. Although the porters may have found it easy to climb up the pole, it was a different story for me! It had been in the place for many long years, judging from the polished nature of the notches hacked into the pole I found myself climbing! I was glad to grab hold of a stake as I neared the top—it was a bravish distance to fall!

On first entering, coming in from the sunlight, everything was in darkness. In the far distance there was a similar open space to that which I had entered, and there was a passage-way running right through the centre, like a village street. On either side of me there were doors leading into small rooms. In some I noticed very elderly ladies, recumbent against the partition, in another, someone was leaning over a fire with a fan persuading some dying embers to burst into flame. As we approached the middle of the passage-way I noticed a big open space on either side, and it was here that my porters were unshackling themselves from their loads. Ituk soon got to work putting up my camp bed and mosquito-net, and I was glad to lie down and rest awhile after quite a nasty journey.

It was already late afternoon. We had still been on the march when the usual thunderstorm had occurred; my clothes had dried on me, but I obviously needed a bath and change. There was a small stream nearby, so I grabbed a towel, some soap and a dipper, and ventured once more down the slippery pole. After that I felt quite a lot better, and was in a good frame of mind to exercise my best Malay and greet the village headman when he returned from the *ladang*.

As darkness fell, there was quite a hustle and bustle as all the villagers in groups went down to the stream and bathed. In each of the small rooms in the long-house women were busy preparing food. The men slowly began to take up a place in the 'village square', and I noticed big jars being brought into the centre. Ituk, in the meantime, emerged from one of the rooms, having cooked me a meal which I was looking forward to, as by this time I was quite hungry. It was just as well I had eaten well, as I hadn't appreciated the drinking session that lay ahead.

Very soon, the headman, or *orang tua*, came over to me and invited me to drink with him. The formalities were dispensed with, and we struck up an amiable, but rather limited, conversation. I was bidden to start the drinking session! I noticed that there was a long bamboo cane protruding some ten or twelve inches above the neck of the jar, and within the neck there lay a leaf of a banana palm held in place by a split bamboo cane which, in its desire to be straight, pressed itself firmly inside the neck of the jar and held the palm-leaf stretched against the edge. Another but shorter bamboo cane just appeared above the banana leaf. I took a long suck through the higher of the canes and had my first taste of *tapai*, native rice wine. It was potent stuff. The *orang tua* indicated that I was expected to drink the *tapai* until the level reached the bottom of the leaf. Water was then poured again into the jar up to the top of the neck. It was then his turn to drink until the *tapai* reached the bottom. If this was to continue, I thought to myself, I must slow up the rate of progress!

To establish good will, I had brought along presents for the villagers. These took the form of tobacco, which they enjoyed smoking as a change from betel-nut chewing, and salt which the villagers badly needed, being so far from the sea. If they didn't have salt in their diet they were prone to goitre, from which some of the women I noticed were suffering. Having established good relations, it was not so long before I had the usual queue of 'old age pensioners' wanting to obtain remission of poll-tax! To retain a certain authority, I felt it right that I should not automatically approve each case, so I refused, rightly or wrongly, some of the applicants who seemed to me to be still capable of work.

It was Government policy to try and persuade the Muruts to abandon their *ladang*

Tapai drinking.

cultivation, which meant that every seven years or so a good few acres of virgin forest had to be felled and burned off, and persuade them to move down into fertile plains nearer the Keningau area. If they agreed to make this move, they would benefit more readily from the social services the Government could provide. First and foremost, medical facilities would be more readily available, as the periodic census of population indicated that the Muruts were a dying race. The next important argument was that of education. It was quite impossible for the Government to provide any form of educational facility whilst the hill tribes remained in the jungle. These were the arguments I was trying to get over to the *orang tua* as we sat by the side of each other with the *tapai* jar in front of us! They weren't fools, and they recognized the force of the argument, but they had their reply. 'We are hunters!' they always answered. 'If we go down to the plains, there is no game near us. We would have to return to the jungle for the animal food we need. Here it is all around us.'

There was, of course, force in their point of view. I tried to counter it by arguing that hill cultivation depended entirely on the weather, and that if they came to the plains there would always be streams to water their *padi*-fields. At that point there would usually be discussion amongst themselves; they recognized that what I was saying had truth in it. But they ended the matter by saying that the stars always indicated to them the time of year in which they should plant. It was a point which could only bring an end to any further discussion on the topic. Whatever village I visited in Murut country, I usually raised the same subject, but I was always met with the same answers.

So my journey went on, travelling from one village to the next, slogging my way often ankle deep in mud, balancing on tree trunks, fighting leeches: 'jungle-bashing' was righly named! There was one incident I still recall with some trepidation. After meeting up again with our ponies at Pendewan, we travelled back to Sook. There I was to encounter my first real obstacle. The Sook river was in flood. It had been a long day's journey, we were all tired out, and it seemed impossible that we could cross it. All my lads were busy having a conference amongst themselves, while I was meditating on the possibility of staying on this side of the river and building temporary shelter. Ituk and the rest of the lads thought differently.

'The horses can swim across,' Ituk explained to me. 'You must hold on to your pony's tail.'

I thought I could do that all right. We all had ponies, so theoretically we could all get across. I made an attempt, but Firefly jibbed a bit and he didn't seem to be the one to lead the way. Seeing my difficulty, Ituk offered to go first. He had had his pony much longer than I had had Firefly and could handle him better, so I agreed. Ituk slid over the rear of his pony as he urged him into the water, but I wasn't adept enough to do that, so dismounted and persuaded a reluctant Firefly into the fast-flowing water. He followed, and I grimly clung to his tail. My body was swept clean off my feet as soon as the current began to bite; I just hoped that Firefly would go in the right direction, and find the opposite bank as soon as he could! We were carried downstream quite a bit, but had allowed for that, and

Firefly just managed to reach the grassy slope before being swept into nasty undergrowth. We had made it! I was very relieved, and I had a double whiskey in a hot cup of tea as soon as we all had sorted ourselves out.

On my return to Keningau, George asked me to do a written report on my tour. This, and the closing of the monthly accounts, kept me quite busy until early the following month, when George asked me to organize a trip to take me into Bokan country. This was more inland and to the east of the Dalit area. This time I was to be away three weeks. If anything the country was even rougher and more hilly, but it was a repetition of the Dalit tour.

Frankly, in retrospect, I think jungle-bashing was beginning to bore me! It was at this point in time that there was a certain foreboding about military events in Europe. Things were not going well for the Allies. The British Army had been pushed out of Europe, and what little news we received didn't seem to augur well. My father, who was in Tanganyika, had told me by letter that if I felt so inclined, he thought he could get me a commission in the King's African Rifles. Fate seemed to be pointing me in this direction, for I could not see that the sort of work I was doing at that juncture could help at all in the war effort. My colleagues in more responsible positions than I must have had similar misgivings because the Governor felt it necessary to issue a circular to all officers, and at the same time arranged for it to be published in the *Straits Budget*, in Singapore, dated 15 August 1940. In it he referred to the restiveness among young officers to go to the main theatre of war and throw themselves into the fight.

> I have sympathy with that very natural desire, but I must once again make it plain to these young men that they are better serving the cause which they have at heart by remaining at the work allotted to them in North Borneo . . . It is not for the individual to decide where or how he can best give his service to the cause or whether he should be privileged to fight in Great Britain. The desires of individuals must very definitely be subordinated to the general interest. I must ask that that be accepted by everyone.

Reflecting back now on the situation at that time, it must be remembered that in writing those words, the Governor possessed the knowledge of the information in the secret telegram stating that it was probable that Japan was joining the Axis powers. That would certainly come into his mind when he issued that circular, and obviously I had no knowledge of any further developments of which he may have had top secret information. If this development occurred I could see that we would be needed.

I was therefore experiencing somewhat mixed feelings when George instructed me to proceed to Pensiangan on transfer. This was the most southerly and remotest station in the Interior, nearly on the border with Dutch Indonesia. No European officer had been stationed there for years. In fact Wittie, the last officer to be stationed there, who left his mark by writing a dictionary of Borneo Malay into English, was murdered as District Officer, Pensiangan, and the previous station Rundum, which it replaced, was pillaged and burned to the ground by the natives!

However, it was all in a day's work, so once more Ituk and I set off with the usual pack-ponies, which I was allowed to keep with me for the duration of my stay. It was five days hard going to reach there. It did really seem like the back of beyond.

It seemed to me that the site of the station had been chosen with defence in view; perhaps this was quite natural with the destruction of Rundum fresh in the mind. It was sited on a hill at the junction of two rivers, each flowing in an easterly direction. The smaller tributary flowed in from the west and ran behind a row of five or six shop-houses, joining the wider river Tagul as it flowed south to the Dutch border. Between them was a small *padang*, with higher ground rising to the north whereon was sited the Government buildings: first, the Police Station and police quarters, with the District Office and Court, then the clerks' quarters, and on the highest point the District Officer's house. Of course, it hadn't been lived in for years, and it was in some state. I couldn't very well stay in the Rest House whilst my own quarters were cleaned, because there was none, so I had to make the best of it. Ituk again proved his worth, and it was not long before he had the one living-room of the house in some respectable order. I rejected the idea of using an old mattress which was there and decided to use my camp bed.

I didn't attempt to go into the office and meet the staff on the day of my arrival; I felt in no state to do so, and consequently followed my normal jungle routine. This was my first station, and I was determined to establish standards. I was well rested and smartly dressed when I made my first appearance the next morning. First I met the clerk-in-charge, and became acquainted with the work in hand, and then I called in the Police Sergeant. He was an important man on an out-station, and here in the remoteness of Pensiangan, there was a sergeant-major in charge, sporting a wide red sash over his shoulder. He was the officer who had the most contact with the public. He received all the reports of any untoward occurrences; his training equipped him to judge if an offence had been committed, and the action he should take. Native Courts had long been established and these had jurisdiction over matters concerning inheritance, where native law and custom were involved, and the most frequent crime of all, adultery! Oddly enough, theft, which was common on the coast, was entirely unknown. It was seldom that an offence occurred requiring trial in a magistrate's court, the nearest being Keningau. If such a case did arise, the accused, the complainant and all the witnesses would be brought in under escort and walking on foot, possibly a journey of some seven or eight days.

There were two Native Chiefs in Pensiangan, each covering a different area. There was Native Chief Akoi, and Native Chief Enduat. Most of my travelling was to be done with Enduat; I came to know him very well and I think quite a mutual friendship developed.

There obviously was little work in the office to be done; mostly it was just a case of sending up copies of the accounts at the month's end, and, of course, of sending a report on my activities. There was no typewriter in the office, and I doubted very much if the clerk in charge could type. So my work was to be mostly travelling, which I believed to have been the reason for my posting.

The one saving grace, I thought, was the telephone. There was a single strand of copper wire between the office and Keningau, well over a hundred miles away. There was an extension to my hillside bivouac, so at just about sunset, when I knew he would be in his house, I rang George to tell him I had arrived. His voice was very faint, and I don't really think I could have passed on any vital information. Coming along the bridle-path I had noticed the telephone wire, and whilst in Keningau I had come to know the telephone gangs whose job it was to hack down the undergrowth below the wire, but any falling tree or branch could have snapped it at any time.

The travelling I had to undertake was to be totally different from anything I had done before. There was to be no jungle-bashing, for which I was very grateful. It was to be done mostly along the rivers, using dug-out canoes. Immediately after meeting Native Chief Enduat, I had arranged my first trip, and over the next three months he was to be my closest companion. I owe much to him, for the information he gave me regarding local customs and legends; in fact, I doubt if any European officer had ever learnt so much about the Muruts before, and certainly since. I was to be the last European officer ever to be stationed in Pensiangan.

To assist in the preparation of my monthly report I decided to keep a diary, and it became a ritual with me to write it up every evening after I had had my sluice down in the river. I would record, with the aid of my compass, the general direction in which we travelled, the number of hours we spent on the journey and whether we were going upstream or downstream, and would attempt to map the region I travelled through, with Pensiangan as the starting point. I venture to think that I was not so very far wrong! In this diary, I also kept a record of folk stories written up immediately after they had been narrated to me. This was a subject that had interested me for some time. I think the origin of the interest may have been the stories told me as a child by my maternal grandmother, who was a Cornish lady and was steeped in local legends, all of them having in them more than a germ of truth. I had concluded in my mind that if I collected folk-stories, it would add to our knowledge of a fascinating and little known race. I was dedicated to my diary, and would write it up too, the last thing at night, whenever I had learnt stories of particular significance from the local folk. I always wrapped it in waterproof material to preserve it against rain and the torrents of water which seemed to flood us from time to time as we went over rapids. I pride myself that it was a worthwhile exercise, but, alas, in a year or so's time, I was to lose it at the hands of the enemy.

There were one or two events which occurred in Pensiangan which I remember with great clarity. It was the end of the month and I had closed the accounts which were to go back to Keningau by safe-hand of a policeman who was being transferred. I had returned to my quarters and was drinking a cup of tea, when I looked down the path and noticed Native Chief Enduat coming up the path. I offered him a tepid bottle of beer for which he seemed grateful. He was, of course, barefooted as all natives were, he had a red loin-cloth, or *chawat*, around his waist, and over his bare body he wore a drill jacket that had once been white. His grey-black hair, unlike that of most Muruts, was closely cropped in modern fashion, and his genial wrinkled face broke into a smile as the beer slipped down and he felt more relaxed.

'Great news, Tuan,' he said, 'I have just heard that the *orang tua* of Kampong Selalir will cast *tuba* into the upper reaches of the river tomorrow morning. Perhaps, if the Tuan will not be long in this district, he would care to be my guest at this celebration? The honour would be great and would give me much pleasure.'

In this gracious little speech, the Native Chief had brought to a formal conclusion the many hints and signs of preparation that I had noticed going on around me in the last week or two. This feast was probably to be one of the most important events in the social calendar of the Pensiangan Muruts.

'I am honoured,' I replied, 'to be invited and shall be most pleased to accompany you.'

One of the principal items of the Murut's diet, being so far from the sea, was river-fish, bony and unpalatable to the European, but tasty enough, I dare say, in the Murut cuisine. By salting and sun-drying his catch after the fish-drive, a villager could secure in a single day sufficient for his requirement for many weeks, or even months if the drive proved to be successful. It was an ancient method, but it was a great boon to the natives.

Tuba is an indigenous name for a poisonous jungle-root. There are several varieties, of which the most common may be three or four inches in diameter, sinuous and very thorny. It is found commonly in the jungle; in some areas one variety may be more prevalent, elsewhere another. If it is not plentiful in the area, growing wild in the jungle, it is frequently cultivated, for the sole purpose of fishing. Large quantities of the root are needed for a successful drive, and it is collected over a long period of time. On the day selected, when all the stars are right, the women beat it into a pulp on which water is poured, causing a poisonous milky-white fluid to drain from it. This flows into the river, and after some minutes, has the effect of stupefying the fish which rise momentarily to the surface. The aim of the natives is to spear the fish whilst they are leaping, almost like a salmon jumping a weir, or to catch them in nets at this instant. As the poisonous extract passes through the reach in which it is intended to make the drive, the poison becomes so diluted that in the lower courses of the river, say two or three miles from the starting point, the poison has no effect. I was assured that the poison was not deleterious to the edible value of the fish!

When I had journeyed upstream some two weeks earlier, I had noticed natives busily constructing a bamboo barrier. They had driven stakes into the river-bed, and were securing split bamboo lengthwise to them, both below the water and above to a height of some three or four feet. There was still a passage through which canoes might be paddled, but this, I was told, would be closed later when the barrier was needed. It was described to me then simply as a fish-trap. I had encountered other signs of animated activity, and I had anticipated the event almost with the excitement of any native, together with a curiosity for a sport in which I had not taken part before.

Dawn, the morning following the Native Chief's visit to me, found me in his canoe, not the Government canoe in which I normally journeyed, paddled by some sixteen or seventeen men all in high spirits! All around a mass of canoes were making their way slowly upstream. It is an arduous business, poling or paddling against a fast flowing stream, and sometimes we had to step out whilst the boat was dragged over a shallow, rocky shelf. But everyone was eager and gay. Along the river-bank in front of the scattered long-houses, villagers were busy on the beaches, some launching their canoes, others pushing off. Soon we hauled the boat through the confined rushing water of the gateway in the barrier, which would later be closed. 'Clonk, clonk, clonk . . .' rubbed sixteen paddles in regular rhythm against the side of the canoe. Finally we rounded another bend to see a vast throng gathered on the beach, shouting and singing, with banners flying above them.

Native Chief Enduat became as excited as a little boy. 'Here is the headman coming to meet us,' he exclaimed.

A fine specimen of a native greeted us. He solemnly raised his hand and placed it on his heart after we had shaken hands.

'Welcome, Tuan, to my poor house and frugal hospitality!'

He was dressed in a brilliant yellow loin-cloth. His hair was long and done up in a bun, held in place by a long pin of fashioned bone. After leading the way to a palm-leaf hut, especially erected for the occasion, he described the celebrations which had begun at dusk the previous evening, when all the villagers of his *kampong*, and those of another nearby, had commenced feasting and drinking. At midnight they had come to the beach and started to pound the *tuba*.

The headman explained an interesting division of labour between the villagers of his long-house and those of the neighbouring village just a mile upstream. His men for the last month had been gathering the *tuba* root from the jungle and had brought it down to this beach. And last night his villagers were the hosts, the womenfolk providing the food, and the men the *tapai*. In exchange, the neighbouring village had constructed the bamboo barrier downstream and were pounding the *tuba*. Next year the roles would be reversed; his men would build the barrier, and those of the other village could collect the *tuba*.

The three of us had a drink of *tapai* together, and then went outside and made our way through the crowds to the centre of activity. Men stepped aside for us until we came up to two great mounds of reddish ochre-coloured *tuba* root, each heap about ten feet long by four to five feet wide, and beaten down to a height of some two to three feet. Around one heap women with long clubbed sticks were battering the root into a fibrous tangled mass. Adjacent to them men were similarly engaged attacking the other mound. Never did the two sexes mingle and work at the same mound. Whilst raising and lowering their clubs they chanted and laughed, joking amongst themselves, and seemed goaded by a feverish excitement and by the remarks of the older men standing around.

One of the men, noticing us, dropped his stick and came over to our party. He exchanged a few words with the Native Chief, who introduced him to me as the headman of the neighbouring village whose task it was this year to pound the *tuba*.

'It's nearly finished now, Tuan,' he explained to me, 'the sap is just beginning to run. It's been a hard job, we've been beating it all night.' And drinking too, I thought to myself, for the old Murut was rather unsteady on his feet, and a strong smell of *tapai* and sweat exuded from him. But he confessed to it as he went on: 'If anyone has tired, he has dropped out, rested and refreshed himself with *tapai*!' I smiled to myself as, judging by the sleepy merry look on their faces, most of them had done their fair share of sitting out!

Just at that moment, one of the women shouted out to the headman. 'She is exhausted!' said Enduat, turning to me. 'She says the *tuba* has been sufficiently beaten!' The woman dropped her stick and the headman went over and examined the root. There was a brief discussion in which the experience of the Native Chief was sought. Then the headman called to all to stop. There was a cheer from the workers, which was taken up by all the crowd waiting around.

Enthusiasm reached fever-pitch. Slowly the natives began to move back to the boats for the next stage of the ceremony, which would take place at the river-bank. Suddenly several people shouted and pointed at a bird which was hovering briefly amongst the trees on the far side of the river.

'A *nahagan*,' Enduat said to me dramatically. 'It is what we all hope to see when we fish in this manner, for it means that the sap of the tuba is deadly, and the fish in the river are plentiful. The omens are good.'

Whilst we were once more settling ourselves in our boat, the natives were already carrying the pounded *tuba* from the heaps to low bamboo platforms built over the river and running adjacent to the bank. As soon as the greater proportion had been shifted, men, bearing bamboo-*poreng* water containers, stood on the edge of the platform and poured water over the red tangled mass of *tuba* root. This went on continuously until all the *tuba* had been treated in a like manner.

After a few minutes, when the water had percolated through the pile, a white milky fluid began to drip from under the bamboo staging into the river below. The natives stirred restlessly in the boat. We were in mid-stream; a gentle movement of a couple of paddlers prevented us from drifting with the current. The rest of us picked up barbed spears, or nets fixed firmly to a pole, in construction resembling shrimping nets. As the minutes passed there was a silence of anticipation—a silence curious among these people who had been chattering and shouting on the banks a quarter of an hour earlier; now they had settled themselves in scores and scores of canoes of all sizes. Some had drifted down to deep pools in the river-bed, where they said the big fish would be found; many were still holding fast to the river bank in readiness; others, like ourselves, lay off in mid-stream, waiting. All were breathlessly silent, with eyes staring fixedly at the water, anticipating the momentary rise of the fish to the surface.

The milky whiteness spread gradually over the width of the river, and then downwards with the drift of the stream. Hushed moments slipped by; then there was a shout, a sudden movement, and the sun glinted on a metal spear as it was held high and thrust into the water. 'Whao-oo!' shouted the natives in the nearby boats as a man proudly raised a gleaming fish on the end of his spear. The first catch of the day! Then another shout, then another! The poison was having its deadly effect. I strained my eyes; suddenly, just a yard away, there was a flash of white as a fish rose and turned on its back to dive again. A splash, a quick twist of a net, and a fish was twitching at my feet. An alert native had captured it whilst I was too surprised to move.

The poison was drifting down with the stream; with it, too, drifted the boats. It was beginning to have a fuller effect on the fish as more and more sap from the lacerated *tuba* root was washed into the river. In all directions fish were being netted or speared, or even caught by hands. Soon fish of all sizes and kinds were lying thick in the bottom of our boat. The alacrity and skills of the natives were quite outstanding. This was sport indeed, for no amateur like myself could catch any except by the remotest chance!

Down and down we drifted, excitement and expectancy ever at the same tension, until, as we approached the barrier, it reached its peak. Here the wisest and strongest fish, as Enduat described them to me, had swum ahead in advance of the poison, until they had been driven by the wall of polluted water into the barrier, and ultimately into the nets. Meeting the obstruction, they would try to jump it. Many succeeded and disappeared downstream; others, less lucky, were caught by the swift and agile natives. The boats thronged so closely that occasionally the fish merely leapt from the water into a canoe, to the accompaniment of screams from the women and whoops from the men! Every square foot of river seemed covered by a waiting spear or net.

Morning wore into afternoon, and the afternoon into evening, until the boats, loaded with fish, began gradually to disperse. All agreed that it had been a most successful drive, and they thanked the villagers in the first place who had gathered the *tuba*, and then those who had pounded it with such effect. In token of their gratitude, they each selected the best fish from their catch and, following an age-long custom, handed them to the two headmen of the sponsoring villages, who in turn would divide them amongst their villagers. So all were pleased and a good day came to an end.

I was to learn that many, European officers included, criticised this method of fishing as wasteful and injurious to a permanent fish supply for the native. It was said that it is a practice that should be forbidden by the Government. In coastal areas where tribal authority has largely broken down, owing to the influx of alien races, it is a practice that has been forbidden. But in the Interior, amongst a community where native law and authority are still strong, fishing by this method has not been interfered with. The natives, after all, are wise enough to guard their own food supplies. Enduat explained it all to me. In the first place many of the stronger fish escape, and recover from the temporarily stupifying effects of the poisoning. Secondly, different river reaches are used in rotation, many years elapsing before the same reach is again poisoned. Finally, against which there is no argument, it is a custom which has been carried out by the natives of this region for centuries—and I was not impressed by the lack of fish on the day I went *tuba* fishing!

Shortly after this interesting interlude, I received instructions from George that I was to proceed down the Sembakong River and inspect the boundary stone marking the frontier between Dutch Borneo and British North Borneo. I didn't really think this was going to be much of a contribution to the war effort, but mine was not to reason why. I did what I was bidden, and when I found the stone, I endeavoured to carve my initials on it; I noticed that others had done it before me. (I was, I believe, the last European officer to do this.) We had travelled downstream on a fairly fast-flowing river; it was a different story going back up again!

One incident I remembered well. Native Chief Enduat and I had disembarked whilst the Muruts manhandled the boat up over some rapids. It had been a difficult walk over stones rubbed smooth by the passing of time and rushing water; it had been a difficult job for the natives too. When they had secured the boat, they came ambling over to the patch of shade where we were both seated. A savage looking lot, I was thinking to myself. Most wore only red or black *chawats*, their long hair held up only by a long curved bone; their breast and arms were tattooed all over with strange designs the like of which I had never seen before. Each one wore a deadly *parang*, secured to a locally woven ornamental belt around his waist. It was at this moment that Enduat chose to tell me that it was on this same sand-spit that the older pioneer of the Chartered Company by the name of Wittie had been speared to death. I recalled the name he was trying to say as that of an older Chartered Company officer who had written a Borneo Malay/English dictionary; in fact I had a copy! It was a work of great value when studying the language, as I was. I had read too of his death, so I hastily changed the subject.

On my return to Pensiangan, I found another letter awaiting me from George, instructing me to do a tour of another part of the Bokan country and then return to Keningau. Strangely, I had mixed feelings about this. I had grown accustomed to these likeable Muruts and found I was liking them and Enduat in particular. He was forever telling me folk-stories; he had a fund of them! Not only did I enjoy listening to them, but by hearing them in his version of Malay, I discovered I was not only getting better and better at understanding the language, but also at speaking it! My log-book was rapidly filling up, as every night I would write up something of the day's events and of the legends I had been told.

Enduat came with me through the Bokan country, even though strictly it was Akoi's territory. Over the few weeks that had passed since being in Pensiangan, Enduat and I had developed a rapport which, I like to think, was mutual. He had certainly taught me much about the Muruts in times past, and how, for example, they disliked the Brunei tribute seekers. They were in fact quite hostile to the Bruneis, a point which I noted and included in my report on my attachment to the District advising that care should be taken not to post a Brunei clerk or policeman in the area. I felt that any such posting even now could give rise to friction.

There was a good deal of planning needed for this last trip. At some spot I would emerge from the jungle and join up with the bridle-path. I wanted, if possible, to name the halting bungalow nearest to this point. I could then arrange for my ponies and my pack-ponies to meet me there. Nobody, however, seemed to be able to give me any exact information; it all seemed to depend on the state of the rivers, whether they were in flood or not, whether a certain village had changed to its new location and so on. So I had to stipulate twenty days, and twenty knots were tied into a length of *rotan*. I sent the message that my ponies were to meet me at Sepulot in twenty days!

There were two events of which I still have a vivid memory and which occurred on this trip. The first was my encounter with a springing dancing floor. As usual, the village in which we were staying had made merry with *tapai* in celebration of my arrival. The usual exchanges of gifts had been made and it had so happened that the village headman was a very affable character. He was busy shouting out instructions to his various henchmen and I didn't follow what was happening at all. At one point I was being pressed to partake of food which didn't appeal to me, for the answer I received in response to one question I asked was 'pickled rat'! I settled for dried meat of a *pelandok*, or mouse deer, which was not all that unpalatable. The main concentration of the headman, however, was the state of readiness of the evening's main attraction: the springing dancing floor!

I had been told of the existence of this by Enduat as we journeyed towards the village, but I hadn't given much attention to it as I did not know what was in store. Evidently few villages had them, but the possession of one added greatly to prestige, hence all the excitement now! A few more shouts from mine host—I noticed it was already eleven o'clock by my watch—and the women gradually emerged in ones and twos. The young girls were already animatedly looking down on the scene from the virgins' loft above and to the side of the dance floor. Then the gongs struck up, and slowly the women began to go on to the dancing floor, moving their weight in the rhythm of the beat, with their backs to the inside of the circle; then with the concerted movement of the weight of their bodies and their feet keeping time with the gongs, the floor began slowly to move up and down. The men then all joined in facing the women in an outside circle, and all began singing a sort of chanting song, the women moving slowly in a clockwise direction, and the men circling outside them in an anti-clockwise direction. All the time the floor was moving rhythmically, up and down, up and down. I felt that ultimately I would be entreated to join in. I was!

Every so often, a man would grab a woman from the inner circle, and some time later they returned, seemingly rather sheepishly! That gave me a clue as to the purpose of this rather ritual occasion. All night long the gongs were beaten endlessly: all night long the springing dance floor moved up and down, up and down! Eventually, I was duly bidden to join in the circle. The younger girls in the inner ring appeared to me to be bashful and a little coy. Perhaps they were scared of me; perhaps they wondered if I was going to pick on any of them. Nothing was further from my thought! I was merely wondering how on earth I should sleep that night, because my camp-bed was only on the other side of the 'village square' of the long-house: in *coro publico*!

The knots on the *rotan* cane were rapidly being untied, and eventually the day came when I should emerge at Sepulot. It had been a vile afternoon; the thunder and lightning had been continuous, the rain never seemed to stop and darkness descended quickly. I wondered whether there was any village nearby but received a negative reply. Eventually we hit the bridle-path, by which time it was already dark. For a long time Enduat had been saying that it wasn't much further now, and I felt that surely he must be right. At long last we turned a corner, and there were lights ahead! But I had forgotten one thing: we had to cross the River Agis before we could reach the halting bungalow!

This wasn't an easy job. The path took us to a wire suspension bridge, and this was the second event of which I have an all too vivid memory! I recalled that the first time I had crossed it on going down to Pensiangan it wasn't in good repair, and I had left instructions with the local bridle-path *mandor* to have the decking replaced. I didn't think my carriers were any too happy as they walked across ahead of me. Certainly I wasn't!

I persuaded the policeman to go ahead of me, with Enduat and Ituk following. The policeman dangled a storm-lantern hitched to his uniform: it was lashing wind and rain and the river, in flood, some fifty feet below, was a roaring torrent as it dashed against the rocks below. I didn't like it one little bit! I clung like grim death to the supporting wires at shoulder height on either side, but they were wobbling up and down and every way as the bridge was swung this way and that by the wind. When I was nearly half-way across, I felt like turning back, but I had already sent the carriers across so all my camping gear was already safely on the other bank. There was nothing else for it except to hold on tight and hope for the best. Gingerly, I put each foot forward, testing each piece of the stretcher for strength—it was made mostly of tree-bark if I remember rightly—to make sure it would take my weight; a snapped wooden lath and I must surely slip and a plunge into the river would have been inevitable. It meant certain death, so I clung on desperately hard! At last I felt the decking begin to firm beneath each footstep as we climbed to the twin posts supporting the 'bridge'; I nearly ran the rest of the way, I was so thankful to get over the worst! I quickly made for the halting bungalow and dived for the remaining whiskey I had in a bottle. It went down without touching the sides! I think I had just lived through the worst moments of all my jungle travelling.

That evening, after Ituk had produced some excellent *nasi goreng*, I felt very tired, and instead of going to the back of the bungalow and chatting to Enduat and the porters, I wrote up my diary and straight away disappeared under my mosquito net. The next morning I was feeling very out of sorts, and I did toy with the idea of resting here for the day. But, I argued, if I was ailing for something, it would be foolish to stay here. So I bade a fond farewell to Native Chief Enduat, and thanked him profusely for all the help, guidance and tolerance he had shown me throughout all the weeks I had travelled with him. In reply, he took from his waist the *parang* he was carrying and insisted, in spite of my remonstrations, that I accepted it in memory of my stay amongst his people. Throughout all the subsequent vicissitudes of war, it still remained with me and to this day hangs on my sitting-room wall.

My syce had arrived with Firefly the previous day; the pony looked well fed and had rested so I could look forward to a fast trip back to Keningau. The pack-ponies and their syce had travelled with Ituk, and the latter was busy supervising the loading of my *barang* into the ponies' pack-saddles. He signalled that all was ready. I mounted

Firefly, and Enduat stood ceremoniously by and raised his hand in farewell as my caravan began its journey northwards. I was never to see him again, and as I moved off I felt I had lost a friend.

I pushed on as fast as I could, and when I eventually reached Sook, I was lucky in not finding the river in flood. We crossed much easier than on a former occasion. I was glad of that as the day's travelling had increased my weariness and I became suspicious that I was running a fever. I took my temperature and it was well above normal, but as I now had only a long day's journey ahead, I felt a quick journey back to base was the answer. Ituk had appreciated my lassitude and said: '*Tuan ada sakit domum.*' A common enough complaint in the villages but I now understood its meaning: I had fever, he had said.

We did make an early start, but even today, I recall how lousy I was feeling. Fortunately, I was beginning to recognize the terrain and instinctively felt we were nearing Keningau. I seem to recall having passed the sixth milestone, when I must have passed out and slumped in the saddle. The next thing I remembered was lying on a make-shift stretcher and being carried up the hill to Keningau station.

I had hoped Marcus Clark might not have been travelling and that he would be on the station, but no such luck! He was in the jungle too. As it turned out he had entered Bokan country, the same area I had just come out of. But the dresser was fortunately available, and at first light the next morning he came over to my house, took a blood slide, and checked on the dosage of quinine I was taking. It was malaria all right, benign tertian, so he told me later. Personally I couldn't see anything benign about it! One moment, I was shivering and calling out for every blanket that Ituk could lay his hands on; half an hour later, I would be sweating streams! I do remember George calling in to see me one day on his way to the office, but I cannot recall anything he may have said to me!

Ituk was excellent. He was always trying to tempt me with food, but food seemed to be the last thing I needed. I craved for liquid: inevitable, I suppose, as the body needed to replace the water it had lost in sweat. He remembered the recipe for a cordial I once taught him: the juice of three limes, three cups of sugar and three cups of water, all boiled together! Add ice and water and it would go down a treat! It seemed to be just as much a cure for fever as the quinine.

After about three days of this, during which I hadn't cared whether it was Christmas or Easter, the fever slowly began to subside, appetite began to return, and I began to take an interest in life again. Later on, in my Borneo experience, I remember old hands saying that once the malaria bug is in you, it never leaves the body, and I have a very strong feeling that they are right. Years later, whenever I had had a strenuous time, I would always have a bout of malaria, and I would never have been near the jungle.

When, eventually, I did get back to the office, it was, typically, to close the accounts. It was then that I began to catch up with all the news. It was stimulating to learn, first of all, that the Battle of Britain had been fought and won, and I was anxious to get down to reading the weekly *Straits Budget*, to which I subscribed to help keep me in touch with world affairs. But there was an event which had occurred closer at hand, here in Borneo, which had riveted my attention.

My mind went back to the day I arrived in Sandakan, when I had noticed a small vessel moored against the inner berth of Sandakan wharf. It bore the name *Kinabalu*, and obviously being of much shallower draught than the *Darvel*, for example, was meant for coastal waters. It belonged, I learnt later, to the Sabah Steamship Company, which was a subsidiary of the Straits Steamship Company, and which served the smaller East Coast ports to which the main line vessels did not sail. Once a month it came round to the West Coast, picking up any cargo from Labuan destined for the East Coast, and would then call in at Jesselton and a small township called Usokan which was the sea-outlet from the Kota Belud plains, and the principal cattle-rearing area of the West Coast. Here it would load cattle for slaughter in Sandakan, and then continue its journey round the ports to Lahad Datu and Tawau.

My friend Peter Edge, who had first met me when the *Darvel* called in at Jesselton, was being transferred to Lahad Datu, and it was a matter of convenience for him to board the *Kinabalu* on her West Coast trip, and travel around the ports with her to his destination. Among the passengers were a group of twenty-two northern Chinese, formerly soldiers in the Chinese Army, and to that extent disciplined, who had been recruited as labour for Bangawan Estate, had committed an affray on the Estate's pay-day, and had been sentenced to a term of imprisonment.

After sailing from Jesselton, the *Kinabalu* made her usual call at Usokan, picking up some forty head of cattle. The skipper took the vessel out to sea again and correctly set the course for Balembangan Island where he would turn east and south to enter Kudat harbour. He had made the trip scores of times, and he had no hestitation in leaving the wheel to the capable hands of the *serang*. He himself had had a hard day, and turned in. However, he had failed to take into account that the tail-end of the north-east monsoon would cause a strong rip tide to beat against the Philippine Islands, and cause a drift, the effect of which on the *Kinabalu's* passage was to move her slightly off course, although the compass bearing remained the same. He had also failed to observe that it was high water. This combination of circumstances led to an unexpected disaster. In the vicinity were the Batu Mandi Rocks, normally clearly visible by the ring of foaming white surf beating around them, but which were that night hidden by the high tide and their looming presence passed unnoticed.

The inevitable happened! The *Kinabalu* hit the Rocks at full speed! Peter, who afterwards related the tale, was thrown out of his bunk, was completely dazed, grabbed for his torch in the darkness and found his way to the deck where pandemonium had broken out. He found the Chief Officer helping the passengers into life-jackets; he managed to get one for himself and had just secured it when the ship gave a severe lurch, and Peter was thrown into the sea. Below decks, the police officers in charge of the Northern Chinese prisoners had the presence of mind to release their prisoners, who being the only semi-disciplined group did sterling work in rescuing people and helping them to a life-boat which they were able to launch before the ship foundered. As for Peter, he feared that any immediate sinking of the vessel might well suck him underwater. He therefore struck out as fast as he could to get as far away from the ship as possible. Dawn was breaking, and he was able to see the outline of the coast in the distance; but he was not a long-distance swimmer, and the swift currents were stronger than he. So he just decided to float. All day long in the tropical sun he drifted, and as the sun was setting he noticed that the currents were bringing him much closer to the shore. After about three or four hours he felt his feet strike some coral; this activated his body and he remembered wading ashore well up a sandy beach, where he collapsed, to be found the following day by search parties which were sent out as soon as the stranding of the *Kinabalu* had become known. He must have had a very nasty time, and when I reflected on that and related it to my own experience in the Bokan and Dalit country, the realization came to me that this was indeed a tough country, in which one had to have strong resolution and not a little courage.

It was at this juncture that a Government Circular was received notifying me that the next Malay and Law examinations were to be held in Jesselton in November. I advised George of this; he couldn't object so said, grudgingly, I thought, 'Well, you had better go!' So I wrote off booking a room in Jesselton Hotel, and notifying the stationmaster at Melalap. I also told Ituk, since Government, in its wisdom, permitted one to take a servant at its expense. Ituk would certainly be useful in carrying my bag, and washing my clothes whilst there. As for the examinations themselves, I felt that with the vocabulary I had learnt whilst travelling with Native Chief Enduat, both my spoken and written Malay would be good enough to pass; it was only the Lower Malay examination I had entered. But I did have doubts about two papers: these were the writing of a bit of dictation of Malay in Arabic script, and the translation of a passage of Jawi, that is Arabic, script into English. This was easier than writing it, which I found horrific! Wherever I had been, I had enlisted the services of the local headmaster of the vernacular school to teach me Jawi, but I must confess I found it hard going.

As regards the Law Examinations, I had entered for the Second and Third Class grades of these, which comprised the Indian Penal Code, the Criminal Procedure Code, the Civil Procedure Code and Local Ordinances. I had no worries about the Third Class examinations, as in these the Government permitted the use of the law books themselves, but this was not so in the case of the Second Class examinations. This concession in the use of books was really like the sword of Damocles: it was as much in the Government's interest that one passed as in one's own interest, for until an officer had qualified in Third Class Law he couldn't preside over his own court. And if he wasn't a Magistrate, a District Officer could only do half his job!

The examinations were held in the Education Office, which was in the same block as the Resident's Office, and overlooking the sea. All seemed to go well, even the Jawi dictation, which secretly I was dreading. Once again I was summoned to lunch with the Resident, Dick Evans, whom I began to like very much indeed, and quite a contrast to George!

My real introduction to Borneo social life began at the Jesselton Hotel. My visit had coincided with a planters' meeting, and apart from the elder statesmen of their clan, who were staying with the Manager of Harrison and Crosfield, their agent, the remainder were staying at the Jesselton Hotel. On the Saturday, before returning the next day to Keningau, there was quite a lunch-time session! We always worked on Saturday morning, when I had had my last examination, so my tongue was hanging out when I arrived back in the hotel. They were nothing if not one of the most hospitable crowds one could ever meet. They all lived isolated lives on their rubber estates, and when they gathered for one of their meetings they were determined to enjoy themselves. It was a small place, and they all knew who I was even if I had never met them before!

After a few preliminary beers, we got down to the serious drinking of gin *pahits* (pink gin, alias gin and Angostura bitters) with ice and only a little water! Nobody could remember whose round it was, so we all started playing liar dice for drinks. No wonder the boy was always on hand ready to serve the next round! Then there was a good curry tiffin, at which we all sat around one table. Whilst we were having lunch, a short bespectacled elderly Chinese gentleman came into the room.

'Hi, there, Dr Lai!' He was affectionately greeted by many of them who seemed to know him well. 'What can we do for you?'

He carried a tray of flags with pins in them, and was obviously collecting for something.

'Would any of you gentlemen care to buy a flag to help war victims of the Sino-Japanese war?' he enquired.

Most of us put our hands in our pockets, and he went away well satisfied. I gathered from the ensuing conversation that he was a fully qualified Chinese doctor who had studied medicine in Europe and had an English wife, whom he had met in the course of his studies. He was in private practice in Jesselton, and was also medical officer to various rubber estates in the vicinity of Jesselton.

'They live near Signal Hill,' the planter sitting next to me was saying. 'He was born in Shanghai, and is virulently anti-Japanese; don't blame him, his family had a very nasty time at their hands: half of them wiped out!'

It had been an excellent curry, and all were in a convivial mood, either cracking jokes, or telling stories of one sort or another. Nevertheless, we were all beginning to feel the heat of the afternoon catching up with us, especially with our alcohol-laden stomachs. It was mooted that we should all proceed to the Club that evening; the motion was carried unanimously, and after a good sleep until almost dusk and a light dinner, so began my first introduction to Jesselton Sports Club, on the hill overlooking the *padang*, which was to be the scene of many, many events of my life, one or two rather foreboding in the relatively near future, unbeknown to me at that time, but later on fantastically enjoyable!

It had been a very welcome break, and I was beginning to enjoy Sabah life, but once back in Keningau, George was his usual self! We were both in the office together, when the Chief Clerk brought me a note from him which instructed me to proceed with expediency to Ranau, the most northerly District of the Interior and dominated by Kinabalu, where I was to be stationed. All the provisions I had ordered from Ban Guan had come up with me from Jesselton, so I knew it was only a question of packing, which with Ituk wouldn't take long. I refused to abide by all this nonsense of notes, so as soon as I received it, I got out of my chair and went over to him with the note and said: 'Right, I'll be off tomorrow, if I may have the use of the pack-ponies!' I think that took the wind out of his sails a bit. He glanced up from the papers he was working on, looked at me for a moment or two, as if thinking up another riposte, but said simply: 'Certainly!'

At lunch, I gave Ituk the news, and asked him to pack *lekas-lekas*, with all possible speed. He didn't bat an eye-lid. '*Baik-lah*, Tuan,' he said, 'Certainly, Sir,' and then went on to suggest that as Ranau would be five days' pony-ride away, it might be as well to buy another pony and send it on ahead, so as not to over-tire Firefly. He obviously had a pony in mind, so I agreed. When I returned in the afternoon, all the kitchen equipment and food, camp-bed, mosquito net, blankets etc. had been packed in the saddle bags which he had got from the store. I only had to select the clothes I wished to take, which was simple! After tea, I didn't attempt to accompany George on his walk-about that evening, but got on with my packing, and wrote a few letters home whilst I still had a chance of posting them. I then went up to the office, managed to raise Tambunam on the telephone and asked Geoff Hedley, the A.D.O. there, if I could stay with him for a night on my way through to the north. Fortunately he happened to be on the station, so all was ready.

It took a little while to get loaded up in the morning; my new pony was brought for my inspection, with another syce, whom it was necessary to recruit. I didn't really know a great deal about the points to look for when selecting a pony, but I lifted and examined each of its feet in turn, ran my hand along its back in a professional manner, and found I now owned two ponies and had engaged a second syce. I straight away sent them on ahead, the new syce on his pony leading my new purchase.

The first night was spent at my initial jungle sojourn, Apin Apin, but that was still two days travelling from Tambunam. The next morning I was able to see how my bridle path reconstruction had progressed. It had weathered completely, to my satisfaction. Moss and weed had grown over it, and bushy scrub on the sides of the slopes were all helping to stabilize the new cutting. I could see no danger of that slipping again. I felt well satisfied!

The path to Tambunam followed the foothills of the Crocker Range: it was largely secondary jungle and very unlike the Bokan and Dalit country through which I had travelled when stationed in Pensiangan. Half-way from Apin Apin to Tambunam we made a stop at Kitau, another bamboo halting bungalow like that at Apin Apin. The next morning I gave Firefly a rest, and tried out the new pony. He seemed a bit sluggish after the usual impatience of Firefly to get away to a trot, but I had to try him out before I could give him a name! He very successfully got me out of the foothills and we soon reached the Tambunam plain, when he broke into an easy canter. I spotted the D.O.'s house very easily: it stood on its own hillock surrounded by tall coconut trees, with the station on park-like land around it. We were already on higher ground and as I looked northward I could see the tender-green of the newly-planted rice fields, lying as if on a lake bottom, like a drowned river valley, with steep hills rising east and west and *padi*-fields stretching north as far as the eye could see. The path took me up to the station, but as it was midday, I headed straight for the D.O.'s house.

Geoff Hedley, pipe in mouth, was at the top of the verandah steps to greet me.

'Ah, come in!' he said, 'you are just in time for a cold beer!'

He had anticipated my arrival and had had his cook prepare lunch for me too, which I considered thoughtful of him. We were soon seated in cane chairs, enjoying our beer. He was anxious to have the latest information on the war in Europe, and I was able to tell him what I had learnt from the *Straits Budget*, personal letters and the occasional news telegram which George received and which he would pass on to me. Then I talked to him about Pensiangan, a station to which he had not been posted, and he was keen to chat about Ranau, a station which he had been visiting once every two months.

'Could do with somebody there,' he said, 'it's quite a big station really. I haven't the time to do any travelling in the District, but nobody, as far as I know, has ever been to Merungin and Tampias—they are both four or five days away from Ranau, if not further, and I simply haven't the time. There's quite a lot going on in Tambunam itself. I've had to build quarters, offices and a laboratory for a new malaria research station three miles north of here. You'll pass it, tomorrow. The doctor appointed to lead the project insisted on bringing his wife with him. No European woman has ever been up here before, and that has led to all sorts of complications!'

After a sluice down, a change of clothes, and another beer, the tiring journey was forgotten. After lunch, Geoff said that he would have to go into the office for a short while in the afternoon, and then, perhaps, we would go for a ride after tea. I was quite ready to fall in with whatever he suggested. (I knew I couldn't fall into the same trap as I had done with Mr Mackaskie! Geoff had neither a car nor a chauffeur!) By this time, I was as much at home in a saddle as I was sitting in a chair, and I much preferred to be out and about.

After a rest and a cup of tea, the body was very refreshed for a ride around the station. Geoff took me up to Kampong Sensuran, a big sprawling village just on the edge of the foothills of the Crocker Range. Having come from Murut country, a land of jungle and long-houses, here I was now in open country villages of individual houses, with pigs rooting here and there, chickens abounding, coconut trees and banana palms in clusters, but with few people around. The men evidently had not returned from the fields—we had passed a few on the way—and the women and children were in the houses, from which a curl of blue wood smoke was arising, indicating they were busy cooking a meal.

Tambunam was fantastically beautiful. As we rode back amid the yellowing rays of the setting sun, the valley reminded me somehow of Switzerland as we approached the red roofs of the Catholic Mission set amongst the delicate green of the *padi*-fields, then up the hill to the station. When I had got to my room, I found that Ituk had laid out my clothes, and no sooner had I entered when he tapped on the door, calling quietly, 'Tuan!' It was a nice habit he had of coming to me usually about dusk, to see if I wanted a drink and to receive any instructions for the following day. I enquired about the ponies, and in particular the new syce to ascertain that he had somewhere to sleep, and I gave him instructions that the pack-ponies and my new horse were to leave at first light, and that Ituk, the syce and myself would leave a little later, after I had had something to eat.

Geoff was already sitting in his cane chair having a quiet smoke when I appeared. 'Time for a whiskey-water!' he said, and called out for his house-boy. We had a very pleasant evening together, telling each other how each had landed up in the service of the Chartered Company, and I asked for as much information as possible about my new station. I learnt that the name of the Native Chief was Kabindong, a wizened old Dusun, who was nonetheless quite active and much respected; that the main snag of being stationed in Ranau was the wind—it never stopped blowing off the mountain and that it was jolly cold at night as a consequence; that the telephone line would be frequently down; that you were only able to get meat once a month when they slaughtered a buffalo on *tamu* day. The *tamu* was a native market which was traditionally held at periodic intervals, always in the headquarters of coastal districts and at certain places in the Interior. He also told me that there was no Catholic mission there, but that a new organization calling itself the Borneo Evangelical Mission had established itself, and was staffed by a Somerset man by the name of Trevor White and an Australian called Alan Belcher. Geoff expressed the opinion that they were harmless enough, but generally speaking I received the impression that unorthodox missionaries were not particularly welcomed by Government. 'You never know what seeds they are going to sow in fertile minds!' was his way of putting it. I gathered that a missionary of some indeterminate sect had once persuaded a community somewhere in the Interior that the Day of Judgement was at hand, and they had all burned down their village, and awaited Eternal Life!

Next morning, I was away well before the sun had risen high. The Malaria Research Station which Geoff had mentioned was on my left, on its own hillock. I did not notice any particular form of activity being pursued and hastened on my way. It was a well populated plain and every bit of land seemed to be under cultivation. I noted that they had also learnt the art of terraced rice fields and irrigation, so different from anything else I had seen anywhere in Borneo before. After ten or twelve miles I reached the Pegalan River. It was a wide rocky stream, but by no means a torrent, there was shade by the side of a few clumps of bamboo, and it was here I decided to rest a while before pushing up into the hills. Ituk quickly got a fire going and I searched for a can of beer which I was carrying in my rucksack. We had made good progress and I was well pleased, but the best of the day was over; as soon as we started climbing into the hills, we also climbed into the rain—it poured and poured! There was nothing for it but to carry on as cheerfully as we could.

At long last we got to Kirokut. Only one more night before Ranau! The pack-ponies were already tethered and all baggage was under cover. They had got a good fire going and Ituk was soon bringing me a cup of tea which I laced with a double measure of whiskey. This quickly drove the cold away and revived the body. A sluice down with hot water and a change of clothes quickly put me right.

It had stopped raining by morning, but the secondary forest through which we were travelling was drenched, and the path very slippery for the horses. We could only proceed with caution. The path was intersected with deep valleys which ran into the central ridge. We would drop downhill along the hill side to a clear rushing stream, cross it cautiously with the ponies feeling their way between the rocks, and then climb up the other side of the valley almost parallel to the section by which we had entered; then we would bear right around the ridge and repeat the process!

The next night we spent at Rendagong. We had climbed high now and seemed never to be out of cloud. I remember that many years later, I stayed a night in a Government rest-house in Ceylon in the centre of the tea growing district of Nuralia and I was reminded of Rendagong. It was cold and damp; outside it was swirling mist—one seemed never to be out of cloud!

The next morning brought its reward by its surprise! Immediately before me was the morning splendour of Kinabalu, towering just a valley's distance apart. I think it was the most inspiring sight I have ever seen. In retrospect, I think it was even more inspiring because it was so unexpected. I could only stand and look at it in awe. Cascades of water rushed down its sides and glistened in the yellowing rays of the early morning sun. It became another one of those unforgettable moments. Magnificent, unbelievably magnificent!

The next afternoon we reached Ranau. The approach sloped down through a *lalang*-covered plain, with ominous black rocks protruding as if lying scattered after a tumultuous flood. As I neared the station, I noticed a large bamboo house on the left, most unlike a native construction. There was a board at its entrance which read: 'Borneo Evangelical Mission'. So this is what Geoff Hedley had told me about. There was nobody around, and I just carried on. Soon we were passing the police quarters, easily recognizable as they were all of the same design, then various quarters and the office itself. The sentry on duty came smartly to attention as I passed. I saluted in return. I had arrived at my next district!

The house was in a nice position at the head of the promontory on which the station had been built. Just below it were two vernacular school buildings and the school garden, and a little beyond, winding its way through the plain, was the river.

Ituk and I worked together, trying to get the place tidy before nightfall. We hauled the mattress out into the afternoon sun to give it a good airing, as I didn't fancy sleeping on it as it was. It had only been laid on planks, and we scrubbed these down and put them too out in the sun. It didn't take long, but before sunset I had unpacked everything and made the place habitable.

At six o'clock that evening, I noticed the Sergeant coming up the path from the office. He had come to present his report on any events that he felt I should know about, and any applications for police leave. I had noticed that in Tambunam the Police Sergeant had come to the D.O.'s house in the same way. The Sergeant-in-charge at Pensiangan had also come to me, but the distance was great and I suggested he should phone me instead.

Again, there was little work in the office, so that I could see my time would be spent mostly travelling. There was, however, court work to be done. I had been gazetted as a Third Class Magistrate, so I knew I had passed that examination satisfactorily! I fixed with the Clerk and the Sergeant to hold Court once a fortnight; I felt that might be a satisfactory interval, at least until I had got the feel of the district better. It would enable me to travel at least twelve days on a tour. Then I asked to meet the Native Chiefs. There were two of them and they held Native Court once a week. They dealt mostly with fairly common native disputes over matters of inheritance, marriage and divorce, and adultery, a very common complaint. Running back through the Police Report Book, I found that the Native Courts had pursued one or two cases over which they had no jurisdiction, for example theft, a common enough complaint here, though unknown in Murut country, which was an offence under the Indian Penal Code and should, therefore, have been tried by a Magistrate. It had obviously been a question of time; I remember Geoff telling me that he was only able to visit Ranau once every couple of months. In that two months, he would spend six days just travelling between the two stations, so he would have had little time to spend here, let alone sit in court. I very soon was to learn that that was a very time-consuming task. Very, very few of the witnesses spoke Malay, they only spoke Dusun, and working through an interpreter who could only speak Malay to you was not a quick way of arriving at the truth, or the version that one hoped would be the truth!

Native Chief Kabindong was the younger and more agile of the two Chiefs, and it was he whom I took with me on my travels. I remembered Geoff's remarks that a village named Tampias needed a visit. Arrangements were made, porters were summoned and in a day or two I was off! There was no canoe travelling as there had been in Pensiangan; it was all foot-slogging. There was one advantage in that being at a higher altitude it was cooler, and I felt we seemed to cover the ground rather better. That I think was the only advantage, because in Murut country not only was one sure of a welcome in the village one visited, but there was good shelter in the long-houses. The Ranau, like the Tambunam Dusuns, had abandoned their long-houses in favour of family dwellings; possibly they were a more settled community, and felt more secure as a family unit, whereas the Murut, with his head-hunting tradition, regarded the long house as a place of safety: a defensive position from which the village was all together in the event of an attack. Hence, probably, just the small slits here and there as windows in the long wall of the house.

When we came to a village to spend the night, the porters first had to construct *sulaps*, jungle shelters, with leaves as the roof over our heads! They were to a certain extent satisfactory, but as they were open one was prey to all the jungle insects, animals and reptiles. Tampias was a rather larger centre, and the villagers had built for their visitors a bamboo shelter not unlike a bridle-path halting bungalow. I was resting on my camp bed in the late afternoon when we arrived, when a green snake which had been in the rafters fell on my stomach. I think I moved quicker than at any time in my life! Kabindong said that it was harmless and that it wouldn't bite, but I never believed in that theory. To me any snake was a dangerous one!

It was also at Tampias that I experienced the most frightening thunderstorm that I can remember. The village was sited at a river junction, and I always had a theory that water attracts lightning. During the storm, there was a blinding flash accompanied by the loudest thunderclap I have ever heard before or since. It had struck a coconut tree right by us and seared its bark from the top of the tree to the bottom, cutting it open some four or five inches its entire length. The fibres of a coconut palm are extremely tough for a man to cut anyhow.

Merungin was a different kind of village. The inhabitants all lived in separate houses, but there were no pigs rooting around or dogs, and the grass was all cropped close by the many goats. Then when I espied the villagers I noticed that the men all wore '*songkoks*' (more popularly known in English by its Turkish name: 'fez'). They were Moslems! I later ascertained that it must have been a very recent conversion, as the fact had not been noted by any previous Government Officer. Their origins indeed, were not Dusun, since they were more related to the *orang sungei*, or river people. At that time it was the most eastward penetration of the Moslem religion, and it came as a complete surprise.

Christmas was approaching, and I had been wondering how best I could spend it. I had ordered from Ban Guan tinned food which I would not normally order, sweet biscuits for example, and I decided that I would spend a few days in Bundu Tuhan, the highest village on the slopes of Kinabalu. There was a job of work to be done, as the Government had planted an experimental tea garden there and periodically it had to be inspected to ensure the fencing was being maintained properly. The headman of Bundu Tuhan was responsible for its maintenance. I also toyed with the idea of making an assault on Kinabalu.

The mountain was sacred to the Dusuns who believed that it was the resting place of the souls of the dead. If one trespassed there, one had to placate the gods by the slaughter of a cow (which ensured that the guide's villagers had a free meat supply for a month) and also a white hen which had to be taken to the top and slaughtered there! The guide had to be paid too, so it was quite an expensive operation. It would be a three-day climb from Bundu Tuhan, spending one night on the slope and the second night in Pakka Cave. From there one would make the assault at first light to see the mountain before it clouded up, and to ensure too that one could make the descent before that happened. It had to be a well organized and rather time consuming activity. The two-day Christmas holiday fell in mid-week, so there was no alternative but to ask George for three days' local leave. 'You haven't yet earned it!' came the reply. He was right, of course. Official Regulations said that an officer was ineligible for local leave until he had completed one year's service. But it was a lost opportunity, and one which I never had again until many, many years later when I had the responsibility of building a transmitting station 10,000 ft. up on a spur of the mountain.

Nevertheless, I kept to my plan, inspected the fence of the tea garden, picked up some tea-leaves just to see how they would dry out and, amidst the blanketing cloud around the foothills of Kinabalu, found the rest-house! Everything in it was damp—that, I think, was inevitable—but there was a fire-place. It wasn't long before we had a good fire going, and a stack of wood next to it. As night fell I couldn't see the point of going into another room to sleep: it would be too damp and cold; so I set up my camp bed near the fire.

When I awoke in the morning, I expected to see the magnificence of the mountain before me, but I was looking in the wrong direction. The valley, on the slopes of which lay the village of Bundu Tuhan, was definitely chilly, and for comfort I had to put on a sweater. I went outside, and there behind me, looking up to heaven, was the most awe-inspiring sight I had ever seen: the glory of Kinabalu. It was spectacular! One of the most wonderful mountains in the world, towering 13,450 ft. above the flat plains below. Torrents of water cascading off its side gleamed in the early rays of dawn. But in a few short minutes, as the heat of the tropical sun began to make itself felt, already wisps of cloud were rising in the gullies, and within fifteen to twenty minutes as I watched spellbound, the entire mountain was lost in cloud. Later in the morning, as the heat made itself felt in the valley below, the mist gradually rose and enveloped the rest-house, and as it rose in the foothills of the mountain it turned into rain. It became cold, really cold, and I searched for warmer clothing.

Naturally, it was a quiet Christmas, but the influence of the English family Ituk had served before lingered in his memory, and he laid on the best food I had ever known him to cook. I kept warm around the fire, lazed, read a little, and wrote up my diary. If I had had any premonition of what the following Christmas would be like, perhaps I might not have rested so easily.

I was kept busy on the station and time went by very quickly. I made the acquaintance of the two missionaries and it was quite a change to talk English again. But the characteristic of the station was the wind: every afternoon it started to blow strongly. The pioneers of the past had recognized that *atap* roofs would raise their fronds in such a breeze, and so giant bamboo, split into two and laid one half over the other, like primitive tiles, provided the best roofing material.

One morning when I awoke, I noticed that the two school houses in the river valley below the house were both leaning over at about an angle of 80°–85°. I hastily summoned the head teacher, showed him what was happening and told him to take class in the Court House. With the Sergeant and the telephone *mandor*, who happened to be on the station, I managed to get hold of a team of buffalos, and in a joint effort, with the aid of ropes, we slowly manoeuvred the buildings until the main posts were in an upright position once again. Then, with poles, we braced the building so that it couldn't happen again. The cause of the mishap had, of course, been the wind.

It was whilst we were in the middle of this operation that George arrived, without any previous notice, entirely unannounced! I don't know whether he thought I would be in bed or not, but he was sorely mistaken! As he had surprised me, I rather rounded on him by asking why the station was so starved of money for current repairs. This took the wind out of his sails a bit, but I must say that when I wanted a further allocation in the vote, on any future occasion, I usually got it.

Although anticipating events under another 'Flag', whilst I am writing about Ranau, it is not out of place to mention that in just a very few years, this District was to be the scene of probably one of the worst war-crimes perpetrated by the Japanese invaders. It was here in Ranau that the massacre took place of those few remaining alive out of five thousand Australian prisoners of war belonging to the Eighth Army Division of the Australian Army. They had been captured by the Japanese at the fall of Singapore, moved later to Sandakan and, after a lengthy imprisonment there, when at last the Japanese Armies were beaten back, their prisoners were marched very much along the same route as I had taken when in Tampias. On reaching Ranau, the Japanese captors made their prisoners dig their own graves and then machine-gunned them. It is one of the lesser-known war crimes of the Japanese Army except in Australia. There is an Imperial War Graves Cemetery at Labuan Island commemorating them, and also a well sculptured statue in the present Kinabalu National Park.

Many years later, I was present at the ceremony when representatives of the War Graves Commission unveiled the memorial. The Australian Government had flown up the four survivors to be present at the consecration. I talked to one of them, who related to me that at the time of the shooting he was fortunate in that he only received a flesh wound. He retained the presence of mind to feign death and allowed himself to fall and be buried with his comrades in the shallow grave that they had all helped to dig. He was able to breathe and hours later contrived to work his head above ground. It was already dark, he told me, so, managing to free his arms first and using these to uncover his body, he was able to extricate himself from his grave; he then set about attempting to recover the depression left by his body. Anxious in case anybody was around he immediately hid in the nearby scrub. He edged gradually away, as far as he could, and hid himself as well as possible just as the sky was beginning to glow. Neither dog nor man passed anywhere near him and at nightfall, having obtained his bearings from the setting sun, he pushed into the jungle. The other three who had survived had managed to escape into the jungle whilst on the march, and had eluded their captors. All four managed to survive on jungle roots, and sometimes were lucky enough to find banana palms left behind by a deserted village. All of them had the sense to realize that the Allied Forces, in their drive towards Japan, would relieve the East Coast first, and that they should move in that direction. Looking back now, over all these years, it seems incredible sometimes that the minds of so many Allied prisoners of war, in whatever state of destitution or desperation or however bad their health or physical being, never, never lost confidence in the ultimate Allied victory. The only question in everyone's mind was 'when'. I'm sure that this confidence did give strength and saved many lives. It could, of course, have been that 'hope springs eternal in the human breast'.

My own days as Cadet, Ranau, were fast coming to a close. Returning to George's unexpected visit, when we were back in the house, Ituk got together a remarkably good breakfast at such short notice, and in a short discussion with him I sorted out suitable dishes for the rest of the day and sent him off to the market to get fresh vegetables, chicken, fruit and so on. I then put George in the picture regarding my activities during the past month or so. I had sent him written reports, of course, but verbal amplifications, now I had the opportunity, were better. He seemed well pleased, then suggested we had a look around the station. He went to the office and inspected the Sergeant's Daily Report book. I think this was mostly to check up on the action I had taken on each report. Every order given to the Police had to be recorded, of course, and followed up before the case could be closed. I had brought quite a number of cases to court, and the procedure was that at the end of each month, the case dockets were sent to the Chief Justice for scrutiny. George went through every docket awaiting despatch. He made no criticism, so I think I must have passed the test! In the evening we took out the ponies and I showed George all the work that had been done by the various gangs in the maintenance of paths and bridges and so on.

I was quite relieved to find George relaxed and even talkative on the evening before his departure.

'You're getting on very well with your Malay, I notice. You'll be pleased to learn that you passed your Malay and Law Examinations. The *Gazette* Notification is in the next mail for you. You couldn't have passed them at a better time really, as Geoff Hedley is being transferred to Kota Belud, and the Resident will be appointing you to be Assistant District Officer, Tambunam.'

That was excellent news! I think it was the main purpose of George's visit, to tell me this. I was delighted, as it was a Grade III posting, and I was to be in charge of a much bigger sub-district than Ranau. Not only that, but it also made a difference to my emoluments. I would be Acting in a higher grade than a Cadet, and would be entitled to half the difference in salary between those appertaining to a Cadet and the higher salary enjoyed by the Grade III posting.

George left at dawn the next morning; he wanted to do the journey back to Tambunam in two days, instead of the normal three, and then go on to Keningau in a day and a half. He had left his pack-ponies and his camping equipment at Kiau, and he aimed to get back there in the first day's travelling. I do give him credit for this; he may have been a hard task-master, but equally, he never spared himself.

There was one last tour I wanted to do. When I was at Bundu Tuhan, I noticed a very large village on the opposite slope of the precipitous valley. It was Kampong Kiau, and I figured out that by visiting there, I could follow the track of an old bridle-path and rejoin the existing one at Rendagong. Native Chief Kabindong agreed with me, and it was decided that he would come with me as far as the path, and take his leave of me at Rendagong.

On the evening before I left Ranau, I was in for a suprise. On leaving the office, the clerk-in-charge said that all the Government staff, the Police, and the Chiefs and local villagers wanted to give me a party: a *dindang*, they called it! It was most unexpected, and I was amazed at the work that had been put into it. The Court House had been selected as the venue for the party and, surprisingly, it had been decorated with coconut fronds; when lit up with lights, it looked an entirely different place to that to which I was accustomed. Someone had prepared an excellent curry—I suspect it was one of the Police wives—and in truth it was vastly superior to any curry that Ituk cooked. He was, of course a Murut, and curry was not his natural food; curry belonged to the coastal natives, mostly the Bruneis.

I was offered beer when I arrived, but I noticed a jar of *tapai* was available for those who preferred it. One or two of the shopkeepers whom I had come to know were also present, and I daresay they had contributed the beer! Then, from the direction of the Police quarters came the food. That, for the moment, quietened the murmur which was beginning to rise! Then the fun was to begin in earnest. Gongs appeared from somewhere, and the dancing began, not ball-room dancing, but Kedazan *sumazau*: a man would face a woman and both, with outstretched arms, would raise their bodies on to their toes, and lower them by bending their knees, all to the beat of the gongs! Quite simple, really, once one had got into the rhythm of it! I, of course, had to be a pioneer and had to take to the floor before I had properly understood the movements. It was all good fun, but I wasn't going to get away with it all that easily; speeches had to follow and I had to reply—in Malay! Apart from summing up a court case before delivering sentence, I had not made a formal speech in Malay before, and this one had to be witty! Anyhow, they all laughed, probably at my bad Malay.

It was midnight before I could get away, and I had to leave again at six o'clock the next morning! I left, as intended, and in spite of twenty-seven years residence on the West Coast subsequently, I was never to visit Ranau again. In later years, when I was to undertake a big project more than half-way up Kinabalu, the approach from Jesselton was always from the Kota Belud coastal plain.

It was after I had visited Kg. Kiau, and we were walking through fairly open country with Kabindong behind me, that he let out a yell, and leapt on to my back! I was taken completely by surprise, and hastily looked round to ascertain the cause, to see a king cobra just disappearing off the path! I hadn't noticed it, but must have trodden very near it. I think walking along, with fairly similar scenery all the time, and in a heat to which one is not accustomed by birth, one's attention tends to be less concentrated, and I must have passed over it without particularly noting what it was. It was just as well I hadn't stepped on it! Oddly enough, on the next leg of the journey, after I had bidden farewell to Kabindong at Rendagong, almost the same happened to Firefly. We were going up the side of a mountain, and there was an almost perpendicular fall on my left-hand side for some 200 ft. or more; it was hot and sunny, it was a bit of a trudge uphill, and Firefly, as was his wont, was trudging uphill with his eyes apparently closed. I spotted just ahead of me, very fortunately apparently asleep in the drain, another king cobra. For a moment I was petrified, but every step that Firefly took brought us nearer to the reptile. I knew that if my pony spotted it, he would be terrified and rear on to his hind-legs, with every chance of slipping over the edge of the path down the precipice. I very slightly averted his head, and we passed safely. I glanced around and noticed that Ituk and the policemen were, like their animals, all seemingly dozing in the noon-day sun. We all passed the hazard unnoticed, with the cobra still sleeping.

It was good to see Geoff again. He was all packed and ready. Evidently he had been posted to Kota Belud. It was the prize district for the younger officer; it was all open country in magnificent scenery, with Kinabalu in the distance, not dominating the scene as it did in Ranau. It was polo and buffalo country! Geoff was looking foward to polo; previous D.O.s there had taught the sport, and quite a coterie of natives who were *aficianados* of the game existed. The Resident, Dick Evans, liked a game, and Benita also, I believe, played it. Kota Belud was quite a good district for stag-hunting, and Dick had imported and maintained at the station a pack of hounds. It was to be only a short posting whilst the substantive D.O. took short overseas leave to Australia. He felt sure he would be returning to Tambunam, so I didn't buy off him various items of his which he had bought to embellish the house, the normal practice of an incoming D.O.

After Ituk had unpacked, and I had got the house to my liking, I was very pleased and happy with my new posting. On one of my first evenings, I called on Dr and Mrs MacArthur at the Malaria Research station. They were both very hospitable people and very glad to welcome a new face. They had settled down very well, and had a young Eurasian woman to do the cleaning etc., or rather to help Mrs MacArthur, for I fancy she did most of the housework and the cooking. Dr MacArthur was a little depressed, for after a year or more's work, during which he had trapped, dissected and examined under a microscope literally thousands of mosquitos, including the particular species known to be vectors elsewhere, he had not yet found one carrying the malaria parasite. It really must have been depressing for him, for malaria was rife everywhere, and even an untutored person like myself could tell that the spleen rate among children was abnormally high.

I was returning from their house one evening when an event took place which could have turned into a very nasty occurrence. I was chased by a swarm of hornets! I had to come out of a canter as Firefly was going over a nasty bridge, and they swarmed all around me. I didn't know quite what to do, but they seemed to be going for my head. I was wearing a tropical helmet at the time, which they appeared to be liking, so I thought I might distract them by taking it off and throwing it behind me. The subterfuge worked! I went out early the next morning to retrieve it, and found it shredded with tiny perforations, many of which still had the hornet's sting in them. Not many months later, I had to conduct an inquest on a nun who was similarly chased by bees; they had become entangled with her habit, with disastrous results. She had died. I reckon I was lucky!

Tambunam was a busy office; the district had been settled a long time, so there was a substantial rent-roll, larger even than that in Keningau, where a considerable proportion had been hived off to provide funds for the Native Administration area of Bingkor. There was also a large poll-tax register. It was early in the year, and little had been collected. Geoff had advised me of his intentions in public works, which were sound, and I intended to carry them out as he had planned. Travelling was limited, as the population was concentrated mostly on the plain, and one could get out to the villages and back all in the same day. I did have at the back of my mind the possibility of visiting the eastern part of the district, which, as far as I could judge, had long been neglected, largely because of the scarcity of the population living in the area. The main attraction appeared to be the mountain Trus Madi, which apparently only Dick Evans had assaulted, years before, when he was District Officer in the Interior. I remembered him saying that it was more difficult to climb than Kinabalu. That proposal only remained a possibility!

My first really tough assignment was not long in coming. George rang me up one evening and asked me to inspect the trace over the Crocker Range to Penampang. One had already been cut, but he wanted me to find out if it was being used at all by the natives, who might have found it a short way to get into Jesselton. I had instructions to improve it wherever necessary, and popularize it in the district to establish the route.

I assembled the usual 'caravan', except that there were no pack ponies. The only established path along which I could ride Firefly was to Sensuran. I climbed reasonably quickly to what I thought might be the ridge, but it was already about four o'clock in the afternoon, it was raining and the chaps had to construct *sulaps* for themselves and for me against what obviously was going to be a wet night. The next day we went from ridge to ridge in a seemingly unending pattern; progress was very slow indeed. These jungle traces were far worse than following native paths. The latter went straight up a ridge, along it and down again, but a future bridle-path or road wouldn't be able to follow a route like that. A trace was a cutting through the jungle, supposedly two yards wide. It was not a well-trodden path by any means. I think that answered George's first query: only the beginning and the end were being used!

The following day was nearly all descent. In the early afternoon, we came out of the secondary jungle and picked up a better used path which led down to a river. This seemed a likely camping place, so I asked one or two of the bearers who had done this journey before, how far it was to Penampang. They all agreed that it was something short of an hour's journey. This was approximately my own estimate, so I decided to find a nice spot and make camp there. Then, with a policeman I had brought along with me, I proceeded into Penampang, found the District Office, which was unmanned except for a few clerks and the duty policeman, and, following George's instructions, duly rang him from there! It was a very bad line, but I recognized his voice, and I daresay he recognized mind. Duty done, I returned to the camp-site I had chosen.

I was anxious to get back to Tambunam so left early the next morning. The going was a little easier as we had only to follow our own trace back, and towards sunset we were well beyond the spot we had camped the first day out. We were passing through what seemed to be a little clearing, which I thought would make a good camp-site. What I had not noticed was that it was old jungle; it was only on the next morning that I noticed that the trees had old bark on them. After dinner, we had had the usual camp-fire, during which various yarns were told and I and most of the others turned in, I suppose, at about nine or ten o'clock in readiness for a dawn start. It was moonlight, and being a clear night a strong wind must have sprung up in the early hours. I remember being disturbed by the noise of cracking and falling trees, but I took no particular notice of it; I was half asleep anyhow! When I next came to life, to my horror I was in the cold night air, having been pitched out of my bed through the leaves of my shelter. A tree had fallen right through our camp! Miraculously, the trunk had fallen through the middle of the camp, and only the branches had broken across the *sulaps* where the rest of my party were sleeping! A branch had hit the bottom of my camp bed, which had tossed me aloft! Being a cold night I must have been sleeping with my legs curled up, and this had saved me. Very fortunately, nobody had been hit, but there was no more sleep for any of us that night. We quickly brought the fire back to life, and Ituk brewed some tea for me; that at least steadied my nerves a bit, but we all sat huddled around the fire and at the first glimmer of light, we were off.

It was early evening when I returned to the station. I was glad to get out of the saddle and was looking forward to a bath. When I entered the house, however, I found I had a visitor leaning over the bookcase. It was Father George O'Connelly.

'Oh! I've just dropped in to borrow a book; you don't mind do you?' he said.

I asked him to sit down and gave him what he really wanted: a whiskey-water! He was a very nice fellow, and later I came to know him well. I always found the Catholic priests in Borneo to be very helpful individuals. Usually there were just two of them together on a station, and not very far away there would be a convent. The priests had a very meagre stipend; at that time they received from their Bishop only $10 *per mensem* on which to live, but they were permitted to retain a proportion of the church collection. Their parishioners, very often Chinese, were, however, generous to them, and at the time of Church festivals donated many gifts to assist in their daily needs. It was a wise D.O. who entertained the Catholic priests, for they often received in conversation with them information of help in the administration of their district, particularly in relation to the public: their needs, aspirations and opinions. Furthermore, they knew the inside relationship of any family matter, especially of any dispute, on land for example, which might have come to the notice of the D.O.

Father O'Connelly told me he was a Liverpool Irishman, and had lived in Tambunam for twelve years, coming here direct from England. We chatted away and eventually he stayed for dinner.

Whether it was the exhaustion of the previous days of jungle foot-slogging, or whether I had been stimulated by a long conversation in my own language, I know not, but that night I had a very fitful sleep. I vividly recall hearing footsteps slowly walking down the long corridor which ran from the back to the front of the house. I remember breaking out into a cold sweat: the person wore shoes as the steps were so distinct. I was determined to find out the cause of the intrusion and, grabbing my torch, got out from under the mosquito net, went to the door, the direction in which the steps had moved, cautiously opened it and shone my torch up and down the corridor. There was nothing! I went to the front door and opened it, and shone the beam down the path. Nothing at all, yet I remember even now hearing those steps most distinctly!

The next morning, I related what I had heard to Ituk. 'Yes, Tuan,' he said, '*ada hantu sini dalam rumah*': there is a ghost here in this house. After further enquiry I was told the whole story. Evidently, many years back there had been a District Officer stationed here by the name of Baboneau. He had taken a fancy to one of the policemen's wives, and, sending the policeman off to a distant village to serve a summons, he arranged an assignation with his wife. After his return, the policeman learnt of the affair, went up to the house and shot Baboneau dead as he stood in the doorway. Ever since, his ghost has haunted the house. I am very certain I can confirm it, even though close on sixty years have passed. I can still hear those steps, just as I heard them then.

Not many weeks passed before George rang me one evening, and said that Geoff Hedley was on his way back to Tambunam, and that I would then be on transfer to Tenom. I knew I would not be long in Tambunam, but when my remaining days here became numbered, I was very sorry. Undoubtedly, I liked the place very much. In spite of ghosts and falling trees, my time had passed quickly and enjoyably.

Geoff, when he arrived, had enjoyed himself immensely at Kota Belud, and he, too, was sorry when Sam Chisholm had returned from leave. Sam had tried to join the forces when he was in Australia, but the Chartered Company had caught up with him and he was hauled out of the Army and sent back to Borneo. We had a good cheery evening together, and the next morning I was off.

In Keningau, George very kindly invited me to stay with him on my way through, probably in return for my hospitality to him in Ranau. He made me feel very welcome, and by now I felt I really had joined the Service. I left at dawn, in order to catch the 7.30 a.m. train from Melalap, little aware of the circumstances in which I would see Keningau next time.

Tenom had been the headquarters of the Interior Residency before Keningau was selected. There was much more activity in Tenom. It had the country's largest rubber estate, Sapong, just five or six miles distant across the Padas River, and Melalap Estate was also in Tenom District. There were far more shop-houses in the township and there was a big Chinese land settlement scheme under way in the very fertile Tenom–Melalap valley. The land was being opened up, by felling and burning the forest, and maize was the first crop to be planted; the land was so fertile that enormous cobs were produced. Groundnuts were another favourite crop, but for the longer term, quite a few acres of coffee was being grown, of excellent flavour too. Tenom coffee became renowned throughout Sabah, and it retains its reputation today.

I took over the District from R.S. Abbot who was on transfer to the Customs to take over the vacancy caused by Peter Edge's transfer. He was affectionately known as The Bot! There was a Government owned rest-house in Tenom, and I stayed there until The Bot had vacated the house, moving in immediately afterwards. It had a magnificent position on a hill between a quarter and a half mile away from the office. Every morning at dawn a policeman would walk up to the house and hoist the Sabah Jack, coming up again at sunset. If I were on tour, the flag would not be flown. It was a give-away really!

The District Office itself was, of course, a wooden building, but it had an extremely large stone-built safe with an iron door and huge old-fashioned lock. One had to carry the keys of the safe on one's person, at all times, so the Official Regulations said. It was a bit of a bind; one felt one was a gaoler! There was a lock-up near the Office and in the same compound a Post Office. Not far away there was an Old People's Home, where the down and outs could find shelter. In all, it was quite a big station, and a very busy one too.

My syce had brought the two ponies down from Keningau and had taken two or three days on the journey. Ituk, since he was coming a long way from his village, brought his wife and children, so it was quite a sizeable party who wended our way up the hill to the house. It was quite a long climb, and one that I didn't fancy doing two or three times a day, so I was glad to find that the stables were on the hill-top near the house.

There was far more activity going on in the office than there had been in Keningau. One was flooded with land applications, nearly all lodged by Chinese, all of whom seemed to come from a certain area in China. Strong family connections existed between the settled Chinese and their families back home, so there was a constant flow of money orders going from Tenom to China. Land settlement seemed to take up a large proportion of my time, as every application meant a visit to the site, to ensure there were no native rights involved. So often, highly decorated wooden erections marked the graves of Muruts who had once lived here; oddly, these graves, although in the jungle, were highly ornate, and when one came across them, it was obvious they were still visited, as they bore little triangular red or other coloured flags, and there were remnants of offerings of some sort. Obviously, land with graves like that on it could not be alienated to anyone. They were part of the native rights which the Chartered Company was pledged to preserve.

When rubber estate pay days began to approach, the managers would send in their senior assistants to collect money from the Treasury to pay the wages. They would bring along a cheque drawn on the State Bank, against which I would issue the cash. They would always say in what denominations they wanted the money, and it was my task to unlock the 'vault', count out the cash, bring it out and hand it to them. They, naturally, would go through the counting process again! It wasn't peanuts! The Estates were extremely busy producing as much rubber as they could, as the war had brought a big demand for it; consequently, their pay roll was very large. If I remember correctly, the Sapong Estate cheque was of the order of $20,000–$25,000 each month. This was in excess of the station's revenue, so with two large estates to supply, every month I had to ask the Treasury in Jesselton to send up money. In the Official Regulations, this operation was known as the

'Transfer of Treasure', and could only be undertaken by an armed escort of one NCO and one policeman. All had to be counted out and signed for, and an official receipt given to the NCO in charge. It was quite in contrast to the manner in which the estate assistant would take it away: usually in a haversack slung over his shoulder!

It was not only cash which was stored in the walk-in vault, there was ammunition for licensed shotguns and also *chandu*, or opium. Government rigorously controlled the licensing of shotguns. Each applicant to hold a shotgun had to be recommended by his village headman, and the purpose for possessing a gun, like the protection of crops, had to be well defined. Similarly, Government alone could sell ammunition, an operation conducted through the District Office, only five cartridges at a time, in exchange for five expended cartridges which later the District Officer had to certify as destroyed. The sale of *chandu* had historical and medical reasons. Many of the early Chinese settlers were already opium smokers when they arrived in the country. Such immigrants were immediately registered, and, recognizing the medical need for such people to continue their practice, Government decided that they were the only fit organization to sell it. In out-stations this operation was conducted by the Post Office, with the District Officer holding the stock, issuing five boxes, each of a hundred phials at a time. At no other station in the Interior Residency was it sold at all, but, unlike the other stations, Tenom did have a large immigrant Chinese population. It was only the older generation of Chinese who indulged in the habit, and as each one died, his name would be struck off the register until ultimately the import of *chandu* would have been totally prohibited.

It was in connection with the sale of opium that I made my first blob! To this very day, I do not know how it arose. Not long after my arrival, I had an audit visit. The Government Auditor was a very pleasant fellow by the name of Penlington. All audits were surprise visits; I only heard of his arrival when the afternoon train had reached Tenom. We met the next morning in the office. Naturally, he went through the books from the date of the last audit, and arrived at the figure of cash that I should be carrying. I opened the safe, and he counted the lot. Fortunately there wasn't a cent out! I think it took the best part of two days for all that to be accomplished. Next, he went through the land revenue registers; there was as usual a certain amount of quit rent still outstanding, and he suggested that notices should be issued to late payers. Finally he checked physical stocks: the ammunition was correct, but I was one box of *chandu* short. How this happened, I simply have no explanation. Both the postal clerk and myself counted the boxes very carefully when they were issued, and we were only dealing in small numbers: we couldn't have made a mistake. I came to the only possible conclusion, that the error had existed before, and that at the handover, possibly in my eagerness to take over a big station, I had failed to check the number of boxes carefully enough. My salary, however, was surcharged for the selling price of one box of *chandu*. The Government was quite correct, but I was mad with myself at the time, because somewhere along the line, the fault had been mine! In a way, it was a lesson, as I was always extra careful in future, and never made a mistake again.

Having become accustomed to the routine in the office, my attention turned to my first love, that of travelling; the geographical position of Tenom made it nearer certain areas of Murut country than Keningau had been, but there were other priorities than, as Ituk would say, '*pergi* round': going on tour. I also wore the hat of that of Assistant Protector of Labour, and the largest rubber estate on the West Coast was less than ten miles away. So I wrote a polite letter to the Manager of Sapong Estate acquainting him of my proposed visit, and suggesting dates. I tried to avoid pay days as I knew the estates would be very busy then, but the Manager replied suggesting I came the day after pay day, and that I would be welcome to stay over the following weekend in a private capacity. I felt this was a genuine welcome, and that by falling in with his suggestions, I would be starting off on the right foot.

I left in the late afternoon, in readiness for an early start to the inspection the next morning. It was only a mile or so walk to where the ferry, which was operated by Sapong, crossed the Padas River, where the Estate bus was waiting to pick me up. It was a relatively short drive to the headquarters, where I found Ray Crosland waiting for me in the office which was quite large with a number of clerks busy at their desks.

'Nice to meet you,' he said. 'Johnnie Baxter has asked me to put you up at my house, so if you would like to come with me, we'll be in just nice time for a cup of tea.'

Johnnie, he told me, normally only entertained the Visiting Agent, or the Resident, and perhaps the District Officer. (I was only an A.D.O. [Acting]!) Nevertheless I felt at home with Ray immediately, and he made my stay very comfortable. Before dinner, he told me that the Assistants usually went along to the Clubhouse for a drink to talk over the day's events and that Johnnie Baxter, the Manager, would be waiting to meet me there.

I was pleased indeed to meet Johnnie Baxter; I had already heard a lot about him as the man who ran the largest and best-run Estate on the West Coast. He was a tall, broad-shouldered man, with a very welcome smile and a handshake which gripped you like a vice. His uniformed boy was in attendance dispensing the drinks. As they arrived I was introduced to Harvey Coward, Senior Assistant, and Ray Barret. There were now only four Europeans on the Estate, which before the world slump of the early 1930s had employed twelve. Hence the need for a clubhouse equipped with a billiard table, which was a rather excessive luxury for a staff now comprising only four!

Johnnie naturally dominated the conversation, the main topic of which, of course, was the war in Europe. It had been fought now for some eighteen months, and although we had been pushed out of Europe, it seemed as if Britain had won the 'Battle of Britain'. There was renewed confidence now that Churchill was at the helm, but of the Japanese threat, nothing was spoken. I could say nothing about the secret telegrams to which I had had access a year or so previously, so it became quite obvious that a state of complacency existed among commercial Europeans. Without seeming critical of my hosts, I felt their thoughts were more concerned about the price of rubber and the bonus that each would receive after the Company's Annual General Meeting than they were about Britain's struggle for survival and the forces lining up against her, envious of her position as a world power.

The next morning I undertook my inspection in company with Johnnie Baxter. The official part of the visit mostly concerned the health and hygiene of the labourers and the size of their living quarters. (The Labour Ordinance laid down the minimum size of a single worker's quarter—there weren't many of these—and a married man's quarter.) Facilities for the sick had to be noted, and also an inspection of the Estate shop was demanded. This latter requirement went back to the early days when the estates were first opened, as the workers were frequently paid in coin, with the Estate's name and the value of the coin embossed upon it. These coins could only be spent in the Estate shop; they were not legal tender, and in later years they were made illegal and their use banned. Nevertheless, the shop still had a monopoly, and there was no law to prevent the shopkeeper giving advances to the labourers. ('*Minta pinjam*': Can I have a loan please?) The labourers, especially on remoter estates like Sapong, were very much tied to these Estate shops, and the only recourse to prevent exploitation was to take note of the prices being charged, to see that they were in line with similar commodities in the townships.

When we were in the Club that evening, my inspection having been concluded satisfactorily, Johnnie Baxter invited us to his house to curry tiffin the following day. I felt that this was going to be something special. It was! Johnnie, in common with many Managers of the larger Estates, employed a curry cook, in addition to his normal cook. The curry cook did not necessarily have the rest of the week off. He shopped personally in Tenom, getting the correct spices, and Friday and Saturday would be devoted to grinding them on a special stone (*gulingan batu*) with a round stone roller. Some spices required a stone pestle and mortar. To achieve a good curry was a time-consuming matter, and it was a matter of Estate pride to endeavour to have the best curry cook! Down the line, on Estates nearer Jesselton, Estate Managers would frequently join a circle in which they all became guests in turn on each other's Estates for the one social event of the week! Even crimping of curry cooks was not unknown!

It goes without saying that Johnnie's curry was supreme! We had assembled shortly after noon, and first slaked our thirst with delightfully chilled beer, and then turned to gin *pahit*, i.e. gin and bitters, the ward-room drink of the Navy. Lunch was possibly served about three o'clock, and I think we were all ready for it.

Farewells were said all round. I returned to Ray's house for a short lie-off and, about half an hour before sunset, I mounted the bus that had been laid on for Ituk and me, crossed the river just as darkness fell, and walked the few hundred yards to the office, where Firefly and my syce were waiting for us. After that curry, I needed little else to eat that night!

I only made one jungle trip whilst in Tenom, and that was along an old and no longer maintained bridle path to Kemabong and Tomani. It was the path which led to Rundum, when the Residency Headquarters were at Tenom. The only real rebellion which the Chartered Company had to face was in fact the Rundum rebellion of 1915 when the rioters, some Muruts who had possibly drunk a little too much *tapai*, burned down the Government station at Rundum. After a punitive expedition, the Government never sought to rebuild it, but instead developed a new and more easily defensible site at Pensiangan, a site with which I was well acquainted!

There was a very delapidated halting bungalow at Kemabong, and I almost wished I had pushed on to Tomani, where a long-house might have offered me hospitality. It was, however, a good centre and I was able to pay brief visits to a number of villages. Time was the limiting factor; there was an impressive quantity of work waiting me in Tenom office, and it became no longer possible to plan a tour, nor was there a Native Chief attached to the District. In the Government hierarchy, it was more regarded as a Chinese land settlement area, and the administration of distant Murut villages was better looked after from Pensiangan. I think their priorities were correct.

One event I shan't forget was when the circus came to town! The Chief Clerk came into my office one morning saying that a Mr Wang Wang San would like to meet me. He was shown in and I offered him a seat. He obviously was not one of our local Chinese, so I wondered what had brought him here. I was quickly to learn the reason. Mr Wang was a circus proprietor, and he came to enquire whether he might have permission to bring his circus to Tenom and erect his tent on the *padang*. This was quite a new one on me! I know of no local ordinance I could refer to from which I could ascertain the procedure. Somewhere in the local law, I felt, there must be a fee prescribed for such an event. We talked round the subject a bit, whilst I tried to resolve the issue. My mind went back to the time when, as a boy, Robert Foster's circus used to come annually to a field opposite our house, and I had visions of horses and caravans, and trodden rings on the grass when they had all departed! By no means, I thought, could I allow them to mess up the *padang*: to me that was Tenom's pride and joy!

'Very well,' I said, 'You may come on the five nights, as you request, but you must leave the *padang* exactly as you find it, and clear up totally all litter and the smallest trace of your presence. You must also make a donation to a local charity.'

A large beam spread over his face. 'Thank you, thank you,' he said. 'We will do everything you ask!'

Goodness knows what George will think of that, I thought, but I have to make decisions for myself, and can't refer to him all the time. When it was all over, and I made mention of it in my monthly report, he might well have blown his top, but I didn't get to hear about it!

The next Sunday's train brought the circus. There were no animals, and I was grateful for that. When I rode down to the office the next morning, the tent was already up, and gave a note of gaiety to the town. The die had been cast all right; there could be no withdrawal of permission. In the afternoon, Mr Wang came along again to the office, and invited me to come as his guest for every performance. 'Each one will be different,' he promised. And they were! There was a band of sorts; there were conjurors, tumblers and acrobats, and trick cyclists riding one-wheel cycles (on the rough Tenom *padang*!). I did go down every night to enjoy them. I thought the last night might be an occasion on which I could return Ray Crosland's hospitality for the night. He gladly accepted my invitation, and after the show, I invited Mr Wang and the principal members of his cast to come up to the house and have a drink! Ituk had made lashings of curry puffs, and I asked the local shop to send up a case of beer, and lemonade for the ladies if they preferred it. It was quite a good party, the first I had ever thrown in the country, but I think they all enjoyed it. I don't know whether it did my reputation any good or not.

It was very shortly after that I received a letter from George, advising me that I had been appointed to act as District Officer, Papar, and that I should proceed immediately I had handed over to my relief. He was to be John Macartney, whom I had met before in Beaufort. The Resident had made this appointment with the knowledge that in the event of war with Japan, the European women and children in Jesselton would be evacuated here, and that the Constabulary would defend the Gorge. A senior officer and one with more experience than I would be required to cope with that responsibility.

Having met before, the hand-over was comparatively easy, and John had only come up the line from Beaufort. I had arranged with the stationmaster for a horse-truck in which Firefly and my syce could travel down the line, and soon Tenom was behind me and I was looking forward to my new District: a piece of the territory in which I was to be the longest serving officer!

Papar was very much regarded as the rice-bowl of the West Coast. Its very name is that of the Malay word for 'flat' or 'smooth', and there were vast acres of *padi*-land to the east and west of the railway line as it proceeded on its southward track from Jesselton. It was also one of the earliest stations to be settled when the Chartered Company first began its administration of the territory, and was an area where the main races of the country became contiguous. It was the furthest penetration northward of the settled Brunei community who always kept to coastal areas, as they were fisherfolk before becoming agriculturists. Just north of the town was the most southern of the Bajau villages, whose origins lay in the southern Philippines, whilst inland with rice fields coming almost down to the railway line and extending westward to the Crocker Range were the Dusuns as they were then called, but who now prefer themselves to be known as Kedezans, their own native name. On the islands out at sea, there were sea gypsies calling themselves Binadons, an Islamic race linked to the Suloks and the Illanuns, who were the descendants of the notorious pirates who terrorized local waters almost until the founding of the Chartered Company.

I could see from the beginning it was not going to be an easy District to administer. Almost all the races were old enemies once upon a time, and one quickly gained the feeling, even in the tone of voice of a man of one race describing another, that the old animosity lingered on. Thrown into the middle, all in the immediate neighbourhood of the town, some of the earliest of the Chinese settlers had made their home; they were the shop-keepers and small industrialists, businessmen with enterprise. They too had cast their seed, and over the years there had developed yet another race of people: the Sino-Kedazans. Perhaps of all, these were the balanced race; they better understood both sides to a problem. Certainly they were fine-looking people; a young Sino-Kedazan girl could enter a world beauty competition with a good chance of becoming Miss World!

Having changed at Beaufort, the train finally brought me to Papar, where the station was thronged with fruit sellers, who almost before the train had stopped were selling all varieties of fruit in season to the passengers leaning out of the train window. I was met by an extremely affable Malay-Indian gentleman who introduced himself to me as Abas bin Haji Hassan. He spoke excellent English and took control of everything, including the unloading and the carriage of my baggage, even telling the stationmaster where the horse-box conveying Firefly should be left after the train had departed. He then took me down a metalled road running parallel to the railway, but separated from it by a white fence which was the station boundary and a broad grass verge with flowering shrubs, to the Rest House.

'We've arranged, Sir, for you to stay here for the first few days, until you can get your house as you like it. You see, Sir, the house hasn't been lived in for a few years. You are our first District Officer for quite a long time! The Assistant District Officer from Jesselton, Mr Hiew Sin Yong, has been coming up once a week, staying one or two days, taking cases and so on. We have been very short-staffed, and we have been awaiting your arrival for quite some time!'

I was very glad indeed to hear that someone needed me. When, as I thought, I had been trudging, aimlessly and wearily, through the jungle for so long, it more than once entered my head that there seemed to be no real purpose in being in the country. At last, someone wanted me: I had a job to do! Little did he realize it, but Abas's kind words encouraged me enormously.

The Office building was very old and was built on high stilts, with the Court House joined to it by a covered walk-way. Under a section of the Court had been built the Post Office. My office was to the north, off the general office, and on the extreme southern side lay the section reserved for the Sergeant and the Police. Along the verandah, just south and to the west, the adjoining jail was located.

The approach from the town was by a path which ran past my window around to the front of the Office; from this path smaller paths led off to the Court and to the Post Office. A broad staircase led up to the Office and there was a wide verandah where members of the public usually sat waiting their turn either to speak to the Sergeant who would be laboriously writing reports and questioning witnesses, or to pay some fee due to the Government like quit rent or poll tax. In one corner, screened off from the others by wire mesh, sat the Treasury clerk. On the left, as you entered the Office, there was a big desk piled high with files, behind which sat the gentleman who dominated the office: the Chief Clerk. His chair backed against an inner office wall, by the side of which swing half-doors led into the inner sanctuary: the D.O.s Office!

On the night I arrived I had a quiet night to myself. At sundown the Sergeant had come to the Rest House and reported to me. He, in fact, was a Sergeant Major

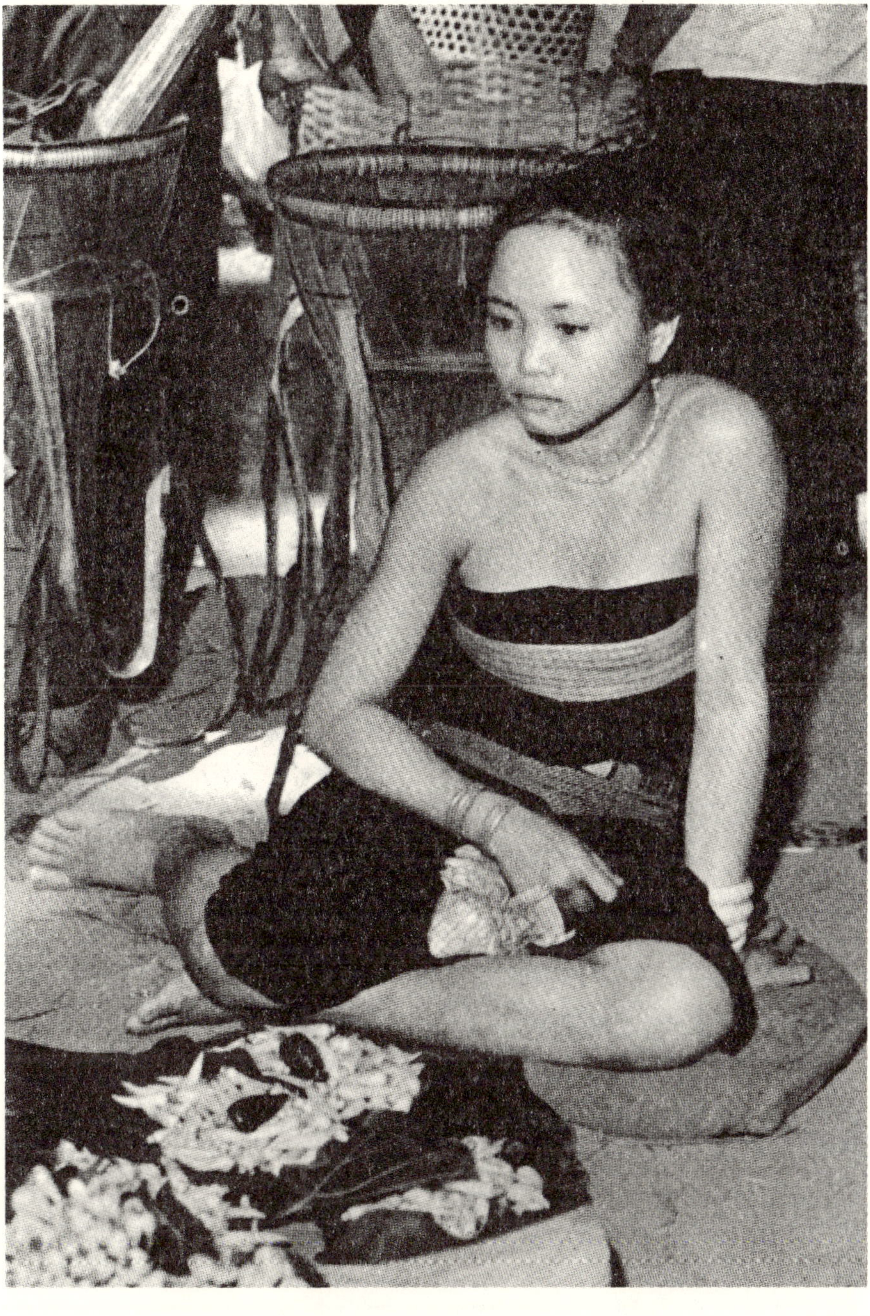

Kedazan lass at Lota Belud Tama.

and wore a broad red sash acros his breast, with a large golden tassel dangling from it. He was a smart chap, and I felt a little reassured; obviously, we would be able to assess reports as they came in by discussion, and he would not remain dumb and provide me with the opportunity to issue doubtful instructions. The Sergeant, after all, was the man who had met the complainants, and he was in a better position to judge the veracity of the reports.

I was up very early the next morning, and had walked around the town even before the townsfolk were properly awake. I could see curious eyes peeping at me from most of the shops, but the main activity was the arrival of the fishing fleet. The Brunei fishermen were just beginning to arrive up river, and were unloading their catch and bringing the fish in baskets to the Chinese fishmongers. They were loudly haggling over the prices being offered, and my presence went unnoticed.

The vegetable market, too, was a hive of activity; Chinese Hakka women were busily arranging the display of fruit and vegetables on their stalls, shouting out the day's gossip to each other as they worked, or so it seemed to me! The meat market, next to the fish market, was already doing trade. The pigs and buffalo must have been slaughtered before dawn, and the poor bedraggled chickens were cooped up in rattan-woven baskets; they, of course, would be sold alive. I walked quite a distance following a cobbled road which at first followed the river and then branched off to the right across the *padi*-fields, first passing through a mixture of large double-storey Chinese homesteads and plank-built native houses with *atap* zinc or galvanized–iron roofs. This kind of roof was a status symbol amongst the natives. Before you were told the number of buffaloes (or wives) he may have had, if he had an *atap zinc*, you were told that first! Although they may not have needed renewing every nine or ten years or so, the house inside became beastly hot in the afternoon, whilst the sago-palm *atap* did provide cool if not refreshing air inside the home.

Fortunately, the District Office had a shingle roof: wooden tiles made by splitting *belian*, the hard timber for which Borneo is famous. Doubtless, the process of cutting the timber and splitting the log was a very laborious business, but the result was a roof made to last which best reflected the heat of the sun. The Rest House had a similar roof, but not, unfortunately, the D.O.'s house!

My first morning was spent meeting all the office staff. I called them in one by one, and by chatting to them, slowly assessed their ability. As soon as I had met Abas the previous day, I had asked that messages be sent to the Native Chiefs of the District to come and meet me. In view of the mixture of races in the District, it seemed to me to be important to establish good relations with all the Chiefs. Orang Kaya Kaya Matjakir was the Brunei Chief who lived only a couple of miles from the office; Native Chief Daniel was the local Kedazan Chief. The morning train brought Native Chief Sahal from Kinarut—he was the Bajau Chief—and in the afternoon the Pengiran from Bangawan arrived. The Chief from Benoni, the very large lake village about six miles away, was reported sick.

O.K.K. Matjakir was the first Brunei that I had met, and I took to him immensely; he was an elderly man, possibly in his middle fifties, and he carried an air of authority around him. He was a Grade I Native Chief, one of the most senior in the country, and the Chairman of the Native Court. We had no difficulty in engaging in conversation. We spoke about the *padi* crop; he said it had all been planted in the nurseries, and when the rains came, probably next month, then people would be very busy ploughing, and planting the rice. We discussed his area of jurisdiction; I could only follow him by a close study of the District map, and by picking out the villages which he named. One thing which immediately struck me was that all the land in his area had been settled many years before, and that I would not have the land applications to deal with, which had been my main work in Tenom.

Next I met Native Chief Daniel. He was a Kedazan, and lived at a village called Limbahau, about ten miles to the east of Papar. His people were the farming community of the District. Although Matjakir had spoken about the progress in *padi*-planting, his people's main contribution to the economy was fishing; the Bruneis went to sea daily, leaving about 3 a.m. and bringing in the catch at dawn. They were all Moslem, and lived only in villages on the coastal fringe. In contrast, Daniel's people were the real farmers. In origin they were the pagans of Borneo, but here on the coast, many had been converted to Christianity, mostly by the influence of the Roman Catholic Missions. There was a strong Catholic presence in Papar, and in Limbahau, Daniel's home village, there was a convent, and a Catholic girls' school. Daniel's area of jurisdiction extended right into the foothills of the Crocker Range: it was, indeed, a large area, but most of the activity was concentrated in the first nine or ten miles from Papar.

Native Chief Sahal was not of the same order as the Chiefs I had met earlier. He was a Bajau, on the fringe of the District bordering Jesselton, also a Moslem, but he did not give me the impression he travelled much in his area. Conversing with him and looking at maps, I ascertained that Dinawan Island was within his jurisdiction. Because I hadn't been near the sea for so long, and as I felt Sahal needed to get off his backside, I arranged with him to visit Dinawan during the following week.

The Pengiran from Bangawan arrived in the afternoon, but again I was not impressed. He had travelled on the afternoon down train to Jesselton. He had seniority, but he seemed to me to be a 'yes' man, unwilling to contribute constructive ideas of his own. In my mind, I rather wrote him off.

Reflecting on the situation: I had two good Chiefs, two lazy and indolent, and one unknown. It was this question mark that I decided to examine first, so the next day I again asked Matjakir to the Office and invited him to make arrangements for me to visit Kampong Benoni as soon as possible. This he did. It was my first outing on Firefly, since he had had the chance to breathe Papar air! It was good to be astride him again. I think there is a rapport between horses and men, just as there is between dogs and men. Firefly definitely enjoyed being ridden again. We soon arrived at Mile 5 along the Bukit Manggis road, where there was a deputation of three natives awaiting us.

Benoni was obviously different. The epithet: 'The Lake Village' sprang immediately into my mind. There was a vast expanse of water which stretched from the roadside, which acted as a bund, to jungle far in the distance, and in the middle, on higher ground, was an island dotted with houses and coconut palms, attractive as a picture postcard!

The introductions over, I asked the guides to lead the way, which they did along a sort of walkway, of roughly hewn planks perched in the V shape of a triangle made by sticking two posts in the bottom of the lake in the form of a X. The tops of the crossed posts did have connecting hand-rails, so it wasn't entirely a balancing act! When we had reached a point about two-thirds of the way across, the planks had rotted apart, but there was a dug-out moored into which the five of us managed to descend. It was then but a short paddle to the island village.

More men had gathered around to greet us, and there was hand-shaking all round, and then we walked, so I assumed, to the Native Chief's house. I then understood why the Chief had not come to Papar at my request to meet me, and why so many of the Police Reports, which I had noted from the Report Book, had their origin in Benoni. The Native Chief was old, effete, and most certainly was not earning the monthly stipend which the Government granted him. We had a long talk, at the conclusion of which I suggested he should retire in favour of a younger and more vigorous villager. One could never have a talk in private: there must have been twenty or so of the menfolk sitting around listening to the conversation. I was, however, surprised and pleased to hear murmurs of 'Tuan', 'Tuan', coming from the lips of the onlookers. I think I had aroused a mutual chord of agreement!

I knew that only the Resident could appoint Native Chiefs, so I could not take my thoughts much further at that stage, but after looking around the village, I called on the old man again, and asked him to think of persons who would make a good Chief in his place. This he agreed to do, and I received the impression that he would be thankful to be relieved of his post. Accordingly, on my return to the office, I wrote to the Resident, quoting the number of Police Reports received at the office which had their origin in Benoni. I ascribed it to the decrepitude of the Benoni Chief, and reported on the action I suggested should be taken.

I quickly received his reply, agreeing with my recommendation and saying that he would like to meet any suitable replacement I may have in mind on his next visit to Papar. I felt very pleased that my recommendation, on really a major issue, should have been accepted so readily.

Native Chief Matjakir was in agreement on all my views. His comment merely was: 'Well, he's an old man, Tuan!' When I told him of the Resident's reply, I asked him to arrange a further visit in the very near future with that specific intention in mind.

Within a few days, Matjakir came along to see me again. He had done his homework well. 'There are two people, Tuan, who are willing to take up the post. If Tuan would like . . .' I immediately agreed with his proposals and arranged a date when I should visit the village again.

One of the suggested two names had been a *wakil* or stand-in for the resigning Native Chief, and the other was an entirely 'new' man, by the name of Oman. I took an instant liking to Oman. His eyes were straight and fearless; he was of medium build but strong. I judged him to be a man of great fortitude and determination. The *wakil* may have had a wider range of experience in acting for the Chief, but he seemed to me to be a rather shiftless man, who appeared to be looking at his feet most of the time, and kept on shuffling them on the grass. In my own mind the choice was obvious. I had a word with Matjakir, and I told him my views, but added that I wanted the appointment to be as democratic as possible. 'Leave it to me, Tuan,' Matjakir said. 'I understand your wishes!'

He then bade them all sit down on the grass. He spoke to them for a while in local Brunei, which I didn't understand, but I was fully aware of his message when the crunch line came. Then, calling on the *wakil* to stand by the side of a certain building, he asked all those who preferred him as Chief to arise and stand by his side. Only a few stragglers rose to their feet and went over to him. Then he called on Oman to move over towards the Mosque by which we were standing, then bade those who preferred Oman to rise to their feet and move in his direction. The whole of the village as a body rose to their feet and moved towards the Mosque. It was all done in silence, with scarcely a word spoken, but the verdict, without any doubt, was unanimous!

The village had spoken, and I felt they were quite right in their decision. I knew now that the village was behind their new Native Chief, and I hopefully anticipated that the village of Benoni would cease to feature in the Sergeant's Report book!

Oman then invited Matjakir and me to enter his house, which was close by, to *minum kopi*, have a cup of coffee. It was the first time I had been invited into the home of a Moslem, and I felt it to be a rare privilege. It was, in fact, to be the first of many occasions in which I was to enter his house. Following custom, I removed my shoes before going up the steps. Although the house was on stilts, they were about a third as tall as those of a Murut long-house, and there was no slippery notched tree-trunk to ascend. A race altogether more civilized, I felt!

We all sat cross-legged on locally made mats, the women sitting quietly in the shadows. We talked of this and that since Oman, I felt, was a little over-awed at his unanimous election, and was not as forthright as later he was to become. I explained that the election would have to be confirmed by the Resident, whom I would like him to meet on the occasion of the Resident's next visit to Papar. After a few more pleasantries, Matjakir and I took our leave.

I next turned my attention to Kinarut and Native Chief Sahal, whom I also suspected of being a weak link. I had already arranged with him to visit Dinawan Island, off the Kinarut River estuary. I was eager to see the sea again. This visit proved to be quite unique. After an hour's paddling out to sea, we reached the island where we were surrounded by young children, each of whom had a model boat of some description with which they were playing! A little crowd of men gathered around, all speaking to Sahal in a language unknown to me. It was Sulok, he told me later. We went under the shade of some coconut trees, and one of the youngsters shinned up it with utmost dexterity, and seizing a *parang* from his waist, cut off three or four coconuts. These were pounced upon, and the first one to be opened was handed to me. I was glad of its refreshing water, as it had been hot coming across the short stretch of sea. I didn't enter into any of the houses, but I did notice some of the womenfolk, seated in the shade, weaving gaily coloured mats from a kind of straw, which I ascertained later was *pandanus* fibre, from a tropical plant which grew in abundance on the sandy soils of a large part of the West Coast.

Sahal went up in my opinion, after this trip. As we went up-river on the return journey, we passed through an area where *nipah* palms grew in abundance. These trees would grow in tidal estuaries, and if you tapped the fruit at the right spot, and collected the juice and boiled it, you could obtain a sugary liquid, not unlike *gula mallaca*, which was traditionally used with sago as a sweet after curry. *Gula malacca* was similarly obtained from the spathe of a coconut tree. Sahal took the trouble to explain all this to me as we went along; he also said there were quite a number of crocodiles in the reach through which we passed. I don't think he needed to have told me that: at least, not until we were well away from the swampy area in which they lurked! We were only in a small river boat, and I didn't like it all that much when we were half-way between the shore and the sea; it wasn't a sea-going fishing boat at all. The craft we had seen at Dinawan Island were entirely different; their out-riggers turned them into fore-runners of the modern trimaran. I was told they would often go to sea for months on end in craft like these; they were quite large vessels, each needing a crew of three or four to man their sails.

I also learnt that just down the railway-track past the station was an Englishman living on his own on a small rubber plantation. I had a little time in hand before the train left to take me back to Papar, so I asked Sahal to show me the path. I first passed through a small coconut *kebun*, the local word for a planted crop-bearing garden of any description, whether vegetables, bananas, coconuts or rubber, and quite contrasted to *padi*-land, on which only rice would be grown. *Padi*-land would be wet land, here on the plains, but a *kebun* would only bear crops on higher dry land. The path through the *kebun* bore right and, turning a corner, there in front of me was a one-storey black-painted bungalow. I went up the path and tapped on the door. Hearing a voice shout '*Masok!*' (enter) I apprehensively opened the door, and there facing me was a Gordon's gin bottle on a table, with a white-haired European gentleman seated behind it. I introduced myself but Sahal was obviously well-known to him.

'Sit down,' he said, 'you're just in time for a drink! You must be the new D.O. I've heard that there was a European D.O. in Papar. About time too!' And that is how I first met Harold Read. He was a character, such as Somerset Maugham would take delight in drawing.

Later I learned his story, and it was quite a remarkable one too. At about the age of fifteen or sixteen, he ran away from home and joined the Merchant Navy. One of the ship's masters with whom he had sailed was Joseph Conrad; he had sailed around the Horn with him, and it was Conrad who introduced him to the Far East, a part of the world with which he was to fall in love. It was just at the time when rubber companies were opening up on the West Coast, and he was successful in obtaining a post as an Assistant Manager on Lok Kawi Estate. He must have done well, as during the world slump he was the only European to be retained by the Company as caretaker Manager. It was during his time here that he had bought the land on which he planted and developed his mixed coconut and rubber *kebun*. He returned to the United Kingdom every so often, and became a member of well known London Clubs, like many Estate Managers from Borneo, but it was always Borneo that called him back. He must have come from a good family, as he had such a strong character; his brother was King's Harbour Master at Falmouth, and possibly it was the Cornish connection which had attracted him to me.

I came to call on him regularly whenever I was in Kinarut in future, and he, like the Roman Catholic priests, was able to pass on much information which would not otherwise come to my ears. He lived very close to the people; they liked him very much and they were prepared to confide in him their knowledge of events in the area.

As well as a written monthly report, the Resident would frequently ring me up, possibly once a week or so, and talk over less formal events. One day, he asked if I would cut a trace over the Crocker Range to Keningau. He was obviously very keen to establish a route across the Range, either from Penampang to Tambunam, or from Papar to Keningau. Both were possible, but knowing that I had done one, he possibly thought that if I did the other one too, I would be in the best position to recommend the better alternative, whenever money became available for development.

Recalling my experience on the mountain top before, I wasn't enthusiastic about the idea of a further journey quite so soon. Anyhow, I appeared willing and at the first opportunity organized the trip. It was a wearisome journey, and I was glad when the time came to conclude the expedition. When we were out of the foothills, my guide suggested that if we kept to the Bangawan Estate side of the river, we could walk through the Estate paths, and so avoid the marshy and somewhat boggy ground on the Kimanis side. I readily agreed, knowing only too well the numbers of leeches waiting for us on terrain like that.

I duly submitted my report to the Resident, together with a sketch of the route taken, including compass bearings, but almost before he could have had time to read it, I received a letter reprimanding me for trespassing on Bangawan Estate land without the Manager's permission, and for not meeting him as I passed through! Recalling that the Manager had a bit of a reputation, I duly wrote to him apologizing, and at the same time suggested that I should pay the Estate a visit as Assistant Protector of Labour when I would have the opportunity of making his acquaintance. Nothing really like a bit of tit for tat, I thought!

He arranged for me to stay with Gerald Beers (whose family in the UK were indeed brewers) and he introduced me to the Senior Assistant, Paul Van Veen, a Dutchman who had come originally to Borneo as a tobacco planter.

Gerald told me that we had all been invited over to the Manager's house to drinks that evening, so whilst it was still daylight we walked over to his rather palatial establishment, fortunately not too far away; when we arrived, he shouted down from an upstairs verandah for us to come up. We duly obeyed and I was introduced to the already notorious (from what I had already heard of his activities) Bertie Thomson. He was not at all the kind of man I expected to meet. He was outspoken certainly, and he probably was a little boastful.

'Look at the sunset,' he said, 'the best there is in Borneo! Never see a sky like that anywhere else!'

But the verandah only overlooked rubber-trees, and one could not even see the distant hills! He had kindly asked along also the other Assistant, Harvey Coward, who was a big-built, quiet and pleasant man. The Estate had no club-house like Sapong, but the land alienated to it originally was only a quarter of the size, so there was no intention of employing a large number of European Assistants. Evidently it was their practice to meet every Saturday evening, each taking it in turns to bring a bottle of whiskey, staying there until it was finished! The next day I completed my inspection, but I did not write an adverse report.

I felt it my duty to liaise with all the European Managers of the Estates in the district, as the potential war situation in the Far East was deteriorating. Although Britain was holding its own in Europe, the battle in the skies having been won, Japan was beginning to make angry noises in the Far East, and although most hostility appeared to be against America, it was obvious that their population explosion would make them look elsewhere for *Lebensraum*. The garrison in Malaya was certainly being strengthened; the Eighth Division of the Australian Army was in the Peninsula and active measures were being taken for its defence.

My thoughts were echoed by another Estate Manager whom I met when I visited Kinarut Estate, not far from Harold Read. He was Dick Jones who lived in a beautiful Estate house with his charming wife. I spent a delightful weekend with them, and Dick showed me his dream holiday house on the beach at the edge of his Estate. It was nearly completed, and they both very kindly invited me to share with them their first weekend there. I was delighted to accept and looked forward to it immensely.

The next Estate I visited was Kimanis Estate, where Jock Riddel lived with his wife in a very beautiful mansion, high on a hill with a most beautiful view of the Crocker Range, and at sunrise and sunset the ever present Kinabalu. In neither Tenom nor from my house in Papar did I have a glimpse of the mountain, and it was so refreshing to sit at sunset, *sa-tengah* in hand, and once more rave over the glory of its ever-radiant colours.

Kimanis Estate was linked with Papar Estate where Robin Lutter was Manager. I had met him in Papar when he had come to the Office on some matter or another and we had gone to the Rest House together and had a drink. I was to see him more regularly in future, as he frequently came down to Papar and I was in the habit of inviting him up to the house for lunch. I had a darts board there which I had sent for from Robinson's in Singapore, and we also went to listen regularly to Don Bell who broadcast an excellent Far Eastern news bulletin from Radio Manila at 12.45 p.m. daily. Every Englishman or American living in the Far East at that time will remember him. He was an excellent newscaster of Far Eastern affairs, and left any other station cold.

Robin Lutter also invited me to spend weekends with him on the Estate, and I was very glad to accept any such invitation so kindly offered to me. By moving around the District and meeting the people, I was able to learn what they were doing and thinking, and I comprehended that there was a certain amount of apprehension regarding Japan's intentions. Although endeavouring to exude confidence, as a Government Officer should, I began to nurse private doubts. I didn't like the reported massing of troops in Saigon and the Americans didn't seem to be taking the threat seriously: they weren't in the war, and had no experience of dealing with warmongering, totalitarian states.

The only person who seemed to share my views was Dick Jones. He and I thought that the Japs possibly aimed to capture the Philippines, and if they got as far as achieving that, might even aim at the Celebes and Australia, but we couldn't see why they would aim for the jungles of Borneo. The Miri oil-fields were, of course, a possible target, but everyone knew the difficult sea conditions adjacent to the oil-fields, and they were being defended by the Indian Army. We were further heartened to hear that Churchill had agreed to the despatch of the *Repulse* and the *Prince of Wales* to be based in Singapore. That was good news: things weren't so bad after all! With the Royal Navy in such great strength in the South China Sea, what could the Japanese do? After all, not many years before, it was the Royal Navy that was training their fledgling officers.

The Government, however, began to take things seriously, and the Resident called all nearby D.O.s down to Jesselton and discussed his plans in the event of hostilities breaking out in the Far East. The worst that could happen, he thought, was a raid on Jesselton, with the object of destroying and plundering. All women and children were being advised to leave the country and take passage to Australia, but those who remained would go to the Interior. The Armed Constabulary would defend the gorge. Everyone was to stay at his post, all travelling should be cancelled, all movements were to be reported to him, and we should always be in in reach of the telephone. In coastal districts, we were to select coast-watchers and have somebody on duty day and night, with quick means of transport to District Headquarters.

Undeniably, a sense of alertness and urgency dominated our thoughts and actions. In no way were we despondent. 'Let 'em come! We'll give 'em hell,' was the attitude. Obviously the local people were not fools; most of them had wireless sets, and they heard the news coming over the air. The unfortunate point was that Radio Malaya could scarcely be heard in Borneo, and it was only by the grace of God that one managed to pick up a BBC Overseas Service transmission. And then it was only a fifteen minute newscast which was the heart of the matter, and related in the main to the European theatre of war. On the other hand, Japanese broadcasts in Mandarin, understood by the local Chinese, came in loud and clear.

The North Borneo Volunteer Force was mobilized, two companies in all, one on the East Coast and one on the West Coast, both companies being under the command of Managers of Companies or Rubber Estates, each Company Commander having had military experience in the First World War. Government Officers were allowed to join, and most of the European Officers in Jesselton who were not in key posts did so, and the clerical staff of both commercial organizations and Government offices were the main force. Because of transport difficulties, I think I was only able to attend two training exercises.

The last weekend of November, I spent at Kinarut Estate with Dick Jones. He was already living in his beach bungalow, and surprisingly comfortable it was. There had been a stream near the site which he had selected, and this not only supplied the house with water, but he had built a small dam and narrowed the overflow into a fast moving channel along a split bamboo *poreng*, which provided a sufficient head of water to drive a Pelman wheel, the axle of which he had embedded on concrete supports. This in its turn drove geared wheels with sufficient power to activate a 12-volt dynamo which charged batteries and provided a constant electricity supply to the house, free from charge. The main thing was that he was self-sufficient, and not dependent on imported supplies of kerosene which would obviously cease. He was also experimenting, as I had been, in trying to burn coconut oil instead of kerosene in his refrigerator. Both of us only had moderate success!

The Sunday morning started off with one of Dick's marvellous cooked breakfasts for which he was justly famous, followed by a delightful cool swim in the crystal clear sea before the sun became too warm; this was a prelude to a nice cool beer accompanied by gorgeous curry puffs. Leisurely talking and beer drinking was the prelude to the serious gin-slinging, and then the loveliest of curries which was to linger in my mouth for many a long day!

This was to be a fitting end to the period of relative tranquility that the country had enjoyed so far whilst Britain had been at war. In the following week, all hell was to break loose. On the Monday morning, the Resident advised me that emergency measures were to be taken, and that all essential supplies were being moved out of Jesselton to various out-stations up the line. I would have to plan and prepare to receive a large quantity of limed rice which had been imported as emergency food supplies (by covering the rice with lime it prolonged the life of the rice, so we had been told), all the West Coast supplies of benzine, or petrol, and kerosene, and all the West Coast supplies of flour. Papar had been chosen since there were a number of rice-millers in the district, each of whom had storage space for the rice, and possibly flour, but I was advised to construct a bamboo store for the kerosene, and decide on a dumping ground, outside the town and preferably in the jungle, for the petrol. The Locomotive Superintendent would advise me of the approximate times the special trains carrying these supplies would arrive, and I would have to arrange labour accordingly. A new vote would be created to meet the cost of all these emergency measures, but in the meantime all expediture for porterage, depot construction etc., should be charged to this new vote to be called 'Emergency Expenditure'.

As always, Dick Evans was brief and to the point. Those were my instructions;

there was no amplification and no discussion. The implication was simple: 'Get on with it!'

First, as I regarded this as most important, I called in the rice-millers, acquainted them with the plans, and asked them to see to it that there was space in their godowns for the rice supplies. They all agreed that they could make room, and that they would make their porters available to carry the sacks of rice. Next, I called in my head *mandor*, Amit, to get word to all the Government labourers to cease all other work, except for refuse collection, night-soil removal and the cleansing of the markets, and concentrate on the collection of bamboo *poreng* and using it for the construction of a kerosene store on the *padang*. This was the only space I could think of which was clear, and reasonably removed from a concentration of population. Then I looked at a map of the district and, relying on my memory, chose a site near the railway line which would be suitable for dumping the 66-gallon drums of petrol.

All the Native Chiefs were due to sit in the Native Court on Wednesday, so I arranged that they should meet me before they opened the Court session. Although as yet they were not directly involved, I felt it was correct to notify them of the situation which was developing, assuring them at the same time that there was no cause for alarm since the British Government had sent out a Battle Fleet, with the strongest and most powerful battleship the world had ever seen, to defend the South China Sea. All would be well!

Everything went ahead as planned; December had come, and a Japanese plenipotentiary was in Washington negotiating a peaceful settlement.

That much was known; the world did not know, however, that the main Japanese fleet had already set course for Pearl Harbour with orders for a perfidious attack on the American Fleet, that the Japanese Armies were already on the march towards Malaya and Burma, and that they had loaded their transports in Saigon and were already *en route* for the oil-fields of Miri! Even Hitler could not have acted with such treachery.

At 7.30 a.m. on 7 December 1941, one hundred and fifty Japanese bombers and torpedo-carrying aircraft unexpectedly attacked the American fleet in Pearl Harbour, Honolulu, and sank nineteen warships as they lay at anchor. When I heard Don Bell announce this, I, like everyone else in Borneo, listened to his newscast with incredulity. But the death-knell tolled a week later, when we heard, aghast, that the *Prince of Wales* and *Repulse* had been sunk. This was the unthinkable: we had no defence.

At 7.30 a.m. on 9 December 1941, the longest train ever seen in Borneo pulled out of Jesselton Station. It carried all the European women, none of whom had taken their Government's advice to leave the country and proceed to Australia, and their children, the entire staff of the Lands and Survey Department and their families, the Land records and maps of the country. All the Chinese who had relatives 'up the line' also boarded the train with their cash boxes, their wives' jewellry and their families. Although it was only a distance of some fifty miles, it did not reach Beaufort until 4.30 p.m. in the afternoon.

The freight section of the railway was also busy. In Jesselton throughout 8 December, every freight train of the rolling-stock was pushed into service, and all Jesselton's stocks of limed rice, sugar, flour, kerosene and petrol were unloaded at Papar under my supervision and put into store. Further stocks of rice were also sent up to Tenom. Possibly the major responsibility fell to the lot of the D.O. Beaufort, at that time an officer by the name of Hugh Sykes. He had the responsibility of building an internment camp at Membakut for all the Japanese on the West Coast: mostly, these were the fishing folk on Banggi Island, but also included Mr Sakai and his family.

By about the middle of the month, everything was mostly in place and we were able to breathe again, but the hardest job was just waiting, wondering what next would happen. The coastguards I had appointed as look-outs regularly reported to the Sergeant and myself: '*Tida'ada apa-apa Tuan!*' So far all was well, but the tension was building.

One night, about eight or nine o'clock, the phone rang and the Sergeant, who had already made his evening's report, said excitedly: 'There's a fire at sea, Tuan, they don't know what it is! It's unusual!'

I went down to the Office and questioned the look-out. From what he said, and judging from his rather frightened bearing, I decided that something unusual must be happening. I rang up the Resident, reported the news that had just been brought me, and told him that I was going to Kuala to investigate. I brought a Corporal with me, went back to the house and saddled up Firefly, and with a torch with which to try and follow the path, set off for the Kuala with some trepidation. It wasn't at all a nice journey; we had to go through swamp where I knew there were iguanas if not crocodiles, and adding to our troubles there were some heavy thunder showers. We pushed on, and eventually reached the hard white sand which meant we were near the shore. It was easier going then across to the beach where the look-out post on the only hill had been established. I could see a clear red glow in the sky; there was something unusual happening! I climbed the hillock as fast as I could scramble, and reaching the look-out post, grabbed the glasses from the other look-out who had waited there whilst his companion came back to the Office to report. Sure enough, there was something unusual happening for which I could find no explanation. There was undoubtedly a fire of some kind or another out at sea; every so often I could see a shower of sparks flying into the sky. The source of the fire wasn't moving. In the tenseness of the moment it seemed as if a Japanese munitions vessel had caught fire. Very apprehensively, I urged my posse back to the Office to report to the Resident.

This event occurred just before Christmas, and it didn't seem to bear glad tidings! On the contrary, it seemed to be a portent of things to come. At that point I could not guess what it was, but years afterwards I was told by geologists that it had been a mud-volcano erupting on Pulau Tiga, a group of three islands just visible from Papar and in the direction of Labuan. I often was to fly over it in later years, as it was in the flight path of the Malayan Airways plane from Jesselton to Labuan, and I would always look down on the big wide circle of different vegetation that had grown in the crater of the volcano, and inevitably recall those rather apprehensive moments whilst it was happening without finding it possible to ascertain the reason.

It was then that the cable came from GHQ in Singapore telling that the Japanese had landed at Miri. Panic set in, so it seemed. Telegram after telegram came from the Resident's Office emanating from Singapore, which he had transmitted on to all his District Officer *en clair*. Destroy all petrol supplies; destroy all kerosene supplies; sink every boat over ten feet in length. Apply a scorched earth policy throughout the area. Burn all rubber stocks in Estate warehouses. The cables never seemed to stop coming.

I could appreciate the point about the destruction of petrol, and immediately set out with a gang of men and the Sergeant, wondering how best to achieve this in as quick a time as possible. I didn't fancy opening six hundred drums. But we did it! I did entertain the idea of building a big fire, and firing into the drums from afar to cause a spurt of petrol to jet on to the fire and blow the lot up, but it seemed a bit of a dangerous experiment!

On my return to the Office, I pondered in my mind about the efficacy of the other orders I had received. I simply could not agree with the one concerning the sinking of the fishermen's boats. Obviously the events in Malaya differed from conditions here; I could appreciate the point in mainland Malaya, as the Japanese were using any craft they could lay their hands on to infiltrate behind our lines and attack from the rear, but here the situation was different. Their line of advance would be the railway track; it was the only means of north/south communication available to them. So I decided that the more sensible method would be to hide them.

Regarding kerosene, that too was a commodity of use to Chinese and native alike; it would be plain stupid to destroy it. So, on my return to Papar, I sent for the three local Native Chiefs asking them to bring along every adult male they could muster, and through the Captain China I sent a similar message to Chinese households. They didn't know the purpose of my demand; I might have been calling them in to issue them with rifles for all they knew! I reckoned there were approximately two natives in the District to one Chinese household: a simple ratio of two to one.

Sugar, flour and rice were the only stocks left which would be of use to the enemy and which were Government owned or controlled. Of these, sugar was the only stock of use to the natives; they didn't eat flour, and they had their own stocks of rice. The division here was obvious: I would give almost all the sugar stocks to the natives, and the Chinese could retain the flour and rice. I looked through all the telegrams I had received, but read no mention of these obvious commodities. From what I could gather from news coming over the air waves, the Japanese Army hadn't worked out their logistics, not in the same way as Eisenhower was destined to do in 1943 and 1944; on the contrary, the Oriental foe lived off what he captured. So all these commodities would be fodder for his troops. Since the policy was to deny the enemy anything of use to him, I felt I was quite in order to distribute the food stocks in the best way that I saw fit. At times I did entertain doubts as to the rectitude of my decisions; they were all valuable commodities that somebody had paid good money to acquire, and here I was planning in what manner to give them away!

It was already late in the afternoon before the Chiefs arrived, and I saw them together with Chan Chi On, the Captain China. I thought it best to tell them all: the whole truth, as far as I knew it. The Japanese, I told them, by the use of suicide bombers, which we could not have anticipated, had sunk our capital ships, and we had lost the defence of the seas around Malaya, Singapore and Borneo; they had already made a successful landing at Miri, and there was nothing to stop them taking Labuan and Jesselton. (In fact, as I was speaking to them, Labuan had already been occupied.)

I had received orders to destroy petrol supplies: this had been done. I told them the orders to sink all local craft, but I said that I relied upon the Native Chiefs to get the word around and make doubly sure that all boats were hidden and could never be found by the enemy. I then told them that I had asked them to bring men along so that I could distribute kerosene evenly through the villages: one tin per household. I made the Chiefs responsible for carrying that out.

We then discussed foodstocks. Rice, I suggested, should be left where it was, since all natives had rice, and it would be up to the millers to distribute the rice through the shops and account to the Government after the territory had been re-captured. Flour, I suggested, was not an essential commodity for the natives, and I suggested the same process be applied to flour as to the rice. Sugar, I suggested, should be issued at the same time as kerosene, leaving a few sacks for the Chinese. Nobody had any better suggestions to make, so all my proposals were unanimously agreed.

Throughout the discussion, I emphasized that the anticipated Japanese occupation would only be temporary, I made the point that Great Britain was engaged in a much bigger war in Europe, which would have to be won before forces could be released to send to the Far East. It was all a question of time: if not by the end of this year, then assuredly before the end of the next year the British would be back. I would be proved to be a bit wrong in my estimate, but I couldn't guess that at the time.

It was already dark. It had been a long day! I had left the house at first light, had only had a cup of tea and a banana and had gone straight out to get rid of the petrol. That had taken some time, and I had returned to the office. In mid afternoon, Ituk had sent me down some *nasi-goreng* which I consumed as I was working, so that by the time I had spoken to the Chiefs, the sun had already set. It had set in more sense than one. The adage I had learnt at school that 'the sun never sets on the British Empire' was about to be proven wrong.

When the evening sun set on New Year's Day, 1942, I ceremoniously hauled down personally the Sabah Jack. Native Chief Oman stepped forward and asked: 'May I keep it safe for your return, Tuan?' I replied: 'Certainly, with pleasure; it won't be for long!' Little did I know! But it caused me some worry as the years went by, as I gradually came to learn of the inhumane deeds of the then victors.

As a sequel to this anecdote, I must relate how the victorious Australians landed in force on Kimanis Beach only a short distance from Benoni village three and a half years later, and were met by Native Chief Oman with the flags which he presented to them; and for this incident and the help he was able to provide to the Australian Army, he was awarded a Military Medal.

That evening, I felt very lonely. I knew the enemy had captured the oil-fields at Miri. I had heard too that they had invaded Labuan: this much I had learned on the phone from Hugh Sykes in Beaufort, and I had relayed the message to the Resident. I tried the wireless set; I endeavoured to tune in to the BBC, but did not receive any news of the Far East, but did hear the strains of the Looe Fisherman's Choir being broadcast! In time of anguish, it is always comforting to experience a link with one's home town. It seemed to give me strength for whatever was to lie ahead.

The next morning the telephone to the D.O.'s office in Beaufort was not replying. This seemed ominous, and I advised the Resident. My next thought was the railway telephone, and so I went across to the railway station and asked the stationmaster if he had any news. He told me that a special train had been ordered. Japanese troops were on board. It was now only a matter of time.

I went back to the house and pondered what I should do. I tried to eat, but in times of tension appetite disappears.

I returned to the Rest House from which one could see the station. It appeared to be an age but in reality not much more than an hour before the engine heaved into sight. Suddenly there was activity on the platform. The train gave a whistle as it approached. I could feel the blood coursing through my veins. The engine pulled to a stop. What would happen now? Several khaki-clad figures descended from it, and started to urinate on the flower beds. They were all shouting to each other in a language which was gibberish to me. I kept well hidden. They all stood around in groups, lighting cigarettes, laughing and talking together, like any soldiery would do. At last the engine whistled again, they boarded, and eventually the train pulled out of the platform in the Jesselton direction. I had no one to talk to on the phone now, neither north nor south. We were occupied territory!

Naturally, I briefly advised Dick Evans, but on the morrow, bidden to the Station by the stationmaster, I saw him pass straight through, no stopping for 'line clear', with Colonel Adams, Commandant of the Armed Constabulary, accompanied by two armed Japanese.

Under the Poached Egg

WITHOUT any instructions, I was in limbo. I had been working feverishly, almost day and night, for the previous two or three weeks, and now I was cut off, surrounded by the enemy. Native Chief Oman came up the house early one morning, and tried to persuade me to go into the jungle with him.

'I'll hide you, Tuan,' he had said. 'Nobody knows the jungle better than I. I guarantee I will bring you food, and keep you safe. I swear, on oath, I will do this. Just give me the chance!'

It was a very tempting offer, genuinely made, but in no way could I consider it. First of all, I was still on duty, and I had no instructions to abscond from my post whatever circumstances may arise. Secondly, the presence of a European anywhere would stick out like a sore thumb, and I felt that wherever I was, I would be located by anyone wishing to find me. At that time, I had no knowledge or foretaste of the Japanese, but they were the enemy, and they had the guns. It was just as well I reached the conclusion that I did, as a party of Europeans who went into the jungle in hiding in Sarawak were all tracked down, tortured and shot. So I had to stay and await the return of the Resident.

There were no trains; everything had come to a halt. The stationmaster, who was the only link with communication into or through the District, was the one person who might have any knowledge of events, so I used to phone him regularly, once or twice a day, and frequently visit him; he was always seated with the telephone ear-piece to his ear, listening for any glimmer of information which might come to him, and keeping in touch with the Kimanis stationmaster. Jesselton station had gone silent. Then one afternoon he rang me excitedly: 'The Resident and Colonel Adams are coming down the line!' he had said. I immediately went over to the station and, in about half an hour, the rail-car turned the bend and came slowly into the station, drawing to a halt. Dick Evans leant over the door and said: 'We have arranged a truce! Things will gradually get back to normal, but we have to follow the orders of the Japanese Commander.' In a way, that seemed a little reassuring, but there seemed to be big question marks arising from every point of view. There was, however, no time for questions; he was away almost as soon as he had come. I just didn't know what to think or do.

I had been very relieved to see him return, and I managed to get a message to most of the Managers of the rubber estates, who I knew would also be wondering what was happening, and as usual be blaming the Government.

In a day or so the trains started running again, and then I heard that the European women and children who had gone up the line were returning to Jesselton, information that proved to be correct. A week later, the phone rang one evening at the house, and it was Dick Evans informing me that he would be up on the next morning's train 'to put me in the picture'. I was very glad to hear that.

He appeared very strained when he arrived on the next morning's train: that, of course, was inevitable. He told me of the meeting in Brunei, and of the points agreed, adding: 'We were playing for time. If we hadn't agreed to continue the administration, there is no knowing what they may have decided to do. Going along with them to this extent at least helps the people. It is a status quo for at least a short while, and we can get food production organized, and endeavour to replace imported commodities with local substitutes. We can give a lead to the people, and seeing us still around may quell the sense of panic that has set in'.

Certainly his visit helped me enormously; any feeling of uneasiness with the situation which I had entertained was at least softened. I gathered that he did not think it was a situation that would last long, but possibly was the best in the circumstances. He advised me to play down policing and court work, just dealing with any cases of crime which I could not pass to the Native Court, and concentrating on alternative sources of essential foods which were now cut off.

He also asked me to visit all European Managers of rubber estates in turn and advise them of the position. Don't put anything in writing, was his advice; speak only to them face to face. Regarding the Japanese, he could give no indication, naturally, but he said: 'Always bow your head to them, on meeting them. It is their custom, and they, naturally, as victors would want us to bow to them first.' They would bow in return, but they were punctilious about these matters.

When I accompanied him to the station, and walked in the direction of the first class compartment when the train arrived, I noticed that there were two Japanese soldiers also travelling in the first class compartment. This was to be my first close contact with them. I felt sorry for Dick Evans having to travel with them, but they seemed polite enough; they rose to their feet when he entered, he bowed and they politely acknowledged him by bowing in reply.

My chief concern after his visit was the procedure I was to follow in arranging visits to the Estate Managers. They were Europeans, and they had a right to know the true position, as scaremongering rumours were very rife. I thought it best to send one of my policemen to Papar Estate, making sure he left his rifle at the station, as my unit were still all armed! I rehearsed him well in his messages, and the whole programme went like clockwork. I went to all 'up-line' estates first, from one to the other. I think even Bertie Thompson was glad to see me! I emphasized what I felt, that this was only a temporary truce. Dick Evans himself felt that the Japanese did not know what to do with the Europeans that fell into their hands: we were not in their plans! He felt that they would have to refer back to the High Command in Japan for instructions, and that it might well be that we would be shipped to Japan, as we would only be an obvious embarrassment to them here.

My visit down the line was more relaxing. I called on Harold Read before going on to see Dick Jones. Harold, as ever, had a glass of pink gin on the table in front of him. He had ordered a couple of cases of gin in November, and felt he could hold out for a few months yet! He had a boat and a sail, and felt it might be worth a chance trying to sail down to Singapore.

'How about it?' he asked me, 'Are you game?'

I couldn't really concur with him.

'My duty is here,' I said, 'Nobody has relieved me of it yet.' And I tried to dissuade him from undertaking anything so foolish himself. 'Even if you made it along the coast, you'd never make it across the narrows to Singapore; you'd be swamped out in a craft like that. Besides, at the rate they are going, the Japanese would be in Singapore before you!'

Little did I know that I would have been absolutely right on that point.

Dick Jones and his wife were well established in their beach hide-away. They had stacks of tinned food, and were catching fish, so they lacked little, except that Dick admitted the beer would run out soon! His Pelman wheel was nicely charging his batteries but, like me, he wasn't being very successful in making his refrigerator function adequately with coconut oil instead of kerosene. I fear I assisted him in diminishing his stocks of beer. His curry puffs were excellent as usual; his cook that morning had gone out to sea and caught a *tengiri* (a horse-mackerel) and a beautiful smell of curry pervaded the kitchen area. 'We'll be able to hold out until we are relieved!' he said. He was always an optimist!

We had had a lovely swim in the morning, and the good food and drink, as well as the very sociable company, made us forget that we were in enemy-occupied territory. I stayed the night, and left early the next morning to be up to the Estate's rail halt in time for the morning train. Seeing me, the driver stopped, otherwise he would have gone straight through. He had timed his stop well, and the first class compartment halted directly in front of me. I mounted and was taken aback to find three Japanese soldiers seated in the bucket seats. Fortunately, I remembered to do exactly as the Resident had told me: I dutifully bowed my head. They, likewise, dipped their heads in acknowledgement. Obviously, I had put a halt to their conversation. I think everyone felt a bit embarrassed at first, so I thought I'd break the ice. I asked them in Malay if they were able to speak Malay yet, but I drew a blank. One of them said something to the others in Japanese, and they all started laughing. I daresay I was the butt of the joke. Anyhow, it broke the ice, and they continued talking among themselves. Nevertheless, I was very glad when we at last reached Papar station, when I rose, bowed my head, and left the carriage.

That was my first direct encounter with the enemy; my second encounter followed all too quickly on that. I had become used to being told that the train which had passed through carried Japanese. I only hoped that they would continue to pass through! But the day came all too quickly when the Rest House keeper's assistant came over to the office in some agitation: *'Ada Jepon panggil sama Tuan dalam Rest House!'*—Japanese in the Rest House were summoning me to meet them. So the end of these phoney days had come at last, I thought. As I walked over to the Rest House, I figured out that this was probably the beginning of internment.

As I walked up the steps and entered the lounge and dining area, three Japanese soldiers were seated drinking beer. One of them rose to his feet and saluted smartly;

I quite willingly bowed my head in response to such recognition. Out of the corner of my eye, I recognized Sakai, in a Japanese Army uniform. He was obviously to be the interpreter!

I was motioned to sit at the table, so I drew up a chair and sat down with them. Sakai started the conversation by introducing the officer who had stood up when I entered. 'This is Lt. Yamaha,' he said. I introduced myself by name. I was then invited to have a beer with them, and the Rest House cook, with his hair standing more upright than usual, appeared with two large bottles from which all glasses were charged. This will never do, I thought to myself, drinking with the enemy, but, on the other hand, they offered a friendly gesture, and it would have been rude to refuse. It was the officer who set the scene.

Looking back over the years, I think he was the finest and most straightforward Japanese I have met at any time, and I hope he did survive the war. He was the victor and I was the vanquished, but he showed only respect. He was among the spearhead of their Army and, I imagine, among their best fighting troops.

I think his visit was purely to gain information. He wanted to know where the Europeans lived, and on what Estates, who and what nationalities were the priests and where they lived. Was there a convent, how many nuns were there, and what nationality were they? All my answers were copiously written down in Japanese; it seemed natural to me that they would require such information, and there was no reason to mislead them, since they could acquire the same information from almost anyone. One of the priests was a German national, but still they recorded all the information that I passed to them.

In spite of the apparent amiability of this particular officer, I was, nevertheless, able to relax a little more with the departure of the afternoon train taking the Japanese contingent with it. Shortly after this incident, I was advised by Dick Evans that he had decided to transfer me to Tambunam to take Geoff Hedley's place, and that he would come to Papar. Long after, he explained to me that he felt that Geoff had not faced the brunt of the invasion in the same way as the officers along the line, and that I had had a particularly rough time, immediately before the Japanese arrived, handling Jesselton's reserve stocks, and was vulnerable owing to the proximity of Jesselton. I was very ready to go back to Tambunam, and was packed in record time. Ituk was extremely happy with the news too; Muruts seemed always to be homesick, if they were not near their own country.

The first day's stop was to be Keningau. George Robertson was no longer there, having been transferred to Sandakan as Legal Adviser just before the war began. The house had been left empty for the Jesselton wives and children, with Macartney nominally in charge from Tenom. When the wives returned to their coastal homes after the invasion, the house was empty again. It was here that I arrived on 14 May 1942.

The journey to Tambunam should have proceeded the following day, but an unexpected hiatus occurred when the Chief Clerk, new to me and an Indian, reported difficulty in getting labour to act as porters to carry my baggage. I always retain a suspicion that he knew something was afoot, and that the delay was deliberate.

Be that as it may, I was forced to delay a day in Keningau. I used the visitor's room in the house, as after George's departure from Keningau the house had been left empty for the ladies from Jesselton.

The next morning, at daybreak, I was sitting on the verandah looking out over the plains below the distant hills as the early rays of the sun began to warm the earth, and a gentle mist was beginning to rise, when my attention was roused by a hibiscus bush, which I couldn't recall having seen on that spot before. As I gazed curiously at the bush, to my astonishment I saw it move, slowly but surely in the direction of the house. To my amazement, another bush appeared, and that also began to move. It was dawn, I had only been drinking tea! My first reaction was to call for Ituk, but before he could arrive, the bushes had reached the bottom of the steps, and two Japanese soldiers emerged camouflaged in leaves! They rushed simultaneously up the steps, with bayonets fixed to their rifles, shouting: '*Banzai, banzai!*' I really don't know what they thought I was going to do about it! But they certainly needn't have gone to all that trouble. I really think they were more alarmed than I was.

I had anticipated internment; it had been inevitable. But they need not quite have gone to the lengths that they did. Having rushed in on me in that manner, I was forced to sit on the ground against a house post whilst my wrists were tied coarsely with rope behind the post! Having achieved that, one of them stood in front of me, with rifle and bayonet pointed at me, whilst the other went over to the phone, and started ringing and shouting: '*Wisheee washee! Wishee washee!*' at least a dozen or so times. At last he seemed to obtain the reply he wanted, and only then did they begin to relax. The rifle was no longer pointed at me; I was rather glad of that. I felt pretty sure it was loaded, since their nervous agitation certainly indicated this, and the man had his finger too near the trigger for my liking.

After a few further and regular '*Wishee, washees!*' down the telephone, and ensuring that I wasn't able to budge, they began to inspect the house. I think Ituk and any of his family who might have been there had disappeared quickly; I don't blame them! It wasn't their war.

It was certainly a long morning! The calls of nature began to press. I hadn't been gagged, fortunately, so I made my needs heard vociferously. Alas, my message was misinterpreted: all I received were a few bananas thrown at me! My own bananas too, as they had found them in the kitchen. After a few more shouts I believe they began to see the point; they untied my hands from the post and led me to the bathroom, where they did their best to lock me in, overlooking the fact that the bathroom had a door to the back of the house, where Ituk coming up a few steps from the kitchen would bring the bath water. Anyhow, I remembered the loaded rifle, and wouldn't have appreciated a bullet up my backside. By this time, they had discovered the mosquito room in the spare bedroom, and thought this might be a better way to guard me. So I was put in there, with one of them seated outside the door with the rifle on his knee.

When late afternoon came, the telephone rang and once more there was a long conversation, and what I could only interpret as grunts of agreement. Then it was action stations. They clearly indicated that I was to go with them and bring the things that I needed. Fortunately, I had done a lot of jungle bashing, and being packed anyhow, it wasn't difficult to grab essential things like my mosquito net, aluminium saucepan and frying pan, shorts, shirts, underwear, toothbrush and so on. I also had a ruc-sac which I always carried on my own back, and this was soon stuffed full of the necessities of life, including some M&B693 tablets which had just reached Borneo, and which were supposed to be the new sulpha wonder drug. I also had some quinine tablets. I looked at the camp bed, but there was no way in which I could carry the legs!

I packed slowly, thinking hard all the time of any vital necessity I might need—I nearly forgot my reading glasses which were on the table in the sitting room where I had used them the previous night. It wasn't like packing for a weekend, but an indeterminate stay did create problems. I made certain that my compass was in the top pocket of my bush jacket; that is where I normally carried it, with my iodine pencil. At length I could think no more, and the soldiers were getting restive and shouting at me. I refused to let that bother me. Every time they shouted, I turned round at them and indicated with my hand to keep quiet, as I was very busy. At last I could delay no longer and, bidding a fond farewell to the things I would never see again, I shouldered my ruc-sac, picked up the one bag I thought I could carry with ease, and led the way out of the house, along the path, past my first bungalow where I had had fever, and past the office where I felt at least a dozen pairs of eyes were watching me, noticing that the Sergeant didn't stand to attention and salute, as he would normally have done, and walked over to the awaiting bus. I assumed I would be allowed my normal seat by the side of the driver; in fact, that is where they seemed to want me to go. I took off my ruc-sac, putting it on my knees as I took my seat. One of the Japanese soldiers sat next to me by the side of the door, and the other occupied the rear passenger area.

So we drove away from Keningau on a day that was already becoming hot and sweltering, on the longest journey I was ever to make on the North Borneo Railway! On arrival at Melalap, I spotted Horry Lack's face at the window of a third class railway carriage, and immediately noticed that the coach for first and second class passengers had been uncoupled. Two or three other Japanese soldiers were standing nearby. There was much shouting and bantering exchanged between them all, whilst one busied himself shouting: '*Ugh! Ugh!*' at me. I took it to mean: 'Get on board the train!' and did just that, relieved, I think, to meet another European.

Mrs Lack was there too, and the heavily bespectacled Williams, the Assistant Manager on Melalap. We had much to gossip about! At length, already latish in the afternoon, we spotted two of the soldiers climbing into the engine and the others came into the back of the carriage with us. Half an hour or so later, we were in Tenom, where John Macartney was waiting on the platform with another couple of soldiers! Then on to the Sapong Estate Halt. Here there was a long wait, and whilst the engine was blowing off surplus steam, the sun had already set. It had always been a custom with the Railway Service never to let a train pass through the gorge at night. Even rail gangs would inspect every yard of the line at daybreak, in case rocks or trees had fallen across the line during darkness. It was not merely derailment that could happen to the train, there was nothing to stop it rushing into the raging Padas River! It was obvious that the book would not be followed on this occasion.

Eventually, close on eight or nine o'clock at night, we heard voices. The ferry had crossed the river, and had brought the Sapong Estate contingent. Johnnie Baxter climbed into the carriage, looking unperturbed and debonair.

'A bit of a rough crowd, aren't they?' he exclaimed. 'Surely they won't attempt to take us through the gorge by night!'

He spoke with the voice of experience, having long suffered from land slips, line blockages and so on. But they did! I think the engine driver must have been terrified, with the knowledge that this was a thing that was never done, not forgetting the guns pointing at him and his fireman.

To any of us it was frightening enough. Bare wooden seats, not built for European bodies, no room for one's legs at all! We felt every rail joint as we went over it. We were squashed like sardines in a dark canister, as there was no light and we could see nothing at all; it was a clouded night and not even a star was visible. The driver relied on his whistle and his brakes; the engine seemed to screech and scream at every bend. Now and again, when we were in the narrows of the gorge, the roar of the Padas River could be heard in the background, and the white crests of the froth caused by the rushing water lashing against the rocks which were the outer bastion of the rail-track seemed to gleam menacingly at us as we rushed by. It was an eerie sort of journey, like a flight into the unknown.

At length, the flood plain of the river and flatter land was reached and the rush became less hectic. With a long penetrating whistle, the outskirts of Beaufort township seemed to be approaching, and soon the train came to a grinding halt. An optimist among us shouted out: 'Let's go up to the Club and have a drink!' That, at any rate for the moment, put less agreeable thoughts out of our minds!

There was considerable shouting amongst the Japanese at this point. I think the argument possibly concerned the carriage in which we were travelling. To negotiate the bends of the Tenom section, the length of the carriage was much shorter and passengers normally changed at Beaufort to the mainline carriages which had a longer wheel-base. However, the faction which was opposed to our change won the day. We were aware that our carriage was being shunted around, and during this process we passed carriages of the mainline train in which we spotted Europeans from the Beaufort area. It was only a momentary glance, but we realized that a big operation in rounding us all up had taken place. By this time it was gone midnight, and none of us had had anything to eat or drink since dawn. I think we were all rather exhausted.

At length, with more whistling by the engine drivers, we were off. We all felt a little safer on this section of the railway line: although the running of trains at night had never normally been done, it had been done when stores were being removed from Jesselton just a few months earlier. The danger, although slight, was the possible collision with buffaloes which often wandered on to the track. The engines were equipped with 'cow-catchers', but a water buffalo was quite a weight with which to collide! Anyhow, that was going to be the problem of our captors, and not ours.

We stopped at the Estate stations and halts one by one, and could see the planters being forced into the train at bayonet point. Many of them had their wives too. I wondered how poor old Dick Jones, with his enormous girth, was going to fit into a third class seat! In fact, he had to stand! Soon we went through Papar, and I tried to wave to the stationmaster, who had been so good to me relaying information whenever he had news just a little while previously, but he must have handed the 'all-clear' slip to the driver and then kept out of sight. He had been a very friendly Chinese, and obviously would have had no pleasure in seeing the Europeans, whom he regarded as his friends, in a state of bondage.

The Japanese had done their homework well and must have employed about a hundred troops in the operation. They knew too what to do when the engine needed firewood and water at Pengalut, some four miles to the north of Papar. They all leapt from the train, and trained machine-guns on it, just in case any of us should try and escape. I don't think the thought ever entered our heads: we were all far too exhausted. We got the message though! By this time, the sun had nearly risen, and it was quite light enough to see all their antics. At least, they made certain of getting us all. It had been an extremely well planned operation. They had planned to capture us all at exactly the same time and had succeeded.

The rumour went around that we were being shipped to Japan, and that they had not rounded us up before because they hadn't had the shipping to spare. Everyone, of course, had been deeply shocked to hear of the fall of Singapore, but each living in isolation, without many fellow countrymen to talk to, we had had to bear the devastating news which came over the air alone with our thoughts. The outlook was grim.

We had, however, only heard snatches of news. We did not know that some 85,000 British and Australian troops had laid down their arms when Singapore had fallen earlier in February. We had heard that Darwin had been bombed, but had no details. Don Bell of Radio Manila, the universal source of news in Sabah, had gone off the air early in the conflict. If we could have received the BBC with any degree of clarity, we might have heard an outline of the news. We did not know, for example, that Darwin had been packed with merchantmen at the time the attack on that harbour had occurred, that there was little in the way of anti-aircraft defences and that when the bombers had exhausted their loads, the two hundred plus Japanese aircraft involved had used their machine guns on the survivors of the merchantmen struggling in the sea. One of the survivors wrote later: 'What we didn't like was when they turned their attention to the Australian hospital ship, which was clearly marked—painted with white crosses. They bombed and machine-gunned her. That was not war—that was sheer murder.'

It was as well we did not know these events, otherwise we would have descended from the train with greater foreboding.

At nine or ten o'clock, the train halted at Tanjong Aru, the Headquarters of the

Railway: we thought at the time that it might have been to change the points but, looking back, it probably was to telephone ahead to Batu Tiga that the train was about to arrive in Jesselton. The next stop was the Police Headquarters at Batu Tiga, and we quickly realized our destination! A stable block and one married quarters block had a tall barbed-wire fence encircling them; at the entrance was the guard-room, which admirably suited the Japanese for the same purpose.

Around the train there appeared Japanese soldiery with machine guns; it was obvious this was our destination—but the men only, it being made quite clear that the ladies had to stay in the train. I felt quite sorry for Dick Jones and Jock Riddell, for, by this time, I had come to know them both and their wives quite well, and it must have been very upsetting to have to part from their wives, leaving them to journey to an unknown destination.

We all knew well enough where we were to go! At the fence we saw the faces of many that I had met before: the European officers of the Chartered Company, and members of the commercial fraternity. They were there first, and obviously they had chosen the best places! They were in the barracks, but the ex-stable block, with its cement floor, was our lot. Some were lucky as friends had reserved places for them, but I didn't begrudge them that. All I remember is the coldness and the hardness of the cement on the first night. By the next night, I had found some old rope lying around, laced it through the slots in my camp-bed mattress, and tied it to the bottom stable bars: I was off the ground! I had learnt my first lesson in camp survival: scrounge!

We had been very largely, particularly amongst the Government staff, an itinerant community; the job of the administration was to travel in order to keep in close contact with the people whom we served. Others who had to travel were doctors. When we had a roll-call amongst ourselves to ascertain whether all Europeans on the coast were present, we ascertained that John Dingle, the District Officer, Kudat, was missing as was Dr Clarke, the Medical Officer, Interior. It suddenly struck me that he should have been in Keningau and apprehended at the same time as the hibiscus bushes advanced towards me! Nobody had any idea what had happened to these officers. It was always possible that John Dingle might have taken off in a *kumpit* (a large coastal sailing vessel) which often plied between Kudat and the outer Philippine isles: they were American territory, and we believed that Corrigidor was still holding out, but Marcus had simply disappeared. We simply had to wait and see, and in the meantime we were out to make ourselves more comfortable.

What we learnt later was that John Dingle was having his morning bath when the Nips, employing the same tactics as they had done on me, advanced on him. Unperturbed, John, clad only with a towel round his waist, shouted at them to get out and wait until he had put some clothes on. That had not pleased them!

In the case of Marcus Clark, he had been unwise in sending a circular to all his staff, saying what most of us thought: 'This is just a temporary set-back, and very shortly we'll be in charge again!'

About a week or so later, Geoff Hedley from Tambunam, and the two missionaries from Ranau, the Australian Alan Belcher and White, a Somerset man I believe, who comprised the Borneo Evangelical Mission in North Borneo (other members of their mission were in Sarawak) were brought down the line. Evidently, a party of Japanese must have gone up to Tambunam and Ranau with the two who came to apprehend me: hence possibly the cause of so many '*Wishee, washees!*' that I had heard being pronounced on the phone! Geoff Hedley had had a particularly rough time because he was immediately arrested when the party had arrived in Tambunam, and was then confined to his house whilst the rest of the party went up to and returned from Ranau with the two missionaries: that was six or seven days in all in addition to the three or four days to Jesselton. He had almost become a Japanese speaker!

The language barrier was a very real problem in dealing with our captors. On a visit from the Japanese Commander in Jesselton, we were given a lecture on how bad the English had been as colonialists and that a new Asia was being born. He spoke in Japanese but had brought along with him Sakai in his Japanese uniform and we got the gist of the message especially when he announced: 'We Nipponese are like monkeys! We are everywhere!' He paused in his speech when he became aware of a general titter all round. From that moment on, our captors became known as 'Nips'! Eventually, Mark Linggard, a rubber planter on the Weston line who had previously been in the Shanghai Police in the British zone, confessed to being able to speak some Japanese. He was immediately seized upon as interpreter, and relations became a little more comprehensible.

The immediate problem was food, and the means of cooking it. The Nips had dumped a couple of sacks of rice inside the gate, and would daily bring along some salt fish and *kangkong*, a local kind of coarse watercress that grew almost wild on ponds and was normally collected by Chinese farmers and used as pig food. However, it was a green vegetable and would provide some vitamins. There had only been a minimum of fuel available, so the first essential was to obtain firewood and adequate cooking utensils. The Japanese understood this, provided a couple of large *kualis* and said we would be allowed out, under escort, to collect firewood daily. I along with the younger members of the camp volunteered for this duty, but I think only four of us were allowed out at any one time, with a couple of armed guards. Fortunately, we didn't have far to go: the metalled road to Tanjong Aru rounded a corner at the edge of the Police Depot, then ran through mangrove swamp straight through Tanjong Aru to the wireless station and the beach. We had only to cut the mangrove on the seaward side of the road. Mangrove was a very hard durable wood: it made excellent firewood, in fact the railway used it as fuel, but it was arduous work cutting it. The ground where it grew was swampy and full of leeches, and probably water snakes; adding to the dilemma, it was an extremely difficult wood to cut, rather like the wood of an olive tree in more temperate climates!

Local people soon learnt where we were incarcerated and our daily procedure. Various local persons were seen from time to time, either riding bicycles or just walking as if returning from market. Having not been stationed in Jesselton, their faces were not known to me, but they were known to others. When these encounters were repeated, it became obvious that they were not by chance, but had a purpose.

One day one of us found a note in the swamp, which obviously had recently been placed there with the intention that we should discover it. The rumour went around that it contained an offer of help in the provision of food and medicine, and anything else that we might need. Although I did not know the person involved at the time, I learnt later; and although he is now dead, his elder daughter is at present a member of the State Legislature.

Whether or not advantage was taken of this link with the outside world, I am not certain. I believe it was. I think the main point was that a connection with the world outside had been established. Through this link we also learnt that John Dingle and Marcus Clarke had been seen in Jesselton. What, in fact, we heard about them was disquieting news. We were told that they had been led hand-cuffed, with their arms behind their backs, roped to Nip soldiery, and led at bayonet point through the streets of Jesselton for the townsfolk to see them. We had no notion then why they had been singled out, treated in this manner, and kept apart from us.

What really was to become the most pressing question all the years we were to be behind barbed wire was food, or the lack of it! The sudden change from a balanced European diet of meat and fish, potatoes and vegetables changed to one almost completely of starch with just a few vitamins added: in other words, rice and a teaspoon of finely chopped fried salt fish, and about a dessertspoon of boiled *kangkong*. In a comparatively short time our bodies began to react to this deficiency in our vitamin intake. I began to notice this in my own body. I had recovered from dysentery, and regarded myself as fit and healthy at the time of the Pearl Harbour incident. Admittedly, I had been working under severe strain since then, but I was very surprised when a tiny scratch from a jagged mangrove branch began to ulcerate. Tramping through the jungle in the past had caused many cuts and scratches as well as leech bites; they all healed normally, but the sight of the ankle beginning to give me trouble so soon after internment had commenced did give concern.

I was not the only person whose small scratches began to ulcerate in this manner, and one of the rooms in the barracks was soon set aside as a sick bay. Every morning there would be a sick parade, and we would queue up to have our wounds dressed by the doctors with whatever medicine they had managed to accumulate. I regarded it as superficial, something that would soon heal, and I still continued to take my turn on firewood duties, until the doctors advised against it.

I then became involved in food preparation. This wasn't on the style of the Savoy Hotel! Something had to be done about the two-year-old 'corn on the cob' hen food, that the Nips persisted in giving us. Someone thought up the idea of de-husking the grain from the cob by hand and pounding it with a heavy stone, and then slow-cooking it with water and whatever salt could be spared by placing a large saucepan of the gruel into a hay-box which someone was clever enough to construct. This sort of maize porridge, which we started to boil in the evening about 5 p.m. and put in the hay-box about 6 p.m., would be ready by dawn the next morning when we needed it for breakfast. With a spoonful of brown sugar, we didn't consider it too bad!

One afternoon we were busily cooking the evening meal, when there was a terrific explosion from under the kitchen *kuali*. It was like a crack of a rifle, so loud that it brought in the Nip sentry from the guard-room at the gate. Smoke was oozing out of the bar which we had used as part of the supporting grate to hold the *kuali*. Although it had looked like a rusty piece of iron, someone noticed that it was a nineteenth century musket. It must have been loaded, and the heat finally persuaded it to pop off! We could see that the bullet had indeed pierced a hole through the kitchen wall.

Sickness slowly began to play a more predominant part. Poor Sam Chisholm, who had joined the New Zealand Army when he was on leave but had been hauled out of it to return to duty in Borneo, began to develop boils on his neck, and I can't remember that he was ever to rid himself of them as long as he was in camp. In the case of George Moffat, the doctors diagnosed a quinsy, and advised hospitalization, to which, suprisingly, the Nips agreed. I believe he was permitted to enter the second class ward, but the treatment accorded him by the finely trained nurses of the Chartered Company days would have been first class. Unfortunately though, the quinsy had burst when it was least expected to, and nobody had been able to stop him choking himself to death. He was our first casualty. We all felt very sad for his wife Barbara, imprisoned, so we were to learn, just down the road with the other European ladies at St Francis' Convent. They were both very popular members of the pre-war community, both in Sandakan where I had first met him in the Sandakan Recreation Club, and later in Jesselton.

The stable in which I was quartered was, judging by the lay-out of the cross-bars, accommodation for two horses. I shared a stable with Geoff Hedley and Jack Smallfield. There were two other stables on the same side of the building, a central open section in which we had erected a table, and three corresponding stables on the other side. This block formed half the building, with another similar block between us and the front barracks which ran parallel to the road. It had a sort of L-shaped lay-out, at the back of which a barbed-wire fence had been erected to cut us off from the scrub-covered hill behind. This hill would take one in the direction of Penampang and the Crocker Range, with Sensuran and the Tambunam plain directly to the east. The thought of liberty must have been too tempting for Geoff Hedley and Jack Smallfield. One morning I awoke to find that they were no longer where I expected them to be.

Their absence was immediately discovered, and all hell was let loose. We were all lined up in front of the barracks, and harangued for ten minutes or so by the guards who menacingly pointed guns at us, whilst another telephoned their officers in Jesselton. The latter soon arrived in Dick Evans' car flying a 'poached egg', and further harangued us. They visited the scene of the crime, and then demanded to know who the occupant of the third bed was in that particular stable. I confessed and stepped forward. With a bayonet up my backside, I was hustled into the Resident's car, and taken to the Sports Club, which was evidently the Headquarters of the Kempitai, the Japanese Secret Police, dreaded, I was to learn, even by the Nips themselves.

I was made to sit in a chair opposite three fearsome looking people, one of whom claimed to be the interpreter. I learned the gist of the argument: I was the nearest to them, therefore I knew their plans. Where had they gone? I had to do some quick thinking. Scarcely an hour before, I was still in deep sleep, and had known nothing whatsoever of their plans. Now I was being accused of knowing everything, even as to where they were heading! Affirming that I knew nothing was getting me nowhere! I was only getting my ears boxed gratuitously, and making them more angry. In my own mind I felt sure they were heading for the Penampang–Sensuran trace, but the Japanese would know nothing of that. They would only know the railway, and the roads to Penampang and Tuaran. So I suggested the obvious: that they had probably followed the railway line, which, I explained, was the easiest way to the coast. I suggested that they might have managed to secure a native canoe and put out to sea. I thought that might be as likely an explanation as possible. At any rate, they appeared to accept it!

It may have been very fortunate for me that just at that moment Lt. Yamaha appeared from the billiards room of the Club. I had averted my head as I had heard another person enter the room but our eyes met; there was instant recognition! Hopefully, I thought there might be a hint of a smile on his face, Anyhow, he evidently was of senior rank than either of my interrogators who had stood up and saluted smartly on his approach. There was a quick-fire exchange in Japanese between all three of them, at the end of which the interpreter told me I would be taken back to the camp. I was indeed grateful, as I hadn't at all liked the way things had been developing! So I stood smartly to attention, faced Lt. Yamaha, bowed as I had been instructed, and murmured the only few words of Japanese I had yet learnt: '*Arigato, gozai mas!*' A simple 'thank-you'.

Events passed quietly in the next few weeks, and we were becoming accustomed to the daily routine. We had made a mistake! One morning very shortly after daybreak, lorries and soldiers appeared from the Jesselton direction and shouted at us: '*Kurah! Kurah!*'; their rifles had their bayonets fixed, and it appeared that we were in for yet another form of oppression. Mark Linggard approached the officer in charge and asked wht they wanted of us. 'Bring your bags, and get in the back of the lorries!' we were told. Making no haste, for by this time we had decided that it always paid to respond slowly to these Nipponese antics, we packed together what we had (this didn't take long) and slowly carried our things to the waiting lorries, wondering what was in store for us now.

It was standing room only in the waiting lorries, but we managed to get in somehow, and were whisked through a dead quiet town to the wharf, where a very small coastal vessel, with one open hatch, having bridge and crew quarters aft, was tied up alongside. It was hardly the *Darvel*, nor the *Maradu*; it would have been cargo for the well deck of either! There were armed Japanese, weapons at the ready, like a guard of honour protecting our path to the vessel. We wandered slowly out to the wharf; there was no alternative but to get on board the thing. There was no deck space whatsoever, but it was made clear where we were to go. There were vertical metal steps leading down the side of the hatch, and this was to be our lot. When we descended, throwing out bags down first, we found that it was half laden with coal! It was hardly a 'cabin-de-luxe' leading on to the promenade deck. I selected a spot as near as I could to the open hatch entrance, as I figured it would be cooler there than further inside, but imagination helped a lot. It was like a furnace wherever one went.

Immediately we were all aboard, the vessel cast off. It had a diesel-motor engine, which started at the clang of a telegraph, and we were away. A voyage into the unknown was about to begin! All of us hoped that the journey would not be far in this rather knobbly means of transport. Optimists suggested we would be going to Labuan; since that was an island it would be a more secure place on which to imprison us. There was speculation that this was the direct outcome of Geoff Hedley and Jack Smallfield's escapade. There were others who thought we might be taken to Japan. 'What, in this?' we all chorused. It was all pure speculation, of course.

Once we were outside the channel and around Gaya Head, we were permitted on deck six at a time. The guards did realize that we would have ultimately to cook food (we didn't think there would be a waiter service in the restaurant), and relieve nature. That was pretty urgent for everyone, and we all hastened to take it in turns, no more than six on deck at a time, to go aft where there was a box-like construction secured over the stern of the vessel. We were not alone in using it—even the guards, the crew and what looked like the captain obviously had no other alternative.

From what we could observe from our course once we were out at sea, we certainly weren't bound for Japan. Those who favoured Labuan were in the ascendency.

Eventually our guards concluded that we had to be fed. The cooks, not exceeding two, were allowed on deck and conducted to a sheltered area under the bridge, where a couple of *kualis* were built into a clay hearth. They were shown two sacks, one containing rice and the other salt fish. That was our diet for the next five or six days. Although it seemed frugal, it turned out to be the best food we were to have in all the period of internment. The cooks portioned out the salt fish very liberally, and we had about three or four times what had been our previous ration. They had charcoal as fuel, and found that one of the *kualis* was a rice-steamer, so that the resultant product was greatly superior to that which we had become accustomed to eating.

It was night and when finally it became my turn to go on deck to visit the box affixed to the stern, I endeavoured to linger as long as I dared, not merely to breathe in the fresh cool sea-air instead of the hot, stale atmosphere of the hold, but chiefly to glance rather longingly at the dim dark outline of the coast which had been my home for the last couple of years, a home which already I was growing to love. I thought of the pleasurable moments: river fishing with Native Chief Enduat, and the warm welcome I received comparatively recently in Native Chief Oman's house. I was happy that they were all still in their villages, free to wander along the rivers and in the forests, whereas I had been caught like an innocent insect in a gargantuan spider's web. Dominating the northern skyline, from which we were receding, my eyes fell on the outline of Kinabalu, still towering over the silent coast in the half moonlight, ever foreboding, and looking down on our cockle craft with a sinister question mark.

I had no knowledge of the events which were beginning to unfold on the West Coast, no knowledge of the much heralded Nipponese 'co-prosperity sphere' which was bringing forced labour, stagnation of trade, prohibition of movement and starvation to all the people of this lovely country. The 'banana' currency they had brought with them to replace the Straits and the local dollar notes (so-called because the reverse side of the new note depicted a couple of crossed 'hands' of bananas) quickly began to lose its face value; it could buy little, for as soon as the shelves in the shops began to be emptied they remained empty. There were no imports to replenish them.

The Japanese had decided that airports should be built at Jesselton, Keningau, Kudat and Sandakan: all the civil population were being conscripted for this purpose, and all civil servants were made to work one day a week. A once happy country was being raped!

Sleep did not come easy to any of us in the hold that night. A pile of coal is not the most comfortable of mattresses to sleep on. You would move one knob out of the way, to make it a little more comfortable for your back, only to find, on trying to settle again, another knob poking at you somewhere else! I think the most reassuring thought we all experienced was the certain knowledge that if an Allied submarine were around, it wouldn't waste a torpedo on us!

Next morning, there seemed to be great excitement above, and on no condition were we allowed up the ladder! The engine stopped, and then, after a minute or two, there was a bump which would have knocked us to the coal knobs had we been standing, followed by another less erratic bump and more shouting. We seemed to have arrived! It could only be Labuan. We had scarcely been brought alongside with the finesse of the Straits Steamship captains!

For two or three hours nothing happened, and even the optimists among us who had predicted that the island of Labuan was to be our destination began to have their doubts. There was only occasional desultory shouting at the top of the hatch, without any particular reference to any activity we may have generated.

Eventually, the klaxon of a motor launch penetrated the depths of the hold, and we became aware of more activity and excitement above us. Very shortly, the hatch cover opened, and we spotted the white-trousered limbs of a European descending into our midst, followed by another, and another: altogether about twelve in number.

Very soon, old residents of North Borneo made their way over to the group, still blinded by the action of entering the dark hold after being out exposed in the blinding tropical sun. Gradually they began to see and recognize friends gathering around them; people began to shake hands and formally introduce others in the group. It was a bizarre scene, and looking back at it now after some fifty years or so, only the British could have enacted it! Here we were, prisoners of the enemy, in the black hold of a collier, standing on the remnants of its cargo, and virtually in darkness, yet formally standing up and introducing each to the other, with the politeness of a handshake, as if we were meeting a group in the foyer of the Regent Palace Hotel in London!

I observed the events without, of course, knowing any of the newcomers, but word soon spread about their identity. The party was led by the British Resident, Brunei, a Mr Pengilly (a name I remember because of its Cornish origins) and his Assistant, Mr Noel Turner (whom I was to get to know very well in the years to come) and many planters, again with whom I was to become very friendly in the immediate future. They all had their own stories about their capture and their treatment to date.

As soon as they were on board, there was more activity on deck, more incoherent shouting, the engine started again and once more we were away to an unknown destination. That night, when we were allowed on deck, six by six, to visit the stern box, we could see the flares of the Miri oil-fields which had been set alight, before the arrival of the Japanese, to deny the oil to the enemy. There had been a battalion of Punjabis of the Indian Army allocated to defend the Miri oilfields, as it was believed the Japanese Army would attack Miri to obtain the oil with which to prosecute the war. In the debacle which followed the sinking of the *Prince of Wales* and *Repulse*, it was realized there would be nothing now to stop the Japanese advance, and the Indian Army units were ordered to destroy the field and retreat overland to Pontianak, a town in Dutch-occupied West Borneo, where Dutch troops were also stationed, and where, it was thought, a stand might be made against the invaders.

The crate in which we were travelling rolled badly, presumably because, if it had a Plimsoll line, it would have been well under its load level through lack of cargo. The Nips, however, permitted a few more hatch covers to be taken off; this gave better air circulation below decks, and it was not quite as hot as it would otherwise have been. Visiting the stern box, however, without any guide rails to act as bulwarks, was indeed a hazardous operation!

At dawn on the third morning, even before we had had a cup of tea, we noticed the boat changing its motion from a roll to a pitch. This could only mean one thing: a change of course, and most probably the crossing of a river bar. The latter was the correct interpretation. Even I, who had done the journey only once before, realized we had entered Kuching River. The question was, whether Kuching was to be our destination, or whether we were merely going to make a visit to pick up more civilians, and be taken on to Singapore. It was going to be an awful squash if we had to take on more people.

As early as I could I made a lingering call to the stern-box, with the principal reason in mind to survey the terrain. I only remembered it as rather swampy, with a river fringe of *nipah* palm on either bank. This I confirmed, but I also spotted some open ground with villages built right up to the river's edge, like Kampong Buang Sayang in Papar. At the moment I was about to descend into the hold, we were passing such a village; there were children playing around, so I waved my hand to them. They noticed me all right, for they waved back. I thought that would be a sure way of telling the native folk that white men were being brought into Kuching! The Nips never noticed my wave, as just at that moment they were too busy feeding themselves.

Kuching was in fact our destination! We berthed at the wharf, opposite the Astana, where the 'poached egg' was flying from the flag-pole. We were soon ordered out of the hold, with all our bags, and straight into Nipponese Army lorries waiting there for us. Again, it was standing room only, and we all held on to each other for grim death, as it drove furiously through the town, along a road which, symbolically, passed the main Chinese Cemetery, uphill through rubber gardens, then round a corner following the direction of the sign-post which read 'Batu Lintang'. Soon we were halted at a barrier across the road, guarded by Nip soldiery occupying a substantial house, one probably built for an Asian manager or owner of a large rubber estate which we then entered. Uphill for another half mile and we entered a large open area, with typical black creosote Army huts dotted around amidst the rubber trees. We quickly realized this to be our destination!

We were hastily ordered out of the trucks and grouped together in a bunch. Our party was then divided into two, and the first half marched away under escort. I was in the second half, and when it came to our turn, we were led to the hut the furthest away from the entrance. We passed two huts in which we noticed Europeans, but guarded by Nips, as we were escorted to the huts which were destined to be our homes for the next three and a half years!

It was just a bare wooden floor Army hut that we entered, but having been built to British Army specifications, it was well constructed. The barracks had in fact been erected just a year earlier to house the same Punjabi battalion which had retreated from Miri to Pontianak, and the reserve force stationed here, destined for the defence of Kuching, had equally trudged through the jungle to Pontianak!

The construction engineers who had built the camp had, undoubtedly, done their job well. The kitchen facilities were good, with two very large built-in *kualis*, six cement troughs, with taps and a good water supply, absolutely essential for hygiene especially in the tropics, two sets of wash troughs, with running water, a block of eight or nine shower cubicles, and a block of half a dozen bucket latrines. All of the huts were nicely camouflaged by the rubber trees of the estate in which they had been sited.

It was an ideal site for the Japanese to use as a prisoner of war camp. Miles of barbed wire had been used in dividing the area into different compounds, all of which led to the main square. Adjoining us, but separated by a double fence, were British prisoners of war. On our other flank, but well separated by a barbed wire patrol path and a wide stretch of the rubber estate, was the Officers' camp. Immediately opposite us from the main compound were the priests' camp, and the women's camp. In the main square was a guard, who was mounted in a dominating position, guarding all entrances. In front of our gate and a little to the right was a hut which housed the Nipponese administration block, and about a third of a mile up the hill was the Commandant's office and the Nips' own quarters. Opposite the administration block were store houses for the essential commodities: rice and sugar.

I have described the layout of the camp for the reader to follow more clearly the events of the camp life as it unfolded. Three and a half years constituted a long period of time to spend in one place.

The Jesselton contingent was allocated two huts which meant that there were some forty or fifty of us in each building. It so happened that there was no senior officer of the Civil Service to whom we could look for guidance. One of us suggested that we count the number of floor boards along one side. That divided us into two halves, from which we worked out the number of boards which could be allocated to each one of us as our 'living space'. A crude allocation, but it worked!

I laid claim to a space where I had entered, on the opposite side of the hut in front of a window, and there I sat with my bags. When the boards were counted out, I was fortunate in that I had to move only one plank to the left! I had chosen this spot as I thought it would provide a through draught, and be cool. In the main, I was right; the only time I felt sorry about it was during the monsoon season, or *landas*, as they called it in Sarawak, and then damp air constantly wafted over one. It also had the advantage in that it was the farthest door from the main path, so that when the lightning raids occurred, of which the Nips were very fond, they always entered the other side of the hut first: an advantage, as you always had a chance of hiding whatever it was you suspected they might be after!

We soon had the chance of mixing with the Sarawak contingent who were first brought to Batu Lintang. On the morning of our arrival, they were given extra rations and informed that we would be coming. That was unusual, as the Nips rarely mentioned what might be happening. However, it was very welcome news for our cooks who had a chance to sort themselves out first. This was a most welcome break for them, as they had really fed us well, under the most arduous conditions, on the dreadful crate!

The next most important thing was to organize ourselves. Quite a good organization had already been established by the Sarawak contingent. They had appointed a Camp Master, Mr Le Gros-Clark, who had been Chief Secretary to the Rajah's Government. He was a fine upstanding gentleman, tall with broad shoulders, who had grown a ginger red beard! Most of us, in truth, had grown beards of one sort or another, simply because we had no shaving facilities. Even if we had a razor, we had no soap, nor mirror, to assess whether we were cutting our stubble or our lips!

The interpreter was a gentleman named Selous, also, if I remember correctly, an officer of the Sarawak Government, and son of the well-known big game hunter. He had had experience in Japan, and was an excellent Japanese linguist; Mark Lingard was very happy to relinquish his post as camp interpreter!

Le Gros-Clark suggested that we should appoint Hut-masters, as they had done. The easiest way of creating our own camp administration and disseminating information was by a Committee (a typically English way of running things, of course, but in this case it seemed logical!).

We had several doctors in the camp, and they soon established a medical unit and First Aid facilities. I was very glad of that as, without medical attention, my injured ankle had been playing up badly, and had gone septic. At least I could have it dressed, but septicaemia had set in, and I felt pain and a swelling in the groin. The doctors took it seriously, and ordered me to lie up with my foot raised. In a way, it was a blessing in disguise as, being sick, I was exempted from the forced labour which was to engulf most of the fit and able-bodied men in the camp.

The Japanese Commandant of the Camp was a Major Suja. We seldom saw him normally, but he would strut around the camp like a peacock, from time to time, accompanying any visiting General. He was quite arrogant in that he would so often proclaim we were one of the best camps in South East Asia! (May the Lord help the others, we thought!) His Adjutant was a Lt. Nekata; he would frequently visit the camp—a very arrogant man, who had an unpredictable temper. We soon learnt that if he had a smile on his face, it meant trouble!

Another habit of the Nips was face slapping. Whether Suja slapped Nekata across the face, we never saw, but Nekata certainly smacked his subalterns, and they in turn smacked the soldiery, who had nobody to take it out on except us! When they were in a face slapping mood, we all suffered, no matter what the offence!

It took time, but eventually our captors came to realize that it was against the Geneva Convention to treat internees as prisoners of war, so the 'chain gang' finally came to an end. I also think that they realized that we were dangerous people to have outside the camp. They began to appreciate that we all spoke Malay, which they could not, and, therefore, occasionally would be able to speak to any local person who might be around as we travelled to and from the air-strip, which ostensibly we were assisting in constructing.

Instead, they allocated us a piece of the rubber estate, on the left-hand side of the rise going to the Commandant's Office, and told us to make a vegetable garden out of it. This involved cutting out the rubber trees, which we had to carry in to the camp and use as fuel. They did supply axes for this purpose, and one of our axemen, I recall, was an Australian by the name of Bob Kirkwood, who had joined the service of the Chartered Company as a telephone engineer and had arrived about a year after I had done.

He was recruited at the same time as an accountant called Alan Quartermaine, also from Australia where his family had a large apple estate near Perth. He and I chummed up, as we were about the last recruits to the Chartered Company Service. I think I was about a year his senior, so we both regarded ourselves as newcomers!

My ankle was still bad and it worried me, but I suddenly remembered the M&B693 tablets which I had secreted in to my kit at the last moment. They had been taken from a bulk package, so I had no idea of the dosage. There were only a dozen and if I were to take, say, two per day orally, I should soon have none left. I worked out in my mind that the antibiotic was in the granules of the tablet itself, so I pulverised one, and put half the powder on the wound one night and the other half the next morning: it might work. It was nothing short of miraculous! The swelling and pain in the inner thigh, which had worried the doctors (and me too!) had disappeared. In a few days the poison had gone out of the wound and a healthy scab had formed—leaving the doctors most perplexed. I simply explained: 'I always did have a good healing skin!'

I was well enough to join the gardening force, and went with them from the very first day. In the square, *chankols* were laid out in a row. '*Chankol*' was the local word for a digging tool of Chinese origin, but which was universally used in the Far East. The best ones were known as *chop buaya*, the 'crocodile tool', and were made in England! My bridle-path gangs used to use them. I knew they varied in size and weight. In my early days in Papar, I had enjoyed growing a few of my own vegetables, and had become used to using a *chankol*, unlike most of my compatriots! So when it came my turn to grab one of these tools, I went for the smallest and lightest I could see, since I knew better work could be done with a tool which was easier to handle. Fortunately, we were allowed to take them back into camp with us, and the *chankol* that one became accustomed to over the years became a very precious tool!

We were all too individualistic to work together as a team, so instead, by universal agreement, the area allocated to us was divided into plots like an English allotment, and two of us worked together on the plot apportioned to us. My first co-worker was Alan Quartermaine. I was lucky in choosing him, as he was stronger and had a bigger frame than I had. Once Bob Kirkwood, who was our axe-man, had felled the trees, we set to with our *chankols* and dug out the roots. These tools had sharp edges and cut through soft rubber-tree roots like a knife going through bread. Nevertheless, it was hard work!

Once we had cleared the ground, I pointed out to Alan Quartermaine the methods the Chinese would use in making raised beds, so that the heavy tropical rain when it fell could be drained more readily. The next problem was seed. I had already thought of that, and even before the knowledge that we would be allocated a vegetable patch garden, I had been collecting seeds. Sometimes we would be given *kepayas* in the rations, and I had collected the seeds from them and dried them in the sun. They were very quick growing and in three months the tree would be bearing fruit. I had intended to plant them behind our hut, but they were ready now for the allotment. Sweet potatoes were easily grown. Any old bit from a tuber would sprout, and as soon as the long trailing leaves appeared they could be cut into 9″ or 12″ lengths, and planted in a mounded ridge, and in three months the *ubi manis*, to give the sweet potato its local name, would be ready for cropping. Nature gives quick rewards in the tropics!

It was about this time that the rumour went around that more prisoners were to be brought to our camp. One day, our liaison officer for supplies, in fact John Macartney, a Chinese speaking officer whom the Nips were able to understand, was allocated more *kangkong* and salt fish than usual, and was told to expect more arrivals. The rumour quickly went around the camp, and curiosity at least seemed to make the day seem shorter. When we returned from the gardens that evening, we found the camp full of new faces, new only because they were new in Kuching; they were, in fact, our colleagues from Sandakan, all the planters from the East

Coast, and a few Americans who had been caught at the time of the fall of Corrigidor and captured by Nip gun-boats whilst creeping down the East Borneo coast towards Tarakan.

I sought out Mike Edge who had first befriended me in Sandakan on my arrival there, and John Massey. Mike, like the good Police Officer he was, had organized himself well. He told me that Peter, who had taken short leave, was on his way back to Borneo when the balloon went up, and he thought he might have been caught in the fall of Singapore. The experience of officers in Sandakan when the Japanese arrived was quite different from our own on the West Coast. Sandakan had received instructions from the High Command in Singapore, instructions which we never received. Consequently, they knew how to proceed when the Nips arrived. They, quite rightly I believe, refused to visit their offices, except for the doctors who agreed to care for their patients in hospital, the Nips having brought no medical facilities at all. At first they were all under house arrest, so to that extent we were technically in the same category, except that District Officers like myself in Papar were permitted to visit rubber estates in their districts and attend office. Be that as it may, but they were all rounded up more quickly than we were and sent to Berhala Island, at the entrance to Sandakan Harbour where the North Borneo Government had established a leper colony. There were unoccupied buildings on the island and both a women's camp and a camp for the men had been established there. They had the advantage over us, in that, being on an island, they were able to catch a few fish from time to time which had supplemented the rations handed out by the Nips. Their island prison was also helpful in that the Japanese could not guard all its coastline all the time, and local people were able to make contact and occasionally bring a few necessities.

The Governor, they thought, had been given special treatment and sent back to Japan. He certainly wasn't in the Sandakan party, which now occupied the two remaining empty huts in our compound. The Nips had now completed the round up of all the Europeans in British Borneo. It had taken them six or seven months to achieve this, but there were exceptions. There was a party from Limbang in Sarawak, who had decided that a free life in the Interior would be better than life behind a barbed wire fence, and had set off inland, men, women and children to Long Nawan, in the heart of Dutch Borneo. There was no news at all of them, but one of the Brunei contingent, who had a bed next to mine, Bomfrey, had sent his wife with the party, and inevitably as time wore on, and as the Nipponese became uglier, constantly worried over their fate.

There was a reallocation of land in the garden, inevitably, with the influx of more workers, and I figured that I had heard enough about Australia and the way they did things there, and set my sights on a plot a good way down from the road and farther from the spots where the guards seemed to like standing. I asked Mike if he would like to join me to which he agreed, and it was a partnership which was to work well!

Mike related how, when he was young, his family had had a gardener who was skilful in burning all the garden refuse in a fire that he would keep in continuously, without it ever going out: a sort of slow combustion, with clay bricks on the outside and top, leaving just a hole in the bottom and a hole at the top, so as to enable a gentle draught of air to flow through and keep the embers glowing. The whole idea was that when we first arrived in the morning, we would dig up a couple of sweet potatoes, shove them in the embers, and by *yasumi* time—the word yelled at us by our guard permitting us to stop work—the potatoes would be nicely roasted, and give us strength to carry on for the rest of the morning!

A two hours' break in the middle of the day, for a cupful of rice and some *kangkong* soup, enabled us to rest and recuperate for the afternoon slog. It was Noel Coward who wrote: 'Mad dogs and Englishmen go out in the midday sun!' In the tropics especially, it is something to get out of, rather than go in to! Fortunately, in a way, and especially during the *landas* (the Sarawak name for the south-west monsoon) season, it would frequently rain. We built a shelter in our bit of garden like the jungle *sulap* I had slept in on top of the Crocker Range. This time, though, banana palm leaves kept the rain off our backs. Most of the little groups of gardeners had built similar shelters, so that when the thunder and rain arrived, we all dived into them; even the guard disappeared somewhere to keep himself and his rifle dry. Sometimes, we would just sit and talk, or just sit! We wore nothing but a *chawat*, which we made out of any piece of clothing we could find. The skin is the best waterproofing, the Muruts had discovered that, but even though we were virtually on the equator, it could be jolly cold!

When eventually the storm had passed, the principal task then was to see that our fire was still alive. We put banana palms over that, too, to keep the worst of the rain off, but it was essential we kept the fire going. I can't really confess that much work was done in the afternoon during the *landas*!

When we were in our *sulups* during the wet monsoon afternoons, our minds went back to the previous year. The British War Council in Singapore had said the year before that the Japanese wouldn't contemplate commencing a war during the south-west monsoon: 'Absolutely impossible! Couldn't possibly attempt a sea assault at a time like that—they'd never be able to make a landing anywhere!' But that was exactly what they did do.

We did have Sunday as a work-free day. Advantage was taken of this to do our personal chores like washing our *chawats* and night attire. There were good facilities for this with basins and water taps which had been built for the use of the Indian Army unit. Sunday was also the day on which married men had the privilege of meeting their wives for half an hour, under escort, for by this time the ladies from Jesselton and Sandakan had all been brought around. At first the women were housed in huts next to the garden, with only the ubiquitous barbed wire fence between. The contact between the men and their wives was, therefore, comparatively easy—so the women were moved to huts at the far end of the camp. In their place a fairly large contingent of Dutch Roman Catholic priests arrived from Pontianak.

Other free times were the evening. We returned from the gardens usually at 5 p.m., immediately queued up for a shower, and by the time we all returned there was only ten minutes or so to wait, before the call went up from the kitchen:

'Food's up!' Each hut would take it in turn to be first served, but it was always the last hut that was the lucky one. It was not humanly possible to dish out accurately for some one hundred and fifty people, or thereabouts, without some being left over in the bottom of the *kuali*, either of rice or of soup. So the system was devised that a hut in turn should be entitled to the extras! At least, it was something to look forward to about once a week.

From the very first, the Dutch civilians from Pontianak, whom we came to regard as different from us (mostly civil servants and extremely well educated), objected to our way of cooking. So all rations, as they arrived, were divided out between the Dutch community and ourselves, on a *per capita* basis.

Equally, there was a minority of three who also opted out on a *per capita* basis, as they had long been settled in Labuan and had married Moslem girls and themselves become Moslems. They were Sam Cook, Zimmer and one Gus Youngberg, who was an American missionary of some peculiar sect, but who was the kindest and most honest man that I think I have ever known.

Perhaps, on the whole, the minority groups were correct in their insistence, as they did seem to know how better to deal with the rations they were given than were the Britishers. The Dutch colonists lived closer to the people than the British ever did; many of them had native wives, for example, and they had learnt the best way to deal with local vegetables, and any other local commodity, whereas the British were more concerned with dropping cards on their neighbours, employed usually Chinese cooks used to cooking only European-style food, and, apart from the curry parties, never ate any local food. I think that put us at a disadvantage. On the other hand, I had lived in the jungle, had known what wild weeds were edible, and what vegetables and fruit had the highest vitamin content. This is why I had *kepaya* seedlings ready for planting, even before we had been allocated land, and why I took cuttings of a wild *sayur manis*—literally, a 'sweet vegetable' bush—of which one could eat the tender shoots immediately on plucking them; both were very high in vitamin content.

One afternoon when we returned from the garden, I was surprised and delighted to find that my colleagues Geoff Hedley and Jack Smallfield had been returned to us, and were quartered in my own hut, Jack next to his father, Eric, just a few berths away from me on the opposite side of the hut, and Geoff between me and the missionaries from Ranau. Once, apart from the Roman Catholic priests, we had been the only Europeans in some two to three thousand square miles of jungle: now, I doubt if we had more than twenty square feet per person!

Both were completely emaciated, and must have had a very tough time indeed. Each of them was very reticent about the events which had led to their re-capture and their treatment once they had been imprisoned again. They were probably very lucky, as we had all been warned, both in Jesselton and particularly here in Kuching, that anyone attempting to escape would be shot. That they had both been starved was obvious to us all. Their reticence then is a reminder to me now of the effect the Japanese had on their prisoners, and may be judged from the fact that it has taken me over fifty years to write these lines.

Soon it was Christmas Day 1942! For a wonder, our captors gave us a day off work! They even gave us a banana and a ration of tobacco each as an extra ration! Being a non-smoker, I already had a permanent agreement with a 'smoking' colleague to swop my tobacco ration for his banana! The kitchen staff were marvels in that they had put on one side various oddments they had received in the rations, and with these on Christmas evening they were able to give us a *nasi goreng* for Christmas dinner.

If anyone had told us then that we would still be spending Christmas 1943 and Christmas 1944 behind barbed wire, we simply would not have believed them, and I think there may have been more suicides than there were and more of us giving up the will to live.

Gradually, though, our lives settled more into a routine, and we began to get things organized. We could do nothing about the day-time, we had to go out to the garden, rain or shine, but we did have the evenings unmolested, apart from the occasional visit from an NCO with a soldier or two. The Committee thought up the idea of organizing talks in one of the huts one night a week. This caught on fine! There was a great deal of talent and skill amongst us. After all, most of us had been recruited at the time of the world depression of the early thirties, and its aftermath; there had been much competition for each and every post which we held. We were the elite amongst our compatriots, and thus it would come as no surprise that we were not an ordinary group of people, but specialists each in our own field, backed up usually by considerable field experience.

The talks given in Hut 3 were always of interest, and although the speakers might not have had books of reference they knew their subjects. They came from all over the world—Americans, Australians, New Zealanders, Danes, Canadians and even Germans and Austrians who had Jewish blood in them and been refugees from their own country had found a welcome and a livelihood in Borneo and Sarawak. Conrad country, as I have remarked earlier!

We had all made stools of one sort or another, and these we carried with us to the meetings; the occupants of our host hut had the kindness to keep up their mosquito nets, and the visitors were able to see and hear the speaker. Inevitably, the quality of the talks was variable, as some men are born talkers and others are not, but always they were interesting as each had once been master of his subject.

I think it was a talk by Selous which, unfortunately, brought that activity to an end. He was a natural raconteur and a clever wit. He had earlier travelled in Japan and was describing his adventure in the 'outback' of Honshu Island. He chatted about his stay at a country inn where there was only one communal bath tub for both men and women to use. When the water was hot, then it was 'bath' time, and he was so informed. He had not encountered the custom before, but to acquire the true Japanese ambience he decided he would participate and have his bath, so went along the corridor to the bathing room into which he was ushered. It was all very steamy and difficult to see anything clearly. As soon as he had taken off his bath robe, climbed the steps and stepped over the edge to a submersed stool, some Japanese hostesses, always perfect in their role of caring for their guests, appeared out of the misty steam in the altogether and joined him in the bath tub 'to scrub his back'. He mused to himself, but added that he thought 'it was all rather pointed!' I think it was the way he said it more than anything else which, to a male sex-starved community, brought the house down! Unfortunately, laughter like that seemed to indicate to the Nips, always prowling around the camp, that we were having too good a time, and at the very next meeting with the Adjutant, our Liaison Officer was told that large gatherings led to conspiracies and that they would be prohibited in future. (One wonders what they thought the talk was about; of course, they had no clue we were laughing at an incident that had happened in their own country!) From then on, no groups larger than six were allowed to gather together; we weren't supposed to be enjoying ourselves! We were a defeated nation, and should always hide our heads in shame. That was their philosophy.

Always, when any significant order was issued which we didn't like, our immediate reaction was to circumvent it. We overcame this one by initiating 'classes' on any subject we could think of, and persuading those with any knowledge of his subject to impart it to others. The objectives of our Camp Committee were mainly to keep our minds occupied, employ them gainfully, and so distract them from our present situation thus preventing the spread of despondency. These objectives were definitely good for morale.

There were handicaps, however. For example, we had no paper! But, fortunately, just about this time, in response to repeated requests, the Nips provided us with books. They had taken them out of the Sarawak Museum Library (probably so that the local people could not be indoctrinated with decadent Western thought). These were a godsend, for not only did they provide good reading, which helped to take our minds off our present miseries, but the fly-leaves of the books were able to provide us with the paper which we could use as writing material for notes taken in our classes.

Every so often there were searches, at the most unexpected times. Suddenly, in the middle of the night, perhaps at two or three o'clock, we would be woken by the shout of '*Tenku, tenku!*' which meant 'fall in' in the open quadrangle, by the kitchen, between Huts 2 and 3. There we were counted hut by hut. We had to call out our position in Japanese: 'Ichi, ni, san, she, go . . . etc.' and the totals, hut by hut, were reconciled between the Liaison Officer, the Camp Master and the Japanese NCO in charge. Then, if they had decided to make a search, we had to stay there whilst Nip soldiers went around the huts, rummaging in all our things, but I'm sure not knowing what were the objects of their search. Rumour went around that they were after diaries, and we were warned by our own camp officials that the finding of these might well have been their objectives, so we were told not to keep any. I certainly didn't keep a diary; all the relevant items remained in my head. But I did have my compass! When I was first captured in Keningau, I made sure this vital instrument was in one of the top pockets of my bush jacket; this is where I had always kept it when jungle bashing in the now seemingly long ago days of tramping through Dalit country. It had stayed there all the time. I suppose at the back of my mind, I never knew what the future might hold, and I didn't want to lose it. So after the first search, I thought something like this could happen again, not that some of the bovine guards we had would have the intelligence to know what it was, possibly some queer dice game, they might think; but I took the wisest course and buried it in the dry soil underneath my part of our hut. I memorized the place exactly, so that I could find it again if it was ever needed. Very, very much later on, I was on the point of retrieving it, since we were entirely unsure of the intentions of the Nips and feared the worst. As the story unfolds the reader will become aware that we were destined to be moved by the Nips, probably inland, and probably to befall the same fate as that of the remnants of the Eighth Australian Division as the advance of their Ninth Division eventually proceeded into Borneo.

Unfortunately, that was to be still a long time ahead! In the meantime, the question of survival predominated, coupled with the pursuit of activities which would take our minds away from the present. Our leisurely garden activities almost became a thing of the past. In the patch of land between the Officers' Camp and ourselves, there were some poorly growing rubber trees. We were told to clear these, and plant sweet potatoes. That was much harder work! Having done that, after eight or nine months, we were given another plot along the road leading to the guard-house. Here we had to plant *ubi kayu*, tapioca. We alternated between the patches, depending on the growth of the crops and the amount of weeding that had to be done. The first crop of sweet potatoes, grown in relatively fresh soil and used for the first time for vegetables, should have been reasonably good, but turned out to be quite poor. Then we remembered the Chinese methods of fertilization, and ensured that all the night soil was utilized to the fullest extent. We had already been carrying cans of urine accumulated overnight from each end of the hut, and utilizing it on our own patches in turn. The night soil, or *benjo*, removal was not a popular job, naturally enough. If I remember rightly, we took it in turns, a period at a time, but it did have certain advantages in that the Committee decided that *benjo*-carriers, during their tenure of office, should be excused all other work!

The heaviest job of all, however, was carrying rice! A full sack would normally have been about 180 lbs. To attempt to carry one on one's own was just too much. (I remembered how easily the Chinese labourers seemed to do it in Papar when unloading the rice from the goods wagons when we were receiving the limed rice from Jesselton in the early days of the war; all they complained about was the burning sensation of the lime as it came into contact with the sweat from their bodies. Weight was no problem to them, but I fear it was to us.) In the first part of imprisonment, it was as much as two men could do, hanging the sack by ropes on poles which we carried on our shoulders, but in the latter half it took the efforts of four men!

Perhaps the most depressing effect of camp life was the lack of news. Occasionally, the Japanese would pass on to the Liaison Officer snatches of information concerning great Nipponese naval victories, like the Battle of the Coral Sea late in 1942 when the Nipponese Navy must have had ambitions to effect a landing in Australia, and the Battle of Midway in the same year. In the versions given us, the Americans and the Australians must have lost more ships than the total of the combined Allied Fleets while the Nipponese Navy only ever incurred superficial damage! This, of course, was an insult to our intelligence, and we dismissed it from our minds. We would certainly have been more worried in regard to the nature of our captors had we known of the sinking of the *Centaur*, a Blue Funnel boat very familiar in Singapore waters as she had been on the Singapore–Australia run. In fact I remember seeing her in the Roads as the *Darvel* had set sail from Singapore harbour in what seemed to me now the very distant past.

She had been commandeered by the Admiralty and converted in Australia into a hospital ship. Early one morning, whilst darkness still lay around the vessel, herself a blaze of light, lit up by the terms of the Geneva Convention, with a white hull and a Red Cross clearly painted on both her sides, she was suddenly torpedoed by a Japanese submarine prowling in the area. She was on a course to take her to the scene of the fighting for the evacuation of the sick and wounded, and all her staff, doctors and nurses, were asleep in their cabins. The shock for all on board must have been horrific! She was a hospital ship; no one suspected anything but a safe passage. She had sunk quickly by the bows, and out of a 'total complement of 360 no less than 296 including 11 nurses had gone down with the ship, died of exposure or been taken by sharks.'*

When the incident became known, the strongest protest was made to the Japanese Government, but it fell upon the deaf ears of a Government which chose to ignore international law and justice.

Perhaps it was as well we knew nothing of these atrocities and the many like it that were taking place all over the oceans and seas where the Japanese submarines roamed. We were spared the worry of what could happen to us. We regarded ourselves just as prisoners for the duration, and were unaware of the orders that would issue from the Emperor in a year or so's time. Nevertheless, the desire to know what was happening in the world outside was paramount, and this led to two developments. The first, and the most innocent, led to grave consequences, but the second was of inestimable value and always remained a secret.

It was inevitable that in spite of the barbed wire perimeter fences and the patrolled path intervening, contact with the British Tommies in the next section of the camp adjacent to us would be made. Although they were mainly North Countrymen, we were the same race, and we did speak the same language, and however much the Nips may have tried to keep us apart, they didn't succeed. The Army other ranks, without question, had a very hard time. In the main they took over airfield construction work which our Sarawak contingent had just begun when we joined them from Jesselton, but from time to time they were taken into Kuching to do stevedoring on ships. Here, in the true Tommy fashion, they began to make all

---

* Bernard Edwards: *Blood and Bushido*, 1991

sorts of contacts with local people. The fruits of these contacts began to emerge in due course through one or two more adventurous incumbents of our own camp: Horn, one of the Americans who had come down with the Sandakan contingent, caught whilst escaping from Corrigidor, quickly earned the sobriquet of Trader Horn. When trade was in full flush, a new shirt would buy a half *kati* of *blachan* or shrimp paste. They also acquired, and readily passed to us, since they were unable to benefit from them, locally produced copies of the Malay newspaper which circulated in Kuching. It was inevitably censored by the Nips who provided its editor with the only war news he could print. Stanley Hill, who was in the Sandakan hut along with Trader Horn and his American colleague, a man called Webber, likewise a 'trader', volunteered to translate interesting passsages. He was in his second or third tour, and was a fluent Malay speaker and reader of Jawi script.

These gleanings at least gave us an idea of where the fighting was; that the Nips had stretched their lines of communication so far was indeed remarkable, that they would be unable to sustain them was clear, but the long haul from America and even Australia meant that it would be a long time before Borneo would be recaptured. The news was equally bleak in Burma. None of us had ever heard of Imphal, but along with Rabaul and Lae in New Guinea they were going to become very familiar place-names, and, oh, they were such a long way off!

What we did not know, and we had no possible means of telling, were the events that were occuring in the territories which the Nips had occupied: our own countries, and Sabah in particular.

Although it is inevitable for the sequence of the narration that I must recount the events of our transfer to Kuching and the experiences we endured as prisoners of war of the Japanese, nevertheless this work is the story of Sabah, and at this point it is to Sabah I must return. Perhaps in retrospect it was as well we had been transferred to Kuching, for events in Sabah were to take an unexpected turn in which, had we remained there, we would surely have been involved.

The story of these events is not drawn obviously from personal experience but was collated immediately after the war on return to Sabah. Although I gleaned at first hand, when memories were fresh and minds were accurate, many of the stories now related, I am nevertheless indebted to Mr Maxwell Hall, a former Chartered Company legal officer, who returned to Sabah with the incoming Australian Army with their Civil Affairs Unit and recorded many of the details I now relate in a small book entitled *Kinabalu Guerrillas*. He knew a little more of the people and events that took place than I did and I am indebted to him for being able to include some of the incidents and names that I now cannot recall. Apart from this work almost nothing has been recorded in official correspondence or any document of which I have cognizance.

In the lead up to the Far Eastern war, the Nipponese were lauding over the air-waves their Co-Prosperity Sphere which they intended to unleash on South East Asia. After their arrival, they shouted loud and clear that the days of ruthless exploiting imperialism were over. The Japanese had come to free them from the shackles of the Empire builders! It was to be the dawn of a new era under the aegis of the Japanese victors!

I felt at the time that these assertions fell on empty ears as far as the local Chinese were concerned. Japan had invaded Chinese territory in Manchuria as long ago as 1931, and they knew what the Nipponese were like as invaders and occupiers. There was no love lost between the local Chinese and the Japanese invaders from the very start! True, the 'Poached Egg' appeared flying at every Chinese shop overnight from the very day the Nips passed through Papar, but that was an insurance, or, as the Chinese would say, 'protection money'! Not to have flown their flag would have meant hostility and early attention from the Japanese marauders.

To fully appreciate Japanese Army methods, it has to be realized that, apart from their weaponry, the Japanese soldiers carried with them in their battle tunics their supplies of rice and canned or salted fish. To use General Eisenhower's phrase which he coined much later, the Japanese Army had no 'logistics'. They were expected to live off the land that they had captured. This was one of the reasons why the advance down the Malayan Peninsula at the commencement of hostilities had been so rapid. Coupled with that was the penetrating deployment of their troops by captured bicycles and canoes. Hence the order I received in Papar to sink all boats over a certain length.

When the advance through Borneo and the Philippines had drawn the forces southwards towards New Guinea, they were replaced by soldiers of an inferior quality: our own guards at Batu Lintang were, for example, Korean. In Jesselton, the somewhat slender garrison was reinforced by the Kempitai, the Japanese secret police who were amongst the most cruel and sadistic group of thugs the world has ever known; they thought up tortures beyond belief! If anyone ever fell into their hands, whether any offence, however small, had been committed or not, it was unlikely that he ever saw the light of day again.

The Kempitai set up their headquarters in Jesselton in the Sports Club, whither I had been taken at the time of the escape by Geoff Hedley and Jack Smallfield. Fortunately, I was rescued by the only decent Japanese I have ever known, Lt. Yamaha, but even so, I don't think I would have been tortured unduly, as in my case I had committed no crime; they only wanted information out of me which I couldn't provide. Furthermore, their Armies were in the full flush of victory, and they had not yet turned quite as nasty as they were destined to become, like rats caught in a trap.

The presence of the European officers and planters, even when we were still interned at Batu Tiga, was a stabilizing force amongst the local population, but once we had been taken to Kuching, and the news soon spread that we had departed, then Chinese, Eurasian, and native alike felt free to do what they could in the best way possible for their own survival. They were quick to learn that they were up against a race such as they had never seen before. The conscription of their womenfolk to serve as prostitutes for the Japanese was the most telling of all their acts. Asian families always kept their unmarried daughters far away from prying eyes, but when they were forcibly taken from them to be used as prostitutes hostility quickly became rife.

The most frequent offence was failure to bow when encountering a Japanese. This was commonplace, as the folk of Sabah are a proud independent race, unsubservient to anyone. When I was a District Officer, naturally everyone knew me, but I certainly wouldn't have expected them to stand to attention and salute me! I may well have saluted them by way of greeting, and the familiar reply was: '*Tabek, Tuan*'! ('Greetings, Tuan'); of course, if I knew one I would stop and have a conversation; that was the best way of keeping in touch with the people. The Japanese, however, like all inferior beings, craved attention.

All the inhabitants had to bow whenever they encountered a Japanese. If they did not do so, they had to stand and face him, whilst he struck out with the full force of his outstretched arm and hand: not once or twice, but with each arm, and if the victim did not stand up and wait for the next blow, he would be beaten until he could no longer stand. Another common form of punishment was to make the person stand in the hot tropical sun for hours at a time. We ourselves had learnt all about this in Kuching. Often we didn't know why we were being the target of their fury! On one occasion I was just going from the garden back to the camp, having obtained the permission of our guard in the garden, and as usual bowed to where the sentry should have been in the camp square. In fact, he was hiding behind a tree. I hadn't noticed him, but having bowed to the tree, turned towards the camp entrance only to be bawled at. Naturally, I stopped, and went over to him as he was indicating, and received a most awful beating up with the butt of his rifle, of which one of the blows I seem to feel to this day, many years after!

This inborn desire to beat up people was a curious trait. In Kuching we noticed that it would often start with Major Suja slapping the face of Lt. Nekata. He would then take it out on his NCOs, they on the guards and subsequently we would earn a bad day! In a way, it was akin to their smiles. If Nekata came into the camp with a smile on his face, then almost certainly there was trouble ahead.

Back in Jesselton, our poor people were learning about it. The lightest form of punishment was to provide sport for the Japanese. Scores of people were arrested for hardly any offence at all. From time to time any two of the offenders were chosen at random, and tied to one of the flame trees at the bottom of the Sports Club steps. They were given sufficient rope to enable them to move around and were told to challenge each other to a bout of fisticuffs. Anyone who stumbled was beaten with sticks by the enemies' soldiers until he rose to his feet and renewed the fight. The loser knew that ultimately he would receive a flogging, usually with lengths of poisonous mangrove-wood always at hand as firewood. This, of course, was all in view of any member of the public who happened to be passing by. It was obviously intended to be a demonstration of the might of the Japanese! This was sport for them—not serious punishment.

Before I describe other forms of punishment that the enemy meted out to our people, the reader may naturally question the circumstances which occurred to merit so many being punished. There were many. The most essential thing for the Japanese was food, and the constant and increasing demands made on the villagers for rice inevitably developed hostility. Their 'banana' currency very soon became worthless.

They similarly demanded labour. They tried to make it plain that they had come to stay. This was not an occupation of conquered territory but a part of the 'greater' Japan, according to the invaders. It had to be defended. Their strategy may be understood, but their way of doing it was merciless slavery such as the world had not seen for many a long year.

Their first task was to build airstrips. To achieve their objectives all able-bodied men were conscripted into service; even local staff in Government offices had to perform manual work one day per week. Forced labour was country-wide. Airstrips were built not only at Jesselton and Sandakan, but also at Keningau, Kudat and elsewhere. The Japanese surveyed, planned and supervised the tasks but did not themselves work. They were virtually enslaving a defenceless population.

At this point, I cannot help but put myself into the position of our poor people in Sabah. They had lived in a British Protectorate, a territory whose protection had been guaranteed by the British Empire, at that time the greatest power in the world. And when they needed protection most, it was lacking! The world circumstances which caused this debacle are now perfectly understandable to us, but it couldn't have been so easily comprehended by a rather less sophisticated, simple and trusting people. Yet, in all circumstances, they always remained loyal to us, and always believed in our ultimate victory: in short, they were and remain the salt of the earth.

It was a multi-racial society, each pursuing its own way of life, but each participating in and enjoying the other's annual festivities. After the first, or family day, of the Chinese New Year the whole community were welcome to join in their festivities. Similarly, after the fast of Ramadan, the Moslem feasting began and all were welcome to join. As for the Dusuns, any event was an excuse for bringing out the *tapai* jars, just like the Muruts, and all travellers and neighbours were always invited just to sit and chat. It had been a very happy country. Yet at the hour of their greatest need, the British, who by the villagers always seemed to be regarded as *ibu bapa* which can best be interpreted as 'father and mother' to them, had let them down.

With our removal from the scene, they had no protector: no *ibu bapa*, and they were left to fend for themselves in the best way they could. They could not accept the Japanese 'Co-Prosperity Sphere', as even the simplest-minded of the natives was able to see through that fallacy. Robbery and pillaging was a more accurate description.

Then an event occurred which in primitive native minds was regarded as an omen. Reasonably early in the occupation, the Commander in Chief of all the forces in Borneo and at the same time the Military Governor of the whole area, Marquis Maeda whose headquarters were in Kuching, was on a flight to Labuan when the aircraft disappeared. Widespread searches along the coast were made without trace of the plane. The news of this incident soon travelled far and wide:

the Gods were on the side of the people of Borneo! The Japanese were not invincible! It is odd how, from relatively small incidents, big events can develop.

Although born in Kuching, a certain Albert Kwok had been sent by his parents to Shanghai where he studied Chinese medicine and later became well-known for his successful treatment of piles. He received recognition for his skills from some of the highest officials in China, and even earned merit from General Chiang Kai Shek himself. As a consequence of the Japanese invasion of Manchuria and the subsequent Sino-Japanese war, he returned to Borneo and as a bachelor lived with his sister and brother-in-law in a house built over the sea at Karamunsing, not more than a mile from the centre of Jesselton. As his stock of drugs began to be exhausted, his attention turned to other matters: how to organize the local overthrow of the Japanese, against whom he felt that, amongst the local people and Chinese alike, there was a growing desire to rebel.

Not knowing the weak position of the Allies, he had felt that the British had tamely surrendered without putting up an adequate fight. When the first line fighting forces of the Japanese had moved on south to further fields of battle, he judged the garrison that had replaced them were less resistant, and if a sufficiently strong force could be organized could be overthrown. His first action was to endeavour to seek out the pocket of Europeans including Americans and Dutch who had retreated inland from Sarawak as the invasion had occurred. They were a party of twenty-one Europeans including three women and two children who had made their way up-river from Sibu in Sarawak to a Dutch military post at Long Nawan in Dutch-administered Borneo. Four of these went on to Samarinda and eventually reached Australia: they were the lucky ones. Four Dutch airmen and a few Americans escaping from the Philippines joined them, and the defence of the station consisted of fifty Dutch marines. In the party of women was Mrs Bomphrey, the wife of the man who was in a berth next to me in Batu Lintang camp in Kuching. Inevitably, he was constantly worried about their welfare; but alas, his worries had been in vain. The Japanese had heard of this pocket of resistance and made an overwhelming incursion into the jungle, and after a terrific battle, wiped out the entire garrison and the refugees, not before they had taken it in turns to rape the women in front of their children, before shooting them all.

Although Albert Kwok reached Pensiangan, he found that further progress along the rivers, where I had once gone *tuba* fishing with Native Chief Enduat, was impossible. A large enemy force was in the area, all local craft had been commandeered, and the presence of a stranger would readily be recognized. He, therefore, was compelled to give up his attempt, but in any case it would have been in vain. The Long Nawan garrison had already been annihilated.

On his return to Jesselton, he was appalled to read a notice issued by the Japanese during his absence which read:

> A warning to Overseas Chinese!
>
> The Overseas Chinese for the past five years since the China–Japan incident helped the Chungking Government War Fund by voluntary subscriptions.

> The Chinese have maltreated, oppressed and denounced overseas Japanese. Such anti-Japanese conduct is intolerable. Since the outbreak of war in East Asia, the Chinese, acting with Great Britain and the Dutch East Indies, have resisted Japan. They have behaved as an enemy by helping the enemy. When Japanese troops repulsed Great Britain, America and the Dutch East Indies and then occupied Borneo, the Chinese changed their attitude and pretended they knew nothing. Let the Chinese remember that the power of seizing them and putting them all to death rests on the decision of the Japanese High Command. Although the Chinese are now allowed their freedom, it is only temporary to enable the Japanese to watch their movements. Now let the Chinese reflect deeply, and come to their senses before the issue of another notice.

For a while Albert Kwok remained inactive. Later in 1942, the US victory of the Battle of the Coral Sea took place. The attempted Japanese thrust towards Australian soil had failed! In June 1943 an even greater success occurred when the American Navy and Air Forces celebrated the success of the Battle of Midway: the tide was beginning to turn!

In spite of the published threats, the underground swell of anti-Japanese feeling was beginning to rise amongst the local Chinese. They secretly formed a society which went by the name of 'The Overseas Chinese Defence Association' with the immediate objective of preventing their people from collaborating too closely with the Japanese. They had worked it out that any assistance given to the Japanese was harmful to the Allied cause. It was an organization of passive resistance.

It was not only in Sabah that the ground-swell of discontent against the invaders was rising: not far away in the Sulu Archipelago, on islands that could almost be seen from the North Borneo eastern sea-board, violent anti-Japanese feeling was festering. In their rapid sweep southward the enemy had by-passed the myriad of tiny isles which once were the territory of the Sultan of Sulu. Their inhabitants were the pirates who had given the Sultan of Brunei so much trouble and who had made the prospect of secession of his northern territories so very much more attractive to him. Remnants of the Filipino Army, who never had the chance of fighting the Japanese before the surrender of Corrigidor, had retreated here, and were gathering to strike the Japanese wherever it might hurt them most. Their main base was Tawi Tawi and here they found natural allies amongst the piratical Sulu islanders.

Close to the *Darvel's* anchorage in the Malawali Channel lay Tambisan Island, and from there could be seen Sibutu Island which was part of the Sulu Archipelago and was Filipino territory. This was to become the line of communication to be established between the force in Tawi Tawi and the malcontents in Jessleton.

Having been rebuffed in his excursion into the Interior, too late to establish links with the Dutch, Albert Kwok had been advised to explore the possibilities of links with the East Coast and the resistance group in Tawi Tawi. His informant had been the comprador of Ban Guan's emporium, the grey-haired Lim Keng Fatt who had come into contact in Jesselton with an Imam Marajukim travelling in the guise of a trader in sugar. He had once been a Moslem priest but was now turning to more warlike pursuits, and had been enlisted by Lt. Col. Suarez, commanding the 125th Infantry Regiment of the Philippines Army. Imam Marajukim had found the right man. Ban Guan's trade had evaporated and like the rest of the Chinese in Jesselton, he was no friend of the enemy. He invited Marajukim to stay the night with him and in the still hours of darkness he sent a message to Albert Kwok. Together they all met, and by the light of a flickering coconut-oil lamp they planned the first moves of the only rebellion the Japanese were to face in the territories they had occupied.

Albert Kwok returned to Tawi Tawi in the company of Imam Marajukim with the object of meeting up with Lt. Col. Suarez. When they arrived, Suarez was at first suspicious of Kwok, fearing that he might have been sent as a spy by the Japanese, but when Suarez's wife, who had been ill, was cured by Kwok's medicines, mistrust disappeared.

Money was the one thing that Suarez most needed. He saw here a chance of tapping the comparatively wealthy Chinese in Sabah and gaining support for his resistance movement. He gave Albert Kwok a document which was headed 'United States Army Forces in the Philippines. Headquarters: Sulu Sector'.

> In the field: 11.5.43.
>
> To whom it may concern: The bearer, Mr Albert Kwok, of Jesselton, British North Borneo, is in the services of the United States Army Forces in the Philippines in the Sulu Sector. He is especially assigned by the undersigned to Jesselton as my representative on financial affairs. Inasmuch as we are fighting side by side and fighting for the same cause, I am now appealing to patriotic citizens there to extend to us your fullest co-operation either by voluntary contributions or loan, and receipts will be issued and reimbursable by the United States Government of America or the Commonwealth Government of the Philippines, so that we may be able to purchase some military supplies that we badly need in order that we may destroy and exterminate our common enemy.

It was signed by Suarez, as Lt. Col. Suarez, Infantry, US Army. Kwok proudly returned to Jesselton, bearing this letter. It convinced all the leading members of the Chinese community that there was a resistance movement in force in the Sulu Islands, and that their best hope of ridding the country of the enemy was to support it with the funds that had been requested. Clothing and medical supplies were also collected and secretly taken to Suarez.

The Japanese heard whispers of the connection but discovered very little. Wanting nothing to go wrong in the early stages of his plans, Kwok went into hiding in a remote rubber plantation in Menggatal, whilst military police searched for him. They failed but instead turned their attention to the East Coast. Suspicious of what might be happening, the Japanese sent an expeditionary force to occupy Tawi Tawi.

They had an expectedly hot reception. They came under fire for three days and three nights before withdrawing to Sandakan, leaving behind thirty-one Japanese prisoners. The Philippino forces had no intention of keeping prisoners; they managed to get as much information out of them as possible, then took them out to sea, beheaded them, and threw their bodies into the sea.

When news filtered through to Jesselton, it gave a great impetus to anti-Japanese feeling and inspired a desire to take a more active role in destroying the enemy. In its activities the Overseas Chinese Defence Association became more militant, particularly in raising funds. It has been said that the fund amounted to more than half a million dollars. Its immediate purpose was to make rewards for Japanese heads. The Committee of the Association assessed payments for killing Japanese, and priced their heads according to rank: the rewards ranged from $200 to $400 for each skull taken!

It has often been said that the multi-racial society of Borneo detracted from its political cohesion, but this certainly was far from true during the occupation. The hatred of the invaders became a unifying force. Personal assault was obnoxious to Chinese and native alike. Public display of force in which the Japanese troops revelled quickly developed a common hatred of them. The clandestine Defence Association which the Chinese had formed soon gained support from all and the news which had spread from the Tawi Tawi incident gave rise to an urgent feeling to take some positive action to rid the country of its oppressors.

In the meantime, help seemed to be coming from an as yet unexpected source: from the Allied Forces themselves. The success of the SAS in France had appealed to the Australian Army and they sought to recruit any European with any knowledge of Borneo into their ranks, with a view to infiltrating him by means of submarine into enemy occupied territory where his job would be to organize resistance groups and harass the enemy. Major Charles Chester OBE, whom I had earlier met in hospital shortly after I had arrived in Sandakan, a planter on the East Coast who happened to be in Australia when the Far Eastern war broke out, had enlisted with the Australian Forces. He was immediately sought out and trained both for sabotage work and to organize resistance within occupied Borneo.

He had heard of the exploits of Albert Kwok and, aware of the hard core of resistance building up on the West Coast, he was fearful of premature action. He knew the position of the Allied Forces and was well aware that they were still bogged down in New Guinea and Rabaul, and not yet in a position to advance northwards to Sabah, where any insurrection of the local population would have been of inestimable value to an Allied invasion force. He sent messages, therefore, to Kwok that the time to strike was not yet at hand.

Events, however, in Jesselton in the autumn of 1943 appeared to force the hand of Kwok and his followers. Following the custom that they had undertaken in other territory they had captured, for instance in Korea, the Japanese began to issue instructions for the formation of a local defence force composed of local Chinese youths. They did the same in Malaya and Burma where they had recruited former members of the Indian Army under their own nominated leader, Chandra Boos.

So too, in Jesselton, the news leaked out that the Japanese were planning to conscript a force of three thousand local Chinese youths, either for garrison duties or for overseas service. They were to be given a course of intensive and rigorous training in Jesselton immediately they had been conscripted. Kwok and his conspiritors were placed in a quandary: these were the very people whom Kwok was relying on to form his own resistance group. His hand was being forced!

Probably the most telling rumour which was to galvanize the Chinese into action was that the Japanese intended to seize the daughters of local Chinese and enlist them as 'comfort' girls for the new recruits. Their daughters are always precious to the Chinese and they were alarmed at the possible veracity of this rumour. The Chinese normally keep their unmarried daughters well in the background: their place is in the kitchen, well hidden from the prying eyes of males. Moreover, they were well aware of the Japanese obsession for sex: Japanese girls had been imported into Jesselton, and housed in the Rectory of All Saints Church. Another brothel set aside for the exclusive use of senior officers was established in the Basel Mission School and school buildings on Ridge Road, and yet another in Harrington Road. This was common knowledge to all the local inhabitants. The possibility of their own daughters being taken from them for the amusement of a newly recruited conscript force was viewed as a genuine, frightening threat.

Kwok was in a dilemma. He had to assess where he could rely on support. Most certainly the Chinese were with the movement, and the sea-going native population, in particular the Suloks, and the Binadons of Dinawan and the other islands on which they dwelt. He could also rely on the Bajaus with pirate blood running in their veins, but the peace-loving Kedazans, although they loathed the continuous demands being made on their crops, were doubtful starters. He left them out of his reckoning. He certainly drew strength from the few very loyal Eurasian families in Jesselton; they usually held fairly key positions in the Government, and although not numerically strong, were influential in local society. His support was, therefore, fragmentary; perhaps much more could have been accomplished if there had been a unity of purpose in the country as a whole.

Kwok selected an area behind Manggatel, where he himself had gone into hiding, as his headquarters.

The date selected for the uprising was a date of great significance for the Chinese, the anniversary of the establishment of the New China under Chiang Kai Shek: the Double Tenth, or the Tenth Day of the Tenth Month. This was a day of liberation, a day that all Chinese celebrated: the day when the despotism and oppression of the old dynasty were dissolved in the liberal views of a more democratic generation.

The stakes, however, were high, and Kwok had a weak hand. Perhaps as a sort of Commando raid, he might have succeeded. But he and his supporters had no retreat; they had to execute their task as best as they knew how, and then stay and face the music. Although it may appear that the uprising of their own people against a common enemy would have found universal support, this was far from the case. There were many, many natives in the pay of the Japanese who, for the prospect of some favour for the enemy, be it only a bushel of rice, would be willing to give information to the enemy when pressed. And the Japanese knew the best methods of obtaining information: torture and more torture, of a kind unknown for generations.

With his contacts at Tawi Tawi, Kwok had relied on reinforcements from that direction. Some islanders had been sent to advise Suarez and seek his immediate assistance. He felt assured that this would be forthcoming. The islanders were ready and eager for action. His plan was a two-pronged attack: one by the Sulok islanders from the sea, and the second by his own body of men that he would first lead to Tuaran, capture the Police Station there, and obtain reinforcements of weapons and ammunition of which he was precariously short. He felt that that would be a simple and successful objective which would give heart to the more ambitious plan of capturing Jesselton itself. The attack here involved his second thrust: the islanders would attack from the sea, with the Jesselton wharf and the godowns as their primary target, whilst after securing his rear at Tuaran, Kwok himself with his main force would come down the Tuaran Road, link up with the islanders, and then attack the Police Headquarters at Batu Tiga where the main force of the Japanese were believed to be. Another party was to attack the Japanese wireless communication centre which was thought to be in All Saints Church.

The auguries appeared to be good. Fishermen sailing far out to sea maintained communication with Tawi Tawi. Allied submarines had been seen from time to time off the East Coast and agents had come ashore. Overhead, occasional Allied aircraft had been sighted on reconnaissance duty. The time seemed favourable: arms and reinforcements would surely come.

Lt. Kwok had chosen his leaders with care. Much later on, reading about these turbulent times, it was of special interest to me to learn that the officer from whom I had taken over the administation of Papar District, Hiew Syn Yong, D.A.D.O., Jesselton, and later on, D.A.D.O., Kota Belud, had assumed responsibility for the uprising in that area, whilst the Chief Police Officer, who had also been looking after Police matters in Papar until I had come on the scene, was none other than Charles Peter with responsibility for the Tuaran area! To assist him in his task was Subedar Dewa Singh of the Armed Constabulary. The adjutant of the guerrilla force was Jules Stephens who, having formerly been a Sergeant of the Volunteer Force, was largely responsible for the organization of the guerillas from the beginning. An operator of the Telecommunications Department took responsibility for cutting telephone and telegraph wires in all strategic places, and a telegraph orderly undertook to remove an essential part of the Japanese wireless equipment in All Saints Church.

Out at sea, all operations were in charge of Orang Tua Penglima Ali of Suluk Island who had assembled a fleet of craft from Mantanani and Dinawan Islands. As they gathered at Mantanani, they would have sat around the wood-smoke after dark, their kris drawn from their scabbards and whetted on the stones by the sea. The prospect of taking action against the invaders they had come to loathe roused their fighting spirit of olden times! They sailed from the islands by night in order that no suspicions should be aroused, and by day they hid amongst the creeks of the *nipah* palms which fringed the coast. The knots they had previously made in the strings of *rotan* indicated the appointed day. The evening of the ninth day of the tenth moon was soon upon them!

At eight o'clock in the evening, all plans and all eventualities having been covered, Lt. Kwok, wearing his American Army uniform, met the spearhead of the party by the roadside at Menggatal. The final order to kill Japanese was given; they mounted their truck and started racing down the road towards Tuaran District Office. It was defended by four Japanese and some native police. The Japanese were killed instantly, and the guerillas assisted by the police raided the armoury and obtained half a dozen Lee-Enfield rifles, ammunition and also a stock of shot-gun ammunition which the station always carried. Reinforced and encouraged, they embarked on the second stage of their enterprise: the attack on Jesselton itself. On reaching Mengattal on the return journey they were surprised to encounter a Japanese patrol. The guerillas took them completely off guard, made short work of the enemy and killed all fifteen! This enabled the guerillas to reinforce their weapons, and give their motorized cavalry three vehicles! The advance on Jesselton had begun.

The first objective was again the Police Station to capture more arms. This was defended by a few native members of the Armed Constabulary, who put up no resistance, and by a few regular Japanese soldiers. These were despatched without any difficulty and the building ransacked for more arms. In this they were disappointed, but as time was of the essence, they went back along South Road to the unmarried policemen's barracks: a single storey building which they thought might house some Japanese soldiers. Again, this was taken virtually without opposition and all inside, taken unexpectedly, were slain. The guerrillas then turned their attention to the Sports Club, which was the headquarters of the Kempitai. This important post was also captured, and it was from here, sited on a hillock, that they spotted the fires at the customs wharf: the signal that the islanders had captured the wharf and had set alight the godowns. They knew then that a second party of islanders had landed near the fish market, and would be storming through the seaward side of the town, killing all the Japanese they could find in the haunts they were known to frequent. When the alarm was given some Japanese fled into the undergrowth of the low-lying hills around the town, whilst those who had cars sped along South Road to Government Cottage hill and the Police Barracks at Batu Tiga where the main body of Japanese troops were in the buildings we, as internees, had vacated.

Lt. Kwok decided not to give chase. Perhaps it was his intention to consolidate before advancing further, but uppermost in his mind, he was awaiting the expected reinforcements from Tawi Tawi with considerably increased fire power. He was well aware too that messages he had received from the Allies, in particular the one from Major Chester asking for a postponement, emphasizing that the time was not yet ripe for a wide-scale uprising, must always have been present in the back of his mind. His hand had been forced by events, but he must have thought that the gamble might have been worthwhile. He did feel certain of support from Tawi Tawi, but perhaps he had underestimated the effects of the north-west monsoon, and the almost impossible vengeance of the sea against frail craft. This was one miscalculation. On the other hand, his only real problem was at Batu Tiga. Government Cottage could have been isolated; it stood on its own hill, with access along the main drive, with a service road at the rear. He could have ignored that. Batu Tiga presented a more difficult problem, but a surprise attack would have been worth a dozen firearms. There would inevitably have been casualties, but luck had been with them so far; it may well have held.

Whatever the reason, Kwok decided to withdraw his men to Menggatal and await reinforcements from Tawi Tawi. At least he had frustrated the intention of the enemy to enlist local Chinese into a force under their command, and thwarted their intended provision of these men with 'comfort' girls. That much he had achieved. In retrospect, it is easy to conclude that he may have erred in his judgement. Surprise was on his side, the numbers he was up against may not have been all that formidable, and if he had been able to overcome them and hold out for just a couple of months, the Tawi Tawi reinforcements would have arrived and the West Coast would have been once more consolidated in the hands of the Allies. In the island-hopping exercise in which the Australians and Americans were engaged, friendly territory on the West Coast of Borneo might have provided the means of a great leap forward. Much had lain in the balance.

Kwok could not even have guessed this. He had been asked to delay operations, but he had been unable to stop the momentum, fearful that the spies which surrounded him and other events previously forshadowed might have destroyed his plans. There was only one thing he could do: retreat to his hideaway at Mengattal and await reinforcements from Tawi Tawi.

Shortly after midnight he passed the order to his own men and the islanders to retreat to their homes. Kwok and his immediate followers kept together in a band, and went into hiding in the jungle. Assessing their achievements, they knew that they had accounted for over thirty Japanese which they had left for dead and had suffered no casualties themselves. They were well pleased with the result, and hopeful that when reinforcements arrived from the Southern Philippines, all of them together would be able to renew the attack.

It would have been wiser if he had dispersed all his men into the jungle. A single man on his own would have attracted less attention, but with the Japanese out for revenge there were many, either fearful of their own lives and property, or for pecuniary or other personal benefit, who would be ready to give information about the whereabouts of the wanted group of guerrillas. Such proved to be the case. Sympathy is one thing, active support another!

However, Lt. Kwok was not viewing the situation in this manner at all. He had regarded the operation he had conducted as a success. Indeed, he had left a Proclamation posted in all prominent places in Jesselton saying that he and his men had taken up arms to liberate the people from the tyranny of Japanese oppression and sought the fullest co-operation of the public in their mission. He warned all Japanese spies amongst the population that their existence and identity was known, and that the day of retribution was at hand. Signing under a fictitious name, he declared himself to be the Commander of the North Borneo Overseas Chinese Defence Force, and, addressing the Japanese, it protested against their maladministration of the territory, the control of business by Japanese Companies, the surrender by the farmers of nearly all their produce to the Japanese, the reduction of the population to poverty and the dishonourable treatment of women. In a final word of defiance, the Proclamation concluded that his Force were determined to right these wrongs, if necessary at the cost of their lives, and to drive the Japanese out of the country.

In their midnight retreat to Menggatal, the guerrillas destroyed the wooden deck of Inanam bridge by saturating it with oil and setting fire to it to delay any pursuit. Tuaran was already liberated, but he had heard of the presence of Japanese on Tuaran Estate. They were sought out on the next morning and summarily executed. Kwok then turned his attention northwards towards Kota Belud. The telephone line had been cut the previous day, but this would have aroused no suspicion: a single branch of a falling tree frequently snapped the single telephone line, as I well can remember from my days in Keningau. (I think the line from Pensiangan to Keningau was broken for this reason almost half the time I was there!) One of Kwok's Deputies led a party to Kota Belud, and, unexpectedly encountering a party of three Japanese at Tenghilan, took them unawares and readily disposed of them, capturing their arms and the ammunition they carried. Nearing Kota Belud, he was able, with the use of a travelling telephone, to raise the station police sergeant. He learnt that there were four Japanese in Kota Belud, so telling him that Allied relief forces were on their way he ordered the Japanese to be arrested. Hiew Syn Yong, the D.O. in charge at Kota Belud, was aware of the existence of the guerrilla Force and interpreted the message correctly. The Japanese were apprehended and when the guerrillas arrived their Japanese prisoners were promptly executed.

Perhaps at that stage in the development of the mind of the average unsophisticated native there was no grey area. The person who came into their midst was either good or bad. In a way their philosophy was not unlike that of Jean-Jacques Rousseau who believed that people are born naturally good and happy until society introduces evil. So too, in the case of the natives: they were and remain an honest and trusting people, but when the Japanese came into their midst then evil was born. They quickly recognized that their interests lay with the winning side. Scruples and morals they had, but they quickly concluded that guns won the argument. It was a Chinese revolt, not their revolt. They had heard of the Sino-Japanese War, so it was in a way natural that the Chinese would want to carry on the war in Sabah: that was their concern. As yet the effect of Japanese maladministration had not fully rubbed off on to them; their granaries had suffered, that was true, but perhaps that was inevitable. Evil such as they would later experience they had not as yet encountered.

Japanese reinforcements arrived on 13 October. They first engaged themselves in repairing the bridge in Inanam and were sniped at by the guerrillas, but the Japanese had brought machine guns, forcing Kwok and his men to retreat into the nearby jungle. There were casualties on both sides. On the following day more Japanese troops were spotted and it was thought that they were preparing to give chase. The guerrillas had no option but to retreat further and take up defensive positions between Menggatal and Talibong. The enemy then resorted to aircraft to which the guerrillas had no reply. They began bombing innocent and undefended people, splattering machine-gun fire far and wide and bombing any house which offered a good target. All villages between Jesselton and Kota Belud in the north suffered, partly as a measure of reprisal and partly to drive out the guerrillas, but since they knew nothing of the latter's whereabouts, the air attacks could have had no other purpose than to terrorize the countryside.

The guerrillas had no alternative but to retreat upstream to the foothills of Kinabalu. Kwok was reluctant to move too far away from the coast, as daily he expected arms and reinforcements from the Philippines, and it would have been essential to have joined up with them to provide local knowledge and assistance. Every day from their mountain clearing they scanned the seas with their glasses, looking for the signs of any approaching craft; but they argued between themselves that they would not appear in daylight hours, but would only travel by night. But, as time went on, the logistics of their situation got the better of them! Supplies! They had hitherto lived off the countryside, gathering coconuts and grabbing a few cobs of maize here and there, fishing perhaps in the rivers, but as they had to withdraw further and further, the jungle yielded less and less. One by one they elected to return to their homes. Every night, over a wood fire that they would light to keep themselves warm on the slopes of Kinabalu with a chilly breeze coming off the mountain, they would talk it over, but Kwok had to let them go. It slowly dawned on him that he was waiting in vain for help from the Philippines and that the enterprise had failed.

Hunger eventually forced the hard core back towards the villages, towards people whom they thought they could trust. It was to be their undoing: a price had been put on their heads! Someone who had been captured, under interrogation and torture had mentioned names. Not only that, but the Japanese were behaving in a criminal manner against an innocent population. People from all neighbouring villages were rounded up and collected at Tuaran District Office. The women and children were forced under the office, and all the men were herded on to the *padang* and kept in the sun. A handful of rice was given to each as a ration. At night the men were bundled into the local lock-up which normally would never house more than eight or nine prisoners. They would be questioned and beaten daily for any information they could give, especially regarding their own movements. When they could extract nothing, the victim was released and given a 'good citizen' badge, and was allowed to return home. None escaped the ordeal. More soldiers arrived in large numbers, rounding up more people: Bajau, Chinese and Kedazan, beating them up, young and old alike. The villagers all around the countryside, whenever they saw Japanese approaching, obeyed their natural instinct, left their houses and took to the nearby scrub or jungle if it was close enough. If the Japanese found a house deserted in this manner, they would burn it down.

Coincidental to these activities, the Japanese Commander organized two parties: one composed of native headmen and police, and headed by Japanese troops; the other consisting solely of Japanese troops and Kempitai. The former had as its objective the search for the bodies of dead Japanese, and the other was out to search for the guerrillas themselves.

Japanese members of both parties showed no mercy and behaved with great brutality. All the Chinese in the townships of Inanam, Menggatal, Telipok and Tuaran were arrested, and if any of them showed any resistance or attempted to run, they were shot on the spot. The news of the arrests spread like wildfire, and many of the people fled into the jungle. Whenever this happened, the Japanese assumed they were guilty; they were pursued and shot immediately. At Tuaran, many of the Chinese townsfolk assembled on the bank of the Tuaran River. When the Japanese overtook them, they were all bound hand and foot, beheaded and their bodies thrown into the river.

Japanese Proclamations were issued almost by the score, all of them threatening death to any person failing to give evidence, if he knew it, of the whereabouts of the guerrillas. Their names had become known to the Japanese and a price was put on the head of each. Top of the list was the fictitious name Albert Kwok had used when he had successfully raided Jesselton just ten days or so earlier. If the person could not be brought in alive, the reward would be paid even if only his head were brought to the Japanese. Kwok's head was top of the list for a reward: a price of $5,000 had been put on his! Others had prices put against them ranging from $3,000 to $1,000. There were thirteen names on the list altogether, and it was dated 5 November 1943. The course of the war had barely run a couple of years.

In the meantime Lt. Kwok battled cheerfully against the odds with his faithful band of followers. He remained in the foothills of Kinabalu, still in hope that reinforcements from Tawi Tawi would eventually arrive. On 12 November, the birthday of Dr Sun Yat Sun, the father of the Chinese Republic, they celebrated the anniversary by hoisting the national flag and singing patriotic songs and their national anthem. By this time, though, their very existence was precarious; they were hunted men. News had reached them of the appalling atrocities committed by the Japanese Army on the peace-loving local populace. They realized that this was the direct outcome of their raid into Jesselton, and the relatively few Japanese they had been able to kill, whom they regarded as legitimate targets of war, when compared with the scores, nay, hundreds, of innocent compatriots, some of whom had been friends and relatives, whose death had been caused by their activities. They began to wonder whether it had all been worthwhile. The apathy of those with whom they came into contact, and indeed the enmity of the natives, began to persuade them that their revolt had not been worthwhile. Passive resistance may have been the safer course.

Gradually they came out of the hills and made their way towards a settlement of Northern Chinese from Shantung, who had helped Kwok when raising funds for the Tawi Tawi resistance forces. They lived in a village near the Penampong road, too close for safety, but they could be trusted as friends. On arrival they were advised that too many strangers passed that way and it was suggested they should stay in their own Chinese cemetery where the grave-digger had a hut. It took them to within two miles of Batu Tiga, on the landward side. It was a little hilly, undulating, country with sparse vegetation, but unless someone of the Shantung community died, almost no one would pass that way. The person who would bring them food would let them know before the grave-digger ever had to come.

They hid up here for nearly a week, and then a chance incident happened which gave them away. The messenger who brought them their food was an inveterate gambler. He had been given some money to take to Lt. Kwok in case of need, and instead of going straight to the cemetery, he went to the gambling farm, which had opened in Penampang after the occupation had begun. He lost the money at the gaming table! Ashamedly, he returned to their friend who was protecting them, and asked for more money. An argument ensued in the shop-house, and voices were raised. Someone outside the shop, walking along the covered way outside, overheard the heated discussion. He was one of the Japanese spies they had appointed! Straightaway, he went to his chief in the occupying forces and revealed what he had heard. That was enough! Whether he ever obtained the reward he hoped for, no one ever knew. Knowing what the Japanese were like, I strongly suspect he didn't. But the damage was done.

The occupying Army acted on the information he had given them. At four o'clock the next morning, on 19 December 1943, over a hundred Japanese set out from Batu Tiga and surrounded the area. It was said later that they trained machine-guns on the little row of about four shops where Kwok's friend lived, and ordered the latter to find Lt. Kwok and his supporters and bring them to the shop.

It was obvious what would happen if he failed to do so! He had no option but to go to the cemetery and tell Kwok. The Japanese, of course, knew that Kwok was armed, so it was a cunning move on their part. Undoubtedly Kwok would have fought to the end, but to spare the Chinese who had befriended him, he and his men came out of hiding and surrendered to the Japanese.

Ironically, just ten days later, the long awaited reinforcements from Tawi Tawi arrived in the vicinity. They had brought with them a body of picked men, a large number of the latest types of American machine-guns and ammunition, as well as $25,000 in cash. They had arrived too late! They were told by sympathizers that Kwok had been arrested, and they returned to Tawi Tawi.

For his part, Lt. Kwok had anticipated that his surrender would cause the Japanese to cease further reprisals. But he was wrong. The Japanese tiger was not to be appeased with a few morsels. He wanted the lot!

It must have been with a very heavy heart that Lt. Kwok came out of hiding. The delay in the arrival of the long promised reinforcements must have filled him with foreboding. His faith had faltered. His men had searched the horizon in vain. When he realized that he had lost the fight, whatever his faults, he possessed the greatest of all virtues: courage in adversity. Continuously, over an arduous period of two years, the guiding principal of his life had been consistent: to oppose the enemy. His practice had matched his principles, but the end had now come.

Lt. Kwok and his band of followers emerged from the low-lying hills and came out on to the Penampang Road, where the Japanese were waiting. They were tied and bound, and taken directly to the Kempitai Headquarters in the Jesselton Sports Club. There Kwok was immediately put through every possible kind of torture. One of those who were with him, who with luck managed to survive, said later that he suffered quietly and flatly refused to answer any questions put to him. He would only say that he was the sole cause and that he alone was responsible for the Double Tenth revolt. He tried to commit suicide to end his torture but the attempt failed.

One of his band of followers, however, must have succumbed under the physical torment his body had to endure, and in his anguish must have mentioned the participation of the islanders: the Suloks of Pulau Tiga, Mantanani, and the Binadons of Dinawan Island, involved in the burning down of the Customs sheds and the raids on shop-houses in search of Japanese, many of whom they had killed. Gradually the Japanese learnt the whole story.

The number of men the Japanese rounded up totalled over four hundred: not that that number had by any means been involved in the rebellion but who can say what the mind can do in extreme pain. If the mention of a name, guilty or not, eases the pain just momentarily, that name will emerge, and that person would be sought out, arrested and imprisoned with all the others. No evidence exists that any trial ever took place; if a person was arrested, he was automatically guilty. The prisoners were treated like cattle, all crammed into a small jail, built to accommodate at most about fifty prisoners. The last time the jail had accommodated so many had been on the occasion of the riot of twenty-two Northern Chinese labourers who had rioted on Bangawan Estate between three or four years earlier.

One can imagine their terrible plight: the heat, no sanitation or any facilities whatsoever, and very, very little food or water, if any were given at all. The Japanese did not let such a situation prolong itself: they wanted revenge quickly. No more time was to be wasted. The Army Administration decided on a massacre of their prisoners. 21 January 1944 was the day appointed and the place Mile 5½ along the railway line, between Tanjong Aru and Putatan, near a railway bridge crossing the Petagas River. Deep trenches were dug in the white sandy soil found there. Traffic on all roads was closed for three days to prevent any person seeing what was being prepared.

In a fairly futile endeavour to justify their actions, just a few days before the event, the prisoners were brought out of jail and photographed. They were made to sign a document admitting to the charges brought against them. As it was all in Japanese, none of them knew what they were signing. Then they were made to stand and hold a card bearing their name, and then they were photographed. If it eased the conscience of the Japanese mind, it would deceive no one else.

No records exist which might give an indication whether any trial ever took place, or whether the prisoners were ever charged of any offence, or brought before a Court Martial. There is no evidence at all, unless the Japanese themselves kept any record of events. What did happen was that at 3 o'clock the next morning (the Japanese always liked making significant moves at night: it added to their Machiavellian enjoyment) the prisoners were marched out of the Police gaol and forced into six covered trucks which had been standing at Batu Tiga Halt, on the railway line which passed the barracks. In retrospect it must have been similar to the actions of the allies of Japan, the Hitler Regime in Germany, loading truckloads of Jews to await their death in the gas-chambers of Auschwitz. Man's infinite cruelty to man can never be understood by any reasonable person.

The six covered trucks had been located in the middle of the train. In the front were carriages which were for the use of Japanese civil and military officials, and behind were open low-sided trucks for the use of the other ranks of the Japanese Army. On arrival at Petagas, the prisoners were pushed out of the trucks, and made to walk in the direction of the mass grave. The Japanese soldiers surrounded the area, whilst the officers selected a particular group for special treatment: these were Lt. Kwok himself, Charles Peter, and three other Chinese who had been leaders of the resistance movement. They were all bound in a row, and a photograph was taken of them; a copy of this photograph was later found by the Allies when they recaptured Beaufort. They were then beheaded. The rest of the prisoners were shot by machine-gun fire, and their bodies dragged, pushed or kicked into the trenches. It was said at the time that there were some amongst them that were only wounded, that they lingered alive for two or three days, and that their cries could be heard in a nearby village. No one, though, dared venture near the spot. It must have been a forerunner of the massacre of the Australian prisoners of war of the Eighth Division of the Australian Army at Ranau, which was to take place a year or so later.

The hatred of the Japanese amongst the people of the West Coast was so great, however, that the news of the massacre did not deter them from planning a second revolt. The leader of this movement was no less a person than Dr Lau Lai, whom I mentioned earlier in connection with the collection of money for the cause of Chinese Relief in the Sino-Japanese War. The Japanese had learnt of his pre-war activities, probably from Sakai, and he was already a marked man. This, however, had not stopped him from raising, either in cash or promissary notes, some $250,000 to finance a further revolt. No move against him was immediately made, possibly so that he might lead them to the involvement of others. They did, however, require him to move into town, where they could more easily keep a watchful eye on his movements, and those who might visit him.

In the meantime, the Japanese turned their attention to the Islanders. They knew full well from the burning down of the Customs House and godowns that this attack had come from the sea and that only the Suloks and Binadans could have been involved. From the torture and questioning of other victims they had already put to death, their assumptions had been confirmed as correct.

The first island to receive attention was Suluk. On spotting the arrival of the Japanese, the islanders, frightened, came out of their houses to meet them. Their shock was short-lived, as the Japanese straight away shot them all by machine-gun in front of their children and women-folk. They next burnt down all their houses. Uncertain what to do with the women and children, they divided them into two parties. Leaving half of the numbers behind, they took the remaining thirty with them to the mainland. These they put into forced labour camps, but very few of them survived to tell the tale. Those who did, later related stories of their brutal treatment. The favourite pastime of the Japanese appeared to be pricking the women in the womb until they died. One has to try and imagine what their crime could have been: being married to a person who may or may not have taken an active part against the atrocities of an enemy?

Virtually the same fate awaited the inhabitants of Sapangar Island, opposite Menggatal River estuary. On Dinawan Island, where some two or three years before I had visited the islanders by canoe, paddling out of Kinarut River, and watched the children playing happily with their model boats, the Japanese tactics varied slightly. They took the men away for questioning; it is possible that they wanted to endeavour to trace under torture any possible links they may have had with Tawi Tawi, but in a few days they were returned to Dinawan Island, where they were machine-gunned in front of their women and children, whose houses were later burned to the ground.

Mantanani Island was left to the last; this island was situated much farther to the north and well out to sea. The Japanese had always suspected it had links with Tawi Tawi; their foray in that direction had ended in disaster for them. They had concluded, correctly, that one of the links towards Tawi Tawi must involve Mantanani. In February 1944, four months after the Double Tenth revolt, between twenty and thirty Japanese arrived at the island in a small flotilla of boats. They virtually surrounded the island with their boats, and those belonging to the islanders of which they assumed control. The Japanese first interrogated them, then captured them and took them back to Jesselton, but not before they had tied up the women and children, removing the gold sovereigns they wore on their *bajau*, or blouses, and killed them all by machine-gun fire. Fortunately, the Japanese officers responsible for this massacre were later identified, put on trial in Singapore in 1946, sentenced to death and duly hanged.

As for poor Dr Lai, covertly planning a second rising, his every move had been carefully watched. Whether anyone ever gave him away will never be known. By the Japanese he was considered a dangerous character: he had collected money before the war for the Chinese War Relief Fund. There is no real evidence that a harmless peace-loving old man could really be plotting a second revolt, but this was the reason given by the Japanese when they arrested him one evening at a dinner party they were giving for prominent people. The next day he, with some other Chinese merchants, was sent to Batu Tiga prison. Here he suffered extreme torture. He was hung by his arms and burned with embers of a charcoal fire. Alternately he was given the 'water treatment': he was forced to drink two buckets of water, and then stamped upon, until water burst from all orifaces. At length, after twelve days of continuous torture, night and day, when every fibre of resistance had been driven from him, he admitted complicity in the revolt. With his confession everything was disclosed and the names of many others were revealed.

The Japanese had always distrusted the poor old man, but now that they had extracted a confession, they thought up one of the most terrible of their atrocities.

They had two buffaloes brought to Batu Tiga: they tied Dr Lai's feet to one buffalo and his arms to the other, then drove the buffaloes off in opposite directions. This account was subsequently told to me by an eye-witness, and it has been confirmed recently to me by Mike Edge, my friend in Australia, who was also told the same story by another eye-witness.

After the return of the former British officers of the Chartered Company, the mortality amongst the civil occupation during the Japanese reign of terror was assessed. It was concluded that beheading, machine-gunning and torture had accounted for one thousand deaths, all of course, without trial; this was 4% of the population in the area of the revolt. Starvation and sickness had caused three thousand deaths or 12% of the population, so that out of the 25,000 persons living in the Jesselton, Tuaran and Kota Belud coastal area, 16% had perished as a result of Japanese torture and punishment. Some Co-Prosperity Sphere!

A retired North Borneo Legal Officer, Mr Maxwell Hall, to whom I have referred before, has written:

> The cruelties inflicted on the civilian population were contrary to the laws and usages of war. They were contrary to the laws and customs of war on land, which was signed at the Hague in 1907 by nearly all the nations, including Japan. It was not permissible for the enemy to work his will, altering the existing form of Government, upsetting the constitution and the laws, and ignoring the rights of the people. Reprisals are allowable as an extreme measure, but they may not be excessive.

He also comments that:

> The Japanese reaped the whirlwind. Many hundreds of Japanese officers and other ranks were subsequently brought to trial and convicted. Their punishment included death by hanging, death by shooting or imprisonment for terms extending to life. Many lived to regret they ever came to Borneo!

It had been a revolt which had had no equal in any other territory occupied by Japan. No other territory, however oppressed the people, had stood up to and challenged the oppressors. That is beyond doubt: it is a fact. Malta, for its bravery, had the George Cross awarded it to honour its people, but little recognition of the sacrifice of the people of Sabah has ever been made. A few places were given to members of the Volunteer Force at the Victory Parade in London, and the tardy award of a Defence Medal was made late in 1946, but there was little, if any, expression of thanks. Unless the bread-winners had been in Government service, the families and widows of those who died received no pension, and when destitute were treated as deserving poor. The volunteers and those of their families they left behind deserved better than that!

Although the revolt militarily had not been a success, it nevertheless produced results. The Japanese halted in their paces. The Double Tenth revolt had an effect like a stone being thrown into a quiet pond, with the ripples extending to the edge. For the first time since the beginning of the Occupation, the Japanese began to think. Two major decisions emerged, and they were clever enough to have spotted the truth. Firstly, they abandoned all attempts to coerce the Chinese and did not continue with their plans to conscript three thousand men for service in their Army. They recruited as many as they could into the Police Force, but that was not the same thing. Secondly, the Chinese and native girls henceforth remained unmolested, and girls were imported from other countries to serve the needs of the troops. These had been the flash points of Albert Kwok's timing in the start of the uprising. To this extent, then, the purpose of the revolt had succeeded.

Not only that, but the campaigns of forced labour in the pursuance of air-field construction ceased. About three thousand Javanese were brought in from the Dutch East Indies in their place. The forced labour of the local population ceased to be demanded. Privation continued and worsened as the Allied sea forces gained a stranglehold on the movement of enemy vessels over the oceans. There was another outcome which was ultimately to affect us in Kuching: the Japanese Commander for the whole of the Borneo area, General Baba, decided to move his Headquarters from Kuching to Sabah and established new Headquarters on Sapong Estate, bringing with him, naturally, all his Headquarters Staff, a considerable force, and all Army communications.

Back in Kuching, we, too, experienced this stranglehold in that supplies of food had become less and less. Instead of the two half coconut measures of rice we had had, one at midday and the other for supper during the first year and a half, and a mug of *bubor*, or rice porridge, which was our breakfast, we were down to sago, not treated sago such as one can buy in a grocer's shop in England, but raw liquid sago of a blue–purple coloration, which nourished the stomach but little. It just went straight through the body. The midday meal was just a bowl of thin *kangkong* soup, reinforced with potato which we ourselves had grown in the garden. Only at night were we able to have just a little rice, with a teaspoon of powdered salt fish, and the inevitable *kangkong*. The cooks did what they could with the meagre rations supplied, and they always tried to give a good supper on Sunday night. It was, though, an uphill struggle against odds for survival. In vain did our liaison officer and camp commandant ask for Red Cross parcels to be sent us!

The complete lack of nutrition had very telling effects on our health. Any scratch, as I have mentioned before, would turn septic. We all had beri-beri; ankles and legs became swollen out of all proportion, and the body lived on its own flesh, as we became thinner and thinner. Even the potatoes we had grown in the garden and eaten after we had cooked them in the overnight fire, we could no longer have, as the Nips had made us go to other areas, to fell another clearing of very poor rubber, and plant up tapioca.

The barter trade over the fence with the Other Ranks flourished, nevertheless, and those who had been able to bring in more shirts than others when they were captured won out! For a shirt one could trade a half *kati* of *blachan* or half a dozen eggs. Two of our fellow internees, both Americans, developed good contacts. Unfortunately, my own wardrobe was not large—the Nips who stood over me whilst I packed had been a bothering presence, and I had not foreseen the time when a shirt may have meant the different between life and death! I had nothing to trade except my tobacco ration.

It was over-the-fence trading which led to the arrest, torture and death of many of our colleagues. It had all seemed so completely innocent; nobody could have guessed that the Nips would react in the way they did. One of the soldiers who was in a working party in the town obtained a fairly out of date copy of a Malay paper in Kuching. He passed it to his contact on our side of the fence, who gave it to a Sandakan Government Officer, who obviously was a Malay scholar—none other than Stanley Hill who was berthed just opposite to the contact in the Sandakan Hut. Stanley translated it, and the 'news' it contained, which in any case was far removed from the truth and told of Japanese victories on all fronts which had never occurred, was circulated around the camp. By some means or other, caused through an incident which had arisen in the Other Ranks camp, the Nips came to hear of this and, as ever paranoiac about communication between the camps, arrested all those, one by one, whose names had been given by means of torture. The soldier involved had given the name of Webber (the partner of 'Trader Horn'), and he, in his anguish, passed on the name of Stanley. He was called to the office in the Japanese Administration block in the main square, and we never saw him again.

The 'punishment' cell was in the Guard Room, at the entrance from a public highway and leading up the main roadway into the square. The cell, made of bamboo *poreng* struts, was about the size of a two-seater settee with bamboo frame spreading over the rectangular open framework, almost like a large bird cage on its side. Hence the name given it. The victim was pushed in at the side which closed on him, and he was unable to sit up, or to lie out straight. A plate of food was allowed to be brought down by one of the older men in the camp twice daily. No spoons or forks were allowed in assisting him to eat. When he was let out, if they ever permitted him to go to the latrine, the victim was frequently beaten up, depending on the mood of the guard. They also made sure he was unable to sleep, by prodding him continuously through the night. When the term of 'imprisonment' came to an end, the 'offender' was usually unable to stand, and men from the camp had to be sent down to assist the victim to walk up the road and back to camp.

Webber occupied the cell when they took Stan away, and it may have been for that reason that they took him elsewhere. Then our patriarchal figure from Sabah was arrested: G.C. Woolley. He was one of the very first Chartered Company officers to have been appointed, and had come to Sabah in the 1880s. He was a brother of Sir Leonard Woolley, the archaeologist, and had retired in Jesselton. Geoffrey Woolley was a well-known man in his own right, and nobody knew the native tribes of Borneo better than he. He had been Resident and Commissioner of Lands and, after his retirement, elected to stay in the country he loved so much amongst the people he knew so well. To give himself an interest and to remain active he had, after he had retired, taught in All Saint's School. He was an eminent Malay scholar, and it was because he was so well versed in Arabic script that Stanley had asked him to give a hand in the translation. Or, since we all had passed our examinations in Arabic script, Stanley, without realizing any danger involved, may have just asked for his help out of kindness to give the old boy an interest. Stan was like that. Who could possibly anticipate the Nips would react in the way they did, through just reading one of their own papers!

Woolley's name must have emerged under someone's interrogation of torture, and one day he too was sent for. He too was put in the cage. In a way, the Japanese respected age, and I believe that because of his age, he was released after about a couple of weeks. People were told to go down to the guard house to collect him, because he was too weak to stand and walk up the hill on his own. He collapsed on his return, but the kitchen staff did what they could by way of giving extra rations: nobody minded!

It was the thirst for news which needed to be assuaged which brought a solution of which none of us could have dreamed. One of our older men had had a deaf-aid which had run out of batteries and was no longer of use for its purpose. This became known, and an idea was conceived which maintained our spirits and gave us the will to exist. The deaf-aid had a valve!

Other 'bits and pieces' may well have come over the wire from the Other Ranks camp and skills were in our camp aplenty. The result was a cunningly built clog, such as we all wore as footwear, and within which was built a small radio receiver utilizing the deaf-aid's valve. This clog, with its mate, was left quite openly in a place where the Nips never searched: in the dead embers of the fire under the *kuali* used for cooking rice and hidden by bricks.

The aerial was a piece of copper wire strung between the posts of the kitchen shed on which various odd pieces of kitchen towelling would always be hung to dry. It was a perfect camouflage and it was such a secret, I don't think anyone of us knew for sure who invented it and who operated it. Nobody ever spoke about it, as anyone arrested and tortured could have revealed names, and then the secret may well have been out. All we knew was that a very knowledgeable gentleman, with an amazing memory, would every Sunday afternoon when there was no work, with watch-keepers fully alerted in all directions, visit each hut in turn with the up-to-date news of how the war was progressing. Too often it was Rabaul and the Soloman Islands, and Imphal in Burma of which none of us had heard before. But gradually the news came closer and stirred our hearts beyond belief. The operators were the unsung heroes of our camp, and went only by the name of 'Aunt Aggie'.

In place of the weekly talks, which had been forbidden because we were enjoying ourselves too much, we organized ourselves into groups of six, the limit that was permitted. Most of the Government Officers had degrees or qualifications of one sort or another; if they hadn't they wouldn't have been appointed to their posts. So there was a wealth of knowledge amongst us which the Committee tried to turn to our advantage. The Assistant Resident, Brunei, for example, had a First Class Honours degree from Oxford in history, so every week he would visit a group of six at one end of a hut and give us a course on English history. We had naturally hoped he wouldn't get further than the Norman conquest, but he did bring it more up-to-date than that!

Our newly recruited accountant from Australia, Alan Quartermaine, ran a course in book-keeping, but lack of paper was a bit of a handicap in this. If we had had some paper, I may have been better at keeping accounts than I am today!

A Sarawak Government officer was proficient in Russian and regularly gave Russian classes; I was one of his pupils, but I fear I have retained little of what he taught me apart from the basics. His description of the Moscow Underground made more of an impact, and I still retain a desire to see it!

One couldn't receive without giving, and, utilizing my Oxford degree in Spanish, I put into practice my own philosophy of the way to help a beginner to comprehend a Romance language new to him. I think I had only five or six takers, but numbers didn't matter (as long as they were below six!). The main thing was that it kept the mind occupied, like all the other minor activities, and for a short time during the week took us away from the ills and evils with which we were surrounded.

More entertaining were the bridge schools which came into being. One member of our hut had been able to bring into camp a couple of packs of cards, and this school met regularly once a week.

Then there was chess. It was comparatively easy to shape chess pieces out of any bits of wood we could lay our hands on, and to dye one set a darker colour. Making a board was a bit more difficult, but pieces of black paper from book covers were possible to find, and from time to time it was black newsprint from American papers which the Nips used to let us have with the tobacco ration.

Most exciting, and passing the time more quickly than anything else, was a poker school, organized by a Brunei rubber estate manager by the name of Montgomery, or Monty for short. 'No relation to THE Monty,' he would always say! He kept the 'book' for payment after the war. We always played on Sunday afternoons because there was no outside labour, and it was a time we had free and normally undisturbed. We had two sessions, one in the afternoon and the other in the evening after we had had our 'dinner', until about 9.30 p.m. The lights were always put out by the Nips at 10 p.m. The cards were pretty dog-eared by the time 1945 had come, and one was getting to know the face of the card from its back! It was, however, strange to find how evenly divided the odds were over a longish period of time. I, in fact, won nine dollars which was paid to me, post war, as agreed, by Jock Riddell, one of the school who had lost nine dollars. The biggest loser lost only forty-five dollars as far as I recollect, so cards must fall fairly evenly on the whole.

These are recollections of the brighter side of an incarcerated life, which took our minds off gloom and despondency. The unexpected call of '*Tenku!*', at an hour we least thought about it, was always there to interrupt our lighter moments. These could happen at any time, and usually at night. If Nekata appeared himself, with a smile on his face, you knew instinctively that there would be trouble, grave trouble!

There were two particular incidents that I recall, one of which had a little humour. Tris Speedy, our Director of Lands and Survey, had arthritis of the neck joint connecting the collar bone to the spine. He brought into camp with him a neck brace; whenever his pain mounted to an unacceptable level, he could hang it from a nail in the hut rafter and, putting his head and neck into it jump off the edge of his bed, and the fall would break the growth of calcium at the top of the spine which was causing the pain. I think this was the theory of it!

He needed help to put his feet back again to the edge of the bed so that he could stand on the bed and detach himself from the neck brace. One day whilst this operation was in progress we had an unexpected *tenku*, and if anyone was in the hut they were possibly quite unaware of Tris's needs and simply did not notice that he needed assistance to free himself. The hut when we were counted was one short. That caused a Nipponese furore! Guards were sent to the hut, and, of course, entering from the door furthest from Tris himself, simply saw a body hanging and rushed back with the news. 'Someone has hanged himself!' they were obviously excitedly chattering to each other! The hut-master received expletives from the guards, which he could not understand, and at length he was taken down to view for himself. None of us had missed Tris, and we couldn't understand the reason for the excitement. As soon as the hut-master arrived, all became clear, at least to us!

The other episode concerned John Dingle and Marcus Clark, later brought down to us and whose incarceration and punishment in Jesselton had brought them close together. Some of us had concluded that the making of 'hootch' might, in the manner of *tapai*, supply the body with vitamins. I managed to get hold of a glass bottle made into a jar by cutting off the top by some more technical fellow than I. Into this I had put some potato cuttings, and from time to time some rice, if ever I felt I could spare a few grains from my ration. I also added a teaspoonful of brown sugar, topped it up with water, and waited for results. I was patient for a week or so, and then swallowed a dessert-spoonful per day. It produced a slightly sour tasting liquid, whether or not it contained any vitamins! Marcus Clark, however, with his scientific background, went one better! He started a distillery!

I was never let into the secret of how this was done, or what primitive materials he had been able to squander for its fabrication, but it remains a fact that he succeeded. I do not think it was intended to be a food supplement, but rather an excuse to celebrate an event best known to John Dingle and himself! The night of festivity certainly came, but most of us were quite unaware of it until later.

The product must have had an unexpected potency on bodies unused to any alcohol whatsoever, and the increasing hilarity of the two participants must have attracted the attention of a passing guard. He was fascinated rather than angry, and he was a 'sugar-baby', known to John and Marcus as not such a bad type. (Out in the garden one had got to know the guards a bit, especially when it rained, when they would seek shelter in the various *sulaps* we had made, and in so far as language permitted, we would try and exchange views, always with the purpose, from our point of view, of gaining some information that they might give in an unguarded moment.) They invited him to a taste. He too enjoyed the stimulating effect of alcohol! As he did not return from his patrol, the Sergeant in charge of the guard sent out another to ascertain what was happening. He similarly fell for alcohol, and all four of them seemed to be having quite a party. When that guard didn't return, the Sergeant really did begin to worry, and reported the matter to Nekata. He came down with half a dozen off-duty Nips, and then there was hell let loose. All four were hauled away! What happened to the guards we never learnt, but we didn't see them again for a long time. They must have got into bad trouble, because it could have been a well planned ploy, from the Nips' point of view. Their weapons and ammunition could have been taken from them without any difficulty, and an ugly situation could have arisen. I have a feeling that they fared worse than either John Dingle or Marcus Clark! Although they had their usual beating, they weren't detained in the guard-house more than a day or so; the Nips, for once, must have appreciated the human side of the episode.

Malnutrition and general debility, towards the end of the second and certainly in the third year, had taken its toll. The death rate, which had begun at one a week, slowly rose to two and sometimes three a week. At times a high-ranking Japanese officer would visit us. There would be an unexpected *tenku*, when we all paraded, and told how lucky we were to be in the best administered POW camp! (They forgot that technically we were internees, and not war prisoners: it simply made no difference to them.) Having said that, we were always told that Japan was winning the war, and that we would never see our countries again. We knew, of course, that they would never win, but we often wondered what their intentions were towards us had they won. I think they would have eliminated us, and I think that as the end came nearer that intention became clearer.

In the meantime, they endeavoured to go through the motions of attempting to provide medical facilities in view of the increasing death rate. One evening after work, we were all paraded, and Nekata, accompanied by the camp doctor Yamamoto and two or three orderlies, announced we were to be inoculated against dysentery, which was one of the big killers in the camp. Personally, I had never heard of an inoculation which was anti dysentery, and this was borne out later by our own doctors. However, there wasn't anything we could do about it; we couldn't become conscientious objectors! So we all had it; as far as we could tell later, it did us no harm, likewise there was no obvious beneficial result. It seemed to be a typical Japanese ploy, at one moment advising us that we had no chance of seeing our former lives, and at the next, going through the motions of being model captors!

In their campaign for better health, we were told that they intended to establish a hospital. As it was, the doctors in our camp had manned in turn a dispensary on the road between the women's camp and the main square, and a sick parade would leave every morning at ten o'clock to see the doctors, who could only dress our wounds, which simply meant bathing in water and re-tying the same bandage, and giving advice. There was no medicine of any sort available. However, I suppose just having the wound dressed by a professional was a bit of a reassurance!

The hospital turned out to be the same hut in which the morning's dispensary was held. It had been cleared out, and the doctors were given new quarters in this building by the side of the dispensary, while the rest of the hut was given over to patients who could no longer walk from the camp on the daily sick parade. The facilities and the food were no better: in fact the poor doctors, if I remember rightly, had to cook their own and their patients' food. In my own hut, Hut 5, we definitely lost out: I, in particular, because I no longer had Dr Deuntzer as my berth mate on my left-hand side. We had become good friends, and there were all sorts of little things that we did for each other. He had taught me much about medicine in a simple way; coming from a medical family on my father's side, I always had a receptive mind towards medicine, and much that the good doctor passed on to me then has stood me in good stead over the years. We also lost Dr Sternfeld from our hut. He had been a specialist in Austria and as he was a Jew, he had fled to North Borneo at the time of the Anschluss. It was Germany's loss and our gain, because he was a wonderfully patient doctor, and often I saw him sitting at night by the side of the bed of one of his patients who was irreversibly ill.

The hut emptied considerably with the loss of the bed patients and the doctors. It, too, was their loss: the patients had gained nothing, really, as far as medical treatment was concerned, and they had lost the help of their friends in beds next to them. The Nips had a 'hospital' to prove that they cared for their prisoners!

On the next, of about three, Red Cross cards we were allowed to send the whole time we were in camp, the first line of the twenty-four words we were allowed to write had to begin: 'The Japanese are treating us well and we have a well stocked hospital with doctors in attendance, tell everybody . . .' and many of us added: ' . . . especially the Marines!'

When we had arrived in the camp some years before, there was a small black and white goat running round. He was an odd little creature, and seemed to like company. More often than not, he would appear in the square at *tenku* time, as if to say: 'Count me in: I'm present!' Sometimes he would get hold of somebody's *chawat*, and chew it up; he wasn't then so popular with the person concerned! On the whole though he seemed to get by better, in terms of food, than we did. Although we had been reduced sometimes to eating fungi that grew on rubber trees, not knowing whether it would give nourishment or poison to the body, he instinctively knew what to eat and where to find it. Unfortunately, his days were numbered. Our Camp committee decided that on Christmas Day 1944, he must go in the pot. I don't think we had given him a name; if we had, he may have been more of a pet and been spared the pot. I think most of us were a bit reluctant to say we had enjoyed Christmas dinner, 1944!

By now, we were all at a very low ebb. The death rate was climbing, most noticeably in the soldiers' camp where the death toll was four or five every day. We knew because the Nips did permit a priest from our camp to go every afternoon to conduct the funeral service. Our own camp did not have a death daily, but it was an occurrence which was happening far too frequently. I think our full strength at the beginning had been something over two hundred. By now nearly half had died. Then an event occurred which struck at all of us. Selous, our interpreter, had been taken away for questioning. No one knew any reason why this should have happened. He seemed always a very quiet man, and not a great mixer. The following day at *tenku*, we were told to collect his body from the guard house. He had committed suicide. He must have been let out of the cage to visit the toilet, taken a bottle of water with him, smashed it, and with the broken glass cut the veins of both his wrists. He had fainted and must have bled to death without pain. None of us could think of any reason why he should have been questioned. It was pure speculation that the Nips may have been on to the source of all our hopes, 'Aunt Aggie', and, rather than give the show away, he took his own life. I don't think anyone knew the reason or could guess it. It could only have been to prevent himself revealing information which would have involved others.

Very occasionally, there was a little light to brighten the gloom. The soldiers in their camp had organized a concert party. In the barrack square there was a platform and the Camp Commandant, in a gracious act of generosity, did permit the concert party to perform on the stage once in a while, and we would then be permitted to go out of the camp to the square and sit in a space allocated to us, heavily guarded by extra soldiers who had been brought in from elsewhere. Mingling, obviously, was not allowed, and guards paced the perimeters of our allocated sitting space. It was quite amusing to see some of the Tommies dressed in 'drag'! There couldn't be a comedy without a woman! Somehow, they managed to form a sort of band with quaint, home-made banjos and drums. They had developed a theme song, the words of which I still seem to remember: 'When we're sailing down the river to the sea, we'll be free!' All joining in and singing the chorus, at least, buoyed up our hopes!

But our greatest uplift occurred on 26 March 1945 when a distant roar was heard in the skies, getting closer, ever closer. The noise was unmistakable; it could only mean one thing, that Allied planes were approaching. Then the Nips gave the show away by running madly all over the place, twirling rattles in their hands, and in the distance, coming obviously from Kuching, a siren sounded. We were driven hurriedly into our huts, where we strained our necks out of the windows, and there they were: five gleaming silvery Flying Fortresses. We had not been forgotten! Mike relates at this late date that they bombed Kuching airstrip, but I have no recollection of bombs having been dropped. The impression I retain was that they were on a reconnaissance mission, since they seemed to fly in a direct line. We were coming into the picture at last! That was the important thing. There was much chattering in the supper queue that night.

The incident must have made an impression on the Nips, because the very next day, we were made to dig trenches in which we had to shelter in any future air-raids. There were more raids, the next within a couple of weeks, and by then they did mean business. The second and subsequent raids were by smaller, light-bomber type of aircraft. That indicated they were operating from a shorter distance than hitherto, and that gave us great hope.

There were other indications too, nearer at hand and to our detriment. The rations became less and less. It is possible that the people of Kuching had taken to the jungle in fear, and that there was little food in the market place. Then the power supply began to fail, presumably for lack of fuel. So when the sun had set, that was it for the night. Lack of fuel also meant that the water pumps could no longer operate, and we had no water. This was a very serious matter for us with dysentery so rife everywhere. Fortunately, near our original gardens there were some

Chinese fish-ponds. They were terribly weedy and overgrown, but we were taken there for the purposes of washing the body, and we were able to bring back sufficient water, dank brown water, which enabled us to cook and drink boiled tea, coloured more by the water itself than the tea it contained! Suddenly we realized how lucky we had been in the past to have been housed in a camp built by the British for the Indian Army.

As the weeks went by, the raids became more frequent. That they had spotted the camp we were in no doubt at all. On many occasions, they flew right over and did a victory roll on their way back. Twin fuselage planes, new to us, were being used now, and it seemed clear that they were operating from a base not too far away. Hopes grew!

The Nips were obviously getting jittery. We were, of course, unaware of what they heard and what our guards had been told. Working in the garden or planting *ubi kayu* came to a halt. We were allowed to go out first thing to collect sweet potato leaves, and some potatoes if they were ready to lift, and then we were kept in. Obviously, the Nips didn't want us to be spotted by any cameras that there might be in the planes. The Nip jitteriness spread through all the guards. Some became ugly tempered; others usually of a more genial disposition became fractious, and one never knew which way they would react.

It was at about this time that we were all called up to Nekata's office, one by one. They took several days about this. When it became my turn, I was asked what work I did in camp, and told them that I carried *benjo*. Instead of putting them off, as I had hoped it would, there was immediately a lot of scribbling taking place. I noticed, too, that the doctor, Yamamoto, was present at the meeting which impressed me as being a bit odd. And there was a bit of laughter amongst themselves, and that alone was always sinister. If a Nip had a smile on his face, there was bound to be trouble in the offing!

I didn't like it at all. I recalled the frequent Japanese remark that 'you will never see your country again!' I felt sure that something was afoot and, that evening, I retrieved my compass from where I had buried it; they no longer seemed to be interested in what we possessed, but rather in our physical fitness. In my own mind, I felt that they were going to move us somewhere, and that 'somewhere' was not going to be better than where we were now.

We learnt later that the Japanese plan was that five hundred of the fittest POWs, internees and probably officers were, on 17 August, to be marched into the Interior beyond Kuching, to be held in a camp that had already been mined, ready to be blown up as soon as the Australian forces arrived. Those remaining were due to be shot.

A few anxious days passed; I knew something was afoot, and I sensed that people in the camp knew something that others did not. We pressed our hut-master for information, but he was like a clam, until finally we were told that 'Aunt Aggie' had a special message. 'She' had gone to ground of late, and we judged that the news might be too 'hot' for us to be told generally. But we felt some people in the camp were in the know! There was a feeling which one could sense. The air incursions were now so frequent that something was due to break: the Allies must be very close by.

The message came to us in the greatest of secrecy. Our own men, acting as guards, were posted everywhere to spot any prowling Nipponese soldiers. Our 'newsman' with his great memory repeated it almost word for word in every hut. An 'atom' bomb had been dropped by the Americans on Hiroshima and Nagasaki, and the Emperor had called on his forces to stop fighting. The Pacific war was over! The pilot and crew of *Enona Gay* had executed their mission with accuracy!

We were instructed that for our own safety, above all, we should keep calm and not breathe a word! We did not know whether the Japanese themselves had learnt any news. We tried to act normally, but life was very difficult indeed until, finally, about two days later, all prisoners, officers and internees were called at the same time to assemble at Colonel Suja's office at the top of the hill. It was a long, hot climb, and we wondered what we would be told when we reached there. All of us were allowed to mingle, an occurrence which had never happened before! Tragedy struck one poor fellow, just ahead of me. His clogged foot must have stumbled on a stone; he put his arm up to catch his fall and held on to a wire stanchion supporting an electric standard. We had had a shower just before, the wire was wet and it must have been live: the soldier was electrocuted immediately—and died. This was a grim reminder that all was not over yet.

When we had arrived outside the Major's office, he was told by one of his henchmen that we had all come. He came out on to the verandah, and said we could all sit. Such an act of clemency had never occurred before! Then, speaking through an interpreter, he told us that the Americans had acted unfairly, and had dropped atom bombs on Hiroshima and Nagasaki, and that the Emperor had called upon the Japanese forces to cease fighting. Then he added: 'The Japanese Army is not defeated; it will never surrender. But the position of prisoners and internees is not certain. You must be patient, and wait and see.' That is all we were told. But later that day, we were told to send men to collect Red Cross parcels! They had had them all this time and had never let us have any. So this was a strong indication of how the wind was going to blow.

The next day we were not sent out to work, and at midday a big Australian transport plane flew fairly low over the Camp. It circled and two men parachuted from it and landed in the square. They carried on their back transmitting equipment. They were two members of the Australian Army Signal Corps. It was over; we were free! At the same time Catalina seaplanes of the Australian Air Force landed on Kuching River. We did not know at the time, but this plane had brought Australian Army officers with plenipotentiary powers and had met in Kuching with the Japanese Commanding Officer of the West Borneo Region, who signed the document of surrender.

With the Red Cross parcels came rice which the Nips had had in store all along. There was one parcel amongst every two people: Spam, something we had never heard of before, chocolate, cocoa, milk powder and even I believe a can of butter. I remember letting Gus Youngberg have one of my tins: I can't remember what it was. It may have given him some contentment in his last few hours of life, for he died very shortly afterwards.

Then Australian Air Force transport planes parachuted food supplies into the camp: fresh baked bread, Australian apples, cans of meat and powdered dried egg, food which we had never seen for years: some never before! One very young boy who had not been much older than a toddler when war had broken out, looking at a loaf of bread for the first time, asked his mother: 'What do we do with this, Mummy, do we have to peel it?'

Sometimes, in the midst of happiness, tragedy strikes. One day after the morning's bread delivery by parachute, another transport plane followed with bundles of clothing: without parachutes. At the time I was just leaving the shelter of the kitchen to return to my hut, when I spotted these bales hurtling to the ground. 'Look out!' I yelled to everyone around. Some others had spotted them and took cover: I took immediate shelter, holding myself tightly to the trunk of a rubber tree, but a fellow I knew well, a member of my Spanish class, was unlucky. He had his neck struck off as if severed with a sword. What a tragedy to have happened when liberation was just a few days away!

Almost the same thing, but without tragic results, occurred in the 'hospital' whither Tris Speedy had been moved just six months before. He had just returned to his bed from getting up and looking out of the window up at the transport planes, and where he had been standing a bale hurtled through the roof, and went straight through the floor boards! Knowing the dry humour of Tris, he must have had some tale to tell to his friends in New Zealand when he reached his home town!

Then they arrived! A staff car led the way flying the Australian flag on its bonnet. It was followed by truckloads of Australian soldiers. The message went round for everybody to assemble in the square. How wonderful it was to see so many bush hats, and tanned healthy six-footers smiling at us. Brigadier Eastick with his aides climbed on to the camp platform and said:

'It's been a long fight, chaps! It's taken a long time to get here, but we've had you under observation for the last few weeks and months. The moment we spotted that the Nips were about to move you, we'd have done a parachute attack and surrounded you! Hospital ships are on their way, and we'll soon have you all up to Labuan, where a field hospital is being established to receive you. Everything you will need is coming from Australia!' And then, concluding his speech, he added: 'A special War Crimes Investigation Unit will be here shortly, and we shall be asking you to give evidence to them; we know what these Nips have been like, and we'll make them pay for it!'

The cheers before and after his speech must have been heard in Kuching! They were certainly heard in the camp hospital, for in the excitement, our District Officer in Tawau, B.R. Coles-Adams, expired in his own personal happiness at the prospect of freedom. His was the last death which took place at Batu Lintang, but tragedy had struck thrice at the moment of our greatest happiness.

Then a medical team arrival with all the medicine we could possibly need. When they took over the Japanese medical stores, they found a quantity of medicine which we had desperately needed but which had purposely been withheld; even basic essentials like bandages and iodine had been in their cupboards. The Australian medical team did a wonderful job. They regarded us all as patients, and their main aim, apart from immediate first aid, was to divide us nominally into two groups: stretcher cases and walking patients. I was, fortunately amongst the latter.

Australian Army engineers quickly brought in essential POL supplies, and very soon the water and electricity services were restored. Fortunately, we weren't destined to appreciate them much longer at Batu Lintang! The Australian Hospital Ship *Wanganella* was soon to arrive at the mouth of Kuching River. We were told that it was on its way, and almost the next day we learnt that arrangements were being made for us to board it that afternoon. Relief in all its forms could not have been organized quicker! Now, fifty or so years on, I still admire and thank the excellent organization of the Australian Army. Their promptness, readiness and willingness in all things at all times will always remain worthy of every possible admiration and gratitude.

The camp song, 'When we're sailing down the river to the sea, we'll be free!' was coming true. When we reached the mouth of the river, there, lying at anchor, was the white painted hospital ship, glowing in the evening sun, with a large Red Cross standing out on its hull! I think, without any doubt whatsoever, the moment I stepped aboard that ship was the happiest moment in my life that I can ever remember!

We heard later that on the evidence obtained from the Officers' and Other Ranks' camps, as well as the evidence we were able to supply, Lt. Nekata and the failed dentist Yamamoto, posing as a doctor, were duly hanged. There are varying tales concerning Major Suja: that he committed *hara kiri* with a table-knife whilst on the plane taking him to Labuan; or that he died similarly in Labuan and that 'he took twenty minutes over the job, with the aid of his batman'! He avoided being brought to trial, where undoubtedly he would have been sentenced to death.

Under the Australian Flag

If ever on this earth one could meet angels from heaven, without any doubt whatsoever we met them when we came under the care of the nurses of the Australian Army! It is trite merely to record that they gave us every care and attention: they were wonderful! Nothing was ever too much trouble. As walking patients we were the last to come aboard. Entering the hull of the ship from the brightness outside, we could see row on row of white-clad uniformed nurses waiting to receive us. Each nurse took four of us, and led us on to the promenade deck, canvassed in on the seaward side, but equipped with four rows of built-in swinging cot-beds. As far as I can remember there was an aisle in the middle which provided the service access to the two cots on either side. A pair of pyjamas was laid out on every cot. The nurse looking after the four of us who had come on board together showed us our lockers in which we could keep our things, then asked us to get into our pyjamas ready for supper which would be served very shortly.

Very soon we felt the vibration of the ship's engines, and a warm gentle breeze floated through the deck space. We were away! In less than no time, nurses were again with us, handing us cups of hot chicken soup. Then we were given some lightly boiled fish and sauce with some mashed potato; the nurses insisted on helping us to eat, virtually spoon-feeding us. They said we would be on a strict invalid diet as our stomachs, used to being starved of any nutrition, would react adversely if we had too much rich and fatty food. I could accept the logic of that. A little custard and banana followed, and we were promised a hot milky drink later on. Over the loudspeaker system they played quiet melodious music: I remember one piece they played. It was 'Lilli Marlene', which I believe was a German marching song in origin!

After supper, the Matron and the doctor spoke to each one of us telling us, in general, that medical facilities were available twenty-four hours out of twenty-four, and the procedure we should follow if we felt we needed attendance. In two days' sailing we would be in Labuan where a field hospital had been established ready for our reception. Shortly afterwards all lights were extinguished, and we rapidly fell asleep.

When we awoke to the sound of Reveille being played through the speaker system, it seemed all a dream; it was so unbelievable! I for one had slept the sleep of the just, a deep restful sleep in the knowledge that we no longer would be woken up by the cries of '*Tenku*'! We were at peace! We were still treated like patients in hospital, and I was content to let it be that way. The next day, possibly in the knowledge that it would be our last full day on board, renewed strength and curiosity made me wander a little through the ship, and below the main deck I peeped into the wards where the sick were being cared for. These were our very ill colleagues and mostly British Army Other Ranks, who had really had a bad time, and were in a worse condition than ourselves. But they were being cared for now all right. Everywhere nurses and doctors were busy. They were professionals, dedicated to the job they had on hand.

Dawn after the second day at sea brought us to our destination, Labuan. We heard the engines stop, and the short blasts of hooters as tugs busily nudged us alongside a freighter, a Liberty boat, we were told later. This time, it was the turn of the walking patients to disembark first. We grabbed our gear and, saying a big thank-you to any of the nearby nursing staff, walked to the disembarkation point where a gangway led us to a new kind of boat, a DUKW, which I believe was an acronym for 'Dual Utility Craft Water'. We thought it was just a landing barge, and were amazed to find that it didn't head for a jetty, but landed straight on to the beach and proceeded up an unfamiliar main road, which we noticed was named Mountbatten Highway. Sign-posts indicating smaller by-roads, all in Military terms and meaningless to most of us, pointed to the HQ of this or that Group, and one could see a bevy of well camouflaged tents in scrub terrain. We climbed over the main ridge of the island, skirting a vast air-strip with planes continually taking off and landing, with others parked here and there under fibre netting. Finally, we emerged on to the northern casuarina-clad coast, and drove about a mile along a sandy track to a vast encampment of marquees. This was the field hospital, and our immediate destination!

It was like the arrival aboard the *Wanganella* all over again! There was little point in trying to keep close to one's friends and associates. As we arrived so we were herded into a big marquee, each named A Ward, B Ward and so on. Basically, most of us ex-internees managed to keep together, but no longer in the groups of huts to which we had so long been accustomed. It took a while to accustom oneself to the geography of the encampment. It had everything. In one tent there was a Post Office adjacent to a writing tent, with tables and chairs and stationery. There was another tent used as a mess, with more comfortable chairs, and lashings of reading material: Aussie newspapers and magazines, which introduced us to another world. New expressions, new vocabulary: it was like being born again a few years hence. We ourselves acquired a new name; we became RAPWI standing for Repatriated Allied Prisoners of War and Internees. Every morning we received the Ninth Division's newspapers called *Platypus*, containing mainly Australian news, but also news from Europe as well as a page of local events in the Division's sphere of activity on Labuan itself and from Sabah which it had regained some time before.

The Japanese had put up very strong resistance in Sabah and it had been the scene of some ferocious fighting.* Naturally, we were all keen to have news about

* The last VC of the Second World War was won in action at Beaufort by Pte. Starcevich, a farmer of Western Australia in peace-time.

events in our own locality. I was not to be kept in doubt for long, as I had a surprise visit in a day or two from two very good friends who had been very close to me at the time of the Nip invasion: my house-boy and cook Ituk, and Native Chief Oman of Benoni. Evidently the Aussie Army ran a service with an LCM (Landing Craft Military), from Beaufort, down the Padas River and across Weston Bay to Labuan. They had learnt that former Chartered Company officers had been brought up to Labuan, and had taken the LCM service in the hope of finding me. I was much touched at the pleasure of seeing them again and by their thought in remembering me and making the effort to journey so far, particularly so in Ituk's case as he was never really happy away from Murut country. Such loyalty and devotion from the people of Sabah! I learnt much from them about the devastation that had taken place in Sabah. All either would say was that everything was *habis*, a word in Malay meaning quite clearly: 'Finished, devastated, ruined!' And so it was. All enquiries led to one conclusion: everything had been flattened; not a town, not a building was left standing! I learnt, too, sadly, of many local friends who had been killed. Ituk and the Native Chief and their families, however, had survived; I had nothing I could give them in return for their kindness in coming to see me, only a promise that I would be back, whenever the Government so decreed.

In the meantime, we were all being examined by Medical Officers, weighed and photographed. All personal details were recorded on a medical record, which I think followed us whilst we were in Australian hands.

Dick Evans and Colonel Adams, having established their credentials with the Army Chiefs, were flown in a light plane to Keningau, landing on an airstrip constructed by the enemy. Their intention had been to endeavour to trace the whereabouts of Stanley Hill, R.S. Abbott of our own Service, and others whose whereabouts could no longer be traced. They returned without any good news. We shall never know the extent of the torture and suffering endured by Stanley, Abbott, Webber and others, including, I believe Dr Stookes, Sandakan's pre-war 'flying doctor' who serviced Estates and lumber camps of the East Coast and who had hidden in the upper reaches of the Labuk River on the arrival of the enemy.

The headquarters of the Japanese occupying forces had, after the Double Tenth uprising, been moved from Kuching to Sapong Estate, above the Tenom Gorge. Because of this, our fellow colleagues who had had the misfortune to have been arrested were moved from Kuching to the Japanese headquarters at Sapong for a so-called trial. Whether such trial was ever held and any sentence ever passed we shall never know. The Japanese Army may have kept some records but these were undoubtedly destroyed in Sabah, and it is very much doubted if any copy, if such were their practice, ever reached Tokyo.

Some natives had told Dick Evans that Stanley had died of dysentery and malaria, others that all the Europeans brought to the Interior had been shot. We shall now never know the true circumstances, but we can conclude that their suffering was extreme, and out of all proportion to their offence. It will be remembered that in Stanley's case, it was merely the translation of a Japanese newspaper written in Malay that attributed to his arrest.

Above: Sandakan before the War.

Below: Sandakan after the Allied bombing.

News of the mainland gradually filtered through to us. We learnt that after the recapture of Labuan, the Australian Ninth Division turned their attention to the mainland, landing in force on Kimanis Bay in June 1945 and, having established their bridgehead, advanced north and south, mainly along the railway track, which was the easiest means of communication.

Prior to the invasion, a certain amount of confusion and destruction had been caused by parachuting British Military Intelligence Officers into the area with the object of gathering information as to the disposition of the enemy forces, and stimulating the local population into co-operation with the Allies shortly due to make their attack on the mainland. One such officer was a Chartered Company man who had been on leave at the time war began, and who was seconded to the Australian Army when the reoccupation of Sabah was being planned. Whether or not he inspired Native Chief Mohammed Yassin to perpetrate one of the most brilliant coups of the last days of the occupation, I do not know, but this true account of the actions of a very brave man must never be forgotten. Patterned no doubt on the Japanese style of inviting the top men to a *makan besar* and then arresting them when they were guests, Mohammed Yassin, at a very appropriate moment when the tide was turning against the Japanese, invited all the local top brass to a *makan besar* at his house for curry. They all duly arrived, and as they came to mount the steps of their host's house Mohammed Yassin greeted them pleasantly, saying as he did so that it was not the local custom to bring swords and firearms into a host's house, and would they mind leaving them outside? Obligingly, not willing to upset one of the few men who had offered them hospitality, they did so. The women of the house brought in succulent curry and rice, which seemingly they much enjoyed. Just as well they enjoyed it, since it was to be their last meal! At a given sign, Mohammed Yassin and his hencemen drew their *parangs* and killed them all.

Another action which was to be of considerable embarrassment to the Japanese was carried out with the assistance of a submarine. By this time, the Allies were well in command of the South China Sea, and submarines now freely entered the shallow and rather treacherous waters. Major Chester, whom I had met several years previously when in hospital, was a Special Operations officer and was air-lifted from Australia to an advanced submarine base. He led a party of three who were landed from a submarine at the mouth of the Papar River and at low tide went up the river to Papar railway bridge and fixed timed explosive charges on the main supports of the bridge. He and his party were well away and out at sea again by the time the charges went off with immense success, completely destroying Japanese lines of communication.*

All these activities did not go unnoticed by the natives of Sabah. Their own deprivations resulting from the demands of the Japanese on their own resources had

* This is local legend although Australian Army records indicate it was bombed by Australian Air Force planes.

not endeared them to the local population, and especially not amongst the traditionally warlike nature of the Muruts under whose influence Japanese domination had now fallen. This had resulted from General Baba's transfer of his headquarters to Sapong, itself situated in Murut country, not far from Tomani, once a Government station before Pensiangan was established.

A Murut ringleader in opposition to the Japanese was Dualis, a retired Chief Inspector of the Armed Constabulary. He became a worthy successor to the participants of the Double Tenth uprising. His ancestral head-hunting instincts fitted well into jungle guerrilla tactics. He interrupted lines of Japanese communications and attacked their reconnaissance parties, not leaving one alive to report back to Headquarters.

The excitement of the battle and the chase reawakened the alertness and vitality of the Muruts, completely reviving their warlike motivations. Their new energies were a tonic to them! Japanese dumps, patrols and stores were being attacked all over the West Coast and Interior on an ever-increasing scale from 1944 onwards until the end of the war. When the end did come, the Muruts did not learn about it, but they did notice that the Japanese were falling back from Pensiangan, and they also noted an ever-increasing number of Allied planes passing over them. This seemed to them to be their opportunity!

Whilst we were all in the Australian Field Hospital at Labuan, the Japanese were following out instructions and withdrawing from Pensiangan to surrender to the Australians. The Muruts were not aware of the surrender; they noticed only the withdrawal. The Muruts were masters of the route extending some two hundred miles from Pensiangan to the railway halts in the Tenom Gorge at Saliwangan and Halogilat, where, getting into the train at Tenom, I had encountered the first Muruts I had ever seen, when I undertook my first journey up the Gorge, with Marcus Clark shooting at crocodiles! Now, five years later, the same Muruts were harassing the retreating Japanese; their dead and dying were littered along the whole route they had taken. When they reached the point arranged for their surrender, the survivors were suffering from wounds, exhaustion and all forms of tropical disease. It was the 'death march' for the Japanese. Possibly a just retribution.

We were between two or three weeks in the field hospital in Labuan. Rumours were rife. The most prominent was that we would all be shipped down to Australia for final recuperation. With the approach of winter in Europe, one felt that Australia as a destination was an easier option. Mike chose that option and was flown down to Sydney. I had had no news of my parents for all the time we had been in Kuching, and I felt a duty to them to return to England. My father had been in Tanganyika when I had last heard from him, but a detour towards East Africa seemed impossible, so I elected to return with the mob to UK.

In due course we were told that we would be travelling on the Australian hospital ship: *Morotoi*, a sister ship to the *Wanganella*; both had been employed, I believe, pre-Pacific War, on the Australia–New Zealand route. The day soon arrived when we were told that we would be embarking. This time, it was a little different. There were no DUKWS to take us alongisde; we were fitter people, although still very much underweight. Possibly with a little sadness, we left the field hospital which had been established for us and, moving by conventional Army transport, were taken down to the wharf, where the *Morotoi* lay alongside. Again, as walking cases, I and those with me were allocated cot bunks on the main deck, and the same evening we set sail for Singapore. In a way, we were all sad to see the summit of Kinabalu, all aglow with the evening sunset, disappear into the twilight. We all felt, I think, that we wanted to get back and carry on where we had left off.

The *Morotoi* was organized in the same very efficient manner of the *Wanganella*. Nurses brought along our food, but by this time there was no need for them to tarry to help us to eat! The food was excellent, still invalid dishes which suited us well, but one could not have been treated better. I emphasize this as the Australians were in the midst of a bitter campaign, with the enemy making last ditch stands everywhere, when the war had come, fortunately for us, to its abrupt end. Yet in a matter of a few short weeks, they had liberated the Batu Lintang Camp, had given us first class care and attention, moved us all the way to Labuan where they had set up and administered a field hospital for us, kept us there for two or three weeks whilst we regained some of our strength, and then taken us down again to Singapore.

On arrival, we had to wait in the roads for several days, because there was no vacant berth to receive us. It was a bit warm, otherwise everything was satisfactory. Then one morning, we heard the engines start up, and we started to move in the direction of the harbour. Although this does not enter the story of Sabah, it is not out of place to mention briefly how we fared in Singapore, and the experience we suffered after leaving Australian care.

In retrospect, one must bear in mind that the British forces had only recently occupied Singapore themselves, and were not as well organized on the ground, possibly, as the Australians were who operated from a forward but established base. Nevertheless there were several notable differences which are engraved deep in my memory. When we eventually landed, I feel certain that the mode of transport from the docks to our temporary accommodation was in the back of Army trucks, just as the Japanese had moved us when we arrived in Kuching. And our accommodation was in Meyer Flats, very close to the Sea View Hotel, but on concrete floors, similar to that allocated to us at Batu Tiga stables at the commencement of internment. The Sea View Hotel, however, was allocated to Army officers, also ex-POWs from Kuching, where they were housed two men to a room and were served food in the Hotel's elegant restaurant. We, on the other hand, were dished out virtually uneatable food, prepared by Army personnel: possibly all right for privates who hadn't gone through hell for three and a half years, but not for sick stomachs just emerging from a state of starvation and deprivation.

I remembered I had an account with the Chartered Bank in Singapore, and possibly had a chance of getting some money. The next day I and one or two others went into Singapore, and took the opportunity of calling at the Chartered Bank. They were amazingly wonderful! Handwritten ledgers of all the pre-war accounts they had had in Singapore had been hidden at the time of the Japanese invasion; they had survived the occupation, and were readily available for depositers like myself wishing to draw money! I drew a sum sufficient to enable me to lend some to friends in a less fortunate position, and we all then tried to enjoy ourselves a bit on our first day of freedom in a city! We found a place where they had some beer, and tasted our first alcohol for the best part of four years. We also found open some restaurants where they served far better food than that being offered to us in the Meyer Flats!

Fortunately, we were not long in Singapore. Priority naturally had been given to those who had been imprisoned in Changi Prison in Singapore, and to any Army personnel there may have been on the Island, but a sizeable number of us were shipped out on what I have always described as the 'hell-ship, M.V. *Celicia*'. The ship may have been all right, and it did get us back to UK, but she was, I believe, a cargo ship converted to a trooper, or else just built as a trooper. We were housed in the forward hatch, differing from the Japanese collier which had taken us from Jesselton to Kuching in that there were bunks six deep, but the deck space we were allocated was confined to the forward hatch. If we went up the forward companionway we were confronted with a notice reading: 'Deck Space Confined to Officers Only. KEEP OUT!'

I had grabbed a bunk, one below the top, and it was a bit of a strain getting in or out of it. But the worst aspect was food. To obtain anything, one had to join a queue for an hour, and descend into the bowels of the ship, to a hot sweaty mess deck where a line of 'chefs' slopped out an apology for food! It was absolutely uneatable: just slops and stewed canned vegetables. The steamed rice we had had on our Japanese collier was infinitely more wholesome! Fortunately, they did hand out rolls, and an apple or orange, and this is all I could eat for the whole voyage.

Fortunately, we put in at Colombo, and that, having been an established base, was well organized. We were kitted out with some different clothing from Australian Army uniforms, given a good meal ashore and told we would be picking up some winter clothing in Suez. The British ladies of Colombo went out of their way to do everything they could to help us. We even had facilities to write letters home which would be sent free of charge. We were certainly made welcome here!

It was nice to be out of Australian Army uniform, and we felt more at ease in shorts and open neck shirts, particularly in the hell-hole of accommodation allotted to us. It was just as hot if we went on the deck of the forward hatch. There, in addition to the exposure of a hot tropical sun at sea, we experienced the insult of Army officers, some of whom had been in the Officers' Camp at Kuching, but who, because they had no forced labour, were in much better shape than ourselves, looking down on us from the shelter of the promenade deck. We felt they were very smug and wondered what made them feel so superior! Over the years, I well believe time changes attitudes, and I am quite prepared to accept that the officer of the modern Army is quite a different type of man.

Eventually, we were sailing up the Red Sea, fortunately not at the height of summer but at the beginning of October, when there was a fresh breeze making the forward hatch a little more bearable. On arrival at Suez, where we went alongside Army installations, we were informed that we should go along to a certain store to obtain winter clothing. Our first issue was a kit-bag which was sensible enough. Next was a pair of Army boots, and a pair of stockings. When it came to trousers and shirts, the 'Tommies' behind the counter started asking for sizes, but none of us knew our present girths even if we remembered what we once were! So we were given anything. When it came to pyjamas, James Cooke, who was next to me, spotted a white pair which he preferred to the stripes most of us were receiving. Back at the ship, we were anxious to get into warmer clothing, because, as the sun went down, it was quickly becoming colder: something none of us had felt for six years at least! That evening we were all keen to get into something warmer before bedding down for the night. James Cooke, who still wore his bright red beard from Kuching days, came to put on his warm pyjamas and found he had drawn a white night-shirt! He had to put it on, and a lad with a sense of humour near me shouted out: 'Jesus Christ!'

Once through the Suez Canal, the weather took on a nasty wintry turn. I ventured out on the well-deck once or twice, glad to put on the warm woollen scarf given me at Suez, on which a label had been sewn: 'A Present from the Ladies of Wyoming, USA'. I was grateful to them and wore it for many a long day.

As we approached the Channel, we were anxious to know our port of arrival. We had hoped it would be London, as a group of us were planning a night together in the West End. Our hopes were dashed when we learnt it was to be Liverpool—of all places, as far as I was concerned! It might just as well have been Glasgow.

It was a very cold autumn dawn when we did arrive. Everything looked very bleak and battered and not at all welcoming. We were among the first of the batch of returned POWs and Liverpool must have experienced a sense of exultation. I believe the Lord Mayor had come to meet the boat, certainly there was a band playing on the quayside: that, I quite well remember. As soon as we were alongside, a whole host of people came aboard, and for the first time during the whole voyage we were allowed on the promenade deck and given access to the public rooms previously reserved for the exclusive use of officers. In the saloon a whole row of officials were seated at tables. As I went up the companion-way, a Naval Officer with lashings of gold braid accosted me and asked: 'Have you seen Noel Turner, anywhere?'

'Yes,' I replied, 'He's down there!' indicating the forward hatch. 'Says his father's an Admiral!'

I received the reply: 'That would be my son, and I am an Admiral!'

Having been put in my place, I continued on my way as we had been bidden to the main saloon. Here, a half dozen or so officials were seated at various tables. Queues were starting to form so inevitably I joined in. When it came my turn, I had to give my name and intended address in UK, then I was given a Royal Message from His Majesty the King welcoming us all back, a ration book, a £5 Victory Bond (tax free!), clothing coupons and a third class rail ticket to the nearest station to our address.

When I finally arrived back in Cornwall, I found that my father had retired from Tanganyika, and that in response to his enquiries, he had been advised by the Chartered Company that they had received a communication saying that I was safe and well. Money was, of course, an immediate necessity, so I wrote to the Secretary of the Chartered Company advising them of my return. They gave me an advance of back salary and a 'welcome back' message, with a sting in it, indicating that under changed circumstances there would be no guarantee of future employment.

Anyhow, the immediate task was to get fit again! Various medical checks revealed a suspected duodenal ulcer. I'm sure it had been the lack of any good food after we had left Australian hands that had caused this. Thorough medical examinations and X-rays by the Australian Army health officials had revealed nothing. If there had been, they would have discovered any symptoms and taken remedial action. As it was, recuperation in the UK took longer than I had hoped. There was one amusing incident which I still recall, showing how out of touch we had become with life in the UK. I was spending some of my clothing coupons in an effort to find something which fitted a bit better than the Suez hand-outs, when I saw a queue, enquired what it was for and was informed 'chocolate'. Not having had any for six years or so, I fancied some and joined in the queue. When it did come to my turn at last, I proffered my ration book and was asked: 'Where's your green book?' I then learnt that children had green books, and that the chocolate was only for them!

Good Cornish food and a healthy climate ensured that my health slowly recovered, and the day eventually came when I was passed fit to return to duty. If I recall correctly, the Chartered Company had advised me that I would be assigned to the British Military Administration of the territory, and that my passage would be booked by the Crown Agents. Eventually I was advised that 'standee' accommodation would be available on a trooper the name of which I have forgotten, and soon the air of the Far East was in my nostrils again!

The description of the accommodation had worried me a bit, with the recollections of the *Celicia* still in my mind. However, it turned out to be a converted deck house, with bunks only four deep, and there was a dining saloon in which we were adequately served British war-time food. However, there was a canteen in which we could buy in reasonable quantity canned food not easily available in the UK. Having heard on the grapevine that supplies were extremely difficult and scarce in Sabah, which was quite understandable, I bought a couple of cases of canned food which were to serve me in good stead. On arrival in Singapore, the only dock labour available was Japanese prisoners of war: a lot better fed, and in much better condition than we had been kept. The groceries in wooden boxes must have been quite a weight to carry, but the Jap did it manfully, without the semblance of a complaint and stood to attention, saluting smartly, when his task had been completed.

I soon learnt from our agents that the Straits Steamship Company was not yet operating a passenger service to the Borneo ports, only an occasional cargo service, and that the RAF were operating a weekly Sunderland flying boat service for passengers. I left all my gear, therefore, with the agents, and early the next morning I found myself being driven northward across Singapore Island to Seletar RAF base. We saw the plane being prepared by the crew and what was obviously mail being loaded into its hull. The only baggage we could take was what we could carry with us. Shortly we were asked to go down the pier to the launch which took us to the aircraft. We all sat along the sides of the aircraft, facing each other. There was a dreadful cacophony as the four engines started up, and we began splashing through the water until we were airborne.

I had not before travelled in a service aircraft, but have done so subsequently on several occasions. Passengers on civil aircraft these days travel in a comfort undreamt of in military aircraft. Flying in a Sunderland was certainly an experience! I noticed pink oil dripping from the overhead control wires of the wing and tail flaps on to the tailored dress of the lady sitting on the seat in front of me; it was also dripping on to my suit! Talking was out of the question, the level of the engine noise was so great!

We dropped in first at Kuching. There must have been a sufficient lengthy straight stretch to enable them to land and take off. Brigadier Eastick had arrived in a Catalina flying-boat, a much smaller version than a Sunderland, I believe. However, we made it! Was it hot there, waiting for a launch to come alongside and pick up the mail and drop the passengers! I felt like a frazzled sardine! There was a similar short stop at Labuan, and then we were off to Jesselton. It was late afternoon by the time we splashed down and Kinabalu was just peeping out of the clouds in the evening sunlight. How wonderful it was to be back again!

When the launch bringing us ashore tied up at the patched up wharf, Dick Evans was there to meet me. He had a former Australian Army staff car to drive us to his temporary split bamboo structure on the site of his old house which had been destroyed in the course of the recapture of the territory. Of Jesselton town itself, there was almost nothing left. The old Post Office and Treasury building, built of permanent materials, was still standing and in operation. The block of stone construction in the Lands and Survey Department was similarly still standing, but the land records, housed in a concrete block which it had been destined to protect, had been destroyed. Only the stone piers of the Resident's Office and the administration block, so picturesquely situated by the side of the sea, remained. Temporary wooden buildings housed Government Offices, and one-storey shops built of split bamboo had been permitted to be built temporarily by the land-owners of the pre-war shops. Miraculously, but possibly because it stood well back from the town and was hidden by trees, the old Sports Club was still standing.

Dick Evans had much to tell me that evening. Of greatest personal interest and satisfaction to me was that he was posting me back to Papar! He was doing that as a matter of policy so that 'informers' during the Japanese period could be more readily brought to justice. I had one or two scores to settle on this account and was pleased at the news. John Dingle, who had managed to get down to Australia after liberation, was holding the fort at Papar till my return. He would then be going back to Kudat where a new man to me, one Rex Blow, an Australian who had escaped from Sandakan POW camp, and had virtually retaken Kudat single-handed at the time of the Japanese capitulation, was holding out as D.O., Kudat in the meantime. Everything was beginning to fit into the picture!

Dick Evans advised me that his office had reserved me a seat on the morning's rail jeep. I raised my eyebrows a little at the mention of that, and he said that there

The pre-war Jesselton Post Office.

wasn't a single engine left serviceable when the Nips surrendered. The main-line locomotive had been blown up by the Nips in Pengalut tunnel. In fact, the last engagement of the war had taken place there. The Australians, having landed at Kimanis Bay, had pushed north towards Jesselton. Having found the tunnel blocked by the railway engine, they had mounted an attack by the use of jeeps mounting the ridge through which the tunnel had been drilled. This had taken the Nips by surprise all right. They hadn't bargained for a mounted light cavalry attack!

When fighting had ceased Australian Army engineers discovered that the axles of the jeep, if fitted with railway track wheels instead of their rubber tyres, would exactly fit the metre-gauge railway lines. So yet another use was found for the universal jeep! Its engine was powerful enough to haul a railway top-side wagon loaded with goods. The only problem, Dick said, was when there was a buffalo on the track: brakes were useless, and the driver had to put his engine into reverse. All the passengers and the driver then had to jump, as the weight of the truck behind it inexorably pushed the jeep into the obstacle before it!

The trip took about as much time as the old steam train used to take. There were still the same throngs at the stations, even though the passengers in the back of the jeep could be numbered on the fingers of one hand.

We raced down the slope as we came out of the Pengalut tunnel and soon the rubber gardens of Papar came into sight. The driver began to put the jeep into progressively lower gears until he gradually brought his load to a halt at the station crossing the river over a new Bailey bridge built by the Australian Army.

A row of bamboo shop-houses had been built on the river bank; I did not readily recognize anyone, but the same ubiquitious Chinese children were playing in the road and running in and out of the shops. I got out on the station; that was just the same, but in need of a coat of paint which after five years of neglect wasn't to be wondered at. It was still the same stationmaster who came out of his office to greet me! It was almost as if time had stood still, and the intervening period just a very bad dream.

When I entered the Rest House the same familiar face of the same old 'cookie' appeared, and again I experienced the same feeling: that I had never been away. But as I stood on the Rest House steps and began to look around, then I was aghast! There was not one of the old shops still standing: just the fish and vegetable markets as they had been before, but looking scarred and weary.

I could see the Office on the other side of the *padang*, and shortly a jeep appeared driven by John Dingle whom I immediately recognized.

After the usual salutations had been exchanged, he invited me to dinner with him at the old house. He said as he went that he would send Ah Choi down with the jeep to pick me up. Things seemed to be looking up!

Promptly, round about seven o'clock, I noticed the lights of a vehicle coming from the direction of the house; it came around the *padang* and stopped at the entrance to the Rest House. I made my salutations to Ah Choi, and was initiated into the experience of driving in a motor vehicle along a path designed only for ponies. I was amazed to see the house again; it was a blaze of light—no longer the hurricane lamp! When Ah Choi switched off the motor of the jeep, I heard the sound of another engine, which could only be a generator. I mounted the steps, and then John explained that it was a small generator left behind by the Australian Army. As I mounted the steps, my attention was drawn to a notice above the doorway: 'Officers' Mess: Keep Out. This Means You!' Amazingly, little had changed. Even the *rotan* cane chairs and the circular drinks table seemed the same. The old magneto-type telephone was in exactly the same position as when I had left it. Just after I arrived, the Sergeant presently in charge rang to present the evening's report, just as his pre-occupation predecessor had reported to me on the evening the Nips had first arrived, passing through Papar on their way to Jesselton.

Very soon I was picking up the threads of the events which had occurred in my absence. On the whole, I felt Papar as a District had not suffered quite as badly as some other areas which had been more intensively occupied by the enemy. Papar was very much a place one passed through. It was true that it was the rice-bowl of the West Coast, having been one of the longest settled areas, with extensive *padi*-fields; even so, the people had had to yield their quota to the enemy more than most, but they had had food reserves in sago, and particularly in well established fruit gardens which the enemy did not know about. Like everyone else, when the reoccupation and the bombing of the towns began, the townsfolk had fled to the jungle to save their lives, but when they had emerged after the cessation of hostilities, they returned to nothing, absolutely nothing.

They were exactly in the same state as ourselves when we were relieved. No homes, no food, no clothes, absolutely nothing! The Australian Army had taken care of everything. They had handed out rice, flour, sugar and fats, and by introducing a new currency to Borneo, the Malayan dollar, had gradually stimulated an economy.

The British Military Administration was quickly established as soon as the war had ended and had assumed control of all civil affairs including supplies. A Main Supply Depot was established in Jesselton, on which Civil Affairs Officers would draw rations for their Districts of which they were in charge. These Civil Affairs Officers remained in the outstations until the Cadre of the old Chartered Company Officers had returned to their posts. Gradually the Australian Army units returned to their base in Labuan leaving behind some of the lighter equipment like jeeps and generators. As the Australians finally withdrew, Labuan became a happy hunting ground for abandoned equipment, much of which the Australian Army had been under instructions to destroy. Nevertheless, stories did reach the mainland of new jeeps, spared from destruction, but which had been sunk out at sea by the Australians in their haste to dismantle their own base as quickly as they could.

The Australian Army, Ninth Division, had recaptured Labuan, North Borneo, and Brunei against a foe with his back to the wall, fighting fiercely all the way. They had done a terrific job, efficiently and well, and will for ever earn the gratitude of the people of Sabah.

Under the Union Jack

QUIETLY, and without fuss and the blare of trumpets, Sabah became a Crown Colony on 15 July 1946. The British Military Administration ceased and civil Government resumed. A senior officer of the pre-war Federation of Malay, Mr J.C. Calder, was substantively appointed Chief Secretary and sworn in as Officer Administrating the Government. On that day, too, Labuan was incorporated into the new Colony and was no longer administered as a Straits Settlement. The capital of the new Colony changed from Sandakan to Jesselton; to ease administration the two old pre-war Residencies ceased to exist, and a new Residency, the Labuan and Interior Residency, was created, with Keningau as Headquarters. Later on, as Tawau increased in importance, a fourth Residency was established there, which included Lahad Datu.

Understandably, the old Chartered Company staff in London, who must have been aware of the Crown's intentions, could only be somewhat cagey when they wrote to me on my return saying that there would be no guarantee of future employment. In the event, as officers who knew the territory, we were greatly welcomed back, not merely by the people of our districts, who knew us, but by the in-coming representatives of the Colonial Service, who did not know the country. Even so, we were very thin on the ground. Mr Rutter, the Resident, East Coast, before the war, did not return and I feel the country lost a lot with his absence. B.R. Cole-Adams, who had been a Senior District Officer, had died in Kuching with the arrival of the Australians. The key figure remaining was undoubtedly that of Dick Evans.

For my part, I was extremely happy to find myself back in Papar and, foreseeing that the British Government would have available far more resources than the old Chartered Company for development purposes, boldly started planning schemes which I felt the District needed most urgently.

We needed roads—all would have agreed with me on that issue—and we needed more land reclaimed from the jungle, to enable the country to be self-sufficient at least in rice, the staple food of the country. The land was there, the potential was there, and the willingness of the people existed. What was lacking were the capital resources to finance the technical skills and the capital costs of all the modern machinery that would be required.

Papar, in particular, cried out for the services of an irrigation engineer. As the virtual rice bowl of the West Coast it was obvious that we should never be dependent on seasonal rainfall; millions of gallons of water flowed regularly into the sea, and we needed means of harnessing that water and diverting it to the *padi*-fields when times of drought threatened. We also had a particular problem in Benoni, where the low coastal fringe appeared to be sinking, allowing salt water from the sea to come further up the rivers on the high tide each year with ensuing devastation of otherwise flourishing crops. It was all very well for the Agriculture Department to introduce higher yielding rice seeds, but unless their successful growth with the right water conditions existed their intentions would be unavailing.

For the moment these thoughts, which I believe I had dreamed up behind barbed wire to occupy my mind, were all pie in the sky! The immediate necessity was rehabilitation: to house people satisfactorily, to clothe them again and to provide them with necessities to restore their life to some normality. This inevitably did take time. However, in accordance with the practice initiated by the Civil Affairs Officers, I issued notes of authority to *bona fide* traders to purchase essential supplies from the Main Supply Depot. To justify their requirement they had to produce registers of their customers, who in turn had to be in possession of notes from the District Office. In this way we were able to reconstitute our Poll Tax register, and at the same time assess the now existing population of the various villages after the traumatic effects of the war.

Of great concern to the Government, too, was the destruction of the Central Land Register held in the fireproof, but not bombproof, vaults of the Lands and Survey Department. These could only be reconstituted by calling in the titles held by the landowners individually, village by village; sending them down to the Lands and Survey Department, who would copy them, and by noting the numbers of the boundary stones recorded on the plans each carried, eventually match them up and reconstitute the locality maps for each district. Tris Speedy, the Director of Lands and Survey, invited old Mr Woolley to forsake retirement and return to the Land Office to undertake this work. No one could be better qualified; he had himself, many years before, been Commissioner of Lands, was familiar with village names, rivers and townships. After liberation, he had not opted to return anywhere but to Sabah. He had lived for the people of the country whom he had served and was happy once more to be of service. He embodied the true spirit of a Chartered Company Officer.

By sending the District Officers back to their own Districts, Dick Evans had sought to bring retribution on those who had become Japanese spies or had assisted the enemy in other ways during the occupation. They deserved punishment, for they had brought needless suffering to many innocent people merely for the sake of paying off old scores. Obtaining evidence was not an easy matter, but there were those willing to speak in whom one could place the utmost confidence. Gradually witnesses began to come forward, and slowly the true facts relating to those about whom one had suspicions began to emerge. Justice had to be seen to be done. Fortunately, it did not fall to me to try these cases; I merely forwarded the evidence to the authority set up for the purpose and left it to others to prosecute if they thought fit. There were, I believe, two or three deserving cases in Papar whose war-time activities required special investigation!

One of my more enterprising pursuits in Papar was dealing with the war-time activities of cattle-rustlers. The offenders were mostly Sikhs, who were the main *sapi*, as opposed to buffalo, owners on the West Coast. The field of cattle-rustling stretched from Kota Belud in the north to Papar in the south, and movement of cattle had occurred to prevent them falling into the hands of the Japanese. They had all ended up in the open scrubland around Kuala Papar. There were incessant reports to the Police by Sikhs reporting cattle theft which they claimed to be theirs. It was quite impossible to prove, and when I had individual complainants in for questioning, it became obvious to me that they were prevaricating. To terminate the matter I declared them enemy property, which they probably were!

As an *ex officio* Assistant Custodian of enemy property, I decided to run the herd myself. I opened a 'below the line' farm account (that meant spending Government money not out of an approved vote) and set myself the task of running it on business lines. I appointed a herdsman, had a rough timber stabling block built, and told the herdsman to provide daily as much milk as he could get from the herd, and to slaughter one head of cattle every Saturday. I put an economic price on a bottle of milk and told all the staff that they were eligible for milk supplies as well as the hospital. Similarly with the meat. I gave priority to the needs of the hospital, which was paid for from the hospital vote for food, and then any Government officer of whatever rank and from whatever Department was eligible to purchase what he needed. The District Officer usually wanted some for himself too!

It was a very good scheme, as all Government officers were still on pre-war scales of pay at a time when the cost of living was very much higher. The Government in due course recognized this and authorized a scaled cost-of-living allowance pending the appointment of a Salaries Commission, but in matters like this, all Governments are slow to act, seemingly postponing action until forced. There was, though, a good reason in North Borneo's case, because we were receiving grants-in-aid from the United Kingdom Government and were, therefore, Treasury controlled. I am quite sure that Mr Calder, as Officer Administering the Government, would have advanced our case to the Secretary of State for the Colonies, who in turn would have approached the Treasury. Inevitably, matters like these do take time, so in Papar, at least, we were luckier than most.

Another matter of grave concern to the Government was the supply of basic food for the country. We were too reliant on imported rice, an essential commodity which was in short supply in South East Asia in the years immediately following the war. The Government, therefore, decided to implement a local '*Padi* Purchasing Scheme', in which Government stepped in and bought the local surplus *padi* harvest. The onus for this fell very largely on Papar, the really big *padi*-producing district of the West Coast. So almost overnight, I was authorized to purchase the surplus local *padi* harvest, and to build stores in which to keep it safe. It was financed from another 'below the line' account. The scheme was not all that popular with the local Chinese merchants, in particular the rice-millers, because the usual practice was for the shopkeeper to advance money to the *padi*-grower well before the harvest for so many *piculs* at a price well below the going rate which would eventually emerge, depending on the year's yield of the crop.

I have forgotten now the number of thousand *piculs* I had planned that the stores should hold. I had a good clerical officer in one Abas bin Haji Hassan, and I relied entirely on him and Native Chief Oman, both of whom were jewels to have on one's staff in the administration of the district. Oman disappeared into the jungle for a week or ten days, appearing one morning with a train of buffaloes hauling all the round timber one needed for the framework of the store. A local Chinese contractor quoted a price for building it, using planks that he would supply, and we were ready to start!

Obviously, I had never been in contact with such a big operation as was contemplated, but I read every hand-book I could find which might be of any use. What most concerned me was the possibility of any damp *padi* being brought in to increase weight to the seller and, conscious that the *padi* might possibly overheat when stored in such a large quantity that we were planning, I decided that each store should be built in three compartments, and that in the middle of each section I would incorporate two funnels made of mosquito net wiring around a frame a foot square, to act as a ventilator. I argued that such a ventilation shaft would take away any heat that could be building up. Perhaps it was a needless precaution; I have no idea! I do know that we had no trouble and that the *padi* kept in perfect condition.

The doorway or entrance into each compartment also needed thought. I decided that each entrance should be built up by the insertion of a removable plank as the bulk level of the *padi* rose above the level of the floor. Outside this were doors which could be padlocked for security, and the key kept with the Police Sergeant. I don't think I could have done more!

In the event, the scheme was an enormous success. It happened to be a good crop that year, 1947. The first store we built was rapidly being filled and I had authority to build another! The second store itself was becoming full, and when Dick Evans, the Resident, visited Papar on inspection one day, he immediately authorized the construction of a third!

The next event of great personal interest to myself was the announcement that the Secretary of State had appointed Mr Edward Twining to be the first Governor of North Borneo. This was good news, particularly as he had been a good friend of my father's when he had been posted to Mauritius. They used to travel together in the same railway compartment between the residential area and Port Louis, the capital. He was due to arrive later in the year.

In the meantime, my friendship with Oman grew. He undoubtedly was a great character and had tremendous influence in Benoni. It was no longer a troublesome village as it had been when I first arrived in Papar, not so many years ago. He was respected and his word was law. Indirect rule of a calibre demonstrated by Oman took a great load off the shoulders of a District Officer. It meant that one area of his District was well administered, and it relieved the work of the Police contingent. Matjakir, too, was a thoroughly reliable Chief with enormous influence over his people. As an example, I remember one incident very clearly. The path to the Kuala had become subject to considerable flooding at high tides, rendering it impossible for the village folk to use. I discussed this with Matjakir. He told me not to worry. He would arrange it. I wondered what he proposed, but in a matter of a week or ten days, I heard from the Police Sergeant that Matjakir had arranged with all the local villagers to turn out on a given day to reconstruct the path. I rode out early in the morning and was amazed to find some two to three hundred people digging away at any mounds of hard soil they could find, and carrying it in earth baskets to form a path, wide enough to take a jeep and well above high water mark. Nearly a mile of track was reconstructed in a day's work. No one could complain of such marvellous support from the local community! Villages working together in this way was not uncommon: whenever it was beneficial to them, they would drop all other work and give support to the wishes of their Chief. Most important of all, however, was the relationship the District Officer had with his Chiefs. They had all known me a long time, and we had gone through together the most testing time in the country's history. No incoming European officer would have ever been given so much unstinted support. We all understood the suffering the country had gone through; we had experienced it together.

With a new 'jeepable' path out to the Kuala, one could at weekends make the journey to the sea comparatively quickly. On the same hillock where I had established a look-out station before the invasion and from where news had been brought me of the mud-volcano on Pulau Tiga, I erected a small plank-built building where I could camp at weekends, whenever work permitted. My dog loved it; not only could he swim in the sea, but he could bark endlessly with great excitement at the monkeys in the scrub-land and swamp just inshore. It reminded me of Dick Jones' beach-hut and the many happy hours I had spent before the Far Eastern war at Kuala Kinarut with him and his wife. And his magnificent curries which his cook was always able to provide!

Another example of community work was demonstrated by Oman at Kampong Benoni, the Lake Village. The swamp his villagers had to cross to reach their houses was crossed by a pole bridge on triangular supports. Purposely in disrepair during the occupation to dissuade roaming enemy parties, now peace had come, they set about rebuilding it which made access so much easier. So I became a frequent visitor to Benoni and was always made most welcome. I liked the Brunei people, and I liked their Islamic beliefs and their way of life. It suited them. They were a clean-living race and it was a joy to be their guest. The absence of pigs rooting around for anything they could find, for example, and instead a few goats here and there, gave one an atmosphere of well-kept parkland when one entered the refreshing shade of their houses.

I in no way demean the Muruts, with whom I have spent many long hours well into the nights, drinking their *tapai*, but, I must say, trying to avoid their food which was not quite my sort of cuisine! However, they did keep pigs and however well they may look after them, it cannot be said that a pig in a tropical country is a clean animal. Many of the same observations apply to the Kedazans, except that those of the coast have eating habits far more acceptable to the European and I have greatly enjoyed their feasts. The villages in the immediate vicinity of Papar

Town were mostly Moslem, and during the marriage season, I found I was a guest in many Moslem households. Considering that the country was still going through a period when everything was in short supply, my native hosts were always extremely generous. Nor must I overlook the generosity of the Chinese communities in the townships; they were always striving to please and always helpful.

It is possible that I am biased in favour of the people of Papar, but that is a natural reaction when one faced a common enemy, survived amidst great suffering, and together faced a future which, hopefully, had much to offer.

The next event of great importance for the country was the arrival of our new Governor and Commander-in-Chief, Mr Edward Twining. All District Officers were called to Jesselton for his formal arrival and swearing-in Ceremony, which was followed later in the day with a garden party at Government Cottage, Jesselton, in his honour, where we all had a chance of meeting him and making his acquaintance. He went down well with everyone! Here was a man, we felt, who would make decisions immediately and fearlessly, and stand by them once they were made. There was so much to be done, and we had long awaited his arrival; once he had come, we recognized immediately that we were in luck. The Secretary of State for the Colonies couldn't have chosen better. He was the right man for the job.

He was straightforward, quick at making decisions and very determined. But with it, he had humanity and understanding and a great sense of humour. Perhaps this may be better understood if I relate a true story which those who knew him will ever remember. In Sarawak, the British Government had taken over the responsibility of the Administration of Sarawak from the Rajah and had appointed Sir Charles Arden-Clark, almost at the same time as Mr Twining's appointment had been announced. In the next Honours List after their appointments and arrival in their respective territories, Sir Charles Arden-Clark was elevated to a KCMG, whereas Mr Twining received no honour. In a message typical of the man he was, Twining sent a congratulatory telegram, which read: 'Congratulations! What, twice a knight at your age?'

Typically, Twining began to visit the Sports Club, which was mainly European in those days, on Saturday midday—a favourite rendezvous of all Jesselton Europeans at that time, both Government officials and commercial men. He was liberal in playing host to all present, but it was a sure way in which to keep in touch with local European thinking, and to keep his finger on the pulse. Later, when I had developed a closer relationship with him, I remember him saying: 'On official occasions, lay on the pomp and the brass bands, but on unofficial occasions, be yourself!'

Papar was relatively close to Jesselton, now just an hour by rail jeep, so it was natural that I was one of the first Districts to receive a visit from the new Governor. Dick Evans had warned me that there were likely to be several in the party, but I had not anticipated a convoy of two jeeps bearing the Governor accompanied by his ADC, the Resident, the Director of Public Works, the Director of Agriculture and the Director of Education. He arrived in a General's uniform, took the Salute, and then inspected the Guard, dressed very smartly for the occasion. He then retreated into the Rest House where he changed into something a little less formal than a uniform, and then asked me what the problems of the District were. I had these at the tip of my fingers.

'Right. Let's see the place!' he said.

So I drove him first along the Papar Estate road, which was mostly cobbled, but jeepable. 'It certainly gives one a most peculiar sensation!' he said as we bumped along from cobble to cobble on the barely cushioned metal of the front of the passenger's seat. That set the mood of the visit. It was all light-hearted, but had a serious thrust. Afterwards we attempted the Bukit Manggis road after the rain of the previous night which, fortunately, well illustrated my point. In places it was almost a slippery mud bath and one seemed to go backward as much as forward, but we made sufficient progress to reach the less used part of the road where the going was better, and I was able to take the party to Mile 5 or Mile 6, well past Benoni, and show him good fertile land just waiting to be opened up. Returning with Benoni on the Governor's side of the jeep, he was able to see planted *padi*-land not of thriving growth, but yellowing and almost withering when only half grown. I drew his attention to it and said that there was a problem with the *padi* land in the Benoni area in that salt water was penetrating further upstream than normal and entering the *padi*-fields, so causing the wilting of the crops. I was able to add that I thought the whole of that part of the coast in Kimanis Bay was sinking a little, as I had observed water at high tide almost lapping against the sides of the railway track, something which had never happened before the war. We couldn't put the blame on the Nips for that!

'Right!' said Twining. 'We'll return to the Rest House and talk it over!'

The Rest House cookie came in with chilled bottles of tonic water, an ice-bucket and a bottle of gin. I had already learnt Twining's preferences from his Private Secretary and was well prepared. It had been a very hot morning, and all our tongues were hanging out. As we quaffed the first glass, perhaps a little too quickly, Twining, who obviously dominated the party, remarked:

'We'll discuss the whole situation and come up with the right decisions by the time we have finished this bottle of gin. And if we haven't reached them by then we'll call for another bottle!'

In the event, there was little argument. All agreed with Twining's priorities, which indeed I wholly shared.

'We must first metal the Bukit Manggis road; and whilst that is being done we must appoint a Drainage and Irrigation engineer.' And, turning to the Resident and myself, he added: 'Please put up costed plans which I can recommend to the Secretary of State for grants under Colonial Development and Welfare Scheme. These plans must go hand in hand, then we shall get Benoni able to harvest its own rice again, and we shall be increasing the capacity of good land for further development.'

The decisions were reached before the gin bottle was empty but, nevertheless, Twining insisted that the bottom should be seen! I was anxious for my domestic staff who were busy at the house working to my prearranged time-table for a lunch party. However, I ceased to be anxious as I realized that the blur of alcohol would obliterate any defects in the cuisine!

When it was all over, I could at last relax, and I returned to the house exhausted, wanting only a strong cup of tea, and a slice of Ituk's cake. It had been worth all the effort, and I felt I had achieved something for the District and its people. As I contemplated the view over the lawn and down to the river, I recalled the last meeting I had had in the Rest House, in the presence of Lt. Yamaha of the Japanese Army and Sakai! This had happened in 1942, nearly six years before, but it seemed an age. Mostly, one tried to regard the Occupation as just a bad dream, but somehow it always kept recurring. Apart from nightmares in one's sleep, there were always faces one knew who one met in one's ordinary working day that recalled the tragedies that happened to them when the enemy were conquerors. It was one thing for General MacArthur to have said when he left Corrigidor: 'We shall return!' We had returned, but we had to meet the same people face to face, and the memories of the cruelty, suffering and hardship our people had had to bear at the hands of a ruthless enemy were always present, and somehow one could not prevent the feeling that our state of unpreparedness, and our appalling military performance in the Malayan campaign, had let them down.

The Australian Army had re-built the railway bridge, utilizing the framework of a Bailey bridge. That was just as well, since one morning the stationmaster rang me up to say a diesel roller had arrived in a truck that morning, and could I arrange to unload it as the railway wanted the truck. Later, when I opened the morning's mail, it contained a letter from the Director of Public Works saying that a roller was being sent with a driver! I believe it was one of the first to have arrived in the country, other than Australian military equipment. The first thing to do was to locate the driver. I sent my *mandor* out looking for him, and then went to the station to consult the stationmaster and obtain his ideas as to how to unload it. We were presented with a bit of a problem! I tried to take the view that it was the railway's responsibility to off-load it, but he obviously maintained that it was consigned to me, and that it was my problem! I was all for calling the Traffic Superintendent, but concluded that the quickest thing was to put all my labourers on to it. So we pushed the truck into the siding, and hastily constructed a sloping ramp of earth and timber. The driver, a very dark Sinhalese, having been found in a coffee shop, looked apprehensively at the ramp and very cautiously started his engine, and seemed to close his eyes as his machine descended more hastily than he had bargained for, slumped a little on the sagging ramp, but managed to reach terra firma in an upright position! The CD&W grant had been approved, and I was in the business of road-making!

Stone was no problem. There was a good outcrop at Mile 2 along the Bukit Manggis road, and I invited tenders for the supply of six-inch stone for the foundations, and one-inch stone for the surfacing. The Police held stocks of dynamite in their section of the office and this was issued to the contractor as required. A lorry followed the roller up the railway track—an ex-Australian Army lorry so it appeared—and work began in earnest. I employed direct labour for laying the metal and arranged payment to relate to the completion of foundation laying at the rate of two chains per day for a day's work. Everyone seemed happy, and every morning I would meet the *mandor* on the job, inspect what had been achieved the previous day, have a cheerful word with those carrying out the current day's task and measure out two chains for the following day's work. Only Sundays were rest-days, when the men would go to the market with their wives. The Tamu at Papar was second only to that at Kota Belud, some fifty miles north of Jesselton, a very popular meeting place which commenced business at the crack of dawn.

The early stages of the monsoon in October and early September broke the normal routine which had been established. Not infrequently, dawn heralded heavy squally showers, accompanied by strong gusts of wind. All outside work then had to cease. At times, the morning would commence with the usual hot sunshine, and the storm would burst at midday, or even earlier. On one such morning, it was a Saturday, I remember well, I decided I would have a surprise check on the cashier to ascertain that his books had been correctly kept and that the cash balance agreed with the book balance. Leaning on my experience in Tenom before the Far Eastern war, I always insisted that the cashier should ensure he had succeeded in balancing his books at the close of business each afternoon. It was always easier to pick up any errors if that practice were followed! I had just completed the cash balance when I heard the noise of a plane's engine. Normally, I would have taken no notice, as the RAF were undertaking an aerial survey for the Lands and Survey Department and the noise of an aircraft was not unusual. This, however, was quite different. It was the roar of an engine flying very low, below the cloud base; there was a spluttering, and then the engine cut out altogether. It all happened very quickly, but most of the station was alerted by it.

One automatically thinks of First Aid, so I rang the Hospital Assistant and told him to be ready with splints, bandages and all medical equipment he might need and that I was coming immediately to the hospital to pick him up. I brought with me too the Sergeant and another policeman and I drove the jeep as fast as I could along the muddy bridle path towards the *kuala*, grateful that Matjakir's men had so recently rebuilt it.

When we emerged from the swampy area, there, about a hundred yards from the path, was the RAF plane, with a couple of RAF officers sitting on one of the wings smoking cigarettes!

'Never expected to see you here!' one of them said, as I walked along the *padi* bund against which the plane had come to a halt.

'Never thought you would try landing on a *padi*-field!' I rejoined.

'There's always a first time!' they replied, and then went on to explain that they couldn't get through the thick storm cloud around Labuan Island and that the airport there was virtually closed. They were instructed to try a *padi*-field as the softest option. 'Another plane on the same operation as ourselves has come down somewhere!'

I suggested they should sit on the backs of the buffalo that by this time had been brought up to the plane by local *padi*-farmers. This they did with all the kit they had brought out of the cockpit with them, and landed up in the jeep. My driver, who was one of the score or so on the station who, by this time, had left the township to come out and see what had occurred, had anticipated requirements and had turned my jeep, running it along the path until it emerged on the hard sand, where, if the pilot had known the terrain well enough, he could probably have succeeded in landing and saved his plane. As it was, I didn't see the slightest hope of salvaging it from where it then lay.

My immediate objective was to reach the house as quickly as possible, and hope that Ituk had hot water for baths, as we were all soaking wet. I put them in the spare room and Ituk brought along a couple of buckets of hot water for them, and one for me. I also offered them a change of clothing so that they could get out of their soaked uniforms.

I had a quick douse myself, and then made hasty arrangements with Ituk for lunch for our unexpected guests. They soon emerged and got the right side of a tankard of beer! Fortunately, my delivery of supplies had arrived from Ban Guan just a day or so earlier. It was just as well, as I don't think I have ever seen anyone knock back a beer quite so quickly before.

It disappeared! Not one bottle, but before nightfall a whole case! I had endeavoured in vain to persuade them to catch the afternoon train to Jesselton, but once I had reported their arrival to the Resident, they seemed more relaxed and at ease and had no sense of urgency to return to their headquarters. At this distance in time it becomes obvious that they were in a state of shock; they were indeed lucky to have survived an accident like that, and come out of it without even a limb being broken. The pilot must have been very skilled to have pancaked his machine on to flat mud.

The other plane had made a similar landing in the Tenghilan–Tamparuli area. Mike Edge as Chief Police Officer, Jesselton had been deputed to proceed to the site. Both the officers in that machine had also survived without injury, and were taken by Mike to the Jesselton Rest House—and would have had to pay for everything they had!

My unexpected guests eventually went down on the Sunday morning train to Jesselton, with instructions to report to the Resident, by phone, on arrival and await his advice. I never really knew what directions they followed, but Monday morning's train brought their return to Papar, where this time they were accommodated in the Rest House, with instructions to await the Crash Inspector's arrival! I merely learned from them that they had landed up at Government House and that Twining, whom they described 'as a beery old gentleman' had accommodated them. His Private Secretary had liaised with the RAF headquarters in Labuan and conveyed messages to them. Their remark had amused me, as Twining seldom drank beer! Gin and tonic was his mid-day tipple.

In a couple of days, the morning train brought the Crash Inspector, appropriately named, I thought, Ft. Lt. Butcher! I bade Ah Choi, my driver, to take him and his two officers to the scene of the crash, and Ft. Lt. Butcher duly reported to me that he had written off the aircraft. My reaction was that that was maybe all right for the RAF, but what about the landowner, who had lost *padi*-land? The reply was that since the plane was now written off, the land-owner could do what he like with the machine. I remonstrated by saying that it was depriving the farmer of quite a considerable proportion of his field on which he depended for his livelihood. My point was duly noted, but in my memory of events no compensation was ever paid. It poses the question of what would normally happen in Britain, in such circumstances? The answer may be that the plane would normally be removed. In Papar this was not possible, and the claim must have been lost in a file!

As to its disposal in Papar, this was a question I discussed with Matjakir, who with his usual unruffled calm replied: 'Leave it to me, Tuan!' A few days later, he came to see me asking an assurance that the Government didn't want it back. I had received nothing in writing from the RAF, just the verbal information from Ft. Lt. Butcher, but it was obvious that they could do nothing with it, so I wrote to him to advise him that on the day agreed the villagers proposed to break up the plane so that the land owner could make a little more use of his land. I received no reply. So on the appointed day, I gave Matjakir authority to do what he wished with it. The plane was attacked with sledge-hammers and *parangs* and I don't suppose there was a machine in the RAF which has ever been disposed of with such little dignity! Nothing was left except the engine which, I expect, in the course of time sank into the soft mud of the *padi*-field!

Like all District Officers of the Chartered Company era, we were trained to travel in the district of which we were in charge, but North Borneo was a very different country to what it had been before the war. The Secretary of State had teams of Advisors seemingly on every possible subject, and the new Borneo Colonies apparently came in for undue attention. However much I would have like to have gone *ulu*: that is, to travel upstream and visit the villages in the foothills of the Crocker Range, there was always something or somebody in the pipeline demanding my presence on the station! Gone were the days when I could spend a weekend away with Dick Jones at Kuala Kinarut, seldom even could I visit an Estate at all! Not only did the very nature of life change, but unexpected circumstances seemed to arise that no-one could foresee.

One Sunday morning, having received news from the Private Secretary that the Governor's wife was travelling up the line that morning to visit Beaufort, I went along to the station to meet her and organized the Rest House cookie to have tea brought to the railway carriage. We had a pleasant few minutes together as she was a doctor and genuinely interested in native health and welfare and did much to promote Government activity in these subjects.

After the train had gone up the line, I ambled back to the house, chatting to anyone I happened to seek. Ituk brought me a beer, which I felt I deserved! Before I had finished it, the phone rang, and it was the Kapitan China, Ah Chi, who very excitedly told me the bridge had fallen down! I questioned him as I instinctively felt that could not be right! I had just come from the station. 'Come quickly!' he said, so, acting on his advice, I took the jeep and went to the station again, noticing that people were all running in the same direction—towards the river! I reached the shops and looked towards the bridge—but Ah Chi was right! The bridge lay twisted and crumpled, lying sideways in the river!

I was speechless with amazement! Then, galvanizing myself into action, I drove to the station to meet the stationmaster. I first enquired if anything was following on the track. He was more excited than the normally passive oriental could ever be, and was in a bit of a panic as the telephone line which the bridge carried, and the District telephone as well, was broken. Fortunately, he was able to put his hand on a travelling phone, and I drove him to the river which we both crossed with the help of a willing native who had come down in his canoe to the Sunday *tamu* and then had come across to the town bank of the river to buy the goods he needed to take back to his village. Securing his phone to the unbroken section of the wire, the stationmaster was able to acquaint railway headquarters of the event and stop any movement along the rail track. When eventually his conversation came to an end, I managed to raise the Resident and convey the bad news to him.

I wasn't short of assistance; everyone was there. The sudden horror went through me that normally at the busy Sunday morning *tamu* held on the northern bank of the river the footbridge which lay alongside the track was packed with villagers: men, women with babes in arms slung around their shoulders, and groups of children trotting along on their own, crossing between the *tamu* ground and the shops. There would have been no warning when the bridge fell and anyone could have been caught. Nobody knew for certain, but the general opinion of bystanders was that no one was on the walkway of the bridge when it fell. That was merciful; not only that, it was a miracle! There was not a report at the time nor in the days that followed of a single missing person. I was most thankful, as I could so easily have had a major tragedy on my hands.

The bridge that had fallen had been a Bailey bridge, built by the Australian Army whilst they still fought their way northwards to Jesselton from their bridgehead at Kimanis Bay. It had replaced the original pre-war bridge blown up by Charles Chester. Their engineers had done an amazing job in getting the railway operational again after the ravages and neglect of wartime. It must have taken great effort to rebuild the bridge, but they slipped up only in one thing, through lack of knowledge of local timbers. Belion, the iron-wood of Borneo, would have lasted till this day, but they made use of any timber available to them, and this happened to be softwood, of a kind not even used in normal village house construction. It was food to the beetles living in Papar river, and when the piles were eventually extracted, an examination showed that they had been riddled with worm holes. The amazing thing was that it had been high tide when the morning train crossed the bridge, and this must have given a certain amount of bouyancy to the timber, sufficient for it to hold the weight of the bridge; as soon as the tide fell there was no longer buoyancy; some worm must have nibbled its last crunch. Mrs Twining had been on the last train to cross!

The in-coming British Forces and the restored civilian Governments which followed had established a Commissioner-General's Office in Singapore; this acted as a liaison office for all British affairs in South East Asia. It was to this office that the North Borneo Government sent an urgent request for an Army Bridging Company. Fortune was with them! A unit of the Indian Army still had a Bridging Company in Malaya, and before long it was being transferred to Papar.

An advance party came up by an RAF Sunderland flying boat, and a couple of their representatives were sent up to me in Papar to survey the site and discuss their camp requirements. In my mind there was only one area in which they could establish their base, and that would be out at the *kuala*. I shuddered to think of the impact that a Company of the Indian Army might have on the town! It was obvious that transport to and from my proposed site would be a problem; the re-made jeep-path would soon disintegrate under the strain.

I met the reconnaissance party and housed them in the Rest House. As soon as they had settled in, I went over to meet them to discuss primarily the question of the location of their camp and ascertain fresh food needs.

They were thoroughly competent officers. They had already proposed a camp site, and by the time I arrived were working out movement plans and engineering requirements. They possessed maps of the area, and were glad to learn that the hard sandy ground at the *kuala* would be a good camping area. 'We shall bring a landing craft,' they said. A transport vessel could anchor off the *kuala*, unload landing craft which, acting as barges, would first ferry the tenting equipment needed for their headquarters and camping area, and then off-load and transport the girders and equipment to the site. They could make concrete piles on location, and would be off-loading a pile-driver mounted on its own barge. They would ferry their men from the camp-site to the construction area daily by landing craft.

I was impressed that they had worked out their plans so quickly, but I warned them that there was quite a rise and fall of the tide daily and that the *kuala* itself was very shallow and only navigable really through one channel which they could learn from the local fishermen. I suggested that they might like to see the camp site, with which they were wholeheartedly in agreement, so although it was getting pretty hot by then, I took them along the new bridle or jeepable path, which I explained had just been re-made by community labour, to the camping area I had in mind. It seemed to suit them admirably, and they went firm on the decision to establish the camp in that location. I was glad, although in the event, I needn't have had any scruples where the camp should be sited; their men turned out to be extremely well disciplined and Papar could not have had a better unit for the job on hand.

The reconnaissance party of two officers took only a day in their planning work, and then left again to return to Singapore. I heard nothing more for about a couple of weeks, and then I received a signal giving me their e.t.a. I posted notices inviting tenders for the supply of fresh fruit, vegetables and meat for the number of men involved in order that these should be at hand on their arrival.

The day soon came when the same officers reported to the District Office asking if they could stay in the Rest House until supplies were off-loaded and their camp was established at the *kuala*. They also asked if it would be permissable for them to use a couple of jeeps along the bridle-path for quicker communication for the officers between the camp and the bridge site. I naturally offered them every facility I could. Papar was to become a hive of activity!

It was not long before the 'clonk-clonk' of the pile driver as it began its work became a regular accompaniment to one's thoughts as one sat in court endeavouring to unravel the truth in some criminal case which needed concentration. That was of minor significance when compared with the difficulties of meeting VIPs who seemed to come in droves! The Secretary of State for the Colonies seemed to have hordes of advisers, all developing an interest in Britain's youngest colony, at a time when it was least able to cope with visitors. The absence of the bridge meant that one had to cross the river by the barge that the railway had provided and meet the intended guest at the rail-head. Fortunately, telephone links had by now been re-established with Jesselton, so I worked out an arrangement with the stationmaster that he would ring me as soon as the rail-jeep had left Kawang. That I knew from experience would be about twenty to twenty-five minutes away, and gave me just sufficient time to drop what I was doing and drive my jeep to the river-crossing point; with luck my arrival at the rail-head should coincide with that of the rail-jeep's! Similarly, the return journey of similar length took about one hour out of my working day.

On occasions these VIP visits did bring their lighter moments which one could laugh about when they were all over! Because of the vast increase in entertaining I was obliged to undertake, I had tried to make the D.O.'s house a little more 'homely' than it was before the war. I engaged the local carpenter who was quite a good craftsman to construct a built-in corner settee in the coolest part of the room, and designed a couple of easy chairs which he also made. On one of my visits to Jesselton, I acquired some cloth, suitable for curtain material, from the Main Supply Depot, and the local tailor made them up to hang at the house posts by the *tingkaps*, and as room dividers between the lounge and dining area. This had just been completed when I received a message that the Minister of State, Lord Listowel, and his secretary would be making a visit. As usual, I arranged for them to have lunch in the house, but I was a bit taken aback when his secretary turned out to be a lady, and clad in a dress made of the same material as my new curtains! I also received a visit from the Secretary of State's Adviser on Social Welfare, Mr Chinn, a charming man who was right on top of his job and an extremely pleasant person.

I was not alone in having embarrassing moments. A telegram had announced Mr Chinn's arrival on an important East Coast out-station. There had been an error in the telegram and his name had been spelt 'Chin'. Naturally, with an inaccurate spelling and possibly an inaccurate telegraphic description of the officer's station, the District Officer hastily and mistakenly thought him to be Chinese and arranged for him to stay with his Deputy, who was Chinese. On his arrival, arrangements had to be drastically reorganized!

On another station, when social emergencies pressed upon a harassed District Officer, he found he had to entertain unexpectedly at very short notice a 'visiting fireman', to use the colloquial term that grew up amongst District Officers at that time. Domestically pressed with a shortage of adequate staff, his thoughts led to a respectable looking prisoner who had merely been incarcerated by the Native Court for breaking native customary law: probably sexual and not all that serious. So, accompanied by a policeman, he was escorted to the District Officer's house, kitted out in uniform and shown how to wait at a table. All went well, until the last course, when the visiting VIP was presented by the 'boy' with a petition asking for a remission of his sentence!

Meanwhile, in Papar, the welcome I received from the native and Chinese population alike was genuine, and came from the heart without any ulterior motive. Whenever there was a wedding in a nearby village, amongst any family of standing, I was sure to be invited. I couldn't wish for anything better. The marriages themselves may have seemed long-drawn-out affairs, but the opportunity it gave to talk to the people on equal terms was unparalleled. They opened their hearts to you in a manner in which they could never have done in the District Office. Of course, one always gave the customary 'red packet', a ten dollar bill in a red envelope, always red for good luck! But from the point of view of being identified with the people, such occasions were invaluable. I never felt that I was a Government Officer imposing law and order, yet I was. I felt more of a friend and ally, available for advice on any problem they might have.

The village that possibly I most visited was called 'Buang Sayang', which translated means: 'Throw away Care'. It was just on the opposite river bank to Papar, and I was always brought back along the river by *gobang*, a native dug-out canoe, and landed within a couple of a hundred yards of my house. Everywhere I went, I was shown the utmost gratitude, and made genuinely welcome. Possibly they recognized in me a man who did not run away from the Japanese invader, but who had suffered equally with them, and had miraculously returned to them, as I said I would. That they had suffered so much during the 'co-prosperity' period was obvious to all, and I must have symbolized all their memories of their happier days before the war.

At about this time we received news which saddened us greatly: we heard that Twining had received promotion to be Governor of Tanganyika. We were all, of course, happy for him, but we couldn't help feeling that it was possibly one of the weaknesses of the Colonial Service: when a good officer who becomes a highly successful Governor is discovered, he is too quickly transferred to another territory where his skills already proven may be used for greater advantage to the Empire. It was understandable that the hierarchy in the Colonial Office should make such decisions, but it was sad for the territory who was losing such a person.

As far as I recall, the Resident, Dick Evans, summoned all his District Officers to a farewell party for the Governor; the feelings of all District Officers were the same: the country was losing a good man!

In his place, the Chief Secretary, Mr J. Calder, CMG became Officer Administering the Government on 5 May 1949, on the day Mr Twining took his leave. I had not previously met him but he had been a former officer of the Malayan Civil Service before the war, and if memory serves me correctly was elsewhere during the occupation of Malaya. To the best of my knowledge, he had never been a prisoner of the Japanese. Shortly after his appointment as OAG, he made an official visit to Papar, as there was much going on in the District which he wanted to see. The construction of the Bukit Manggis Road was making good headway, and we had built and surfaced the road up to Mile 3. This was the well-worn disintegrating section of the road and to have completed this was a considerable achievement. We had been assisted, however, by the arrival of a stone-crusher, and a moveable bucket belt which lifted the hand hewn blocks of stone as it was quarried to the mouth of the crusher. The arrival of another lorry of more modern vintage also aided the delivery of the stone to the construction site at the roadhead.

As I anticipated, his first official visit to Papar quickly followed on his appointment as Acting Governor. There was much to see in the District and much was going on in the way of development. The Drainage and Irrigation Engineer, whose services Governor Twining had sought, had arrived and he and his team were busy taking levels and planning the scheme: a work which would mostly involve bunding, so it appeared, to prevent the in-flow of salt water. The Indian Army Bridging Company was rapidly constructing the Hamilton Bridge to replace the Australian Army Bailey bridge and Papar was a hive of activity.

Mr Calder and I rapidly become on good terms. His wife Emma was a very dear lady. She was Belgian but spoke good English; unfortunately, she was a little deaf, and she persisted in handing one her ear-trumpet from which it was a little difficult to get disentangled! Mr Calder was an officer who did not suffer fools gladly. Many people did not see eye to eye with him, and as, during his term of office in Borneo, he was Acting Governor as long as he was Chief Secretary, his minutes in Secretariat files became mostly written in red ink—the prerogative of the Governor—and he would just initial a minute 'J.C.'. It was inevitable that he quickly earned the nickname of 'Jesus Christ'! Fortunately, he and I always were on very friendly terms, and I owe much to him for the rapid promotion I was to have in the service in due course. However, I must not anticipate events, but endeavour to narrate them in chronological order.

The recruitment to the Service was now handled, of course, by the Colonial Office, and the normal flow of graduates from the senior universities had in the immediate post-war years not yet begun. Vacancies were filled mostly by transfer from African territories and some, mostly technical officers, came from the Burma Civil Service, as this country was one of the first to receive its independence from the Crown after the war, in 1948. Mostly the civil servants wishing to leave the Government of Burma were Eurasian and were of great assistance in filling the middle cadre of our service to replace many of the Chartered Company staff, patriots like Chief Police Officer Peters and Jules Stevens, who had both perished subsequent to the Double Tenth Uprising, but sometimes they were senior officers. One of these was a veterinary officer. This was a post much needed by the Government, as fowl pest was frequently rife, and the pre-war outbreak of *surra* amongst the Kota Belud ponies still persisted.

I had occasion to call on his services unexpectedly because of the illness of my dog. He was only a couple of years old, but was a dear friend who developed a disease known as 'hard pad'. His feet were not normally heard on the wooden floor, but one day I noticed they were beginning to tap the wood of the corridor whenever he was called in for food. Normally, if one heard them at all, they would sound like a light sponge on the floor boards. He was a very faithful companion. One night he started barking without stopping, and looking up at the rafters on the edge of the roof. I reached for my torch and was horrified to see a cobra curled along the beam, with its tongue spitting continuously. It was not in a position where I could beat it with a stick, so I immediately rang the police and Sergeant Ganiong came along with a rifle and quickly despatched it. So Rambler, then, was a greatly valued friend. He was so named because of his habit of chasing any moving object he might spot from the top of the front door steps which was his favourite daytime position, that is if he didn't come with me on my rounds. This I discouraged as he so often would endeavour to lord it over the town and village dogs and involve me in dog fights!

Rambler, therefore, was rather special and when the Government veterinary officer did arrive, I dealt with all the official aspects of his visit in the office, and asked him to lunch in the house. My purpose was obviously to seek his advice and assistance for Ram. After a good lunch, I asked him if he could diagnose what ailment the animal was suffering from and suggest any treatment. His reply was that he was not recruited by Government for the purpose of treating domestic pets. I exploded! To no avail, of course. Poor Ram's condition worsened until his rear quarters became paralysed, and within a week he died.

His death had a traumatic effect on me, and intensified the antipathy which was being felt by all the old Chartered Company Officers to the new breed of Britisher that was being posted to the Colony. I recalled the incident which happened before my arrival in Borneo, when Dick Evans, who had been the son of a general practitioner in Devon, had diagnosed that a Hakka fruit seller on Papar station was suffering from acute appendicitis. Knowing that there would be no medical treatment for her in time, he had cleared the stationmaster's office, obtained the sharpest knife he could find and successfully operated on her! I am sure Dick Evans had not been recruited by the Chartered Company for the purpose of medical surgery! Yet this new breed of expatriate officer could not even perform the duty for which he had been recruited by Government because the animal was a pet! I hasten to add that later veterinary recruits to the service were entirely different.

Whilst the former Chartered Company Officers recognized that there must be a new intake into the senior civil service cadre, most felt a certain resentment that, with only war-time service in the forces to their credit and often without any academic qualification, new officers were being appointed senior to them on the time scale. It took time for new post-war recruits, academically equal and well selected for the tasks ahead, to be absorbed into the service, but the immediate post-war recruits remained a bit above their normal stations, and stood out rather like sore thumbs.

The Medical Service too, was by no means as good as it had been before the war. This was very much brought home to me by an incident which I have never forgotten. I had become a very close friend of Native Chief Oman of Kampong Benoni. The improvement in the reconstruction of the Bukit Manggis Road, and the Drainage and Irrigation Scheme which had begun, brought me into Benoni more often than hitherto. I was always made welcome and bade to stay to many a village curry party. On one of my visits, I found that Oman had cut himself badly with a *parang*, when in the jungle felling timber for a new bridge on the road for which he had obtained a contract. I knew nothing of this until I met him by arrangement at Mile 3, and found that he had had his arm all bandaged in leaves an inch or so thick. He made nothing of it: 'Just a bad cut,' he told me, and assured me that the village medicine would do the trick! I just hoped he was right. When I next saw him, his arm was perfectly mended but the wound was over a foot long and certainly a European doctor would have used at least a dozen stitches.

Sadly news was brought me one morning at the office advising me that Oman was very ill. I hadn't seen him for a week or so, but immediately went to Benoni, where Oman was lying in the sleeping apartment of his house obviously in great pain. He had been treated with village medicine which hadn't worked, and he had also sought treatment from a very nice Chinese dispenser who had been in Government Service before, but who had established his own medical practice in Papar town, purveying European medicine, and possibly Chinese medicine too. I recognized that Oman was suffering badly and that he required urgent attention. My only thought was to get a European doctor to him as soon as possible, and as that would be difficult, the next best thing was to get him into Jesselton Hospital. This I arranged, telling the doctor by phone of his condition and the enormous influence he had in the District and how much he was valued by Government.

By this time the new Hamilton rail bridge had been completed, and it was with moderate ease that we managed to get him as comfortably arranged as possible in the back of the special jeep I had whistled up from Jesselton where an ambulance was awaiting his arrival.

I advised the Resident and rang the hospital as often as I dared, but it was with great shock and dismay that I learned of his death just twenty-four hours later. Conveying the bitter news to his son Hussein was one of the saddest things I ever had to do in Sabah. I never learnt the cause of his death, but I suspected a duodenal ulcer which had burst and turned septic.

He had been a great leader of his people, an extremely loyal subject of the Crown at the time of enemy occupation, and given great assistance to the incoming Australian relief forces just a few years earlier. To me his loss was a personal tragedy. There was no doubt in my mind who should succeed him: his eldest son Hussein often went into the jungle on his father's timber expeditions and, like his father, was a born leader amongst his equals. The Resident quickly approved my recommendation, and himself came up to Papar to present him with his badge of office.

Kompong Benoni: Ceremony of *Tutop Kuala* (notice Cheif Oman in seen standing at stern).

I mentioned that the new railway bridge had only recently been completed. The Indian Army Bridging Company did a magnificent job in a very short time. Oddly enough, the officer-in-charge came from my home town in Cornwall, and had been at school with one of my cousins. They had caused no trouble at all with any of the townsfolk. On the eve of their withdrawal they invited me to dine with them in their mess, fetching me in their landing barge and returning me back late at night to Papar with the headlights of a jeep mounted in the craft illuminating the river banks. A novel way of travelling, anyone would admit!

My time in Papar was, however, rapidly drawing to a close. I was in fact overdue for leave, but was in no hurry to apply for it. I enjoyed my days in Papar even though it was the scene of enemy occupation and all that that had meant. But the people were friendly, the kindest and most honest people one could ever wish to meet.

I had had a most wonderful office staff, most of whom had served with me before the war. I shall never forget Charlie Kong, the most impeccable land clerk one could ever wish for, and, being a long settled District, Papar had a large rent roll. And then there was Abas bin Haji Hassan, one of the most generous and honest men I have ever known. He had been Rubber Restriction clerk before the war, controlling rubber quota production for small rubber gardens dating from the early thirties and the great depression in world trade, and administering in the District the scheme devised to maintain world prices of rubber. I also well remember Mohammed Said bin Keruak and Nawawi bin Latif, both members of the General Clerical Service, whose posting was under the control of the Resident.

Abas was of Malay–Indian extraction and was always doing good turns for everyone. He was kept very busy when we were buying *padi* as he was the clerk-in-charge of the operation. No longer involved in rubber quotas, he had become food clerk and was in charge of rationing of commodities in short supply: hence his involvement in the *padi*-purchasing scheme. He was full of good will for people. When meat was scarce, he was able one day to acquire a goat for the office staff. He slaughtered and butchered it, and sold everyone their requirements, but when it came to his share, there was nothing left of the animal except its entrails!

Leave was always granted subject to the exigencies of the service, and one day I learnt that Government had selected me to start an Agricultural Co-operative movement in the Colony. This would obviously be promotion as the Registrar, as in other Colonies, would have a super-scale post, i.e. bearing a salary above the normal time-scale. I gladly accepted the offer and was advised that I would be given a period of three months training in agricultural co-operatives, followed by a fortnight's tour in Cyprus. Then I would proceed to Ceylon and undertake a month's tour of the co-operatives there, followed by a fortnight in Malaya. All this would be study leave and additional to my normal vacation leave. I was naturally delighted, but it meant leaving Papar, and that was the rub!

However, I knew I was overdue for leave, having served a full four years after my return subsequent to the war, and it was time that I moved on. I began the horrible task of packing household goods first to put in store at Jesselton. Aware that there were still shipping difficulties and that it might not be easy to obtain a passage, I was surprised to learn that I was being offered a passage on an East Asiatic cargo-boat carrying about twenty passengers. This suited me fine, and I was soon to learn who had been influential in obtaining it. The Chief Secretary himself had contacts in the shipping world in Singapore, and he and his wife were proposing to travel on the same boat.

Sir Ralph Hone had been appointed as Twining's successor and this enabled Mr Calder to proceed on leave. Concluding my work in a District in which I had been stationed for so long was bound to be lengthy and somewhat mixed with emotion. So much had happened since the day I first became its District Officer in 1941—and it was now 1950!

It was with genuine emotion and deep sorrow that I attended the farewell party the office staff and the people of Papar had arranged the evening before my departure. It was not only the office staff who were the hosts, but all the townsfolk had joined in too, headed by Chan Chi On, the Kapitan China, and my dear friend Towkay Chop Bee Seng who was always in the forefront when help was needed, like carrying bags of rice on his back from the rail trucks to the stores before the Japanese invasion, and equally an enterprising man who started a pottery in Papar for the production of rubber cups after the war. I must confess that of all the Chinese shop-keepers, he was my favourite. He was always willing, always ready to have a 'go' at anything, and although his Malay didn't really exist, we always managed to communicate one way or another!

The station was crowded when I left; all the Chiefs had gathered and the village headmen, and it seemed half the population of the nearby villages! There was not time to shake them all by the hand; the stationmaster was anxious to get his train on the way. This I knew was my final departure! No need now for me to give an assurance, though I wasn't so sure at the time, that I would return, for one didn't return in Government Service; it was always on, and hopefully upwards.

Jimmie Calder joined the *Selandia* at Singapore, the ship that had a perpetual list! We played a lot of chess on the way back, and came to know each other very well. Three months study course at the Oxford University School of Agriculture went down well and was an excellent stimulus in provoking thought and seeking ways of helping our native peoples in Borneo. I became a trifle perplexed when I received a telegram from Sabah asking me to cut short my leave, to omit the visit to Cyprus but to do the projected tour in Ceylon. Very soon I was in Colombo and made a most interesting tour of the various co-operative societies established throughout the island, visiting Negombo and Jaffna, taking in the *dagobas* and the ancient city of Anuradhapura *en route* to Kandy. I stopped too at an old Government Rest House at Nuraliya in the damp misty hills amongst the tea plantations before returning to Colombo. On reaching Singapore, a message awaited me instructing me to curtail the tour of Malaya and return immediately to Jesselton. I had become suspicious by this time of Government's intentions and it did not surprise me greatly to be informed on arrival that I was to be posted to the Secretariat as Principal Assistant Secretary!

After a period of leave, extended by study leave in Oxford and a tour of Ceylon, I had been out of the Colony for ten months, and was not *au fait* with all the postings that had taken place during my absence. I took over from Wookey, an old Chartered Company Officer. It wasn't a hand-over that one was used to in a District. I think we only had a morning together, but he had compiled notes on the important work currently on hand, and with a cheering word: 'Mr Vun will always help you, if you are stuck!' he was away! He didn't come to the office in the afternoon, I had no stenographer, and files kept mounting! This was so different from any hand-over I had ever experienced before!

From my short time in the Secretariat on first arrival in Sabah, I had learnt the drill from poor old Stanley Hill. I grabbed a bundle, and quickly went through it. Those that needed work to ascertain precedents, I put on one side. Those that required nothing but short minutes I disposed of quickly. Those files that had come down, i.e. had already been sent to the Chief Secretary and if necessary the Governor and had received their instructions, I put in another pile. These merely needed letters starting with the words: 'I am directed to inform you that . . .' followed by the decision.

The next morning, I was in the office at seven o'clock, and a European part-time stenographer, Peggy Ozimek, the wife of a newly appointed doctor, arrived promptly at nine o'clock, when office hours normally started. Having made each other's acquaintance, we got to work. I promptly disposed of the files with letters that had to go out, dictating ones that were more complicated than the brief minutes of the Chief Secretary which often were only initialled in agreement with what I had to say. When, however, the file had been referred to the Governor, great care was taken to ensure wherever possible that the words he had used appeared in my reply. If I had submitted in simpler cases my own draft reply, and it had been accepted or slightly amended, then it could be passed direct to my Personal Assistant.

The files that 'had to go up' caused the most problems. Mr Vun would put the incoming letter on the most appropriate file and attach any other files which appeared to be in need of consultation wherever any precedent existed. These were the ones that had to be 'devilled', and consumed most time and concentration. They mostly concerned land and forestry, both very important subjects. With telephone interruptions and the noise of typewriters, I found it simpler to take boxes of files home with me and do them at night; at least, that enabled me to make notes and write the minutes when I came up to the office early in the morning. This was the best time for working; the sun was not too high in the sky, everything was fresh and still apart from the twittering of birds. The office was totally open to the elements on my left hand side, and I could look far away to the tops of the Crocker Range before the rising mists of the morning heat hid them from view, across the foothills of the Penampang plain, and up towards Menggatal where not so many years before, Albert Kwok and his band of loyalists had engaged upon their brave attempt to overthrow the Japanese invader, and were eventually hunted down in the very same hills that I looked down upon. So much had happened to the people of Sabah in these few years, and now, although the signs of the past conflict were all around us, at last we were engaged upon a vast process of rehabilitation.

I think it was with intention that the Chief Secretary, Jimmy Calder, had gathered around him as his Assistants a team of men who had all been ex-Chartered Company officers. In the two outer offices, and more accessible to the public, sat John Macartney as Establishment Officer, and in an ante-room to the main office was John Longfield as Defence Secretary with Health and Education also under his wing. We were all in one of the few pre-war buildings which remained standing; it was in fact the old ballroom reasonably adjacent to Government Cottage where, on his visits from Sandakan, the Governor would stay, and the ballroom, on the same hill ridge, was where he would undertake most of his entertainment. John Macartney had the most accessible office, immediately under the porch of the main entrance. That was logical as most callers were Government Officers having personnel problems. On either side of the porch were the two ante-rooms, one of which housed John Longfield and the other the Chief Justice.

On the spur leading up to the new Government House had been two hastily erected *kajang* and *atap* buildings: one for the exclusive use of the Chief Secretary and his Personal Assistant, Justin, and the other divided between the Financial Secretary and the Attorney General. These were entirely new posts when compared with the old Chartered Company Establishment. Our pre-war 'Treasurer' had done the work of both the Accountant General and the Financial Secretary.

Housed around the corner from me on the furthest extension of the spur, also in a new *kajang* and *atap* building, was the Deputy Chief Secretry and the Development Secretary. In pre-war days poor old Stanley Hill, as Under Secretary, had fulfilled the functions of both these officers, and in my judgement, with considerable more efficiency! His great advantage was that he knew his Borneo, as all the Chartered Company Officers did. All had served in the field in some district or another, and didn't have to get up and look at a wall map to find, say, the locality of Lahad Datu!

In fairness to the new order of things, it was not altogether 'Parkinson's law' which created the need for the increased establishment: there was more money to go around and, being Treasury controlled by the British Government, every penny we sought had to be amply justified. Obviously, there were many vastly larger territories which needed money for development in a post war era, quite apart from the voracious demands of a war-time Britain. Borneo was 'small fry' and we had to justify every demand for every penny we sought. It inevitably meant more work as our needs were greater.

It was only here in Jesselton that I appreciated for the first time the extent to which the people of Jesselton in particular had suffered during the Occupation. I was aware, of course, of all the vicissitudes of the 'Double Tenth' uprising, with all its repercussions on the local people. I was all too familiar with the infamous murder of all the adult males living on Dinawan Island, but Papar was the rice-bowl of the West Coast and, with ingenuity in frustrating the enemy, the people had survived. It was a different story in Jesselton itself. The people here had been denied the ready supply of rice from the harvests of the plains around them, and in the closing stages of the war high level Allied strategic bombing had forced them to shelter in rubber gardens and even made them hide in the jungle. Not only had the towns been entirely destroyed, but the middle strata of the local society, the clerks and compradors, had disappeared. Many loyal citizens had lost their lives at the hands of the invaders, not necessarily killed deliberately, although many of them were, but conscripted for work in building air-strips and roads, starved and emaciated by being forced to pursue laborious tasks to which they were not accustomed. So as I looked around me from the 'corridors of power' in Jesselton, I found the reason why Wookey had found it necessary to recruit a European as his Personal Assistant; it was the net result of the fall-out of the higher grades of the clerical service, combined with the recruitment of so many new Europeans from mostly African territories or Burma, wherever the old Empire was folding up. Thus the pattern of the Civil Service at that time seemed to be all tops and no bottoms.

Aside from his normal duties as Establishment Officer, John Macartney's work revolved greatly around the two major tasks of recruitment and training. For recruitment, he had to look overseas not only for the senior staff which would be supplied by the Crown Agents, or by transfer arranged by the Colonial Office, but also for the higher grades of clerical staff. South East Asia was still in the throes of recovering from the Far Eastern war and one of the first countries to throw off the yoke of imperialism was Burma. Here, many well educated English-speaking Anglo-Burmese, not feeling their position secure in a very nationalistic state, were happy to accept contracts in a fresh Colonial dependency. The Commissioner General's Office in Singapore was the liaison in the recruitment of this grade of officer, and their introduction proved very successful. We desperately needed skilled technicians and middle supervisory staff and the Anglo-Burmese as they began to arrive fitted well into the local community. The Public Works Department, the Railway and the Agricultural Departments urgently needed the skills they brought with them. The occupation had dealt a savage blow to the advancement of our own people to fulfil the requirements needed to revitalize the country.

Out of a common need in all the South East Asian dependencies of the Crown for the advanced training of local staff was born the Colombo Plan, a conference convened in Ceylon in 1950 in which Australia and New Zealand played the major parts. This Plan was of vital assistance in the training of our own people. It was of inestimable value in meeting the urgent and vital needs of a country lacking technical skills and a good educational base. Without it, Sabah could never have developed so quickly in the immediate years ahead, either economically or politically. It was a scheme which worked in both directions in that its provisions offered the services of officers who were experts in their particular field, or it accepted students from Sabah and gave them training courses in a university or other professional establishment, whatever their skills might need. This latter alternative was of the greatest help, for the services of professional officers had a built-in time factor: these officers came, naturally, for a limited number of years: whereas the training of our own people became a lasting benefit to the country. To safeguard the value of these awards to Sabah, the officer on accepting a scholarship also signed a document to the effect that he or she would return to Sabah after their training and serve their country for a minimum period of two years. Nor was the award limited to Government officers but was open to any to work in any capacity on their return. They were merely asked to continue their work in their country, nearly always in a higher grade, for the required minimum period.

Our difficulty was in being able to find, not merely select, school-leavers with sufficient basic education to benefit from the scheme. The absence of any sort of education during the war years had exacted a very telling toll. In the Colony's Annual Report of 1951 the Education Department recorded that 'at the end of the year nine candidates entered for the Cambridge School Certificate of whom one has been successful'. Naturally, to benefit from academic or advanced technical knowledge, the Governments quite rightly required candidates for overseas training to have certain basic qualifications, of which the possession of a School Certificate was usually the minimum.

The emphasis of the social services in the early years of Colonial Administration had to be on education, with health running a close second. To obtain the maximum benefit from the Colombo Plan, we had to improve the levels of education. One of the first major projects in this connection was the establishment of a Teachers' Training College at Tuaran. This was funded by a major Colonial Development and Welfare grant in 1952. Plans for this were being handled by the Development Secretary. His function embraced all schemes being sent to the Secretary of State for consideration. It was his office, for example, that had succeeded in obtaining approval for the money to implement the Benoni drainage problem.

My most important subject as Principal Assistant Secretary was undoubtedly forestry. In the early days when the Chartered Company had difficulty in raising money to finance its endeavours to establish a stable and progressive government, it had given a monopoly of timber extraction to one Company: the British Borneo Timber Company. Whilst the Chartered Company may have succeeded in its objectives, a monopolistic policy of development of the greatest natural resource of Sabah was now clearly anachronistic. The immediate wealth of the country lay in its timber resources and the ending of the BBT monopoly was the most certain way of increasing the much needed revenue. Hence the implementation of the Government's forest policy was one of the greater achievements to have occurred during the Governorship of Sir Ralph Hone.

The Timber Company may well have anticipated that the pre-war monopoly would be challenged and had rallied all their resources in their efforts to obtain the best possible terms for yielding their concession—a concession which covered all the great forests of the country of which some 80% carried commercial timber. Harry Keith, who had been interned with us in Kuching, was Conservator of Forests and there was no one better equipped than he to advise on the best forest areas. His Department demarcated four large concession areas, each of some 2,000 square miles, and proposed that these areas be put out to tender for commercial exploitation on a permanent yield basis. This was indeed the important feature: permanent yield.

It was planned that the conceded areas should be subdivided into smaller areas for annual coupes, and that felling should be limited to trees above a certain girth. A return to the same felling area would not take place until the expiration of one hundred years, by which time other trees by natural growth would have attained the same minimum girth and would be ready for felling. In this way, the forests would never be exploited and always remain a natural source of wealth for the country.

There were certain pockets of very rich andesite soil which was extremely good for agriculture. It was decided that the forests could be removed from these small pockets to make way for agricultural production: cocoa was being recommended by the Agricultural Department as an alternative crop to rubber and needed rich soil. Removal of the forest in these areas was known as 'slaughter felling': the same, in fact, as the Muruts had been doing for centuries in very small patches with their *ladang* cultivation. They were accustomed to clearing a virgin area of jungle about the size of a football pitch, burning it, and cultivating it for dry rice for at the most about ten years, then moving on to another area of virgin jungle. The areas demarcated for slaughter felling were somewhat larger, of course, than a Murut *ladang*. It was, however, the provision of these areas which seemed a sensible policy at the time, but which in later years led to over-exploitation for the benefit of the few rather than the many. This could not be foreseen at the time.

The main negotiations were with the British Borneo Timber Co. whose executives were hard headed business men from London, and their local agents, Messrs Harrison and Crosfield. The Government relied on any assistance and advice the Colonial Office could offer. Every letter which came into the Secretariat appeared to carry a 'Priority' tag, and every letter had to be filed with files containing precedents attached. At times it meant research into four or five files. We could not, for example, contain in the licensed areas any parcel of ground to which there were native rights attached. Graves, in particular, could crop up in odd places long since devoid of habitation, but the location of graves of forbears in native eyes are never forgotten, and oftentimes when in Murut country I have encountered in the jungle quite isolated, but perhaps at the site of a former village, a grave with a square roof ornamented with coloured flags and obviously recently tended. The District Officers and Residents were brought into the picture as well as the Commissioner of Lands, with the Conservator of Forests playing the key role.

Meetings with the Governor in the chair were commonplace, some of them taking place at most unsociable hours like six o'clock in the evening. The Chief Secretary and the Attorney General always had to be present to represent Government's views to the business tycoons. In all this, it was my task to be the secretary and produce the notes and decisions reached by noon the next day at the latest. It was hard going!

Sir Ralph Hone as Governor was also keen to improve communications, and he gave priority not so much to roads as to internal air communications. To him must be attributed the building of airstrips in all the major towns, particularly linking the isolated stations of the East Coast, like Tawau and Lahad Datu, to Sandakan and

Jesselton. Land acquisition was necessary to construct these in suitable locations as near as possible to the towns they served, and this actively involved the Public Works and the Lands and Survey Departments. Much land had to be acquired for a public purpose so surveyors, in the main, sought sites in which only moribund rubber trees or coconut palms were involved. In a later phase Kudat and Keningau also had their airstrips. I was the Secretary to receive this correspondence from the Heads of Departments concerned and had to submit it with a recommendation to the Chief Secretary and Governor. Everything seemed to be priority!

High level talks were also going on regarding the establishment of Borneo Airways, a Company to be set up jointly by the Governments of North Borneo, Brunei and Sarawak, holding 51%, with Malayan Airways holding the balance. This was, of course, the first internal air service for public use, but it may be mentioned in passing that before the war, Dr Stookes, Medical Officer to East Coast estates, had been the pioneer in domestic air travel, using his own private seaplane based at Sandakan. He was one of the few unfortunates who had hidden from the Japanese in the East Coast jungles of the Interior in the early stages of the war, but was later caught by them and suffered execution in Keningau along with Stanley Hill and other inmates from Kuching.

Now, however, Sabah was really beginning to be brought into the modern age. Already, Jesselton and Sandakan airstrips were in operation, and we no longer relied on the services of the RAF Sunderlands for the link between ourselves and Singapore. The links between the Colonial Office and the Governor were always maintained by Savingram; these arrived through the night and there was always a bundle of them awaiting attention as soon as the office opened, when Mr Vun began their distribution to their correct files. Frankly, I do not know what the Government would have done without Mr Vun; he had an amazing memory and knew the place of every single document! The Secretariat was a hive of industry at that time.

I think we earned our salary without any doubt at all! I was always up at the Secretariat very soon after dawn, and long before the office opened. I then returned for breakfast, which always was beautifully fresh fish, caught a few hours before, which my cook would fetch from the market, whilst I was doing my early morning stint. Calls from the public interrupted office hours to a certain extent, but not nearly as much as in a District, and telephone calls too were an interruption. The inevitable result was that one took at least a couple of red boxes home every night to read up and make notes to give one a good start in the morning. It was a long hard grind, nevertheless interesting and enjoyable! I had no complaints whatsoever albeit my own social life was limited by it.

Then one morning I was called to the Chief Secretary's office. Thinking it was an urgent matter on forestry which had just cropped up, I was surprised when I was asked by Jimmy if I would like to start an Information Office for the Government. It was the time of the Korean war, and there was a good deal of anti-American and anti-European propaganda which was coming over the air waves, and as a Government we had no means of countering it. On the Establishment side, the Secretary of State had been urging Colonial Governments to establish Public

Relations or Information Offices for the purpose of disseminating the British Government's views and attitudes in the complex attitude of growing world opinion towards Colonial territories and their governance. This in my view was stimulated by the United States through the United Nations, and secretly I have always believed it was a movement born out of envy. Great Britain before the war was the greatest trading nation the world had ever seen; after the war we still retained Colonies, and with Preferential Customs Tariffs, we had undoubtedly retained a dominant trading position in our Colonial Territories, which put other trading nations at a certain disadvantage. We ourselves were in any case committed to the task of bringing about self-government in the Colonial Empire. But there now seemed to be an outside force endeavouring to quicken the pace of emancipation. We were making our contribution in a sure and solid way, gradually building on our achievements and granting independence to countries already able to stand on their own feet like Burma, India and Ceylon where education and political development had advanced to a high degree: they were ready for it, but many Colonies still needed a strong educational basis before they could be introduced to a political scene. Certainly Sarawak and North Borneo, the Empire's youngest Colonies, having endured such a terrible set-back during the Far Eastern War, needed a breathing space for recuperation as development and educational standards slowly began. I readily comprehended the Government's desire to establish an office which would disseminate its point of view and ultimately speed up the process towards self-determination.

I asked Jimmy if I might think it over during the weekend, and also sought his assurance that I wouldn't be leaving the mainstream of the Administrative cadre. Naturally, I wondered why he had chosen me for the job, and it even passed through my mind that perhaps I was not up to the Secretariat post and that he was offering me a tempting way out. I did not believe that, however, as on most Sunday mornings he would come down to my bungalow on the beach, and join me for a swim and a game of chess. We were good friends, and I could only come to the conclusion that he was genuinely pushing me up the ladder.

There was one thing of which I was certain: he knew I could write! There used to be a periodical published in Great Britain named the *Crown Colonist*, and as Information was on my schedule it fell to me to write up events in North Borneo for every issue. Once, I had written a feature article on current developments, which I had submitted to the Chief Secretary, in accordance with Government regulations, on the progress in the country since the Liberation. I know he was pleased with that so I concluded that I was being offered the post on merit. As it would carry a duty allowance of M$100 *per mensem*, which was always worthwhile, I decided in favour of acceptance. It was a big decision to make, since if I applied for a transfer from the post of Principal Assistant Secretary to another Colony, I would be well on the road to a Chief Secretaryship. On the other hand, that would have meant leaving North Borneo, something I did not wish to do. I had chosen to serve here, I knew and loved the people well, and there was to me no better country in which to live! Whatever may have happened subsequently to make me doubt that decision, I still feel it was the right course to have taken and that in no small way, knowing the country as intimately as I did, I was able to advance its progress and enrich the lives of its people in a way that few other officers could have done.

It is always easy in later years to wonder whether at a particular juncture in life, one did the right thing for the furtherance of one's career. It was postulated later by a devious method of interpretation by more senior officers that I had elected to leave the administrative cadre when I established the Information Office: nothing, in fact, was further from the truth! The only omission I had made was not to ask the man in whom I trusted to set the record straight in writing. In fact there was no need for me to have made such a request—the question was never in doubt. Nevertheless, in retrospect, I would advise any Government officer who may read this and be placed in analogous circumstances to have written confirmation of any act that may affect his career in later years. One can never trust the whims of a government!

The first Information Office was opened in a temporary two-roomed building constructed hastily after the war as offices for one of the new trading firms which had opened up shortly after the civil administration had been re-established. They had moved to new and larger premises and, rather than have this building destroyed, the Public Works Department made it available for offices. We only had a small establishment in the beginning. My right-hand man and only office assistant was the redoubtable Tom Willie. We also had a Chinese translator, Madame Cheng Kwok Mee, who came in the mornings, two orderlies, a van and a driver: a small beginning for an office which was to become in a few years a major Government Department with a staff of over 250 officers!

The Central Office of Information in London sent us press releases for newspapers which at that time did not exist, and we had a wire-recorder for picking up information from BBC broadcasts. Tape at that time had not come into existence, but anyone who may recall the intricacies of a wire-recorder will sympathize with the tribulation we experienced in operating such a machine! More often than not, on play-back, the wire broke. Infinite time was taken in writing up a fifteen-minute news broadcast. I was torn between trying to decide whether we would be making any impact at all with international news or whether we should endeavour to concentrate on publicizing activities of our own Government.

At the back of the minds of those in the Goverment in the UK was the Communist threat from North Korea and China. It was demonstrating itself already in the state of emergency in Malaya. Many will remember the attacks on rubber estate managers, the disruption of road and rail communications and even that a Governor was ambushed and killed. The threat of the spread of communism existed even in the Peninsula. Here in this country I was now in charge of Information Services and reviewing the situation in my own mind, I felt that the communist threat would fall on stoney ground in Borneo, at least as far as North Borneo was concerned. Communism breeds amongst a people who have nothing and have nothing to lose. Here in Sabah all our people had land of their own, or access to land. They possessed wealth in their buffaloes, their oxen and their brass. They all had housing adapted to the climatic needs of the country; they wanted for nothing.

I concluded that the greatest threat to the security of Sabah might well be the voices coming over the air-waves. There was nothing to stop people buying wireless sets and listening to the rather crude propoganda being broadcast and beamed towards South East Asia. This had the potential of making an insidious impact on a certain proportion of the less well off of the population: perhaps on the islanders who had little land of their own and lived only off the fruits of the sea. These were the pirates of old and had suffered badly during the occupation. There was only one way in which we could combat hostile thought coming out of the air, and that was by swamping the air channels with our own story of events.

It was out of this thinking that Radio Sabah was born. The Posts and Telegraphs had a spare local transmitter just covering the Jesselton area, and I persuaded the Director to let us use this transmitter for experimental midday news broadcasts. This was agreed and the first of these transmissions broadcast local news in English, Malay and the two most important Chinese language groups: Kuo-Yu and Hakka. These were immediately successful and there was hardly a Chinese shop in the main streets of Jesselton which did not have its set tuned loudly listening to our broadcasts! The number of wireless licences issued during 1952 when we started these experimental broadcasts rose from 1,611 to 2,163 in just a few months. Now there was no doubt in my mind where the main thrust of our efforts lay. We had to have our own Broadcasting Service!

My efforts were helped to a certain extent by the planned commencement of the publication of the *Sabah Times*, the Colony's first English language newspaper, early in 1953. This would mean a change of emphasis in the way we distributed news of Government activities. Our own stereo'd midday bulletins could give way to press releases issued to the daily newspaper and translated into Chinese and Malay. That gave me more time in which to concentrate on the insatiable demands for the knowledge of English and the provision of English reading material. The reading-room in the old warehouse at the back of the office was never empty, and I decided that we should start a library. At first we provided a reference library where people could use the books for consultation on the site, but the demand for a lending library was very evident.

It was obvious that I had to submit an early bid for more extensive office accommodation and a broadcasting studio. To a certain extent fortune was with us. The Police had had new barracks built for them and the married quarters of the Jesselton Town force, earlier mentioned in connection with the Double Tenth uprising and where the Jesselton guerrillas killed several Japanese, became vacant. It was in a good position, just opposite the Town *padang*, and suited us excellently. Here and for many years afterwards we had accommodation for a very good reading room and library. Later, we had the kitchens converted into more office space, a film library and a dark-room for photographic facilities.

We were lucky too in that the first commercial hotel had been built in Jesselton

Party celebrating opening of Radio Sabah in old Rest House building. Donald Stephens, as Editor of the *Sabah Times*, standing full-face mid-left.

and this released the post-war Jesselton Rest House on the hillock by the clock tower, which became our first Broadcasting Studio.

I also had the good fortune to obtain the services of the most loyal and honest of men, Abas bin Haji Ahmat who had been with me in Papar before and after the war. His knowledge of English was so excellent that he made the perfect Malay translator and relieved Tom Willie for other duties.

I was aware that I was not professionally equipped to become a broadcaster myself, but I considered it essential that if I was to administer a broadcasting service I must have a basic technical background to comprehend and advise others. I therefore made enquiries at the BBC and they offered me a place on one of their Staff Training Courses. As I was due for leave in the near future, I sought approval for study leave which was added to my earned leave and this enabled me to accept the kind offer of the BBC. This course was invaluable, and my head was full of ideas which could be put to great advantage in Sabah. I couldn't get back quick enough to implement them!

Foremost in my mind was the conception of a new building designed for broadcasting to serve as our headquarters: a Broadcasting House for Sabah. We also had to have our own engineering staff and our own transmittors and no longer be dependent on the good offices of the Posts and Telegraphs Department; they had their own priorities and those didn't necessarily coincide with ours.

That brought me to the question of transmitters, and I obtained Government approval to seek the advice of the Crown Agents who provided professional assistance in undertaking a transmitting survey. This survey recommended the installation of a VHF transmitter at a height of some 10,000 ft. on Mt. Kinabalu. The signal would be sent direct from an aerial on the roof of Broadcasting House to the VHF transmitter where it would be relayed to five or six medium wave transmitters situated in the main areas of population density.

I submitted a CD&W Scheme to Government and at the same time asked the PWD Architects' Department to prepare drawings for Broadcasting House. One of my major recommendations to Government was that we should recruit our own broadcasting engineer and divorce ourselves from the technical assistance of Posts and Telegraphs. This met with a little opposition, as if there was any possible way of saving money, Government would do it. However, they saw the logic of the situation and finally agreed. Broadcasting needed specialist engineers. With larger organizations there were engineers who specialized in studios and others who specialized in aerials; we needed an all-rounder.

It was not only in the field of broadcasting that the office was developing fast. Information services were not confined to Jesselton; we had offices too in Sandakan and Tawau supplying both reading rooms and libraries. The widespread desire to learn English had never been greater; English books were in great demand. I felt that the need for the services of a British Council Office in the country would be beneficial and began to raise this issue.

Films and photography also contributed in no small measure to the impact that the Government was making in the country. The Central Office of Information in

London air-lifted every week news-reels for cinema distribution and I managed to secure a wide showing of these in cinemas in the chief towns. Rural areas, however, were neglected, and consequently in the Colony's Estimates I was successful in obtaining money for the establishment of the first mobile film unit which could travel on a regular itinerary around the Jesselton road system, serving the villages of Penampang, Inamam, Menggatal, Telipok and Tuaran. The supply of films from overseas agencies was no problem at all; not only did the COI in Britain let us have many documentaries on various subjects, but the Australian Government also needed its image to be remembered in South East Asia and were willing suppliers of film material. Similarly, the United States Information Services with Headquarters in Singapore willingly supplied films. The cinema shows put on by the travelling film unit were so widely attended that they pointed the way to further growth in this field as soon as funds became available.

The popularity of the Sandakan and Jesselton libraries and reading rooms clearly indicated that other main towns were also crying out for the provision of similar services and in 1954 the Hong Kong and Shanghai Bank, upon removing into new premises in Tawau, generously made available its old building for use as a library and reading room, whilst in Beaufort a newly constructed youth centre very kindly offered space for similar activities. The demand for our services was springing from the grass roots of the youth of the country. This could only be good, but my problem was to convince Government of this and ensure the successful provision of funds. This was certainly not an easy task! The financial authorities did not appreciate that this was a movement and desire for knowledge springing from the fundamental base of society, but regarded us more as just another spending department which would not increase the revenues of the country. I appreciated that Sabah was still Treasury-controlled by the United Kingdom Government and that the Annual Estimates had to be pruned to available resources, so I simply had to bide my time!

In the meantime, the plans for the new Broadcasting House were going ahead fast. The CD&W Scheme had met with approval, and we were authorized to implement it. For the first time Government really began to take a more than passing interest in progress since President Sukarno in Indonesia was making very anti-Imperialist utterances and it was beginning to be foreseen that a situation which was to become known as the Indonesian Confrontation was on the sky-line. We shared a common border with Indonesian Borneo. The need for a good broadcasting service now became apparent to all. My role was rapidly reversing: at first I had had the greatest difficulty in stimulating any Government interest in my proposals, but now I was being questioned about when the new transmitters and the new service were going to be on the air. I was being pressed!

My reply was that Rome was not built overnight! We had to wait until the Crown Agents had placed the orders with transmitting engineers; then they had to be shipped out to Borneo and we had a mammoth job getting the equipment to a height of 10,000 ft. The PWD had done a magnificent job in preparing the site, and plans had gone ahead according to my requirements with the greatest speed. It was not long before tenders were placed and construction had begun.

On the personnel side, my recommendations for the recruitment of a broadcasting engineer had met with approval. The Crown Agents had selected an all-round engineer who had seen service with Radio Malaya, and with his arrival technical equipment for the studios was being ordered and plans made for the transmitting side of the project. This was commenced not without considerable difficulty. Because of the isolated nature of the transmitting site, all equipment had to be duplicated, so that if one transmitter developed a fault, the second transmitter could take over and the service would not be interrupted. Then there was a question of power supply. This had to produce sufficient electricity to drive a 5 kw. transmitter, and voltage power would be lost, the higher one took the cables up great heights like Kinabalu. It was necessary to build a generating station on a site as high as possible on the mountainside, and to achieve this a road had to be built to enable generators to be transported to it, and subsequently maintained for the continual tanker traffic which would be required to convey the oil to feed the generators. When it was completed convoys of PWD trucks were seen moving along it like the never-ending stream along the Burma Road some years before in equally mountainous country.

The transport of the transmitters themselves presented the greatest problem. They all had to be broken down into loads that could be carried on men's backs—and by Government regulation this was limited to 30 *katis*. The sides of Kinabalu in places were almost 80°, usually wet and slippery, so we built a wooden staircase of lateral lying logs to assist the feet of the local Kedazan carriers to get a grip on the constantly wet mountain-side. Inevitably it was a time-taking exercise.

The threat of Indonesian confrontation was already becoming a reality. The immediate reaction of the Government was to form a security committee and invite as members representatives of the armed services. In my role as the 'eyes and ears' of the Government I was also a member, but the main-spring of the meeting was the weekly report of the special branch. This arm of the Police Department had a network of undercover agents who fed in the type of information which the Police needed to receive. With a top secret coding it evaluated the reports that they had received during the week. Sabah was very vulnerable to attack as we had a land border with Indonesia several hundreds of miles long. I knew it—I had been all along its length! It was virtually entirely uninhabited, a terrain easy to penetrate.

Hitherto, our only outside threat was the pirates of the Suluk islands and the Southern Philippines who had raided isolated townships on several occasions. Confrontation with one of our most powerful neighbours was a different and more serious situation. This was recognized immediately by the British Government who deployed the Navy into the area led by HMS *Bulwark*. From its deck, troops were to be flown by helicopter into the border country. Landing pads had immediately to be re-claimed from the jungle to enable troops to be at all strategic points where a threat seemed possible. The Murut longhouses appeared most likely to be threatened, but in the event none were actually attacked even though hostile movements had been reported.

It was then that I came under attack as Radio Sabah was not on the air to reach the 'hearts and minds' of people and calm the fears of our distant communities who might be under threat. I explained the difficulties of transporting the transmitters to the site on Kinabalu and asked if the RAF could assist in ferrying the heavier parts of the transmitter by helicopter to the mountain-side. This would, I explained, save a great deal of time in disassembling them into small parts and assembling them again. The RAF officer present made a note and at the next meeting the following week advised that it was considered feasible and that a suitable machine and its crew were being flown up from Singapore for this purpose.

This was really invaluable assistance as can be judged from the fact that the helicopter made more than fifty sorties from Jesselton airport to Kinabalu. This was all the more remarkable since the mountain misted up very early in the morning, making flying thereafter quite impossible. It could only make one trip in the morning with any certainty and at times in the evenings. It was quite a remarkable accomplishment and made it possible for us to go on the air possibly six months or so before we could otherwise have done. Special thanks are due to the gallant efforts of the RAF helicopter crew who undertook these early morning flights every day for about three months and to the skill of the pilot who had to navigate the plane amidst the treacherous down-currents of wind swirling off the mountain top as soon as the tropical sun had risen sufficiently to stir the dawn air.

In the meantime, the additional Colonial Development and Welfare scheme for new studies had been approved. Plans had been agreed with the PWD architect and myself and they had been put out to tender. The site chosen and allocated by Government was the site of the old dispensary on a hillock off the Tuaran Road which led up to the old hospital. The site was bulldozed and made a sufficiently expansive area for the building proposed and for a further extension at a later date; even at this early date I had television in mind.

It wasn't many months before the building began to take shape, and I was actively putting forward staffing proposals. I had already decided that I would have my office here, as broadcasting, I knew, would fast become the most powerful medium at my disposal. I was certain of its growth in the towns, but I wanted to get at the native population and my mind turned to the natives of the Interior amongst whom I had journeyed so much: to the Ulu people around Tampias, so remote and out of the way, and particularly to the Muruts of the Dalit and Bokan country. They were so far removed by distance and by inaccessibility from the majority of the social services the Government could offer, whereas broadcasting had the potential of entering their very own longhouses. That focused attention on the need for them to have radio receivers, and I recalled having read in the *Crown Colonist* of the installation of community listening houses in various of the African colonies. I didn't think that was the correct approach here, and I rather favoured the 'saucepan' radio: a cheap radio set distributed to villages which, although it would receive weak signals from other stations, would receive Radio Sabah loud and clear when the new transmitting system was in operation. I put a request for such sets to be presented to us under the Colombo Plan, and we would undertake distribution through the District Administration.

Whilst all these plans were being made, it must not be thought for one moment that the information side was in any way being neglected. Far from it. Again, looking to the future, I founded a children's newspaper. I will quote from the 1956 Colony Annual Report where I wrote:

> In May the first number of *Anak Sabah*, a monthly newspaper in English designed to interest adolescents, particularly those still at school, was produced. It aimed at helping young readers to improve their English, to take an interest in their country and the activities of their fellows, and at encouraging young people to write, particularly about Borneo. A circulation of about 1,000 was originally anticipated, but the paper was received with enthusiasm, particularly by the schools, and the circulation rose rapidly to 2,500 and has been maintained at that level.

There were several points of interest which arose out of this venture. The first major point was that it was not a give-away sheet. I held a very strong view that something which is given away is not esteemed, but something which one pays for, however nominal, is held in value. Secondly, I sought to encourage talent. I wanted contributions from the children of Sabah for whom it was being produced. I wanted not merely letters but articles, stories and even drawings or sketches. I edited the paper, which was printed by the Printing Office, myself for the first year of publication, and then when I had stamped my mark on it, I gave the editorship to a European lady of ability who carried on the good work. I may add here with a certain amount of pride that through its columns we discovered a brilliant artist in one Mohammed Yassin, who I believe is now Principal of the College of Art in Sabah.

The next step forward in media publicity to which I directed my attention was born out of the need to publicize the programmes being broadcast by Radio Sabah. The service was now well established in four language groups: English, Chinese, Malay and Kedazan or, as I would have preferred to have called it, the 'native language' programme. The Kedazans were, however, the predominant native race, and it was an all Kedazan staff who were the programme organisers. I envisaged using the magazine I had in mind as a medium of publicity to include useful information in developing an awareness of citizenship. The programme publicity would be the *raison d'être* of the magazine but it could also include useful articles, translated into the vernacular and culled from our radio broadcasts. I was certain it would be a winner for the simple reason that one of the most popular of programmes for which we received hundreds of letters a week was a request programme. People just love to hear their names coming over the air, and I conceived the idea that the request could only be broadcast if the coupon I proposed to publish in the magazine was completed. That simple fact would, I was convinced, ensure the success of the magazine!

I received a set-back when the Government Printer told me he was far too busy to undertake a weekly production of a magazine such as I proposed. I was, however, so convinced that it would be a success, that I approached a printing firm of very high standards in Brunei. They obliged, and the second very popular medium of publicity was launched! I gave it the title *Radio Sabah Calling*. I knew instinctively that this would be a success, and with every issue our distributors asked to be supplied with additional copies. I've forgotten now the price at which it was to be sold but I know every issue paid for itself. It was a four-language magazine, a different magazine for each of the programme services in which we were broadcasting, and it appeared weekly. The programme organizers of the four language groups were responsible for compiling the text of the programme material, but I combined it too with the function of the *Listener* magazine of the BBC by reproducing in written form various talks of an educative nature which had been broadcast. These were nearly always talks on agricultural or health matters, so we were able to obtain maximum educational benefit.

None of the distribution and accounting involved could be done without additional staff, and our two office buildings were bursting at the seams. In every field we had to expand. The simplest method of publicity was by means of photographs, so we had to recruit a good photographer and find space somewhere for a dark room. This went hand in hand with the mobile cinema unit, so I created a Press and Photographic Division within the Department.

Every year the Annual Estimates became a struggle with the Financial Secretary's Office! I was on the ground and felt the pulse of the public. I knew I had to have the money to provide the services the people of the country demanded. I knew I was acting in their best interests by creating the demand, and I only hoped that Government would view my requests in the same way. Although I met with apparent sympathy, unfortunately only some 60% of my requests were normally met! It was natural enough, really; every Head of Department wanted the best financial deal he could get for his own expansion. Always demand exceeded supply, and I was regarded as one of the 'spending' departments: not a department like forestry which was adding to the financial well-being of the Colony's revenue. It was difficult for Government to evaluate the return it would get from Broadcasting and Information Services.

We were put to a critical test when it was announced early in 1959 that North Borneo would be included in the itinerary of HRH the Duke of Edinburgh when he made a visit to the Far East later in the year. Suddenly Government became aware of the value of publicity and realized that the world's press would at least for a short while focus on the Colony.

I was on leave in the United Kingdom at the time, when I unexpectedly received an urgent letter instructing me to cut short my leave and return immediately by air to serve on the Planning Committee for the Duke's reception and programme. This was a great turning point for the fortunes of the Broadcasting and Information Office and the Colony in general. Suddenly, the world's press would begin to focus on a little known back-water in the South China Seas!

There began, almost simultaneously, a political awakening! Because the world's attention was spot-lighting itself upon us, an awareness amongst the people to have a little more say in their own affairs began to dawn. To a great extent credit for this must be given to Donald Stephens who was beginning to exercise an influence on public opinion through his editorials in his newspaper, the *Sabah Times*. The motivator and great political developer who was the instigator of all this was our new Governor, Sir Roland Turnbull. He, not unlike our first Governor as a Colony, then still Mr Edward Twining later to become Lord Twining, was a man of vision. He had previously served in African Colonies, where the 'wind of change' had blown earlier than it had done in the Far East, and so he was more aware of the immediate thrusts necessary to produce political development.

One of his first steps was to nominate Donald Stephens as a member of his Legislative Council. Donald had become, quite rightly, a vociferous critic of Government measures, or lack of them, in cases where he thought action was necessary. By bringing him into the inner circle, he would then appreciate the more fundamental problems with which the Government was being faced. Sir Roland also had the foresight and wisdom to identify in Donald a potential political leader who had the ability to stir political thinking and create the atmosphere and background against which political parties could be formed. Political development was essential if ever the country were able to shake off the yoke of imperialism and become a country capable of standing on its own feet.

The Private Secretary called me unexpectedly to his office one day, saying that the Governor would 'like to have a chat' with me. No subject was mentioned, but as I drove my car to Government House one late afternoon just after five o'clock, I began to wonder what misdemeanour I had been up to! It was, of course, nothing of the kind. I was welcomed with a drink, and bidden to be seated. Sir Roland then began a long monologue which held me spellbound with the quality and imagination of his thought. He spoke of the inevitability of self-determination of the country, and how best this might be achieved. He foresaw a time when political achievement would overtake economic development. He stressed that there was no rapid way in which Sabah could become financially strong, and that political development would be more easily achieved, and would, therefore, precede economic independence. If Sabah was to make its mark politically, it would have to federate with other neighbouring territories under the influence of Britain.

'We needn't look as far afield as Singapore or Malaya,' he said. 'All we have to do is to look at the history of Borneo.' Then he asked: 'Weren't Sarawak and Sabah once part of the Sultanate of Brunei?'

Sir Roland then proceeded to announce his views on the desirability of 'closer association' with Sarawak and Brunei. It then became apparent as he talked that he had already discussed his thoughts on the subject with the Governor of Sarawak, Sir Anthony Abell, and the Sultan of Brunei. 'Neither are opposed to the idea,' he concluded. Then the penny dropped, for I remembered that the Sultan of Brunei had recently paid an unofficial visit to Sabah. Discussions with the Sultan had obviously taken place on this subject. The Sultan held the key to the success of the policy: for him, it would be the reunification of his old Sultanate. He certainly would be in favour of the proposal!

I came into the picture to co-ordinate publicity with Sarawak and Brunei. Prepared press-releases and simultaneous broadcasts would be made by both the Governor of Sarawak and the Governor of North Borneo at the same hour on the same day, and the prepared releases would be given to the press immediately afterwards. It was quite a masterly stroke of co-ordination. After the third or fourth gin tonic with the Governor, I found myself filled with admiration for him and the skill with which he had negotiated it all. I was immediately enthusiastic for the idea. It was original and it was simple, and merely re-wrote the history book as it once was in Borneo.

Sir Roland then asked me if I would give him a personal report on public reaction to the proposal. This, in fact, was the cue I had been waiting for. So many times in the past, I had had to explain that the Department was organized to desseminate information, but had no ground staff to provide a feed-back. I appreciated that this was essential, if we were doing our job properly: we should be the eyes and ears of Government, and to a large extent I was very much aware of public opinion. I had been a District Officer; when out on my rounds I always chatted to people and learnt much from them, and I always had a feed-back on Government measures through the Native Chiefs, all of whom I met regularly once a week on Native Court days. I was, therefore, very much *au fait* with public reaction to any Government measure introduced, but officially there was no feed-back in the way that the Police had in their Special Branch. So I immediately took advantage of the Governor's request, and explained the staffing position, a point which the Governor readily acknowledged. 'You need a listening post!' the Governor said: 'Put up your proposals!'

So I proposed a post with the title: 'District Liaison Officer', and recommended that he should be a Chinese-speaking man for preference. The wheels of Government work slowly, but after a year we were able to recruit an officer who had been a former missionary in China, and spoke Hakka, the Chinese language most widely-spoken by overseas Chinese in Sabah. He travelled widely throughout the country, his reports were always accurate, and his style of writing droll and diverting, and they were read with considerable interest by all the high ranking officers of Government. I was very glad to have him on my staff.

Possibly overshadowing public interest in the country's political development at that time was the visit of the Duke of Edinburgh. This had caught the imagination of the people of the country; that such an important person in the British Royal Household was coming to meet them took on the mantle of a gleaming torch in their otherwise fairly humdrum existence. Although the visit was inevitably to be of short duration, the Planning Committee decided that in spite of the fact that they couldn't arrange for him to see as much of the country and its people as they would have liked, the only satisfactory alternative would be to bring the people to the Duke! It was decided to reproduce on a small scale, a typical house of every major native race of the country. An area of Tanjong Aru beach was set aside for this purpose. Once more, much of the planning for this fell inevitably on the District Officers. Nevertheless, everyone rose to the occasion magnificently! One of the Secretariat officers was given the task of co-ordinating all the arrangements with the Districts, and truly magnificent replicas of houses of all the Interior races began to be built on the beach area of Tanjong Aru reserved for the Exhibition.

All overseas press enquiries received by Government were directed to me, and it became apparent that representatives of all the major British papers intended to cover the visit. This meant setting up a centre where they could prepare and file their reports, and I thought the old reading room which we had recently vacated would be ideally located, being only a stone's throw from the Posts and Telegraph office. Accordingly, I laid out the place in the best way I could and equipped it, in collaboration with the Telegraph Department, with a dozen phones. Singapore, Malayan and Hong Kong newspapers were also to send their representatives. Hotel reservations were made for them all, and transport allocated.

An aircraft of the Queen's Flight brought the visiting Duke from Sarawak and Brunei. He was met at the airport by His Excellency the Governor who introduced him to members of the Legislative and Executive Councils, and then the two of them in an open car, borrowed from a civil servant and sprayed black for its more formal role, left the welcoming crowds at the airport and drove along the streets of the town, and through resplendent arches of salutation built by the Chinese Chamber of Commerce. The representatives of the press at the airport had conformed to the restraints on their movements in the photo coverage of the arrival, and I just hoped that they would be well pleased with the rest of the arrangements made for them.

The Duke's apartment was the visitor's suite at Government House which, with the Governor's Residence itself, had recently been fully air-conditioned, the first buildings in the country to be so treated. A few days later I heard that there had been panic stations at Government House earlier that morning when it was found that the air-conditioning plant had broken down! Dawn calls to the Director of Public Works had brought out engineers who had managed to trace the fault to a transformer at the bottom of the hill. After the visit was over, the word went around that the Duke had found it 'a trifle cool'! Such 'stories' often emerge after an event like this!

In the early evening on the first day of the visit I called in at the Press Centre and found it a hive of industry. Some were busy on the phones filing their stories to Cable and Wireless, whilst others were still busy at their typewriters. As soon as they saw me, I met a barrage of questions, not so much about the arrangements for the visit, but more about the Colony itself. I had realized that to the international press we were a little known back-water, and had prepared a roneoed fact sheet on the vital information about the country which they would seek. These were freely available in packets, with copies of the Colony's latest Annual Report at their Centre. That didn't stop them, however, from asking me a multitude of questions, the answers to which were mostly available in the packs I had prepared for them. Fortunately, I was able to answer most of their questions off the cuff, but it struck me that they were far more interested in the country than in the events concerning the Duke's visit. This I had anticipated as, to the world outside, we were about to be 'newly discovered'! I could not recall a single overseas journalist to have called in here before.

Fortunately, all the arrangements made by the Government went off very smoothly. The people as a whole were enjoying the occasion, and the small shopkeepers and coffee shop owners were doing a roaring trade with all the influx of the Interior peoples which the Colony Exhibition had brought into the capital. The phrase used by local people when they were really enjoying themselves was *banyak ramai*! This was a phrase Ituk had expressed to me when, some few years earlier, he had caught me listening on the radio to the cheers of the crowds in the streets of London on the occasion of the Queen's Coronation. At the same time he had asked me how many buffaloes they might have slaughtered to provide the feast which would accompany any such occasion in Murut country!

After his visit to Jesselton, the Duke was scheduled to fly to Sandakan where he would board *Britannia* for departure to Hong Kong. A separate plane had been chartered to transport the press representatives and the timing of its arrival by direct route would be in advance of the Duke's Flight which was to be slightly circuitous, to obtain if possible a view of Kinabalu. The departure time was, therefore, of the utmost importance. I was to accompany the party, and when all had boarded I did a head count to find that one of the party was missing. It was the representative of one of Britain's leading dailies! I had noticed before that punctuality was not his strong point, but just as I was becoming anxious, he appeared running from the direction of the terminal building. We made it and the press were able to cover the Sandakan arrival.

Forestry being the country's primary industry, visits to the British Borneo Timber Company's headquarters and the Forestry Department were naturally the main events, and the day's proceedings ended with a reception aboard HM Yacht *Britannia* to which I had the great honour of being invited.

My main concern was to learn the impact the country had made on the British press. As far as I could judge, everything had gone very smoothly. No occasion had been marred by adverse weather which can so happen, but predictably the beginning of the year, when the visit took place, usually brings with it cloudless skies, and often a nip in their air during the early morning. The press cuttings from the United Kingdom when they began to come through were universally good, and I received a congratulatory message from the Chief Secretary on all the arrangements I had been able to make to assist the press.

The visit certainly seemed to mark a turning point in the fortunes of the Department. It had stimulated an interest and awareness in the world at large that Sabah existed as a country, and we began to receive visitors not only from the United Kingdom but also from Australia and America. Realizing the value of publicity, almost for the first time, I thought to myself, the Government lent a more sympathetic ear when the next year's estimate proposals were being discussed. We had become a spending Department that had a value!

A number of other significant events appeared to have their origins in this visit. The British Army recognized the value of the Kota Belud plains as a training area for troops, and with the agreement of the Government, arrangements were made for British troops stationed in Singapore and Malaya to establish a training post early

The Royal Yacht *Britannia* alongside Sandakan Wharf.

in the following year. Countries participating in the South East Asia Treaty Organization held sea manoeuvres in North Borneo waters. Politically, Sir Roland's ideas for closer association of the Borneo territories began to crystallize. On 10 April 1958, the subject was debated in the Legislative Council and a resolution was carried unanimously stating:

> whereas in the opinion of this Council, the people of North Borneo welcome in principle the proposal for the closer constitutional association of the three territories of North Borneo, Brunei and Sarawak: Be it resolved that the Council do recommend that the agreement of the Governments of Brunei and Sarawak be sought for a joint examination of the proposal by a body of persons drawn from all three territories, with a view to the preparation of detailed proposals, including any necessary safeguards for the individual territories such as thereafter might be considered by the three Governments severally.

I have quoted this resolution in full as it marks significantly the beginning of politics as such in Sabah.

It was not by coincidence that the next Inter-Territorial Conference was held in Brunei at the personal invitation of His Highness the Sultan. It was held under the Chairmanship of the Commissioner-General for the United Kingdom in South East Asia. The official statement which was released after the meeting laconically states that 'items of common interest to the three territories were discussed'. Looking back on events after a number of years, it appears to me that the United Kingdom Government had other plans for the future development of the Borneo Territories. Although most people in the country favoured the idea, it never took off. No subsequent action was ever initiated to further the concept.

There is no written evidence available to me which gives any possible explanation, but it is not hard to guess that the British Government had other more important matters concerning the Far East to which they had to give prior attention. There were, most importantly, threatening utterances from our southern neighbours, Indonesia, to which I have referred earlier.

The Java story after the war was somewhat different from that which had transpired in Malaya, Singapore and other Far Eastern British territories. The Dutch, the pre-war masters of Batavia, Java and the Dutch East Indies, had never returned to re-establish their rule. The internal forces leading to a near rebellion against the invading Japanese established their own form of Government immediately on the collapse of Japan. The Dutch were not welcomed back as Colonial masters.

Eventually a new and powerful voice was being heard in the Far East, that of Sukarno, the self-styled President of Indonesia. He had long been active even before the war as the leader of an Indonesian Nationalist movement and, with the defeat of the Japanese, emerged as the Indonesian strong-man and virtual dictator.

With a certain foresight and naive circumspection, he had viewed a certain restlessness and upsurge in the Far East amongst the peoples of former Colonial territories. In the north, French Indo-China had virtually disintegrated with the emergence of the new territories of Vietnam and Laos, whilst in Malaya communist insurgents had forced the Government to declare a State of Emergency. After the recapture of the Philippines and the restoration of United States rule, the islands had been granted their independence on 4 July 1946. He knew of the continual unstabilizing effect of the pirates of the Southern Philippine islands, and he must have felt that on the island of Borneo nature had presented him with the relatively simple opportunity of enlarging his own territory and enabling him to enhance his popularity amongst his own people.

One can never guess the thinking which twists the minds of ambitious leaders, particularly of that era and in that part of the world. Logical English thought disappeared through the window. We saw it at close quarters when the Japanese paraded outside the barbed wire, and this experience taught us all that the Asian mind acts differently from Western logic. Kipling was so right when he wrote: 'East is East, and West is West, and never the twain shall meet'. Even though man himself may have much in common, birth and culture remain a great divide.

So was born the undeclared war of Indonesian 'confrontation'. Ambassadorial memoranda to the Foreign and Colonial Offices must have given the United Kingdom Government due warning that Sarawak, Brunei and Sabah were in the front line. We all shared that common border with Kalimantan, formerly Dutch Borneo: an almost indefensible line of jungle running south of all our territories. This sudden threat to British territory became suddenly of far greater importance than any local political moves towards 'closer association'.

Fortunately for us, Great Britain still had its naval base in Singapore, and fighting units of the Army were in Malaya. HMS *Bulwark* was the aircraft carrier which was to serve virtually as the base for operations. Her helicopters flew contingents of the fighting forces into the jungle, where the district administration had prepared landing areas at strategic points. Simultaneously, an unexpected threat arose from an unexpected quarter: the Sultanate of Brunei! Possibly instigated by Sukarno, an upstart named Azahari commenced a small rebellion in Dar-es-Salaam. For a short while the situation was tense, until a unit of Gurkhas were flown in from Malaya, but not before there was an overspill across Brunei Bay and into the Sipitang area, as ever the entry point of foreign forces.

For a short while the situation was tense, but never all that serious and never out of control. The Government's reaction was quick and effective. The threat existed, but it never erupted into conflict. The role and importance of the Security Council was electrified! The lesson had already been learnt in Malaya of the importance of winning the 'hearts and minds' of the people. In Sabah, this was never really a battle: the people had proved their loyalty to the British flag, time and time again.

The Security Council now met weekly and considered carefully the weekly report prepared by the Police Special Branch. Other members of the Council were the Resident, the Chief Secretary, and Secretary for Chinese Affairs and the Attorney General, whilst the king pin was the Special Branch Officer of the Police Department. It was his report which was considered paragraph by paragraph. Frequently my friend Mike Edge would present the report, but if he had the chance he preferred field duties. It was he who had been the first officer to scent out that there was trouble brewing in Brunei.

Suddenly, I found that my department had taken on a new significance in the eyes of the Government. Instead of opposition to every move of expansion I had sought, it was a question of why I hadn't asked for this or that support service sooner! From now on, everything I was to ask for was approved. It had taken years of effort to get funds for Broadcasting House to be approved; now it was a question of how soon we were going to move into it.

The delay in the commissioning of the new studios was almost becoming an embarrassment. Initially, Posts and Telegraphs had cared for the technical side, but as I explained time and time again, they had their own priorities and broadcasting was not one of them! However, the earlier approval of the post of Chief Engineer was soon to bear fruit. I had been suddenly notified by the Crown Agents that an officer with all round transmitter and studio experience who had seen service with Radio Singapore had been recruited and was due to arrive shortly. With his arrival my ill-conceived but necessary 'honeymoon' with the Posts and Telegraphs Department was over. It had been a liaison born out of necessity, but we could now be independent.

Winston Ramsbotham set to work immediately. He was a perfectionist. He had an acoustic measuring device brought up on loan from Radio Sarawak and with the aid of this equipment he was able to adjust the baffle boarding required in the studios to achieve the best acoustics. The wiring of the racks in the control room appeared to be endless! So many wires to be soldered to the correct point, with every circuit to be tested, and of course a shortage of trained technical staff apart from the two technicians of the Posts and Telegraph establishment who had been allocated to work for us and who elected to join our establishment. At the same time, because there were absolutely no local candidates with the required qualifications, we had to recruit such officers from overseas. Once we could start filling our establishment with sufficient school certificate candidates who could receive technical training overseas, the way ahead for the filling of our establishment with trained local officers was much clearer. In the meantime we had to recruit on contract overseas staff with the required qualifications and experience, who often were Anglo-Burmese but who fitted well into the local community. It was a mammoth undertaking, achieved under the greatest pressure.

For me it had been a particularly galling time, as for so many years I had pressurized Government on the very issues on which they were now accusing me of tardiness! The proposal that the Government should establish a broadcasting service had originated with me. I had to sell the idea to Government and it had not been all that easy a talk. Although the Chief Secretary would never admit it, he only had to look in the files and find where the blame lay! If ever, in later years, I felt a sense of antipathy developing between the Chief Secretary and myself, its origin was here. The technical advancement of broadcasting lay now with my Chief Engineer in whom I had the greatest confidence, and Government failed to realize that the commissioning of a highly technical building like Broadcasting House did not end with the completion of the building and the moving in of furniture!

There was very much more to it than that. Even the programme material took time to assemble; a commercial record library of some two to three hundred thousand records of three cultural heritages, for example, cannot be ordered overnight. Each record had to be chosen, not because it was merely popular at the moment: that was an easier thing to do. But our task was to educate and elevate popular taste to a higher cultural level. Music is international and my aim was to bring at least light classical music to be enjoyed by our many varied races of different backgrounds and cultures. Every Straits Steamship Company's vessel carrying surface mail brought its parcels of records, and they all had to be catalogued, racked and identified. Registers of records purchased had to be kept to enable the auditors to trace them from the Crown Agents' invoices through our records and on to the exact location in the record shelf to the record itself. Not that it ended there; every movement of a disc had to be recorded, whether it was to a playing booth prior to selection for broadcast or to the studio itself. Whenever an auditor wanted to see it, we had to know its exact location and produce it for him. None of this seemed to be appreciated by Government in the person of the Chief Secretary, yet he would be the first to jump on one if the auditor had ever found anything wrong.

As broadcasting was our most powerful medium, I had decided to move my own office into Broadcasting House when the building was completed instead of having two offices, one in the old studios dealing with all broadcasting matters and the other in the Information Office. My recommendation to have Tom Willie promoted to be in charge of the Information Office and the press activities met with approval, and gave me great satisfaction as he was a reliable and stalwart fellow; he had been my first clerk in the original office, and had grown up with the development of the Department.

This move freed me from the day to day responsibility of looking after the requirements of the press and dissemination of Government activities through press releases and the output of the photographic section. One sad incident occurred just before my move to the new building. One morning I received a message from the studios that Che Abas bin Haji Hassan, my old friend from Papar going back before the war, had died of a heart attack whilst sitting at his desk. He had done much to establish the popular record request programme amongst Malay-speaking listeners. His death was a great personal loss to me as my friendship and respect for him went back to the first day I had stepped on to Papar railway station as the new District Officer a long time before the start of the war.

My main task now was to implement the new transmission scheme which had been formulated with the help and advice of the Crown Agents broadcasting engineers. A Colonial Development and Welfare grant having previously been approved, the transmitters had been ordered and their arrival was due at any time. Involved with this was the question of the power supply to operate the transmitters on the slopes of Kinabalu. This problem was taken off my hands by the Public Works Department whose duty it was to construct the road along which tankers could travel to deliver the oil to the generating station which they would establish at a lower level. A technical problem arose in that there is a loss in voltage when electricity is used at a greater altitude than the source of power, so that there had to be a generator of not less than 5kw capacity to drive the transmitters situated some 2,000–3,000 ft. higher up the mountain side. There also had to be a spare stand-by generator in the event of one generator failing, just as in the transmitting station we had to have two transmitters, one always being used as a stand-by whilst the other was being serviced, and to be used on an automatic transfer in the event of an unexpected breakdown. All in all it was a very considerable operation, a fact which I never believe was appreciated by Government.

I had foreseen that we would need a large increase in staff to operate and maintain an operation of the magnitude that I had envisaged. Although our recruits had a certain naive sensitivity to the work they were being called to undertake, they inevitably lacked experience and training. I had, of course, foreseen this and had applied to the Colombo Plan for the services of an experienced broadcasting officer, able to undertake the training of local staff in broadcasting techniques. He had duly arrived whilst we were still in our old building and was given the title of Studio Manager. His work was invaluable in staff training, and he also inaugurated, with great success, a seasonal Christmas programme based on his experience in New Zealand: 'Carols by Candlelight', which was to become an annual event. Another annual event which he inauguruated was 'Radio Sabah Talent-time', a festival which was held in the presence of a packed audience in the newly built Community Centre.

'Talent-time' appealed obviously to a popular audience, but I felt we were not fulfilling one of the purposes of our existence if we did not develop a wider appreciation of good Western as opposed to Asian music. With this in mind I founded the Radio Sabah Music Society, whose Committee members were largely European but who were well aware of my objectives. Using the Society as a vehicle, we were able to undertake the sponsorship of international violinists and singers who had been visiting Hong Kong and were on their way to Australia. At times the British Council, which had already established an office in Sarawak, were able to put us in contact with a concert entrepreneur in Hong Kong. In these endeavours the Financial Secretary's office was always most helpful. The fees for these international stars were normally quite high, but if the Music Society did not recover them by the cost of the seats at the door, the Financial Secretary agreed that votes under my control could bear any shortfall. In the event, no recourse was ever made to Government funds. Through these concerts, we were able to learn that members of the local population were appreciating good classical music, and so direct our subsequent programme output. Our cultural objectives were being met.

Before the services of the Studio Manager came to the end of his secondment from the New Zealand Broadcasting Service, I had obtained the approval from Government for the appointment of Head of Programmes on our own establishment. The growth of broadcasting and the demand for our services had amazed even myself. Although I had sent some of my most valued staff on overseas training courses, there existed a big gap in our establishment until these officers began to return. We were fortunate in being offered by the Crown Agents a member of the staff of the BBC in London to fill the vacancy. This took a great load off my shoulders as the programme output now became another officer's responsibility. My task was the co-ordination of the two main branches and the administration of what had now become a large Department. In recognition of this a Salary Commission appointed by the Government had recommended that my post by up-graded to a super-scale post with the title Director of Broadcasting and Information Services. I think it was official recognition that the Department was playing a vital role in the development of the country.

Once I was free of the day to day output of press release and programme material, I could revert, too, to what the District Officer in me regarded as the most important part of my duties: that was to travel and learn what people were talking about in various districts and what they were listening to. Whilst I always received reports through the District Liaison officer, Mr Keeble, and other sources, there was simply no alternative to going out into the country, finding out about the activities of other Government Departments like the Public Works and the Agricultural Department, ascertaining what people were gossiping about and in particular what they were listening to over the air. There was no other satisfactory alternative than finding out for oneself, and reaching one's own conclusions.

Additionally, I was also opening and establishing reading rooms and libraries in all the main towns, and providing mobile film circuits in all areas accessible by road. In Sandakan, we were even establishing a film circuit on a launch, to reach villages on the banks of the great rivers which poured in Sandakan Bay.

It was on one of the East Coast visits that one of the most startling events of my life in Borneo occurred. I had been to a timber camp in the Kalabakang area which was only accessible by launch from Tawau. I was in a forest area operated by Bombay Burmah Trading Corporation Ltd and had stayed the night with the manager of the local felling operation. I had ascertained that our signal was being received loud and clear and that we were being listened to widely. I had no doubts about that. We could offer no other services, beyond the occasional visit of a film unit, as the area was too remote. But from the point of view of external publicity, it certainly was advantageous to send our camera-man to obtain photographs and film of the operations. I was assured that every assistance would be given, and I felt the visit from my own point of view had been worthwhile. The Company, when arranging my visit, had offered launch transport between Tawau and their camp, so my movements had to fit in with the sailings of their own craft.

My return journey was due to commence in mid-afternoon, which gave us enough sailing time in which to arrive back in Tawau during daylight hours. Some delay, however, had occurred with the departure of the launch and I did not think we would make Tawau before nightfall. That in itself didn't worry me, but I had not expected the strong on-shore wind that sprang up after dusk. We were still within the river estuary when the sun had set but by the time we had emerged into Cowie Harbour it was pitch dark and the sea was very high. I asked the *serang* whether or not the launch could ride a rough sea and he did his best to reassure me. The moon rose shortly afterwards and one could a little more easily assess the position. We seemed to be making very little headway, but once we were committed to our course there was no means of retreat. To have attempted to turn a highly built river craft in a heavy swell would have been an invitation to capsize. So I let the *serang* continue his course. Eventually the lights of Tawau showed on the horizon, and my mind was a little more at ease. The confidence I seemed to have in the *serang* was entirely justified until in the face of a particularly bad wave, he let out a scream, let go the wheel and retreated into the hulk of the vessel amongst the sea-sick native passengers! I immediately took over the wheel, as I knew that to let the rudder slip would be to invite disaster. Immediately I rose from the stool on which I had been seated, it fell out through the open fore-hatch. I had to hang on to the wheel to escape being thrown out myself.

There was only one thing to do: and that was to keep the craft head on to the waves. Fortunately the sea was running straight through Cowie Harbour from the Celebes Sea. That made my problem a little easier, but every dip into a wave trough turned the rudder, and it was a battle keeping on course. As we gradually appeared to come nearer, I made out the lights of the *Segama*, the Police anti-piracy patrol launch which was anchored off the jetty. With the launch's signal lamp, I semaphored SOS in the hope that the look-out on the *Segama* would spot it and perhaps come up to us and, being a much better sea-going craft, provide us with some shelter from the onslaught of the waves. There was no reply, however, and I later came to the conclusion that they were all asleep on board! Our greatest fortune lay in the fact that the diesel engines of the craft we were on never faltered. Fortunately, as we neared Tawau, the harbour had widened and the seas were less ferocious. The *serang* never reappeared, so as we came up to Tawau, and steered a wide circle to enable us to come into the inner berth of the wharf reserved for small craft, I rang down to stop engine, and was never more relieved than when I came to the mooring alongside the jetty. Ashore, there wasn't much more than a refreshing gentle breeze, and after I had walked to the Rest House and called for a stiff drink none of the other guests there believed my story!

Reflecting back, I think that if we had capsized, which was quite likely, I don't think I would have been so lucky as Peter Edge when he was wrecked on the Batu Mandi rocks before the war. He was able to swim to the shore which was a sandy beach, and the sea had not been rough. In Cowie Harbour the sea had whipped up a very nasty swell, lashed with foam, and even if I had been able to make the shore, I would not have been able to have dragged myself up on to a beach but would have been confronted with mangrove swamps infested with crocodiles! I immediately tried to put the incident out of my mind and writing about it now is the first time I have recalled it for many a long year.

Governor Hone's policy of improving internal communication by the building of airstrips in all the main towns enabled me to be back in the office by the next morning. At least, I had been reassured that our signal was being received loud and clear right up to our border and probably well within Indonesian territory, and that we were well listened to, even by the teams of hard working timber workers who had little time for pleasure. It was reassuring to have confirmation that our efforts were not only well heard but eagerly sought after, even in remote jungle areas.

Shortly after this I was saddened to hear that Sir Roland Turnbull had decided to retire. He had been unwell for some time, but only those who had been intimately connected with him knew that the strain of his Governorship was beginning to tell. His work had been outstanding for the political development North Borneo was beginning to achieve. He had broadened the base of unofficial representation in the Legislative Council and had inspired the enactment of the Municipal and Urban Authorities Ordinance, under which Rural District Councils and Town Boards were established. In an address in August 1958, Sir Roland had said:

> For a long time the people of North Borneo were preoccupied with the restoration of the very means of living and in those circumstances political evolution does not seem to be of tremendous importance. Standards of living and education have come first, and that preoccupation has had the unexpected and happy consequence that, whereas our constitutional forms remain old-fashioned, the spirit of democracy pervades all our actions. We here in North Borneo are seeking to preface the accepted forms of democracy by its day to day practice, in the deliberate hope that the emergence of a normal democratic constitution will be a natural growth . . . One instance of that natural development, in which we take some pride, is that all education is now the responsibility of a predominantly unofficial Board of Education, representative of all the educational agencies of all races: an arrangement which, I believe, still remains only an ambition in other countries of this region.

Sir Roland was the architect of the country's political reform and advancement and his Governorship will be remembered for the solid base he had created for its political progress and development. The Board of Education which he had established came out strongly in favour of teaching the English language to the indigenous races and felt that it should gradually become the medium of instruction in all the primary classes of Malay schools. Emphasis was to be given to the training of local teachers to achieve this aim. With this in mind, 'Kent College Teachers Training College' had been opened by the Duchess of Kent during her visit in 1952.

On 24 January 1960, Sir Roland unfortunately had to relinquish his post on medical grounds. He must have been more seriously ill than any of us had realized, for immediately on his return he entered hospital for treatment, and very shortly after sending a Christmas message to the people of Sabah, we received news of his death. As a tribute to his memory, in its programme: 'Carols by Candlelight' on the Jesselton town *padang* on Christmas Eve, Radio Sabah included his favourite carol: 'Silent Night'.

Sabah had been fortunate in the choice of men chosen as Governors by the Colonial Office. Twining had been a visionary; he had great plans for the country, but he served too short a period to see any of his plans come to fruition. Hone had concentrated on the economic development, bringing to an end the monopoly on timber extraction and concentrating on the development of communications which would better lead to the unity of the country and not let it remain as two divisions: the East Coast and the West Coast. But it had been Turnbull who had successfully introduced a political atmosphere and had brought about the creation of the country's first political parties. This was a big step in its progress towards self governance.

During most of this time, the continuing link had been the same Chief Secretary, my friend Jimmy Calder. He had co-ordinated all the policies introduced by the three Governors, and had served as Acting Governor almost as long as he had served in his substantive post as Chief Secretary. Early in Sir Roland's tenure of office, and not long after I had been appointed Information Officer, he had reached retirement age, and although there were official parties to bid him farewell, he nevertheless made the time to drop in at my office and wish me a personal goodbye, an act which I much appreciated. He was succeeded in March 1953 by Mr O'Brien CMG whose earlier career had been spent in the Secretariat in Cyprus where he was known to my father. Unfortunately, his period of office had been relatively short, and he had been followed in September 1956 by Mr R.N. Turner CMG, who before the war had been Assistant Resident in Brunei. When we were travelling as prisoners of the Japanese from Jesselton to Kuching, he had joined us at Labuan with the British Resident in Brunei and travelled in the coastal collier in which we had been incarcerated with knobs of coal as our mattresses. We had been fellow prisoners in Kuching. After liberation he had subsequently seen service in Malaya and later in Barbados. He had been transferred to us from there.

The year 1956 was, incidentally, one of historical landmarks for Sabah. It was both the seventy-fifth anniversary of the granting of the Royal Charter to the British North Borneo (Chartered) Company and the tenth anniversary of the secession of North Borneo to the Crown.

Much progress had been made in those ten years. The main towns had virtually been rebuilt in permanent materials in accordance with the latest concepts of modern town planning for tropical areas in countries the size of ours. Our primary products were being diversified and we were economically beginning to be able to stand on our own feet. We had a very favourable trade balance, with exports well exceeding imports, and although rubber had long been the principal export with the economy of the country largely dependent upon its fluctuating market price, it was being quickly overtaken by timber.

Elsewhere, within the field of the Development Secretary's activities, the plan for a new building to bear the name of the Central Government Offices was reaching fruition. This quadrangle-shaped building with wide interior walk-ways overlooking the central courtyard housed the Chief Secretary's office and the rest of the Secretariat, the Financial Secretary's office and those of the Accountant General. These offices were located at the junction of the Penampang Road and the Tanjong Aru Road. The latter led to the airport, the main residential area, and a fast developing industrial district as well as the Police Headquarters situated well towards the Putatan area; the road was no longer a small narrow road leading only to the beach, but it had become the main arterial highway running the whole length of Jesselton from north to south. The country had emerged from its chrysalis stage and was beginning to blossom!

I have noted before how the Duke of Edinburgh's visit had attracted the attention of the world to this youngest of Britain's colonies. Consequently, we received a number of distinguished visitors. The Department which covered the visitors' main interests was responsible, naturally enough, for their reception and hospitality. Journalists and sometimes well-known columnists whose names were household words in the United Kingdom were naturally looked after by me. Most of them, too, were persuaded to broadcast if they were so minded. So I was able to meet many distinguished people from all walks of life.

Among those I had the great privilege of entertaining was Mr Vernon Bartlet, the well-known columnist in the British press. His visit in 1956 had been very stimulating, and as I drove him to Kota Belud it took considerable concentration to maintain a highly intellectual conversation with such an inquiring mind and at the same time keep the car on the correct path along a sometimes tortuous and mountainous road! Whenever it was possible, I began to ask Dullah to assist me in the driving. Later, the Department had its own car for meeting and conducting official visitors, and with Dullah as head driver, the corps of drivers to maintain the ever extending mobile cinema and library circuits became very much enlarged.

One visit of special importance early in 1959 was that of the Countess of Mountbatten of Burma in her capacity as Superintendent-in-Chief of the St John Ambulance Brigade. It was to occur at a period after Sir Roland's Governorship and before the announcement of his successor. The Chief Secretary, Mr R.N. Turner, was the Officer Administrating the Government and had the responsibility for the arrangements for her visit. He called a meeting of all Heads of Departments in any way involved with it so that an itinerary could be prepared and submitted for her approval.

I naturally had to attend. What, I think, none of us knew was that some three years previously Lady Mountbatten had been warned by her doctor that unless 'she dramatically reduced her activities she must expect to be dead within three years. Her response was to take on fresh activities.'* In January 1960 she left on 'a tour which filled her with trepidation and hardly dare to even think about it, as it would be far too exhausting a process.'*

The planning of the tour took place without this knowledge and was, of course, submitted for her approval well before her arrival. We had to bear in mind that first and foremost it was a St John Ambulance Brigade occasion and the local representatives of this association had also to be fully consulted; it was not a governmental visit as such.

* Phillip Ziegler in the official biography of *Mountbatten*, p. 569

Nevertheless, it was a big occasion for Noel Turner as Acting Governor and he was anxious that the visit should go well. Apart from her official St John engagements, there was sufficient time available for her to visit North Borneo's showpiece, Kota Belud, the country's loveliest district, dominated as it was by the splendour of Kinabalu. The presence there of a detachment of the Gurkhas on training exercises was the reason officially given.

It was a warm cloudless day when the Viscount aircraft in which she was travelling banked around Gaya Island and made its approach from the north, finally touching down at 2.15 p.m. on Thursday 18 February 1960. The assembly of cars around the airport would have given the Countess an indication of the reception which was awaiting her. As she descended the aircraft's steps, Turner and his wife stepped forward to greet her. She had a welcome for all, and shook hands with most of the guard of honour. She was accompanied by a Miss Checkley, a St John Headquarters' officer. The Countess, in the company of her host, was driven to the Chief Secretary's house, where after a little rest and tea, her host drove her around the town ending up at the St John Building where she was able to meet all the local representatives of the organization. Later that evening there was an official dinner party at the Chief Secretary's residence.

On the following morning, officially designated in the programme as a 'day of rest', she undertook the spectacular journey to Kota Belud, enjoying the mountainous climb and the outstanding tropical scenery. The welcome by the escort of Bajau horsemen in their traditional dress enthralled her and she entered wholeheartedly into the spirit of the occasion. She duly met the detachment of Gurkhas and their officers, ending up at the District Officer's house for a curry lunch with twenty guests.

On her return to the Chief Secretary's house, she showed the first signs of being tired and said she would rest before going to the official dinner at the Jesselton Hotel where over a hundred guests awaited her for a Chinese dinner party. When speaking she was cheerful and animated and all signs of earlier weariness had disappeared. However, on returning to her host's house, she complained of a headache and retired early.

A heavy day was to follow and in answer to enquiries she confessed that her headache was no better. The Countess, however, insisted on keeping to her programme: first to the Red Cross and then to the Queen Elizabeth Hospital where a coffee party had been laid on. Her state of health, however, was causing some concern to the Turners and they did persuade her to cancel her attendance at a lunch engagement. Her comment was that the cancellation appeared to be 'rather drastic' but she was reconciled to taking an afternoon rest.

Shortly after 4 p.m. the Countess was on parade again in her white St John uniform. At the Secretariat, some sixty members of St John were on parade awaiting her inspection, with the Police Band in attendance. To conclude the ceremony she gave a brief address to the assembled guests. She could not have been feeling all that well as she asked to be excused from attending the tea party which followed. For the second occasion on that day, she consented to a medical examination by the Commissioner of the Brigade, Dr Blaauw, formerly Deputy Director of the

Last photograph taken of the Countess Mountbatten.
Her host may be seen at bottom right-hand corner.

Medical Services but who had retired from Government and practised locally. He had been on the medical staff of the former Chartered Company, had been interned with us all in Kuching, and had had great experience of health in North Borneo. He was unable to make a satisfactory diagnosis but 'thought the patient might have flu or perhaps the early stages of malaria.'*

Her day did not finish there. At 7.15 p.m. some one hundred and twenty guests had been invited to a reception on the lawns of the Chief Secretary's house. It was, of course, already dark, and the grounds were lit with fairy lights: it was quite a party atmosphere, and although the Countess agreed not to meet the guests on their arrival, she insisted on putting in an appearance a little later on when she consented to sitting on a sofa whilst her hostess brought individual guests to meet her. The party ended round about 8.30 p.m. I remember the occasion very vividly as I had been one of the guests who had been presented to her.

My telephone rang shortly after dawn the next day, and I was aghast to learn that the Countess had passed away in her sleep that night. Turner, who obviously was in a state of shock, asked me to have the news announced in the early morning newscasts. I went straight down to the studios, drafting the message in my mind as I drove. It was one of the very bad moments in my Sabah experience.

What is not generally known, and although out of context, it is appropriate to mention that exactly a year afterwards to the very day, the Earl of Mountbatten visited Jesselton and insisted on staying at the Chief Secretary's residence, although the Chief Secretary was no longer Acting Governor. He also requested that the very same guests as those who attended his wife's party be invited to a reception in his honour at the Chief Secretary's house on the anniversary of her death. It was a very uncanny occasion, and the noise of conversation was just a low murmur.

Of no political significance whatsoever, that event appears to me to mark the end of colonialism in Sabah. The Count and Countess had been associated with the end of imperialism in India, and after the tragic shock of her death in Jesselton, it seemed also to toll the death knell of colonialism in North Borneo.

I cannot recall any subsequent event which had an association with the British Raj. There were, naturally, the Queen's Birthday Parades which continued to take place on the *padang*, with a reception, usually on Government House lawns, but they were very few. The final stages of the era began, suddenly and unexpectedly on 27 May 1961 when, at a press luncheon in Singapore, the Prime Minister of the Federation of Malaya, Tengku Abdul Rahman, proposed that a Federation of Malaysia should be created to comprise the eleven states of Malaya, Singapore and the three Borneo territories. It has been said that the British Government had entertained a similar idea earlier on, but considered the move premature. Possibly

* Richard Hough, in his biography *Edwina*, to which I am indebted for many of the details in this account.

Tengku Abdul Rahman had been 'prompted' by the British Government to make this speech; it was in accordance with policy for the United Kingdom Government to divest itself of Colonial territories and Borneo was still remaining a quiet back-water. Only official records to be revealed in the years to come will testify to the truth of this. Certainly a new political awareness had begun to be developed.

This new awareness will certainly be associated with the appointment of Sir William Goode as Governor. I believe it had been the remit given him by the British Government to speed the development of the formation of political parties. Writing the General Review to the Colony's Annual Report for 1961, I recorded that:

> 1961 marked the end of North Borneo's long insulation from party politics. For the first few months of the year there were no indications of impending change in the pattern of quiet and orderly progress in economic and educational advancement that had been followed since the end of the war. Although there had been talk for some time past of the formation of political parties . . . there was an understandable reluctance to take the plunge through realization that they carried with them the danger of communal dissension and a breakdown in the harmony between the many different races, in which the country had always taken justifiable pride.

This paragraph was approved and appeared in the official report for 1961.

A proposal of this nature, coming from the Prime Minister of Malaya, was bound to create a reaction amongst the people of North Borneo. It aroused the political consciousness of the country and forced public opinion to think about the future. At first the lead tended to come from nominated unofficial members of the Executive and Legislative Councils and other persons of standing in the community. There were many difficulties to overcome; not only was there a lack of political experience and a shortage of suitable organizers but also there was the reluctance of many people to embark on the stormy seas of politics. There were, too, opportunists, and it was not long before leaders began to emerge. Being a multi-racial society, it was inevitable that the developing parties began to represent their own races. That was not the problem. Religion predominantly entered into it. The Malaysia proposed by Tengku Abdul Rahman had a Moslem overtone, and the majority of the native peoples were pagan. The Muruts and Kedazans outnumbered other native races and they, apart from the Christian Kedazans, were pagan. Just over one-third of the total population was Moslem. There was no such native racial problem in Malaya where the division was largely into Malay and Chinese. This was not the case in Sabah and there was the inevitable fear of the emergence of racial disharmony. This was something we very much wished to avoid.

Once, however, the wheels of politics are set in motion, it is not possible to stop them. To record the fortunes of the political parties is outside the scope of this work. Basically the parties that began to emerge inevitably represented races. This vitiated against the very policies we had wished to inculcate. We had developed a racially harmonious society, but by fostering politics we were liable to endanger the fine inter-racial balance we had developed. But politics had to come, and we had to endeavour to maintain the balance and not upset the equilibrium. Possibly we were assisted in our task mostly by the racial distribution. Moslems were the coastal communities, whilst the native communities were largely inland people. It was, therefore, mostly in coastal districts where political clashes could occur: districts like Papar and Tuaran where the Moslem coastal villages lived side by side with Kedazans. In broadcasting, I had to be particularly on my guard that the news output of Malay and native language programmes remained politically unbiased and not in any way slanted. Government had to be neutral.

Two natural-born leaders predominated. First and foremost a gentleman with whom I had close relations emerged as a leader of the Kedazans. He was Donald Stephens, the editor of the *Sabah Times*, a Eurasian by birth but who had a Kedazan mother and had close connections with the Kedazans, particularly of Penampang and Tuaran. The other was Datu Mustafa, Kudat born and a strong personality and natural leader who had the support of all the Moslems of the West Coast. Both were members of the Executive and Legislative Councils so both had influence and experience in the philosophy of government. The Chinese had suffered a great loss just a year or so previously by the sudden and unexpected death of Philip Lee Tau Sang, the Chairman of the Jesselton Chinese Chamber of Commerce, long a member of the Legislative Council with considerable governmental experience. If he had lived, his influence would have been considerable and the history of Sabah in its transitional period may have differed. In his place Pang Tet Shung and Lai En Kong of Jesselton and Khoo Siak Chieu of Sandakan were selected to be members of the Executive and Legislative Councils. From the natives of the Interior came the son of O.K.K. Sedoman of Bingkor fame, the experimental Native Administration area of the Chartered Company days in Keningau District, one Orang Kaya Kaya Sundang.

The political leanings of these embryonic parties differed, and it is right that they should have done so. Most natural of all was the attitude of Datu Mustafa. His origins were from an ethnic tribe of coastal people of the north coastal islands and coastal villages who had embraced Mohamedanism many years before. To his party were also attracted the Brunei folk of Papar, Bangawan and Membakut, right down to the Sipitang area. These people many centuries before had come from the Malayan Peninsula. Donald, on the other hand, had greater affiliation with the Kedazans; he gained his influence with them possibly not only by personal contact but through the Kedazan columns of his paper, at that time the only paper to include a Kedazan section. As the originator of the only voice-piece which could be critical of the Government, and of natural ambitious character, he easily gained the support of the West Coast Kedazans, numerically the largest racial group.

On the other hand, O.K.K. Sundang, living in the Interior Residency and away from coastal influences, saw no advantage in joining forces with a Malay dominated society in view of the peaceful economic and to a limited extent political progress through Town Boards and Rural District Councils his people were achieving. Traditionally suspicious of Malays, through an almost inherent distrust, he was naturally opposed to any increase in Malay dominated influence. The Muruts, perhaps the very original inhabitants of the country, had no representative at all!

The Chinese, on the other hand, being business orientated, and having observed the position of Chinese in Malaya when Malays gained political control, were more reticent and unenthusiastic with the idea. Their position advocated self Government before Malaysia.

The fact that there was little reaction in the country of comparable degree, when the proposal of closer association of the Borneo Territories inspired by Governor Turnbull fell on infertile soil, can only have been because the new proposal sprang more from the grass roots of the countries concerned than did the idea of closer association which had come from the top, and may have appeared as something being imposed upon them. Furthermore, the concept of closer association was just possibly a little in advance of any political thinking in Sabah. As events were to turn out, this would have been a pity. If Turnbull's idea had originated just a little later, it might have caught more of the mood of the moment, and would have placed Sabah in a more politically advantageous position than it found itself later on. The secret of this lies in Brunei.

Brunei, both before and after the war, had remained an independent State. By chance nature had bestowed on it great wealth: oil! Wealth beyond its most possible dreams! The Sultan had found the policy of closer association attractive, because it reconstituted the boundaries of his old Sultanate. Brunei would have been re-born. Of Malaysia, he was suspicious. Wealth converted into money assets was transferable. Many centuries previously, his family had been expelled from Malaya and had come to Borneo. His family had never been overwhelmed with gratitude for that act. Although occurring many centuries ago, antipathy of that nature dies hard. Nothing whatsoever has ever been mentioned of this, but I have a strong feeling that historical thought and economic consequences prevailed on the Sultan who decided that Malaysia was not for Brunei. I think from the point of view of the State of Brunei he was absolutely right, as the subsequent course of history has tended to prove.

The skeleton of Malaysia was being formed; there remained the task of putting flesh on its bones! To capture the flavour of the moment I will quote from what I drafted, and which was approved for the Colony Annual Report for 1961. I wrote then that:

> it was natural enough that the first reactions of articulate public opinion to the Malaysia proposal should be ones of suspicion and anxiety, for the realization that the 'winds of change' had reached the shores of Borneo came as a shock to the more conservative elements in the country, who were well satisfied with things as they were. As the basic considerations of the proposal came to be more fully explained and understood, however, some of the community leaders came to regard it more favourably and to wish to examine its implications in greater detail.

Cynically, one may say that the party leaders had come to realize that here was an opportunity of 'jobs for the boys', but I don't believe that to be necessarily true.

All had a realization that one day soon independence must come. It was going on all around the former African colonies, in their neighbouring country Indonesia, which had been independent since the end of the war, in the Philippines, and in Malaya itself. Sabah had to stand on its own feet, and it would emerge the stronger if affiliated with countries of similar origins and backgrounds. Local leaders had to appear. To assist in this process, the Governor announced that the unofficial majority in the Legislative Council which came into force in 1960 would again be increased in 1961 by the appointment of six unofficial members with the object of giving a greater number of people experience in the political field.

In his address from the Chair, the Governor referred to the grave responsibility and decisions of great importance which would face the Council in 1962. He said: 'If we reject Malaysia, shall we be responsible to future generations for failing in courage to grasp this opportunity to safeguard the future of this country? If we accept Malaysia, what constitutional provisions should we seek to ensure that Malaysia will stand up to the test of time and will meet the needs of the future? In the affairs of men and nations, the best is rarely attainable. We must strive for the best, but realize that often we must accept only the best that is possible. Let us not allow conflicting views on what we should do to arouse suspicion and distrust. Let us beware of falling into factions and personal squabbles. Let us subordinate private interests and personalities to the broad interests of this country. This is a happy country and a prosperous country poised to move forward to a great future. May we be worthy of it and guide it wisely.'

It may be opportune to leave the political scene at the moment of the country's early developing stage, and look for the moment at the phenomenal economic advancement it was making. Since the abolition of the British Borneo Timber Company's monopoly, the forest resources of the country, coupled with the high price of hardwood timber, was producing an economic miracle. The value of exports in 1953 was $60 million and in 1961 it was $220 million; for this the amazing growth in the value of timber exports was the chief reason. Of course, agriculture had diversified. Rubber was still the chief agricultural product to be exported, but 3,800 acres were already planted with cocoa and 1,600 acres had been cleared and made ready for the planting of oil-palm. Prawn-fishing had developed considerably, the prawns being deep frozen in one of the most up to date plants of its kind in the world and exported chiefly to the United States; and the Japanese had re-established the pre-war tuna fishing industry on Si-Amil Island. Geo-chemical prospecting for copper had located extensions of previously known copper deposits in the still remote interior. The Sandakan–Ranau road had received a grant in aid and road formation was proceeding apace. Long gone were the days when we were Treasury-controlled. We were well able to balance our own annually recurring budget. Nevertheless, the CD&W schemes, of which there were many, were of the greatest help in progressing development projects in so many fields which the young Colony could not otherwise have afforded. There was no doubt that progress was set fair. It just had to be guided in the right direction.

It was into a tranquil sea of political stability, and into a country where the acquisition of wealth on such an unprecedented scale, especially amongst those engaged in timber extraction, was not merely a novelty but a very desirable objective, that the crystal ball of politics suddenly burst asunder. In truth, I do not think the country had reached that stage of maturity from which the growth of political associations would have naturally formed. A community of interests in commercial fields existed. Most towns had their Chinese Chambers of Commerce—these had long existed—but their influence was confined to the business interests of the Chinese communities.

Town Boards, with a wide membership of public interests outside Government circles, had been established everywhere. Their influence in the administration of the areas for which they were responsible was being felt, but one wondered sometimes to what extent Government under the Chairmanship of the District Officer was steering the boat. Strictly, as long as they were connected to Government officials, they were not independent bodies.

So it was into a cocooned web of comparative tranquillity that political parties were conceived and born. It was inevitable that racial issues, whether or not they had lain dormant hitherto, first began to emerge. Time does not stand still, neither did it do so in Sabah when the formation of political parties appeared on the scene. Almost overnight, the atmosphere in the country changed. It might not have been so noticeable if it were a question of the country growing up and itself seeking independence. This was different. It was a change from one political master, one which over the years had been proved to be benevolent, to one in which one of their own races was to become predominant and, perhaps most important of all, where one all-embracing religion would be that of the one dominating political force. It must have caused grave concern to both Chinese and Kedazan alike, particularly to the Christian Kedazan.

Possibly in his despatches to the Secretary of State the Governor may have conveyed the quiet misgivings of many of the Sabah people, for it was announced in London in November 1961 that although the British and Malayan Governments had agreed that 'Malaysia was a desirable aim' it would be necessary to ascertain the views of the people of Sabah and Sarawak before coming to a final decision. It was announced that a Commission of Enquiry would be set up to carry out this task and to make recommendations. Lord Cobbald, a former Governor of the Bank of England, was appointed Chairman, and there were to be two members appointed by the British Government and two members appointed by the Malayan Government.

The terms of reference of the Commission were as follows:

> Having regard to the expressed agreement of the Governments of the United Kingdom and the Federation of Malaysia that the inclusion of North Borneo and Sarawak (together with other territories) in the proposed Federation of Malaysia is a desirable aim in the interests of the territories concerned:
>
> (a) to ascertain the views of the people of North Borneo and Sarawak on the question, and

(b) in the light of their assessment of these views, to make recommendations.

It must be said quite truthfully that when the Commission arrived in North Borneo it undertook its task with great patience and thoroughness. It held meetings in all major towns and even penetrated to major villages on the Labuk and Kinabitangan Rivers. Altogether over four thousand people from the Borneo territories, which included Sarawak, appeared before the Commission, and six hundred letters and memoranda were submitted by Town Boards and District Councils; associations of many kinds; political parties; Chambers of Commerce; and individuals, some of them prominent in the community, such as Members of the Executive and Legislative Councils, native chiefs and community and religious leaders, and other humbler folk who wished to have their say.

The report of the Commission on its completion was submitted to the British and Malayan Govenments by whom it had been appointed. At first it remained confidential and perhaps amongst the people of the territories involved there existed a little uncertainty and apprehension. It seemed only to be popular amongst the Malays, and possibly to some of the more educated and sophisticated coastal Kedazans, led by Donald Stephens. Elsewhere the idea still seemed to fall on stoney ground.

The conclusions of the report when at length it was published were, in the assessment of the Chairman, that:

> About one third of the population in each territory strongly favours early realization of Malaysia without too much concern about terms and conditions. [About one third of the population of each territory, Sarawak and Sabah, were of Malayan extraction.] Another third, many of them favourable to the Malaysia project, ask, with varying degrees of emphasis, for conditions and safeguards varying in nature and extent: the warmth of support among this category would be markedly influenced by a firm expression of opinion by Governments that the detailed arrangements eventually agreed upon are in the best interests of the territories. [These would have been the views of the more sophisticated coastal Kedazans and possibly some Chinese.] The remaining third is divided between those who insist on independence before Malaysia is considered and those who would prefer to see British rule continue for some years to come. [These would have been mostly Chinese and certainly the natives of the Interior Residency who always looked upon the European as *bapa*, and had little trust towards those of Malayan extraction which went back a long way in their history to the times of the marauding Bruneis!]

The report concluded that:

> if the conditions and reservations which they have put forward could be substantially met, the second category referred to above would generally support the proposals. Moreover once a firm decision was taken quite a number of the third category would be likely to abandon their opposition and decide to make the best of a doubtful job. There will always remain a hard core, vocal and politically active, which will oppose Malaysia on any terms unless it is

preceded by independence and self-government: this hard core might amount to nearly twenty per cent of the population of Sarawak and somewhat less in North Borneo.

The Commission, in spite of their reservations, unanimously agreed that a Federation of Malaysia was an attractive and workable project and was in the best interests of North Borneo and Sarawak, and that an early decision in principle should be reached.

One is reminded that amongst considerations for the future of Sabah, there remained two outstanding territories which were not featuring in these negotiations: namely, Singapore and Brunei. In regard to the former territory, negotiations had been made direct between the Malayan Government in Kuala Lampur and Singapore, and it had been agreed that the latter island colony should join the proposed State of Malaysia by 31 August 1963, subject to the necessary legislation being approved. Different problems were emerging in Brunei. Whilst the Sultan had been known to have looked favourably on the proposal for the Closer Association of the Borneo territories, originated in an earlier year by Governor Turnbull, this new proposal was something alien to him and what he regarded as Brunei's interests. The past must always be remembered, and possibly a diplomat in Whitehall, quite unaware of Brunei's origins as a part of a Malayan royal family exiled to Borneo, may perhaps have been surprised at Brunei's apparent antipathy towards Malaysia. Sensitive issues like that, however, were not forgotten by members of the Sultan of Brunei's family and past history remained part of present day thought. There was no positive reaction to the proposal of a Federation of Malaysia, and indeed other events were stirring which created an entirely unexpected problem.

Rumours had been reaching Sabah from an entirely different source that there was an undercurrent of unrest amongst the population in Brunei. So strong were these rumours reaching the Special Branch in the North Borneo Police Force, that my friend Mike Edge, at that time chief executive officer of Special Branch, went himself to Brunei to ascertain the truth of the rumours, returning with positive information. He reported the existence of a secret military organization in Lawas District of Sarawak, on the borders of Brunei, which was known as the Tentara Nasional Kalimantan Utara led by an upstart named Azahari, the purpose of which was to start a rebellion in the Brunei Bay area involving Lawas in Sarawak and Sipitang in Sabah and in particular Brunei, with the possible aim of overthrowing the Sultan himself.

As a precautionary measure, two sections of the Police Mobile Force were sent to the Sipitang area. This was the spark which lit the fuse of revolt. In the early hours of 8 December 1962 (a date on which a somewhat bigger war had started in the Pacific) an armed revolt broke out in the State of Brunei and neighbouring territories of Sarawak, and about sixty members of the TNKU from the villages of Kampong Lubok in Sipitang and Gadong Padas, near the mouth of the Padas River in the Klias Peninsula, assembled at Kampong Lubuk and Gadong Padas near the mouth of the Padas River in the Klias Peninsula. Armed with seven shot-guns, four home-made cigarette tin bombs and *parangs*, they made their way to Weston, the rail-head of the branch line from Beaufort, the entry point of the Japanese invaders into Sabah in 1942, and started advancing up the railway line. At the police station in Weston they relieved the village constable of his Greener gun, collected about seven more shot-guns and raised the TNKU flag. The next morning, they were joined by a further small party from Kampong Lubok and commenced an advance a few miles along the railway line to Lingkungan where contact was made with a small party of police and fire was exchanged. The police inflicted one casualty which exposed the fallacy of their invulnerability and, discouraged when no further support came to their aid, the majority gave themselves up to the police at daybreak the following day without firing a shot.

In Brunei itself, the position looked a little more serious and a platoon of the Mobile Force advanced into Brunei and proceeded to hold the airstrip and defend the power station until the arrival of Gurkha troops from Singapore several hours later. In the course of these operations one North Borneo police constable lost his life. A police wireless operator who had been sent to Lawas towards the end of November maintained communications between Lawas and Sabah throughout the critical period. Labuan once more became the scene of intense activity as the port of arrival for all large RAF aircraft and troop reinforcements for Brunei. This in fact was the origin of why a detachment of Gurkhas is retained and paid for by the State of Brunei to this very day.

All these events inevitably had their repercussions on the Broadcasting Service and the Press section of the Information Office. We had suffered a relatively major set-back earlier in 1962 when we had been about to move into the nearly completed Broadcasting House. Unfortunately for us, although it was a logical conclusion for Government, the building was chosen as the headquarters of the Cobbald Commission. We therefore had to postpone our transfer at a time when we urgently needed better and more adequate accommodation. The engineers, however, were able to continue with their work of wiring in the control and transmission rooms, and that was of the utmost importance; it was the office accommodation which the Commission needed. It was ironic that I had had to press the Government for so long and so hard to obtain approval to seek CD&W funds for the new studios, and when we were within an ace of achieving our goal, it was snatched away from us for more important affairs of state. However, the Commission had to sit somewhere, and the first air-conditioned office in the country couldn't have been more suitable for its work.

Eventually, in May 1962, we were able to transfer our headquarters and programme staff to their new accommodation. It provided enormous relief all round, as the Information Office was immediately able to move into the old studios and office accommodation vacated by the broadcasting staff, leaving far more room for the reading room and library which was bursting at its seams. The only other sections we left there were the dark-room with its mammoth enlarging equipment, and the 16mm film library and its projectors. We had adequate parking space for our transport

Broadcasting House, Jesselton, 1962.

here in the yard at its side and vehicles were continually increasing in number. I recall we were maintaining two mobile cinema circuits, each with its own Land-Rover and one general purpose vehicle used mostly for communication purposes, collecting mail and transporting staff from the central town position of the Information Office to the new Broadcasting House at the commencement and end of normal office hours. Many broadcasting staff had their own cars as this was advisable for both technicians and programme staff not working normal office hours, but for those who did not, we ran this convenient 'bus' service as the new broadcasting centre was some distance from the town.

Eventually everything came together. The new transmitters were on the air, with a double VHF radio link going direct from Broadcasting House to the Kinabalu transmitting station which again relayed the signals to medium wave transmitting stations scattered around the country in all the main centres of population. At last we had achieved uninterrupted and strong Colony-wide coverage of two channels broadcasting simultaneously! It had been a long, uphill task against a Government not readily willing to see the advantages of a good broadcasting service until these advantages stared them in the face, and then it couldn't come quick enough for them, and I was almost being blamed for tardiness! However, practice did have its reward as there had been a salary commission under the chairmanship of a Mr Bain who recommended that the post of Information Officer should be upgraded and made into a super scale post designated Director, Broadcasting and Information Services, in view of the additional responsibilities the post carried. I was pleased not so much for the new grading which was financially rewarding but for the fact that I now had at my command an organization for the dissemination of news without equal anywhere in South East Asia.

I make this statement with a deliberateness of purpose since no other British dependency in South East Asia had one single authority in charge of its publicity. Not only in Sarawak and Brunei were Information and Broadcasting separate departments but also in Malaya itself. Possibly it was the historical manner in which the publicity departments in other territories had grown up, all separately, but in our case broadcasting had originally been an extension of the information service we had to offer. In my view it was absolutely correct that the officer in charge of Government publicity, or public relations, call it what you will, should be under one single control. I achieved this. Every morning, I would have a meeting with all heads of the various publicity sections: the Press Officer from the Information Office, the Head of News from Broadcasting, and any other officer who might be involved—with regard to photography for example—and we would 'sample' the morning's news and decide on what stories, arising out of any special departmental or Governmental activity, we would concentrate for the day's main output. We all then spoke in our various media in the same voice, and the impact on the public would be all that much greater. I think this was in-born in me from studies at Oxford where I remember Victor Hugo describing the theatre as '*un miroir de concentration*'. Departmentally, we were 'theatre' reflecting Government's activities in the best possible light for the consumption of the public. So often in the days to come other officials did not share the same conviction. We were to be told that we had to conform to what other territories were doing. This was to be of great consequence to me and ultimately to the department.

At this point, we should again return to the political scene. There had not been a total degree of unanimity on the detailed recommendations of the Commission. These fell into four parts: firstly, unanimity on the general desirability of Malaysia on certain general matters; then the recommendations of the British members; the recommendations of the Malayan members; and finally a summary of all the recommendations combined with the comments of the Chairman. The difference of view between the British and Malayan members was not so much about the final form of Malaysia as on the timing and phasing. In brief, the British members felt that the changes to the final form of Malaysia should be gradual, with a transitional period spread over from three to seven years, whereas the Malayan members felt that changes should be made more quickly, on the grounds that delay was likely to prejudice the success of Malaysia by leaving the door open to obstruction and argument, which would increase rather than reduce the difficulties.

In his statement to the House of Commons on 1 August 1962, the Secretary of State for the Colonies announced that the British and Malayan Governments had accepted the unanimous findings of the Commission: first, that a Federation of Malaysia was in the best interests of North Borneo and of Sarawak; and second, that, provided certain conditions and reservations could be substantially met, a majority of the people in North Borneo and Sarawak would accept Malaysia. The two Governments had noted in particular the first of the unanimous recommendations in the Commission's Report that a decision of principle about the future of the two territories should be taken as soon as possible and, in light of the Report and also of the agreement reached separately between the Governments of the Federation of Malaya and Singapore, had decided that the proposed Government of Malaysia should, subject to the necessary legislation, be brought into being by 31 August 1963. The Secretary of State went on to say that, to give effect to this decision, the two Governments intended to conclude within six months a formal agreement which, so far as it concerned North Borneo and Sarawak, would transfer both territories to the new Federation of Malaysia by 31 August 1963, and provide for detailed constitutional arrangements, including safeguards for the special interests of North Borneo and Sarawak, to be drawn up after consultation with the Legislative Council in North Borneo and the Council Negri in Sarawak. The Secretary of State specified that these safeguards would cover such matters as religious freedom, education, representation in the Federal Parliament, the position of the indigenous races, control of immigration, citizenship and state constitutions. So that the introduction of the new Federal system might be effected as smoothly as possible and with the least disturbance to existing administrative arrangements, a transitional period, the duration of which was not specified, was envisaged, whilst a number of federal constitutional powers would be delegated temporarily to the State Governments of North Borneo and Sarawak.

The task of working out the future constitutional arrangements and the form of the necessary safeguards would clearly be a formidable one, and the two Governments decided that it could best be tackled by the establishment of an Inter-Governmental Committee under the Chairmanship of the Minister of State for Colonial Affairs which would include representatives of North Borneo and Sarawak as well as of Britain and Malaya.

Whereas Governor Turnbull's idea of closer association of the Borneo Territories had lingered on, without any other Government or organization strongly backing it apart from the Borneo Territories, the creation of Malaysia was being pushed hurriedly along. No time was lost in implementing the British Government's decision. Perhaps America and the United Nations which, since the war, had urgently pressed for the end of colonialism and self-determination of dependent territories, had galvanized the British Government into a hastier action than would normally have been the case. This was something they obviously thought came from the grass-roots and the time was propitious for hurrying it along.

No time was lost in the decision to bring the Inter-Governmental Committee into being. Lord Lansdown, the Minister of State, and Tun Razak, the Deputy Prime Minister of Malaya, first came to Jesselton and had talks with members of the Executive Council, staff associations, Heads of Departments, and representatives of political parties. Their first decision was to establish five Sub-Committees: one dealing with Constitutional matters; another with Fiscal matters; another dealing with the Public Service; another dealing with Legal and Judicial matters; and finally a Departmental Organization sub-committee.

On 12 September the Legislative Council unanimously approved the decision in principle to establish Malaysia by 31 August 1963, provided that the terms of participation and the constitutional arrangements safeguarded the special interests of North Borneo. The Council authorized six of their members under the joint Chairmanship of the Chief Secretary and the Honourable Donald Stephens to represent North Borneo on the proposed Inter-Governmental Committee and to prepare detailed constitutional arrangements to be laid before the Council. Shortly after, a similar motion was adopted without dissent in Sarawak and the way was clear for the Inter-Governmental Committee to commence its work.

The headquarters of the Inter-Governmental Committee was to be in Jesselton. By this time we were in full occupation of Broadcasting House and, I hope, performing a useful task in keeping the country informed of all developments as they took place. I felt reasonably confident, therefore, that our office accommodation on this occasion would not be disturbed! The Lands and Survey were to suffer; their new building, close to the Secretariat, was very near completion and the Inter-Governmental Committee established its headquarters there.

The Committee duly held what they termed three 'Plenary' Sessions, the first two of which were held in Jesselton in October and November and the third in Kuala Lumpur in December. At the conclusion of their meetings, they announced that they hoped their full report would be approved and laid before the legislatures of North Borneo and Sarawak early in the New Year. The year ended, therefore, with the barometer set fair for the achievement of Malaysia in accordance with the time-table agreed at the London talks.

During this time, the political parties in North Borneo had become more mature in their statesmanship and those that were opposed to Malaysia, particularly the United National Pasok Momogun Organization under O.K.K. Sundang, began to modify their views and reassess their attitudes. It was always a very strong point in favour of the people of Sabah that they did not allow their difference of attitudes to disturb their harmonious personal relationships. It proved possible, therefore, for all the five main political parties to present a joint declaration to the Inter-Governmental Committee, setting out the basis on which Malaysia would be acceptable in North Borneo and embodying safeguards on twenty points which all parties considered necessary for North Borneo on its entry into Malaysia. The document, which became known as the 'Twenty Points', related to fundamental issues as they affected Sabah.

They concerned firstly religion and ensured that, whilst respecting that Islam was the national religion of Malaysia, there should be no state religion in Sabah.

Secondly, they agreed that Malay should be the national language of Malaysia, but that English should continue to be used for a period of ten years after Malaysia Day, and that English should be the official language for all purposes, State or Federal, without limitation of time.

The third point was a constitutional matter. A new Constitution for the State of Sabah should be enacted. The Constitution of Malaysia should be a completely new document, drafted and agreed in the light of a free association of States, and should not be a series of amendments to a constitution drafted and agreed by different States in totally different circumstances.

They agreed, possibly reluctantly, that the Head of State in Sabah should not be eligible as Head of State in the Federation.

For the fifth point they agreed that the name of the Federation should be Malaysia and not, as some suggested, Melayu Raya.

Immigration was always a controversial matter but it was agreed that control over immigration into any part of Malaysia from outside should rest with the Central Government but entry into North Borneo should require the approval of the State Government. The Federal Government should not be able to veto the entry of persons into North Borneo for State Government purposes except on strictly security grounds. North Borneo should have unfettered control over the movement of persons, other than those in the Federal Government employ, from other parts of Malaysia into North Borneo.

The seventh point stated that there should be no right to secede from the Federation.

The eighth and ninth points to a certain extent linked up. The eighth point stated that 'Borneoisation' of the public services should proceed as quickly as possible. At the same time the following point stated that every effort should be made to encourage British officers to remain in the public service until their places could be taken by suitably qualified people from North Borneo.

The tenth point concerned citizenship. This tied in with the Cobbald Commission's Report on the subject, but mainly stated that a person born in North Borneo after Malaysia should be a Federal citizen.

The eleventh point stated that North Borneo should have control of its own finances, development funds and tariffs.

The twelfth point recognized in principle that the indigenous races of North Borneo should enjoy special rights analogous to those enjoyed by Malays in Malaysia.

The thirteenth point referred to the constitution of the State Government. It stated that the Chief Minister be elected by the unofficial members of the Legislative Council, and that there should be a proper Ministerial system in North Borneo.

The fourteenth point stated that the transitional period should be seven years and that during such period legislative power must be left with the State of North Borneo by the Constitution and not merely be delegated to the State Government by the Federal Government.

The fifteenth point stated that the educational system of North Borneo should be maintained and for this reason it should be under state control.

The sixteenth point sought constitutional safeguards stating that no amendment, modification or withdrawal of any special safeguards should be made by the Central Government without the positive concurrence of the Government of the State of North Borneo. The power of amending the Constitution of the State of North Borneo should belong exclusively to the State.

It was agreed in the seventeenth point that Sabah's representation in the Federal Parliament should take account not only of its size in terms of population, but also in terms of its potentialities, and in any case should not be less than that of Singapore.

The following two points were straightforward: the name of the State should be Sabah, and the name of its Head of State should be 'Yang di-Pertua Negara'.

The final point referred to Lands, Forests and Local Government the policy and administration of which it was implied should wholly remain with the State Government.

Whilst the would-be politicians were hammering out these safeguards for the political future of Sabah, departments which were likely to become 'federalized' were holding meetings with their counterparts in Kuala Lumpur and Singapore to discuss their future administration.

Broadcasting and Information Services were obviously Departments which would have to speak with one voice and would become Federal Departments. Preliminary discussions were held by calling conferences of the officers involved in Kuala Lumpur and Singapore, and I duly met my opposite numbers in Kuala Lumpur to which parallel officers were invited from Singapore and Sarawak. These meetings were rather exploratory, and more a process of getting to know each other. The Kuala Lumpur Government proved to be excellent hosts and we were soon all on friendly terms. We all met later in Singapore, and Kuching and I believe I hosted our final meeting in Jesselton.

It was whilst we were conferring at Kuching that HE the Governor, Sir Anthony Abell, invited us all to lunch at the Astana. This building was well away from the airport and had not come under air attack in the recapture, neither had the town of Kuching. It was on the opposite bank of the Kuching river from the town, and fortunately the Japanese had sealed it during the time of their occupation. It had remained, with its contents, exactly the same as it was in the Rajah's day. My mind flashed back to the day I had seen the Rajah step off the gangway of the *Darvel* and into his barge to be taken across to the Astana.

We all gathered at the quay and were taken over the Kuching River where we entered the well-mown grounds and strolled up the tarmac path of the hillock, ablaze with hibiscus bushes, to the porch of the Astana where Sir Anthony was waiting to greet us. After the usual round of drinks we were ushered into the dining room and, if I recollect aright, I sat on the left hand side of Sir Anthony at the very same table at which the Rajah would so often have presided in times past!

In all other territories there was no other integrated publicity service. The reason may well have been historical: the manner in which they had developed. Before the war there had been a Radio Malaya, a station we had strived to hear in Sabah when, in 1942, the Japanese were thrusting their way down the Malayan Peninsula at all too fast a speed! There was also Radio Singapore in the immediate post-war days and Singapore was also the headquarters for the BBC Far Eastern Service: a relay station rather than a programme-initiating station as far as I remember. Information services in Kuala Lumpur, Singapore and Kuching were separate organizations. When meeting my opposite numbers in any of the territories, it was always two to my one!

It rather stood out at the beginning that Kuala Lumpur, being 'big brother', would want a separation of my department in Jesselton. They were too polite to mention this at the time; it was just a feeling that I had. Economy was not their concern. Their Government was very generous in the money it spent on publicity. It was a different situation from a colonial administration; they were a self-governing country, and they had to justify their actions to their own people. Just as they built large airports which would impress the arriving visitor, so they spent lavishly in demonstrating their progress. To look into the future, they would surely wish to further publicity with their own officers in control. I began to accept the situation, although inevitably, having just achieved the highest possible ambition for my department in Sabah, I would be very dismayed at seeing that achievement broken asunder as a political pawn. I think it was the manner in which it was done, rather than the act itself, which hurt the most. However, in this narrative, I must remain chronological! Much was still to happen on the political front before Malaysia could be achieved.

Events in Sabah were not going unnoticed by our neighbours. There was always the claim on the territory being made by the Government of the Philippines in the name of the Sultan of Sulu, whilst south of us Dr Sukarno, who was probably the *bête noir* of colonial regimes and may well have been the instigator and was certainly the supporter of Azahari's poor attempts in Brunei, was making threatening noises, so demanding that they were about to bring about almost a state of war, which went by the name of *confrontasi* or confrontation. This was a term which had earlier been used by Indonesia against West Irian in its dispute with Holland. So vociferous were the voices in opposition to Malaysia both in Indonesia and the Philippines as Malaysia Day approached that it prompted action by the President Macapagol of the Philippines to call a 'summit' conference in Manila on 31 July at which Dr Sukarno also agreed at the last moment to be present. A conference such as this had previously been suggested at a meeting of the Foreign Ministers of the three countries.

This meeting led to a decision to send a joint approach to the Secretary General of the United Nations requesting him to ascertain the feelings and the wishes of the people in the Borneo territories. The meeting, which later became known as the 'Manila Declaration', went further than just an attempt to delay the political process in ascertaining the views of the Borneo peoples, it proposed most importantly the establishment eventually of a state to be known as 'Maphilindo'—an hybridism coined for the proposed confederation of Malaya, the Philippines and Indonesia.

The reasons for this proposal coming from Indonesia and the Philippines were all too clear, but it was a little less clear why Tengku Abdul Rahman lent support to the proposal. The two territories on our borders would have much to gain in absorbing Sabah; over the long years of history each, and particularly the Philippines in the person of the Sultan of Sulu, had had territorial ambitions over Sabah and Brunei. Malaya had never had historical connections. The link with Labuan had been with the Straits Settlements and was, I believe, administered by Singapore. And the original Sultan of Brunei himself had been expelled by other Sultans from Malay States!

It could only have been greed which had motivated both the Philippines and Indonesia in the furtherance of their ambition for the possession of the Borneo territories when the extension of the Malayan influence became apparent with the proposal of Malaysia. Coupled with this there was probably a dislike of Malayan influence extending to their very boundaries; each country had wealth, especially amongst its leaders, but amongst their people they also had extremes of poverty, a fact which they may have noted Malaya was without. It was, therefore, in a way, natural that they should oppose the creation of Malaysia. It recalled the distant echo of Hitler's Third Reich crying out for *Lebensraum*!

Tengku Abdul Rahman was every bit a gentleman and a peace-loving man. His motives in attending the Manila meeting were assuredly meant to resolve the dispute amicably, and ensure that Malaysia would be born with the active support and sympathy of its nearest neighbours. He needed their co-operation, and the talks that they had were afterwards described as 'frank and cordial'. He did not, therefore, oppose their suggestion that an approach should be made to the Secretary-General of the United Nations in person, at that time U Thant. They therefore jointly addressed a letter to him requesting him or his representative to ascertain the feelings of the people in the Borneo territories.

Their conference ended on 5 August and news of it aroused considerable indignation amongst the political leaders in the Borneo States. It had now become apparent that the date of 31 August on which they had all been setting their hopes as the date of the creation of Malaysia could no longer be met. The political parties all felt that free elections in both territories should have been sufficient to convince the world that the Borneo territories wanted their independence. It was, therefore, natural that at a special meeting of the Legislative Council which sat on 8 August to consider the situation, a resolution was carried unanimously that Sabah should declare its independence on 31 August under the name of Sabah, whether or not Malaysia had been formed by that date.

So for a few days, and for the only time in its history, Sabah was a free, internally self-governing country. Perhaps I should have called this work *Under Six Flags*, for Sabah did hoist its own flag on its independence day! The new State Constitution came into being on that day too, and a ministerial form of Government was established. But this state of affairs lasted not much more than a couple of weeks.

The Secretary-General of the United Nations had worked with incredible speed, and on 8 August, just a few days after the Manila Declaration, advised the three Foreign Ministers of Indonesia, the Philippines, and Malaya that he would be willing to appoint a representative assisted by two working teams to carry out the task of assessing the views of the people in the Borneo territories, provided that the British Government consented. Her Majesty's Government agreed to this proposal on the understanding that the investigation was to be carried out by the Secretary-General personally and not by the United Nations; that the Mission would be purely responsible to him; and that his conclusions would not need confirmation by the Governments concerned. Obviously Britain did not wish to veto the agreement which the Malayan Prime Minister had reached in Manila, especially as its responsibility towards the Borneo Territories would automatically cease within a very short time.

Following the consent of the British Government and the Governments of the Borneo States, the Secretary-General announced the composition of the ten-man mission on 12 August. It was headed by two senior members of the Secretary-General's staff who arrived in Sarawak on 16 August whereupon it split into two and the section headed by Mr Janacek, Head of the External Relations Division of the United Nations Office of Public Information, was greeted at Jesselton airport by the biggest demonstrtion ever held in the country. It was, of course, organized by the political parties themselves, who had arranged the transport from all the out-lying villages, and was estimated to number about seven thousand people, mostly, of course, natives. They carried banners and slogans with such words as 'Tengku—Yes: Sukarno—No!' Similar slogans had been plastered on cars, lamp-posts and walls: everywhere, in fact, it was anticipated the Mission would go!

The demonstration was entirely peaceful but was extremely successful and eloquently pointed out to the team the wishes of the people in so far as Jesselton was concerned. Similar demonstrations and rallies met the team in various parts of the country to which it subsequently travelled. Owing to the vexing delay on the question of 'observers' posed by Indonesia, it was not until 26 August that the team was able to begin its work. With the transmitters on Kinabalu and relay stations throughout the country at last fully operational, we were in a position to give up to the minute coverage of these historical events in the history of Sabah. It was as if we had planned it all to happen in time for Malaysia!

In a remarkably short space of time, and having within days travelled widely all over the country, the Secretary-General's representatives were able to report back to him within two weeks. He published his findings on 14 September and was able to report that his Mission found that the elections had been properly conducted and held in a free atmosphere, that the electors had had full opportunity to express their attitudes towards Malaysia and that the majority of them had shown their desire to join in the proposed Federation.

He concluded in his report that:

> the emergence of dependent territories by a process of self determination to the status of self-government, either as independent sovereign states, or as autonomous components of larger units has always been one of the purposes of the Charter and the objectives of the United Nations. Whatever the origins of the proposal of Malaysia may have been, it seems to me in the light of actual events . . . that we have witnessed in Sarawak and North Borneo the same process leading to self-government. I fervently hope that the peoples of these territories will achieve progress and prosperity, and find their fulfilment as component States of Malaysia.

The die was cast. There was nothing left now to do except for the Queen's Representative, Sir William Goode, to take leave of the country and for the new leaders to be sworn in. At a moving ceremony at the wharf, where all Heads of Departments were lined up to shake hands with and bid farewell to the last representative of Her Majesty, the Union Jack was slowly lowered for the last time, to the accompaniment of the National Anthem played by the Police Band. Sir William had boarded HMS *Lion*, and stood at salute as the anthem was played and the ship edged gradually away from the wharf. Immediately, the new Sabah flag was raised and the Police Band played, for the first time in public, Sabah's own anthem, chosen by competition, accompanied by the raising of Sabah's own flag. It was a most moving ceremony to all those who had known Sabah for a long time, and loved the country and its people so much.

On the following morning at a ceremony on the town *padang*, in the presence of Tun Razak, Deputy Prime Minister of Malaysia, the Proclamation of the Federation of Malaysia was read and Datu Mustafa was sworn in as the first Yang di Pertua Negara. Mr Donald Stephens was at the same time sworn in as the first Chief Minister. To witness the ceremony the new Government had invited past notable officers who had served the territory and amongst them was Lord Twining. I was able to have a brief word with him at the celebratory cocktail party held at the new Astana.

However, I did have a surprise visit from him on the following morning when he visited Radio Sabah, on the day it was re-named Radio Sabah (Malaysia), and the World News was relayed not from the BBC but from Radio Malaysia. We had an interesting discussion on what the future might bring, both to the country and to me personally. He very kindly offered to be a referee for me, if ever I needed to seek alternative employment. It was with a great feeling of sadness that I bade him farewell. It represented an end of an era.

Under the Malaysian Flag

A STRANGE aura pervaded the country in the first few weeks of Malaysia. It was difficult to come to terms with reality. People whom one had known for years on Christian name terms suddenly were Ministers of this or that Department, and were being driven to and from the Central Government Offices in chauffeur-driven black Mercedes, with flags flying. It was so much like another 'invasion'. The country one had been a part of for so many years was already becoming a strange place. One didn't know what was happening. Suddenly, one felt one had to be careful in what one was saying and to whom. There had been so many mixed feelings about Malaysia, and consequently one became aware that care had to be exercised if feelings were to give rise to any criticism. It was as if someone were standing over one's back listening to what one was saying. Nothing really could have been further from the truth, but increasing my tension was the appointment of a Psywar Team from Radio Malaysia, Kuala Lumpur. Ostensibly set up to co-ordinate publicity in the war against Indonesian confrontation, nevertheless, it was high-powered and led by a Malaysian Permanent Secretary and a senior broadcasting official. I had to make available to them office accommodation. The only spare office we had was at the end of a corridor passing my office. Without wanting to, I could see various members of my staff passing my door, apparently being called to meet the Psywar team. What I think they were apparently doing was assessing the capabilities of my senior staff and their loyalties or convictions towards Malaysia. No apparent attention was paid to the Information Department.

Inevitably, I was rapidly coming to the conclusion that I was the fly in the ointment! There was obviously a feeling of mistrust in their minds towards a European officer in charge of to them a very sensitive Department. Had self-government arisen in a straightforward and logical fashion, I had already chosen and had trained overseas my locally born successor. He was already in place, but he was Chinese and at that time lacked experience. Just a few more years of training and guidance and he would have been a very suitable successor to whom I would have had the greatest confidence in handing over my responsibilities.

It was of no great surprise, therefore, to receive within a few weeks a letter from the Federal Secretary notifying me that the post of Director of Broadcasting and Information Services was to be abolished, and that the two Departments were to be separated. It was their prerogative, but my edifice crumbled about me! I naturally thought that I would return to the administrative cadre from whence I had come, but to my astonishment, the Chief Secretary, now the State Secretary, advised me that when I was promoted as Director I had left the administrative service. That was entirely wrong; I had never been advised of that. Presumably it was consistent with the policy of eliminating European officers from the service as soon as possible, and mine happened to be the first case which came along. I could have appealed to the Secretary of State, but that was pointless as he would have agreed with the State Secretary. However, it did have its compensations, as it then became possible to receive my terminal payment in one lump sum, as opposed to a number of payments in successive years.

All domestic arrangements, however, were upset as I had to proceed on leave immediately. Fortunately, as a result of a kindness I had been able to do for a Danish friend once upon a time, I was able to obtain a passage on a Maersk Line boat leaving Hong Kong and sailing across the Pacific to Los Angeles which enabled me to meet and stay at Vassar, Poughkeepsie for a long weekend with a cousin on my father's side, sailing on the *Queen Mary* across the Atlantic: a journey which had its compensations.

To my astonishment, and indeed pleasure, I found awaiting me on my arrival home a letter from Donald Stephens, the Chief Minister, in which he said he had not realized the advent of Malaysia would lead to the abolition of my post and my early retirement. Would I consider returning on contract? It didn't take me a moment to decide! Almost by return, I received a letter from the State Secretary offering me an administrative post at the top of the time scale on a two-year contract! Nothing could have worked out better and I instantly booked an early flight back to Sabah! For a month or so, I helped out in the Establishment Office, and then I was offered a new post as Curator of a new State Museum I was to found. This couldn't have been nicer! I was also to regain part of my old Department which was very dear to my heart: that of control of the country's Library Service. This too was a State subject and the two activities of Museum and Library Services fitted together nicely!

This proved to be the pleasantest job I had ever had in the country! I had two locally born Assistant Curators, one of whom had a leaning towards natural history, not my strong point, and the other who shared my own interests. My first task was to track down in the Secretariat the papers regarding the Woolley Collection. I had recalled that the old Chartered Company Officer, who had devoted his life to the country, had left his collection of native artifacts to the Government of Sabah when the time came for a museum to be established. I had no idea what the collection contained but I think it was housed for safe-keeping in the Pitts River Museum at Oxford. I eventually tracked it down and it was duly shipped out to Sabah. This was to form the nucleus of the collection, and has really remained one of the major exhibits to this very day.

Fortunately, I knew a great deal about Brunei brass from my Papar days when I had so freely mingled with Brunei people, and I knew the value to put on a piece when a villager would bring it to us. I was, however, nonplussed when a Bajau came up to the office one day and said that he had brought in two large cannons. Normally one would expect these to be of the bow-chaser variety with a spike under the shaft for mounting on the prow of the craft and readily portable. However the Bajau insisted that he was unable to carry even one up the staircase. The Museum, incidentally, was on the first floor of two adjoining shop-houses with very adequate floor space for our then small collection. I asked Michael Chong, the Assistant Curator, to inspect them and assess the difficulty. When he returned, I was astonished to hear of their size, and went down myself to have a look at them. They were immense, but I immediately could discern they had not been cast in Brunei, but somewhere in Europe. They were huge ships' cannons, originating in a European country, possibly Spain or Portugal. However, they formed part of the history of the country and were of great interest to anyone. We agreed the price, and then came the task of getting them up the staircase. It was a question of getting anyone off the street with the time and the inclination! We paid them quite generously, I remember. Money, however, was not the problem in the State as it had been in the past, and the vote for purchases for the collection was very adequate for our needs.

Henry Tseng was the naturalist, and he occupied one of the shop-house kitchens for his activities. He was in charge of the tanks with tropical fish which made quite an interesting exhibit. He also, however, wanted to stuff crocodiles and became less popular! Certain European ladies with outstanding interests like collecting shells and butterflies were also pleased to denote their collections to the Museum when they went on leave. In particular, Mrs Mary Saul's collection of shells was unique and made a most interesting exhibit.

One of my objectives was to introduce the 'folk museum' aspect. The women of the native communities excelled in handicraft, mostly hat-making and weaving, either of head-dresses or sleeping mats: all exquisite, and all of different designs. An exhibition of this kind of work being done would certainly create interest, and also help to conserve crafts which might otherwise disappear. I also had other ideas. I felt that if we could adapt their crafts to twentieth century needs we might be able to find a market for them and develop a permanent cottage industry which would bring money into the villages. With this object in mind, I set about bringing over some of the ladies from Dinawan Island. They were still suffering from the Japanese massacre which killed all the males. The offer of cash for demonstrating their skills was for them a great opportunity!

This is where the second shop-house kitchen came in very handy; it provided the cooking and living accommodation for the villagers. This 'folk museum' idea caught on very well indeed, and our attendance record of visitors increased five or six fold. I was well pleased, as whilst they were looking at hat weaving they usually had time to look around at items from their past.

I also became involved in anthropology. Being a friend of Tom Harrison, I came to know his wife Barbara, and she suggested that it might be of interest to conduct a 'dig' in the Medai caves near Lahad Datu. I obtained Govenment approval to pay her travelling expenses and she gave her services free. This gave me an opportunity to visit the East Coast libraries and combine it with a day trip to the caves. This was to be the last bit of 'jungle bashing' I was to undertake in Sabah. Strictly it could not be called 'jungle bashing', as the walk was a well defined native track I had to follow; but the leeches were the same!

When I arrived, Barbara was enthusiastic! She had already dug an oblong about six feet deep, and was discovering many shards of pottery which she could assemble into recognizable items of cooking ware. We had a meal together, and I retraced my steps before the afternoon rain started too earnestly. The pieces she found are still in the Museum.

From my experience in my former office, I regularly supplied items of public interest to the press and broadcasting service; our activities were well publicized, and this resulted in good attendances.

The new airport which was being completed offered accommodation for a number of small boutiques. I applied for space for a museum shop, which provided an outlet for native crafts and brought a steady cash flow into the villages. On the whole, I was kept very busy, and time slipped quickly by. Reponsibilities were much less than I had had before, I could see the physical results of my efforts and I was well pleased.

Unfortunately the two years passed all too quickly. Around me, the social pattern of life was changing. Malaysia had brought a different atmosphere for the European; it was still the same friendly country when one was amongst the people—there was scarcely any difference—but town life somehow was not the same. It was with the greatest reluctant and sadness that I came to the conclusion that the end was in sight. The end of my contract would see the end of my service to a country I had come to love and even think of it as my own. Thoughts of buying a piece of land at the hill-station at Kundasan flashed through my mind, but a deeper look into the future and a retirement with nothing to do dissuaded me. The time had come to say farewell, but not entirely goodbye!

Some twenty-three years passed by, spent mostly in England in a retirement occupation. Many, many Sabah friends came to stay with me when visiting England and I always remained in touch and was aware of its progress. I was also aware of its tragedies of which the greatest was an air crash which killed my good friend Donald Stephens and his son. It was not a scheduled flight; there had been a charity walk in Labuan in which many leading members of the government took part. Being a free port, goods were cheaper in Labuan than on the mainland. Whether there was any link, I have no idea, but when the plane came in to land at the airport, it flopped instead into the sea and all on board lost their lives. I heard of it within days, and felt a sense of great personal loss. My links with the country seemed to diminish. Surprisingly, though, the country had not forgotten me!

I was unaware of the passing of time, and was very surprised and delighted when in 1988 I received an official invitation to attend the Silver Jubilee celebrations in Sabah! To quote a popular phrase, 'I was over the moon'! There was a postal strike being called in the UK but fortunately this letter just got through, about eight days before I was due to leave. The Malaysian Airways flight was magnificent, and with some seven flights a day from Kuala Lumpur there was a connecting flight bringing me to Sabah about ten o'clock in the evening where a smiling benefactor was there to greet me. He was Haji Amat Haji Saman, the State Information Officer; Wong

Teng Kok, his assistant; and the State Protocal Officer from the Chief Minister's Office.

I was immediately accorded VIP treatment and ushered into the VIP lounge. There was so much to say after so long a time, and all the surroundings were so different from anything I had ever seen before! Wong Teng Kok soon came through with my bags. There were no passport or immigration formalities; I was a guest of the State Government. We went out into a floodlit area where two limousines were waiting for us. Haji Amat and Teng Kok and I were driven, with flag flying, along lighted avenues into a town which to me was entirely unfamiliar. Tanjong Aru and the race course were all built up areas all the way into the centre. I recognized nothing! Suddenly we turned a corner and the Hyatt Kinabalu International hotel rose before us. We alighted and climbed the few steps and entered the air-conditioned atrium. Although the evening was late, the hotel was a hive of activity, with an orchestra playing somewhere in the background and smartly dressed Kedazan waiters dashing here and there. I signed the register and entered one of two lifts. My hosts were familiar with the building and were able to lead me along the grid-iron plan corridors, confusing by their similarity.

The brochure on the Hotel which I later found in my room told me there were 350 rooms and suites. It also described:

> the Semporna Grill with its panoramic views of the South China Sea, well known for its Continental and local cuisine, fine wine list and impeccable service. If you prefer casual dining, [it went on] there's the Tanjong Ria which features delicious Asian specialities and Western food as well as excellent buffets. And for the connoisseur of Chinese cuisine, the Phoenix Court serves 'dim sung' and other Chinese delicacies specially prepared by our master chefs from Hong Kong. For those who need the extra bit of pampering there's our Regency Club—a selected floor of rooms with special amenities, its own concierge service, an exclusive lounge area, complimentary Continental breakfast and evening cocktails with hors d'oeuvres. For conferences and banquets, the Kimanis ballroom can accommodate 400 people. In addition there are three other function rooms which can take 30–60 persons each. The Business Centre will take care of your secretarial and information requirements and provide an entire office at your disposal.

All these facilities were a far cry from the rudimentary hotels as we used to know them in Colonial days! I remembered our early efforts when I was Chairman of the country's first Tourism Board—the problem always was how to provide the facilities which the overseas tourist would demand. Here, in this hotel in Kota Kinabalu, were comfort and luxury above the standards of three or four star hotels in the Western world!

Haji Ahmat and Teng Kok came with me into the suite reserved for me and I couldn't have been better pleased! It was spacious, and had ample lounge area, and a lovely view of Gaya Island. There was even a refrigerator stacked with all the possible drinks one could wish for. We helped ourselves whilst they discussed the programme for the next day. They told me Jaffrey had been appointed my aide, and that he would call for me at 6.30 a.m. and give me information regarding the official programme. In the evening there would be dinner at the Istana.

Promptly at the hour appointed the following morning, after a good night's refreshing sleep, a welcome shower and a magnificent breakfast of all kinds of rolls and fruit—how lovely it was to have a large slice of delicious *kepaya* again—there was a tap on the door, and in came Jaffrey, who was on the Chief Minister's staff, so he told me. He bore a sheaf of official invitations and I started making a list of the engagements day by day. Of course, tomorrow would be a holiday and, thinking of my immediate financial requirements, I realized that the banks would be shut. I suggested, therefore, after the outline of the programme had been decided, and thinking of my financial needs, that I really ought to visit the bank. It was within easy walking distance, and for the first time I began to get my bearings and recognize familiar landmarks. Inside the same old Chartered Bank, one of the senior local staff recognized me and I him. Straight away I was ushered inside the inner sanctum and had personal service.

The afternoon was free and would give me a chance to rest from the flight in preparation for the banquet at the Istana. On returning from the bank, I found waiting for me in the hotel my old friend Ben Stephens, Donald's younger brother! Ben appeared from nowhere. It was very good to see him and he appeared very pleased to see me. I had last seen him when he had visited me with his wife at my home in England. He was anxious that I should enjoy my stay and was planning to take me to Kundasan—a spot I very much wanted to visit in order to appreciate the new developments there since my time. There appeared to be one free day which only had an evening engagement: a procession of floats. 'What if I take you to Kundasan then?' he asked. I very gratefully agreed! We had much to talk about and soon it was midday and I suggested he lunch with me, to which he readily agreed, although I was not sure in the end who was the host.

I had appreciated the afternoon's rest! As arranged the previous night, Haji Ahmat then arrived to take me to the State Information Office. It took up one floor of rented accommodation in a tower block, built on reclaimed land, and Haji Ahmat's office, where we first sat and drank tea, had his desk and a couple of settees for guests: far more comfortable than anything I had had! A corner picture window looked out over the wharf and the northern tip of Gaya Island. I was then taken to the outside offices where all the staff were waiting. A few I recognized as having been appointed in my time, but most were new to me. As the man who had founded the office I was the object of curiosity! I was genuinely amazed at the vast collection of hardware, to use a modern term—all very up to the minute equipment, quite unknown in my time. Teletext machines were clicking away unattended, bringing press releases and messages from Kuala Lumpur; there was everything that a modern press office required. The office was even equipped with an in-house cinema. Haji Amat told me his staff totalled over three hundred, stationed in all parts of the State. When I left, I had had a staff of just over 250 for Broadcasting and Information Services. Photographs of my visit were taken all the time, and in their reference library Haji Amat proudly showed me the collection of Annual Reports which had represented so much of my work in Sabah. It was almost after hours, at a time which was a big occasion for them and a busy one too, so I made haste to depart although I would willingly have stayed longer and asked more questions!

Back at the hotel, a short rest and then began the preparations for the dinner at the Istana. The dress was optional, but Jaffrey advised that a lounge suit would be appropriate. Very promptly my aide arrived and together we descended to the atrium which, on the eve of the Silver Jubilee celebrations, was a hive of bustle and activity. A moment's wait whilst the driver of the large white Volvo, bearing the number S 63 (which I memorized as there were a number of similar official white Volvos around) caught my aide's eye. Along it came; page boys opened the doors for us and we were soon climbing Ridge Road to the Istana. I recall that on the left was a very large car park and that there were people walking along the drive, but we went straight up to the Istana entrance. Here I lost Jaffrey and, showing my invitation card to one of the ushers, I was taken to where my name was printed on a card bearing the crest. I was aghast at the expanse of the hall, much enlarged since I last had been there, and the air-conditioning was frigid! I was seated next to Peter Lo, one time Chief Minister in the early days of Sabah, and it was good to be able to talk to someone I knew. There was a good deal of hubbub as people entered and chatted to each other, but fairly promptly at the hour stated our hosts, headed by the Yang di-Pertua Negeri, processed to the high table. The hall became hushed. Then an Imam said a rather long-winded grace in Arabic and the murmur of voices recommenced.

Each guest had two cards placed in front of him: one detailed the events of the evening's programme and the other was the menu, or as the card said: *Hidangan*. The first course was 'Sup Asparagus', obviously having been grown at Kundasan. Then a bowl of rice was placed in front of us and before each group of four at least some six different kinds of curry each in its own dish. It was first class food of the highest order. Drinks, as one would expect, were either Coca-Cola or 7-Up. The sweets were 'Krim Karamel' and fruit, accompanied by coffee or tea. Then the speeches began, in a Malay more complicated than I could understand, unfortunately. Whilst this went on, I counted the number at our table, then counted the tables, and came to the conclusion that the number of guests who had been fed so efficiently and speedily must not have been far short of five hundred. Just imagine, I thought, a Colonial Governor entertaining such a number at dinner! It was not possible! Then the native *Sumazau* began, several groups from various districts.

Whilst people's attention was diverted, I slipped out to the rear where I spotted that the toilets were located. I was quite surprised to encounter there another European face. Naturally I started speaking to him. He was an Australian and had come to the back for a smoke! Talking to him, I learnt much of interest. Apparently there is a dearth of beef (*sapi*) meat in Sabah and to solve the problem the State had bought nineteen ranches in Northern Australia and were rearing 35,000 head of cattle to provide a steady flow of meat supplies. They even owned an aircraft for the purpose of bringing up the meat. Brunei also participated in this operation. The Australian gentleman I was talking to was the liaison officer for this operation and came to Sabah and Brunei every three months to discuss policy and progress with the States.

Whilst I was talking to him, all the guests came out of the dining hall, to witness the lowering of one flag and the raising of another. Each movement was accompanied by a Police bugler and I faintly recognized strains of the Last Post coming through as the flag was lowered and Reveille as the new flag was slowly hoisted to the top of the mast. I thought that was the end, but everyone re-entered the hall whilst more speeches were given. Then the high table filed down into the hall and this was the signal for departure. We queued up to shake hands with the Yang di-Pertua and his wife, whose name told me she was the daughter of Native Chief Hasbullah of Kota Belud whom I had known. When it was my turn to shake hands with the Yang, he asked in perfect English if I remembered him. I told him that both his name and face were familiar but that I couldn't immediately place him. He then told me smilingly that he had been my Chief Clerk in Papar at the time I left the district! Some thirty-five years went rolling back and I knew exactly who he was!

The next morning was the big day! Everyone was asked to be in their seats by 6.50 a.m. The official party arrived promptly and the parade started: section after section of the Police, jungle troops, a contingent from the Malaysian Army, women with each squad in differing uniforms, until the *padang* was full. Then the speeches began. My accolade went to the Deputy Prime Minister who had come over from Kuala Lumpur. He spoke without a script; he was affable and humorous and brought a laugh or two from the assembled guests. Next, school-children put on various displays, and when the girls of St Francis Convent appeared and sang songs through which one distinctly heard the strains of 'Bridge over the River Kwai' and 'When the Saints come marching in', then one realizes it isn't all that easy to eradicate all traces of the British influence!

The next engagement was the laying of the foundation stone for the new legislative building at Likas Bay, timed for three o'clock in the afternoon. I couldn't work up a lot of enthusiasm for that especially as the Ministers were a trifle late in arriving and the sun had crept round to expose my chair. I wasn't alone and I quickly followed others who were moving their chairs into the shade. I sat next to a lady whose face was familiar and she reminded me that her maiden name was Irene Prichard who had been a schoolgirl when I was in Papar, and I also seem to remember her as being on the staff of Radio Sabah, but I didn't check on that. She told me she was now a member of the legislative body for Sabah. Soon after I was joined by a very smart gentleman whose face I instantly recognized! I had recruited him for the Kedazan section of Radio Sabah, and quickly realized he had ability. I remember that I had sent him on a course of Public Administration under the Colombo Plan to New Zealand, and he had still been overseas when I had left. He did well and he modestly told me with some pride that he was substantive Deputy Secretary and at that time the Acting State Secretary. I felt very pleased, particularly when he said to me: 'I shall always be grateful to you, Mr Brooks, for giving me my big chance!' The whole visit was worthwhile if only to have heard that remark!

After that rather hot afternoon, I did not feel that the procession of floats scheduled for the evening merited my attendance. I informed Jaffrey of my intentions and had a quiet dinner later on in the Hyatt Kinabalu.

The next morning and afternoon had no official engagements, but it had been arranged with Ben Stephens that he would take me to Kundasan. I was very much looking forward to this. The phone rang at 7 a.m. and I went downstairs to meet Ben. He was himself driving a Range Rover, and on the way apologized that colleagues of his on the Cocoa Board had asked for a meeting whilst they were in Kota Kinabalu for the Jubilee and that he would have to attend, but he had asked his son to drive me. We arrived at his house along Likas Road, next to Donald's house where Junie lived. There was an array of different cars standing in a shelter opposite the entrance. Ben introduced me to his son, a lad of some twenty-four or five who had been educated in England and spoke excellent colloquial English. As we started off on our journey to Inanam and Menggatal, I was amazed that it was a dual carriageway all the way, and all a built up area. It is now a light industrial area where a rotan furniture maker plies his trade next to a tinsmith: not a trace of the swamp that it used to be, and not a trace of the *padi*-field. We passed through well-known townships of the old familiar lay-out, but I thought they were a bit tatty and apparently in need of a coat of paint.

At Tamparuli the low-level bridge has been replaced by a new bridge a couple of hundred yards upstream. Shortly after crossing it we came to a big roundabout with sign-posts pointing to Tuaran, Kota Belud and Kudat. We followed the route leading to Kundasan, Ranau and Sandakan. Almost immediately we began to climb, imperceptibly at first, and the scenery was that of the Borneo all the old hands would remember. We were already in the foothills of the Crocker Range, the road was all metalled and we climbed rapidly; already the air was feeling fresher. It wasn't long before we came to a large sign reading 'Kinabalu National Park'. About half a mile along this road we reached the 'Kinabalu Park Hotel' where we found a convenient parking lot. We first went to the higher level of the building where there was a natural history display area illustrating the butterflies and birds found in the locality. I also noticed one magnificent photograph of Kinabalu which I had left in the Museum. I knew that only three copies of it existed: one was with my former Chief Engineer, and the other I had retained. This copy had the names of the various peaks written neatly on pieces of paper affixed to the picture.

Quite a number of people like us were walking around. Obviously it was a festive occasion and people were having a break from their normal way of life. We went down to the lower floor where smart Kedazan boys in black trousers, white shirts and black bow ties were waiting at tables in the restaurant. I spotted a verandah outside which looked very inviting and we went out there and found an empty table. We ordered chicken curry, and without any doubt it was the finest curry I had eaten for a long time and certainly was the best I was offered in Sabah on this momentous trip!

Next we went on to the golf course, which Ben particularly wanted me to see. Certainly it must have been one of the highest in the world, although I wouldn't have liked to have played on it! Possibly it sprang from an idea of Tun Mustafa at the time when he was friendly with Tengku Abdul Rahman who was a keen golfer. It appeared that the greens were grouped in threes, but the fairways were very rough, just low-cut jungle where one could easily lose a ball! The greens on the other hand were magnificent, and very well kept, as fresh-mown grass lay by their side. All maintained by the State, Ben said. He showed me the site of the club-house, and I wondered how long it would be before it was all finished. Like other projects, such as the Tanjong Aru Hotel, it was the custom of the State Government to pioneer an enterprise until it became commercially viable when a business concern would take it over.

We then returned along the fairly rough road and rejoined the metalled road which took us to the Hotel Perkasa, Mount Kinabalu. As far as I could judge, this was built on the opposite side of the valley to the old Rest House at Bundu Tuhan where I had often stayed when A.D.O. Ranau before the war. At Bundu Tuhan, the mountain was behind one, but here at the hotel it was in front of the building. When we descended from the Range Rover, I noticed that Ben's son was very careful to lock the vehicle. I asked the reason, and he muttered: 'Filipinos!' They must, I thought, be employed here as groundsmen.

As we walked up to the hotel, I looked at the stone troughs standing in front and saw that they were planted with asparagus and strawberries. An attractive welcome, I thought! This was by no means a small building: it was six storeys high and had 74 bedrooms as well as conference facilities. It advertised that every room had a private bathroom, shaver point, in-house video, laundry and valet services. A little different from the Agriculture Department's experimental garden and Rest House of the old days at which they allowed others to stay!

Obviously this was a high day and a holiday, and people may have taken advantage of that fact, but I noted there were some twenty-five cars parked outside. The glass doors were opened for us and we entered a large reception area. Ben's son led the way to the vast restaurant with panoramic windows looking out to the beauty of the mountain. Unfortunately, it was shy, as it usually is in the afternoons, and it was wearing its hat of swirling cloud. But it was not so much the mountain that attracted me, for I had seen it so often, but rather the opulence of the surroundings in which we were seated. We were met by smart Kedazan lassies, wearing white blouses with black bow ties, and black skirts, with the Kedazan lads similarly dressed but sporting smart red jackets liberally trimmed with gold.

They all spoke remarkable English. When I remarked on this I received the reply that there were three hundred secondary schools in Sabah now, and all taught English. This was true because I checked on it later and was given the same information. These boys and girls had all attended secondary school in Ranau and had been taught their English there.

I was still replete after that splendid curry tiffin, so we both had fruit, all tastefully served and cut into bite-size pieces, and Sabah tea. In the background, I noticed a chef, a European, decked in a French chef's outfit, complete with hat: I had to pinch myself to see if I was dreaming! Time, however, was passing all too quickly. The State Banquet was being held at 7.30 p.m. at Tanjong Aru Beach Hotel and I wanted to get some rest in before changing and getting ready for that!

Surprisingly, having initially had to travel at a snail's pace through thick swirling cloud, we descended quickly. I asked to stop at one of the purpose-built wayside stalls, where all kinds of fruit were being sold, and I bought a hand of *pisang mas* (small bananas) for some miniscule sum, and was given, too, a red pepper! Natives here are still exactly the same; they were still chewing betel nut!

I was a little struck at the lack of road maintenance at one point in particular, where on a corner the road had slipped, not just by inches, but by a foot or so, and the only warning given was the presence of tar barrels placed around the danger point. Definitely dangerous if driving at night since the drop over the side was almost sheer.

In less than an hour we were back at Likas, where it was already raining hard. Ben and Emily made me welcome with some lovely Sapong coffee, and then some excellent curry which, they said, they always had 'on tap'. I believe it was Umpah's old recipe. It is surprising how one can recall tastes! Inevitably, our conversation brought us around to talking about Johnnie Baxter, who was Emily's father. Ben endeavoured to ring him, but there was no reply. I would like to have spoken to him, especially as he had invited me to stay with him for a couple of days when he had heard I was paying a visit to Sabah. I had known him for over forty years! There was no reply, and Ben concluded that at this hour of the day he would be out on his constitutional. Apart from sending my good wishes when Ben was next in touch with him there was nothing more I could do. Changing flights seemed very difficult to arrange. Ben mentioned, however, that Johnnie was constantly writing to the State Government advising them how to administer the Interior; normally his letters were disregarded and considered to be the ramblings of an old timer, but he did receive one reply! It so surprised him, he had it framed and hung up in his sitting room!

Far too soon, time was pressing, and Ben drove me back to the hotel in pouring rain. The day had taken a toll on my energies but a shower and a short rest did much to revive me and I was on form for the last official engagement in the Government's programme. This was a State Banquet at the Tanjong Aru Hotel, and a dinner jacket occasion. Every other person seemed to be in a uniform with gold braid draped on their shoulder pads and medals galore! I seemed quite out of place but not quite alone with just a dinner jacket. There were no long speeches at the conclusion, but again the dancing displays by the native communities. Seated at the table opposite me there was a very affable Malay gentleman who told me that he was the Training Officer for the State and had been in Sabah for six years and, he said, enjoyed living in Sabah. In the crush coming out, I met General Ibrahim of the Malaysian Army; we both recognized each other as he had been one of the Malayan representatives at the Security Council meetings just before the advent of Malaysia.

The morrow was my last full day before departure, but I still had a couple of

Sabah Museum.

engagements I wished to make. The first was to the Sabah Museum which I had heard from several sources was now a very splendid organization. It was indeed a magnificent building, more resembling a palace in Thailand than anything else I could compare it with. As far as I could judge, the immediate post war Secretariat site and the old Government House site had been bulldozed to provide quite a substantial area for the three-in-one building which it constitutes. It would have made poor old Tom Harrison turn in his grave with envy!

Michael Chong, still Assistant Curator, was there to greet me and he introduced me to Miss Regis, Peter Regis' daughter, the substantive Curator who had been trained in the United Kingdom in museum administration. I instantly recognized many of the exhibits, but Michael Chong's pride was the magnificent diorama of a birds nest cave, taking up a considerable space, and illuminated by spotlights trained on the nests in the roof of the cave and other features. It must have taken a great deal of time to construct and was most realistic. Neither could I fail to recognize the many items of the Woolley Collection, nor the two great cannons! We all had Sabah tea together and couldn't help noticing the packets of Sabah tea they had on sale. 'They do a good trade with visitors,' Michael said, adding that on average they have an attendance of 6,000 visitors each month which is increasing all the time.

Eventually, I went through to the State Archives and met the State Archivist. My main interest was to see the Woolley Diaries, as I would very much like to see them published. The story he has to tell is a remarkable history of the early endeavours of the first of the Chartered Company officers of whom he was one. Not only was there hostility in certain areas but, of great significance, there was disease, particularly malaria. Unfortunately the typescript of the Diaries which I had arranged in my day had been lost, probably in the transfer of the Museum. I left a tape-recorded message with the State Archivist emphasizing their importance in the history of their country. As Sabah matures the people will look to their history, even though at present it is of less importance to them than is the present and future. They will eventually desire to know their roots and the origins from which they sprang, and there is no greater work from which they can undertake this study than the most valuable information contained in the Woolley Diaries.

That evening was free of all appointments, and I endeavoured to host a Chinese dinner for all my friends who had helped me during my visit. A much larger and more opulent Nam Hing, the venue of many a Chinese feast in the past, I chose as the restaurant for this purpose. The food, as I anticipated, was excellent, far, far better than one can obtain in a Chinese restaurant in this country. The only snag was that Tom Willie, now long since retired, insisted on doing the honours!

My flight was due to leave about 2 p.m. the following day, but I expressed a wish to visit, before I left, Papar and the District which had meant so much to me, and in particular the old D.O.'s house. Secretly, I think I wanted to visit the grave of my old dog, Rambler, but the house and grounds would recall many memories which I treasure (apart from the arrival of the Japanese when they passed through on their way to Jesselton!). I also asked if I could meet my old friend, Native Chief

Hussein of Kampong Benoni, who had been such a stalwart companion after the passing of his father, Native Chief Oman.

We went first to the Office under the control of the Information Department who had arranged the meeting. Native Chief Hussein was waiting for me all right and recognized me, but he had become an old, old man and I think had suffered from a stroke as his speech was all blurred. We could scarcely communicate. However, he would remember that I had not forgotten him and, hopefully, it might have given him pleasure. Certainly, they would talk about it in Benoni, and for a moment he would be the hero!

I then tried to find the D.O.'s house, but in this I was to be disappointed. I don't think our driver, who was a Malay, had ever been to Papar before, and we ended up lost! If I had taken to my feet, I would have found it, but time, when a plane had to be caught in an hour or so, didn't permit meanderings. I reluctantly gave up, and we returned to Kota Kinabalu. I had one more engagement to keep: a curry lunch at Haji Ahmat's house where he had invited many friends of my old Information Office staff who had left Government Service and made their own ways. In particular I was very glad to see Victor Hua, my photographer, and his wife who had been a librarian. It was a delightful lunch party and on leaving, Haji Ahmat presented me with a pewter plaque in remembrance of the occasion. Before leaving for Papar I had also called in at the Library, which had excellent premises in town, and a very modern computerized lending system, but the staff were not known to me, and I had not lingered.

On the way to the airport, I yielded, willingly, to a request of the wife of an old golfing friend of mind, Walter Leng, to visit them. She had also arranged with Junie Stephens to come along and meet me. There were obviously mixed feelings in meeting her, but she was her usual self. As we chatted, I thought to myself that I must be the one European she had known the longest: from the time she had been a schoolgirl on Papar Estate, quite a while before the beginning of the Far Eastern war. It was really good to be amongst old friends and to have a couple of stiff gin-tonics. All too quickly, I had to bid farewell and proceed to the final stop, the VIP lounge of the airport. What a busy airport it had become! My departure flight was scheduled from Gate 4. Whilst waiting, the Chief Minister's orderly arrived with a gift of photographs and books of modern Sabah, which I thought was extremely kind.

It was a visit I shall never forget. I was proud that the country and people I loved so much had not forgotten me on their days of celebration!

Epilogue

ONE country and five flags! But there is one man who stamped his mark on the country more than any other, and he came from the City of London. That man was Sir Neil Malcom, the President of the Chartered Company, whose wisdom and omniscience selected and appointed most of the Chartered Company Officers. They, in turn, provided the paternalism whereby the country was governed in the early days of white rule. They gave the loyalty which the people of Sabah repaid, many with their lives, during the time of enemy occupation. It was they who moulded the shape and actions of the succeeding post-war government, and even today the friendliness of the people of Sabah reflects the benevolence of its founding fathers.

Sabah today is a rich and prosperous country; it has fulfilled the most optimistic ambitions once held by the merchants of the then leading commercial city in the world. It has been found to be attractive not only to the entrepreneurs of the world, but to the new leisured class that has emerged. Its beauty and grandeur has been discovered and recognized by the most demanding of all classes of modern society: the twentieth century tourist!

The infrastructure of a highly successful tourist industry is omni-present. The essential ingredients are communications and hotels of excellence and comfort which will meet the demands of the most fastidious of travellers. Sabah today has everything! There are daily flights from Hong Kong, Manila, Indonesia and Singapore, and at least a dozen flights a day by Boeing 707 from Kuala Lumpur. The hotels are luxurious and they are everywhere, in all centres and places of interest in the country. There is even a car ferry service between the mainland and Sabah.

To meet the demands of the tourist, English is spoken everywhere. There had been no need to make the teaching and use of English as one of the 'Twenty Points' for entering Malaysia. Its use is self-evident everywhere. It is taught in the very centre of Sabah at Ranau Secondary school. And amongst its pupils are the waiters at Hotel Perkakas, Kundasan, in the very heart of the countryside.

Tourism in itself brings wealth, employment and prosperity. To this must be added the growth of industrial activity as a result of the development of the natural resources of the country. It is not possible to quote figures of exports in terms of Malaysian dollar values, as such statistics are combined with pan-Malaysian totals. The increase in the commercial activity since the advent of Malaysia is, however, remarkable.

Although the use of English is outstanding, it does not follow that the British influence has increased in any way. In fact the reverse is the case. The office of the

British High Commission in Kota Kinabalu has been closed and British interests are represented by an officer on the Commission's establishment in Kuala Lumpur. Nor is there a great deal of evidence of imports from Britain.

In contrast, the British mantle has been discarded in favour of imports from Japan. Everywhere, for example, Japanese cars predominate. Even the local buses are no longer built on an American or British chassis, but are sleek imported models from Japan. In fact, the Japanese motor industry is responsible for some 80% of the vehicle imports. The Japanese may even form the majority of the tourist industry's visitors. Nevertheless, the Double Tenth is still remembered and is now named 'Hero's Day'.

Charlie Peter's daughter has recently visited me, and although her memories of the horrendous days of the occupation when she was a child are still very vivid, recalling the very moment the Japanese took her father away from her home to be tortured and killed, one wonders if the younger generation will grow up with similar antipathy and hatred. Time may heal wounds, but modern incidents will enliven memories. Recently, a Japanese tourist, with two large cameras dangling from his neck, entered the Hyatt Kinabalu bearing two large suitcases. The page-boy dashed to assist him, but evidently he needed no assistance. Instead, he slapped the lad across the face, uttering the familiar hissing explosions. Such behaviour remains incomprehensible and furthers the belief that the Japanese character will never change. Just as the Englishman recognizes his modern-day image in the characters portrayed by Shakespeare, so in a like manner the modern citizen of Japan must still reflect the ruthlessness and even barbarism of his ancestors. This is evident especially in the many many demonstrations of violent and unnecessary cruelty of the Emperor's Armies in the Pacific War. The reputation they earned then should, for the sake of the peace and equality of future generations of mankind, never be forgotten.

The cruelty and sadism of the Japanese as experienced in Kuching which has been narrated in this work was not confined to the military forces in Sabah. A former POW put to work on the Burma Railway has recalled in a book he has published, *One God: Too Many Devils*, that one favourite trick was to force men over cliffs at bayonet point. 'I recall one young man,' he has written, 'who was slowing down from heat exhaustion,' was ordered by the Japanese officer in charge of the work-party to move towards the edge of a cliff. The officer 'then attached a bayonet to the end of his gun and literally prodded him until he fell to his death.' This officer at the end of hostilities, refused to surrender and hid in the Thai jungle, later joining the Malayan Communists fighting for the Chinese People's Communist Party. He was one of two veterans responsible for the deaths of hundreds of Allied prisoners. Comparatively recently, the Thai Authorities surrendered him to the Japanese Government and he was given a hero's welcome on arrival back in Tokyo.

The motivations which brought Japan into the last war are still the same today. These can now clearly be seen as world domination of most economic spheres. At first it became noticeable in light industry, such as in the manufacture of cameras and binoculars, following their pre-war tradition, later spear-heading its industrial penetration by the building of car factories in Australia, in Malaysia with the collaboration of the Malaysian Government, and in Europe. Assisting their industrial development was the United States, resulting from the conflict in Korea when, by placing orders in Japan for many of their military requirements, they perhaps unintentionally rebuilt Japan's industrial base. However, it is in Australia, the prime objective of their war aims, where the success of their economic penetration is most to be noticed. There, in addition to their usual industrial thrust, one of their enterprises has been the construction of an entirely new Japanese city.

The dedication of the Japanese work force to the factories which they serve, singing the particular factory's hymns before the commencement of activity each working morning, introduces a concept unknown in the West. When did the world ever hear of strikes or other industrial action affecting Japanese industry? This extremism is part of the Japanese character; just as they defended each Pacific Island they had captured to the last man, so too they will achieve industrial domination by the same mentality. Yet the Western world, if it has become aware of a very real threat, does not express concern over the dangers of overwhelming Japanese industrial competition.

So it is also in Sabah, where imports from Japan and exports to that country are creating a dependence on a trading nation which they may live to regret. Although economic considerations must inevitably take predominance, the State authorities should not forget the hand that nurtured it.

We must now turn to the Australian contribution to the development of Sabah. This has been very considerable indeed and very generously given. The nascent Colony of North Borneo immediately recognised this by incorporating in its new coat of arms the 'T' for Tobruk, the phase of the Second World War in which the Ninth Australian Division played a prominent part. Placed by the side of an outline of Kinabalu, it signifies the reconquest of Sabah by Australian forces and was a symbol of the gratitude of Sabah to Australian arms. In fact, as I have said, the last VC of the war was awarded to an Australian soldier for his part in the fighting to re-capture Beaufort, and I believe a plaque exists on the site to commemorate the occasion.

Later, when the Colombo Plan came into being, it was Australia and New Zealand which contributed most. Numbers of Sabah youth received graduate and technical training under the Plan which as the years have passed have been of extreme benefit to the country, having assisted many of the country's civil servants now in executive power. It is of little importance whether the country recognises this in their current thought, but facts speak for themselves.

As for Great Britain, Sabah was really forced upon it as a Colony at a time when it did not seek to acquire Colonies. The war had impoverished the coffers and the last thing it sought was an unnecessary financial burden. Clearly, however, it was a British Protectorate and the devastation caused by the war meant that the out-moded Chartered Company had not the resources to rehabilitate and reconstruct the country. However, the British Government willingly accepted its obligations towards its Protectorate status, and for many years poured money into the Colony under the Colonial Development and Welfare Schemes. But it was not in a physical and monetry sense that the country was destitute, it was the loss of skilled middle-management man-power, either by murder or torture or just starvation, that was most felt. Those civil servants, or those in commerce, who would have earned senior positions simply did not exist any longer, apart from a few people like Mr Vun How Kiong, the king-pin of the Secretariat. So massive reconstruction had to proceed before development could begin, and emphasis had to focus on education and training before the desired objectives along the road to self-government could commence.

When that day came, it was achieved through Malaysia. This was a good concept and has brought about remarkable development and prosperity. Inevitably, one or two observations must be made on events as they occurred at the time and in subsequent years. It must be emphasized that these are only personal views and are made out of a love for and with a considerable knowledge of Sabah and its country and people.

It appears to me that the focus of the northern coast of Borneo is undoubtedly Brunei. In history, Sarawak and Sabah were its provinces, and by an accident of nature it has become one of the wealthiest countries *per capita* of population in the world. The greatest thinker on the future of Borneo was undoubtedly North Borneo's Governor, Sir Roland Turnbull. His concept of Closer Association between the Borneo territories was the most practical, logical method and capable of achieving the greatest success, and would have led undoubtedly to political union. When this had been achieved, the step towards Malaysia would have been easier, and have been just as, if not more, favourable to Malaya itself. It would have joined as an equal partner, not with just two former Colonies, but as a vast and a very, very wealthy enclave of a unified Borneo territory. For Sabah it would not have meant a change in colonization from Britain as the mother country to an association with a State dominated by Islam, without some of the independence it might otherwise have had.

Inevitably the question of religion does enter into it. Although I personally believe that Islamism admirably fulfils the spiritual needs of the people, even ordering their way of life and their cleanliness leading inevitably to better health, I do not necessarily think it should be allowed to dominate the political and social life of a people who are not basically Moslem. To allow this to happen tends to give preference *inter alia* to those of this faith in public life. Why else should many of its Christian born leaders and several of its civil servants have become Moslem, were this not so? Were this to happen out of religious conviction it would be admirable, but one is led to wonder whether in all cases this is the motivation factor. This brings into question the first of the 'Twenty Points' where it is specifically stated that: 'Whilst there is no objection to Islam being the national religion of Malaysia there should be no State religion in North Borneo.' This clearly does not give preference to those of its citizens who are Moslem, but in practice it appears to have been an influencing factor in the conversion of many leading figures who would otherwise have remained Christian. The omnipresence of mosques, even at Kundasan in the heart of Kedazan country, leads one to think that some unseen influence is helping the spread of Islam. Of course, it may well be, as a Mother Superior once said to me of Kedazan girls: 'They [referring to young male Moslems] often get one of ours, but we never get one of theirs!'

I have come to the end of the story of Sabah, but whether they be Moslem, Christian or pagan; Chinese, Malay, Kedazan or Murut; the good people of Sabah will always remain the salt of the earth, and this book is dedicated to them.

Obituary

M. Granville Edge OBE

Mike has been an inspirational help throughout the writing of *Under Five Flags*. He has told me the details of the wrecking of the M.V. *Kinabalu* on the Batu Mandi rocks, since his brother had sailed on her on that ill-fated occasion. He had told me about the uprising in Brunei under Azahari, since he was the Police Special Branch Officer during the build-up to the Brunei rebellion. He ended his career as Divisional Commander, East Coast.

In Kuching Internment Camp, we shared a small allotment together, and he was the 'stoker' who kept in an all-night fire ready for the sweet potatoes which we would grow and which more than anything saved our lives.

On return to Britain, he entered the Ministry of Defence, and had a roving commission. It was when returning from Rosyth that he had a car accident in which he lost an eye and a leg was shortened. When the police reached him he was still clutching hard to the bundle of secret papers he was carrying.

Eventually, he retired to Australia where his children had been living. We were in regular communication. He died on 27 April 1995. We had been very close friends for fifty-five years.